A Pilgrim's Guide to

NORTHERN SPAIN

Vol. 1 Camino Francés & Camino Finisterre

Andrew Houseley

Pilgrim Book Services Limited

To David Houseley (1931–2013)

© Pilgrim Book Services Ltd. and Andrew Houseley 2023
ISBN 978-0-9569768-0-2

Published by Pilgrim Book Services Ltd., registered at Devon Suite, Dencora Business Centre, Ipswich IP1 5LT, United Kingdom.

www.pilgrimbooks.com

First Edition 2023

Designed by Kevin Baverstock
Cover designs by Fielding Design and Spectrum Graphics
Country Map and Cathedral Plans by Rodney Paull. Historic and Travel maps by Kevin Baverstock
Stage and town/city maps by Kevin Baverstock derived from cartographic base © ign.es, Federación Española de Asociaciones de Amigos del Camino de Santiago, and data available under the Open Database License © OpenStreetMap contributors
Photographs © Andrew Houseley unless where stated at each image
Printed in the European Union

'Collect for the Feast of St James' from Common Worship: Services and Prayers for the Church of England is © The Archbishops' Council 2000. Published by Church House Publishing. Used by permission. rights@hymnsam.co.uk

The author and publishers gratefully acknowledge the assistance of the Spanish National Tourist Office, London, and in particular Manuel Sánchez Domato, who facilitated initial field research. The autonomous communities of La Rioja, Castilla y León, and Galicia, Government of Navarra – who facilitated or provided accommodation and expert guides. The latter include: Carlotta in Burgos, Camino in León, Francisco Glaría (Novatur) in Pamplona; Monica Figuerola – Minister of Tourism, La Rioja – and Marina at RiojaTrek. Xacobeo Valloria Lda, who facilitated the author's first Camino, arrival and stay in Santiago de Compostela. Also the Tourist Office in Santiago de Compostela.
The Confraternity of St James, London, have provided advice and resources. In particular, the late Marion Marples, the Confraternity's former Secretary; also former Chair Laurie Dennett whose paper '2000 Years of the Camino de Santiago: Where did it come from? Where is it going?' [Toronto, 2005] has informed Parts 3 and 4 of this book.
Finally, the encouragement and theological guidance of my fellow author Ray Goodburn.

Cover picture: The restored Obradoiro façade, Cathedral of Santiago – Andrew Houseley

CONTENTS

Part 1
PREFACE

A warm welcome to this guide. Those who regard themselves as experienced pilgrims will probably agree that all the terminology, let alone the experiences of the varied culture and landscape of the Spanish Caminos, might seem daunting to newcomers, and yet at the same time so absorbing! We had better not let on, therefore, that essentially it is about putting one foot in front of the other for a few hours each day. Once near-instantly familiar with the daily routine, what else is there to do? Well, after the months/weeks/just hours! of planning, that is where the pilgrim experience finally, truly begins. I will do my best in a few pages from here to give at least some pointers as to what to expect, both practically and perhaps at a more abstract level – perhaps. For while there are many loyal returning pilgrims who just can't stay away and indeed may have a different experience every time, the call of the Camino is at least as much about those who yearn to set foot for the first time, and may have been thinking about doing so for a while.

As we shall learn, the Camino is not prescriptive and pushes no-one away. You'd do well to read advice and find out what 'most pilgrims do' and there are a few basic rules. But there are many ways of doing a Camino, and this is going to be *your* Camino. You need a method, involving some decisions, you need to plan ahead, ideally! But don't let anyone tell you how it must be done.

There are indeed many different ways any one of us could describe ourselves to others as a pilgrim. What about me?

My father always wanted to produce a guide in our series that included Santiago de Compostela. The aim of our company has been to cover the major Christian pilgrimage sites, at least of the Middle East and Europe. Although several other destinations were at the time much more familiar to us, our scallop shell logo and company name was entirely his choice. As someone steeped in escorted pilgrimage tours, as was my grandfather, he knew that, somehow, if we were to achieve it, we would have to venture onto lesser charted territory: as he said ominously; "... and they *walk* that pilgrimage." So, he knew that it was not so much all about the Holy City of Santiago de Compostela but about the journey. Also, it was not sufficient to produce a brief touring guide that stopped off at the major monuments, and so sooner or later, someone had to take up the bat, or the pack and poles. To put it mildly, it took a while.

This guide and those volumes that follow it, therefore, is the culmination of over 10 years of research and writing, including several visits to Spain, well over 2 000 photographs, cartography, and yes, some Camino walking that has included meditation and so far, only one real day of 'reckoning'. Not only work, then! The instruction, 'Well, I wouldn't start from here,' probably applies. I started in Santander, actually! But finally, we have arrived, with a 'proper' walking guide and map book combined. Will it be everything Camino pilgrims want and need – or at least get them well on their way? Will it also serve in a mostly practical way as inspiration for the journey ahead? I am a publisher as well as author, so naturally at this stage I have no idea; it is literally 'over to you' the reader, user, walker, pilgrim. I can only welcome any feedback received, and make any reasonable changes and improvements in future editions.

Ultreya! – Onward!

Andrew Houseley

Part 2
SETTING THE SCENE

GEOGRAPHY – ECONOMY – POLITICS – HISTORY OF SPAIN AND THE NORTH

In contrast to the deserts and Mediterranean coastline further south, much of northern Spain is characterised by a rugged Atlantic coastline, high rainfall, green fields and woodland, and sizable mountain ranges. And with a fair share of the country's rivers, notably the Ebro and the Duero, the north is well watered. Some exceptions are the high plains found in Castilla y León – warmer and drier most of the year and cold in winter, as can be felt in and around Burgos – whilst La Rioja and its precious vines benefit from a less extreme climate. July, August and September are usually the driest, with more comfortable walking conditions away from the high summer, which is why May and even October can be quite popular with international visitors. As with anywhere these days, the weather seems to throw up ever more surprises, and given the north's more green starting point, they are more likely, perhaps, to be pleasant (if concerning) ones for the visitor.

The *Picos de Europa*, part of the Cantabrian mountains *(Cordillera Cantábrica)*, track much of the northern coast, which becomes less rugged further west along the *Costa Verde* with longer stretches of sandy beach and wider coves, while the Pyrenees dominate the border with France and signal the start of the Spanish side of the Camino Francés.

Spain is the second largest country in Western Europe by area, after France, and nowadays the population has grown to 47 million, of which some nine million live in the area covered by this sub-series of books.

Apart from Bilbao, with some 350 000 people and a metropolitan area of 1 million, there are several medium sized cities with populations of between 130 000 and 290 000 besides a few in the 60–100 000 bracket.

The major industries of the North include fishing – some of the largest fishing ports in Europe are located here to take advantage of the riches the offered by the Atlantic, though increasingly their boats have to widen their search to other seas further away. Mineral extraction, steel, shipbuilding, port handling, agriculture and food production, energy (including hydro and wind power, pushing fossil fuels down to around 53%), banking and finance, and increasingly tourism – all provide investment, income and employment. The transport infrastructure no longer hampers any of these, as modern roads, railways and airports have grown at a phenomenal rate since Spain's entry into the European Union in 1986.

Spain's strong autonomous communities and the two autonomous cities in north Africa brought a lot of devolved funding, and as La Rioja is one of the smallest – half the population of an English shire county – it is easy to spot in its capital Logroño, where elaborate fountains play and the population has practically doubled in 15 years. The funding was severely cut back in a new austerity programme imposed by Madrid's new government in 2012. Spain's burgeoning public sector has been scaled down, unemployment and falling property values became a problem in the North, though on nothing like the scale of much of the South – all as a consequence of the 2008 economic crisis. The amount of power afforded to the more indigenous regions of the Basque Country and Galicia, although significant, is the subject of constant debate and lobbying. The greatest determination to secede can be found further down in Catalonia, where an independence referendum held by the Community government in 2017 was partly broken up by the national police and ruled illegal. In the 2011 national elections, the moderate Basque nationalist party (PNV) lost ground to a more left-wing nationalist and separatist coalition who also had a base in Navarra – but their challenge subsequently weakened. This came one month after the separatist group ETA finally announced a "definitive cessation" of its 40-year campaign of bombings and shootings. In recent times, as in other parts of the world, there has been a rise in far right populism and some far left and regional separatist alternatives, to the detriment of the traditional large parties of the centre-left (PSOE – Socialists) and centre-right (PP – Conservatives). It remains to be seen how that will fully play out in the wake of the severe economic and social shock of the COVID-19 pandemic – which initially hit Spain hard in its first wave, but was brought effectively under control – and the return of high inflation. There were two general elections in 2019, following an earlier caretaker government, and by January 2020 the first coalition government (a minority) since the restoration of democracy.

A HISTORICAL PERSPECTIVE

BC

c. 1 million years • Earliest human remains at Atapuerca caves near Burgos

200 000–22 000 • Neanderthal man

45 000–8000 • Upper Paleolithic period

To 4500 • Neolithic period

c. 800 • Phoenician traders and settlers on the Iberian peninsula

c.500 • Celtic tribes arrive

5ᵗʰ–3ʳᵈ century • Carthaginians arrive

206 • Romans clash with Carthaginians and drive them from Iberia

AD

To 4ᵗʰ century • Roman colonisation in Spain. Important settlements at León, Astorga, Lugo and Pamplona

2ⁿᵈ century • Early evidence of Christianity in Iberia. Bishoprics established.

409–15 • Suevi, Vandals and Alans enter Spain

5ᵗʰ century–711 • Visigothic rule in Spain; driven out by the Moors

711–1492 • Muslim rule in parts of Spain; establish culture (incl. learning, art, architecture and food); fail to conquer mountainous regions of the north, remains of Visigothic nobility join forces

718 • Defeat of Moors at battle of Covadonga under Pelayo

756–88 • 'Abd al-Rahmān I declares al-Andalus an independent emirate

8ᵗʰ century • Christian kingdoms establish themselves, beginning with the north

1085 • Alfonso VI of León (1065–1109) and Castile (1072–1109) conquers Toledo

1094 • Rodrigo Diaz de Vivar, el Cid, conquers Valencia

1104–37 • Moors defeated at Zaragoza; Aragón and Barcelona join

1232–1492 • Nasrid dynasty in Granada

1236 • Ferdinand III of Castile (1217–52 and León (1230–52) conquers Córdoba and (1248) Seville

1252–1516 • Monarchs of Castile and Aragón including the 'Catholic Monarchs' Ferdinand (King of Aragón 1475–1504) and Isabella (Queen of Castile 1474–1504) (m.1469)

1492 • Alhambra Decree ordering the expulsion of Sephardic Jews from Kingdoms of Castile and Aragón, territories and possessions

1516–1700 • Habsburg dynasty; global expansion

1700 • Bourbon dynasty begins

1808–13 • Napoléonic occupation; War of Independence (Peninsular War)

1813–33 • Bourbons restored; Ferdinand VII

1833–68 • Isabella II

1833–40 • First Carlist War

1835 • Confiscation of Church lands under government of Mendizábal

1846–49 • Second Carlist War (Catalonia & Galicia)

1869 • Isabella forced into exile; Provisional government

1872–76 • Third Carlist War

1873–74 • First Republic

1875 • Bourbons restored

1925–31 • Dictatorship of Miguel Primo de Rivera, supported by Alfonso XIII; replaced by 'soft dictatorship' of Gen. Berenguer and Adm. Aznar; Republican opposition grows

1931–39 • Alfonso XIII exiled; Second Republic

1936–39 • Spanish Civil War

1939–75 • Dictatorship of Gen. Francisco Franco. State controlled industrialisation; growth of mass tourism

1975 • Bourbons restored under Juan Carlos I; Constitutional monarchy

1986 • Spain joins the European Union (EEC) signing the Treaty of Rome with Portugal. Modernisation of infrastructure

2014 • King Felipe VI succeeds his father who abdicates

2017 • Catalan independence referendum declared unconstitutional

Part 3
THE PILGRIMAGE TO SANTIAGO AND THE SPREAD OF CHRISTIANITY

NON-CHRISTIAN AND CHRISTIAN ORIGINS

Much of this book focuses on the Christian origins and development of the region. From the excavations at Atapuerca just off the Camino Francés *(see p. 104)* and the cave paintings at Altamira in Cantabria, it is clear that the antecedents of man were here, together, and even capable of abstract thinking as witnessed by the shapes drawn next to the animals. We can only speculate: at that time in the Paleolithic period, were they thinking about the essence of their lives – their food, and water, even the elements of the sky, the sun and the moon? And death too, where dolmens and stone menhirs followed in the Neolithic period. Likewise, the pagan origins of the Iberian peninsula are of course pre-historic, and so the only record is what the peoples left behind, in terms of fortifications, pottery and implements, and places where rituals and worship most likely took place. The Celtiberian tribes who are understood to have come from further east from 800BC and may even have come because of the Phoenicians to mine and trade precious metals with them, have left their fortifications – *castros*. The remains on Cape Finisterre *(see p. 279)* including the Ara Solis rock suggest strongly the 'Celts' were not only into industry, commerce and war, but thinking profoundly of the significance and interrelation of life and death. According to myth and legend, the souls of the dead would gather at this low-lying spot near to the coast. The souls that were worthy would follow the sun across the sea, whereas the unworthy would remain to haunt Galicia as the 'Holy Company' *(Santa Compaña)*. The 'end of the earth' where the sun and souls fall away, may well have been the culmination of a long walked route.

Roman occupation of Iberia was for the purpose of exploiting the area's natural wealth, although, initially it was necessary to defeat the Carthaginians in the Second Punic War (206BC) who occupied the south of the peninsula. Numerous conflicts against the Celtiberian tribes ensued, most notably 181–179BC and against the Lusitanians, and even between the forces of Julius Caesar and Pompey. Eventually the peninsula was subdued after a conflict with the Cantabrians and Astures, so that by the turn of the millennium, the exploitation of the area stepped up and towns such as *Asturica Augusta* (Astorga) and *Lucus Augusti* (Lugo) were established. Trade routes for mined precious metals were plied between towns and ports. The Camino Francés itself follows in large part the easiest, lowest lying route. It was used as a trading route by the Romans, finishing at Finisterre, and to an extent by the preceding tribes. The Romans, also, brought their beliefs to this outpost of their empire and utilised the settings and the elements required for worship and burial. Several worship sites were later Christianised. Germanic tribes such as the Visigoths, who once settled in Spain converted to Christianity, led the start of the long reconquest of the peninsula from the Moorish peoples of northwest Africa, but from the remote north after they had to flee their capital, Toledo.

Historical evidence nevertheless points to Christianity being established relatively early in Spain, and certainly as early as the second century. Historians link it initially to the establishment of Jewish communities in eastern and southern Spain during this time. But was this the first time Christianity was introduced to Spain, or at least concerted attempts were made? Tradition and belief has it that both St James and St Paul preached in Spain. Paul, who is best known for his missionary journeys in the eastern Mediterranean and Aegean which are recounted in the Bible, expresses his desire not to evangelise areas where another man has already trodden (Romans 15:20) but then he does mention his intention to go to Spain (Romans 15: 24, 28). That is as much as we get about him visiting Spain. He is probably writing in AD56. When Paul, who upon arrest in Caesarea exercised his right as a Roman citizen to appeal to the Emperor, finally made it to Rome, there is some suggestion that he was released and able to continue to preach and even to travel, which is where Spain has been mentioned as one of his likely journeys, before being re-arrested or imprisoned, tried and put to death. And of James making the journey to Iberia, there is much less than that!

By the third century, however, Christian communities in Spain were sufficiently established to have their own bishops and ties with the Church in Rome. Persecution of Christians was sporadic until the Roman Emperor Decius ordered the first general persecution in 250, and in 259 Fructuosus of *Tarraco* (Tarragona) was martyred, while later Sts. Justa and Rufina suffered the same fate in *Hispalis* (Seville). Then, early in the fourth century, Christianity was legally recognised throughout the Roman Empire as an official religion, and around 380 became the Empire's official religion under Theodosius I. By this time, Christianity had become well established in Spain, even ahead of many parts of Europe, fuelling the belief that James and perhaps Paul also, had originally sown the seeds as apostles to the region.

JAMES THE APOSTLE AND JAMES THE WARRIOR

James, son of Zebedee and Salome, brother of John the Evangelist, from a family of fishermen, is often referred to as James the Great to distinguish him from James, son of Alphaeus, or James the Less. He was one of the Apostles called by the Risen Christ to be a witness not only in Jerusalem but 'to the ends of the earth'. Travel, therefore, was very much on the mind. Legend has it that when the known world was divided between the Apostles to evangelise, the Iberian peninsula was allocated to James. Unlike the journeys of Paul (accompanied at various times by Silas, Barnabas, and Mark) there is no Biblical mention of James' journey to Spain (with or without disciples), although his death in Judea at the hand of Herod Agrippa is described in Acts 12:1–2. St. Peter's subsequent liberation is further described – though not his death in Rome. As such, James is the only Apostle whose martyrdom is recorded in the New Testament, and is believed to be the first. This is understood to have been in AD44, some four years after legend has it that The Virgin Mary appeared to James – while he was preaching in Spain at *Caesaraugusta*, modern Zaragoza – upon a pillar by the river Ebro. Prior to the intervention of the Virgin, James is said not to have met with much enthusiasm for his teachings, whereupon he was heartened to carry on. *Nuestra Señora del Pilar* is venerated today in Spain's most important pilgrimage basilica, a national holiday on October 12th, and an equal or even greater than James and Santiago de Compostela for the attentions of the Spanish people. One could say a compromise has been reached: while James is Spain's patron saint, the Lady of the Pillar is patroness of Spain and the wider Hispanic world. According to tradition, James spent a few years ministering in Spain, including preaching in Finisterre, the remote northwest tip of Galicia, 'the end of the earth' – a fulfilment of his missionary journey?

As Paul expressed his intention to visit Spain after the date of James' martyrdom, perhaps he regarded the mission to Spain as incomplete. Indeed, why did James return to Jerusalem in the first place, assuming he had taken to evangelising Iberia? In any event, Paul is believed to have spent only two years in Rome before his eventual death. So, under such a timeframe, any visit to Spain must have been short.

After Herod put James to the sword, the story is taken up in legend, that his own followers carried his body by sea back to Iberia, where they landed at Iria Flavia, modern Padrón, on the river Ulla, an area with a series of *rías* – river inlets – inland from Galicia's west coast. The body was then taken to Compostela for burial, but not before a miraculous adventure which we shall come to in a moment. Firstly, another legend has it that angels intervened to take the Apostle's body up from where it had been decapitated, and it sailed unmanned to Iberia in a rudderless stone boat. Upon landing at Iria Flavia, a massive stone enclosed the relics, which were later removed to Compostela.

Returning to the first version, James' followers were on hand, shortly before they landed with the body, to save a bridegroom from drowning. A pagan wedding party was riding along the shore of the river, when the groom's horse stumbled and threw him in. The followers drew alongside and pulled him into the boat. They performed a spontaneous baptism using one of several scallop shells which hung on the groom's clothing, to scoop water. And so, the scallop shell as a symbol of Santiago was later established. The local ruler, Queen Lupa, was not so predisposed to the Christians. When they asked her for permission to remove the body, now resting in a stone coffin, for burial, she refused and imprisoned them. They miraculously escaped and as bridges fell away to thwart pursuing troops, their legend quickly spread, with many pagans converting to Christianity. Queen Lupa then offered a burial plot for James, and told the followers to go up a nearby mountain and fetch some oxen to

pull the coffin. The mountain was a fearsome dragon's lair and the oxen were wild bulls – she hoped the dragon or the bulls would get them. When the dragon appeared, the followers showed it the sign of the Cross, whereupon it exploded. They then approached the bulls, which became calm and allowed themselves to be yoked to move the coffin. Medieval pilgrims believed the site to be at Alto do Rosario, near Palas de Rei *(see p. 230)*. Lupa had herself now become a believer and allowed the body to be buried in a field. A small shrine marked the spot, with two of the disciples, Theodore and Anthanasius buried with James, but over time it became forgotten.

There is some mention of the emergence of a cult of St James, fuelled in part by a 7th century work entitled 'On the Deaths of the Fathers' by Isidore of Seville, a Bishop whose remains were later transported to León *(see p. 161)*. In it, Isidore asserted that James was buried in Spain. But where exactly was *Santo Iago's* tomb? Then, in 814, during the Visigothic rule of Alfonso II of Asturias, it is again unrecorded and so according to legend, a hermit called Pelayo saw lights flickering over the forest. Seeking help, he went to the bishop of Iria, Theodemir, who was himself guided by a star to the spot of the burial, and pushing back undergrowth with his hands, made the discovery *(inventio)* of the tomb 'guarded by marble stones'. Over time, the 'field of stars' or *campus stellae* became Compostela and the name of the city became established. Inevitably, this explanation has been challenged, pointing to a derivation of *Compositum Tella*, or burial ground. And whether this refers to St James' tomb, or to the pre-existing pagan burial sites, or even to those of the former occupying Romans – both present in this location – cannot be known for sure.

Nevertheless, the dating of this legend seems to coincide with the establishment of a pilgrimage route to the shrine. Alfonso had a church built on the site, ceded three miles of land around it to the Bishop, and later a monastery was established to house the Benedictine monks entrusted with guarding the tomb. Alfonso might be described as the first pilgrim, and although his devotion was likely genuine, in an already strongly Christian kingdom, the discovery was also politically fortuitous, as ties with the Frankish lands were strengthened and dynastic squabbles within Spain were, at least in part, put to one side. So much so, that the battles to reconquer lands from the Moors became invoked in the name of St James, the warriors believing that he was with them, leading them into the fight.

A miraculous legend has it that James reappeared to lead the fight against the Moors, in the **Battle of Clavijo** in 844. However, this particular battle is not documented, so historically it did not take place. It was in a much later battle at Jerez in 1231 that the Muslim army declared that they had seen St James on a white charger, bearing a white standard, leading the Christian forces. And so, the image of James as slayer of the Moors – *Santiago Matamoros* – is firmly established and depicted in several paintings and statues, not unlike that of St George slaying the dragon. The veneration of St James became inextricably linked with pilgrims giving thanks, serving penance in return for James, as their patron, joining in battle to defeat the Moors.

Certainly, in the late 8th Century, Hisham I, son of 'Abd al-Rahmān I, commenced a series of raids on northwest Iberia and the Pyrenees from his Emirate in Andalusia. Although the Moors did not conquer the mountainous Asturian lands, the raids destabilised the area and depopulated lower-lying Galicia, Castile and León. However, by 825 Alfonso, who had earlier turned for help to Charlemagne and the French Basques, had defeated Córdoban forces at Narón and even himself raided Portugal, taking Moorish prisoners and encouraging Christians there to move north to resettle the depopulated areas.

OF MONKS, BISHOPS AND HOSPITALS

The first recorded pilgrim from outside Spain was Gotescalc, bishop of Le Puy, in 947. At this time, the *Meseta*, the vast plain of central Spain, was in Moorish hands, though greatly depopulated by war; pilgrims would land by boat, or use the Roman roads such as that along the Cantabrian coast. A Moorish raid of 1000AD on Compostela saw the later church built by Alfonso III in ruins. But the town was rebuilt and the cathedral was begun in 1078. But still, pilgrims had to come via a longer and safer route. The Camino Primitivo is so named because it coincided jointly with a mass desire to make the pilgrimage, and with the inability to make it via the east–west route further south, so that the early way with its infrastructure was the first to be developed. Oviedo, the Asturian capital also became a focus for pilgrims, but was overlooked as the Moors were driven back, and the lower way became safe to travel and began to take off.

Resettlement continued among those Mozarabs – Christians living under Moorish rule – from the South, often emanating from raids and seizure of booty, and the taking of slaves. The Mozarabs were among the most enthusiastic promoters of the pilgrimage, founding several churches and monasteries along the banks of the Ebro in the Kingdom of León, much expanded from its Asturian origins. This had been helped by similar resettlement of the valley of the more southerly great river, the Duero.

The reformed Benedictine order of Cluny, from their federal centre in Burgundy, had established a relationship with King Sancho III (the Great) of Navarra in the early 11th century, and this was expanded under his descendants. A brotherly conflict saw Alfonso VI emerging

THE KNIGHTS OF THE CAMINO

The 12th century heralded the arrival of military orders, such as the Templars, the Hospitallers – the order of St John – and the knights of Santiago, who vowed to protect the pilgrims from attack by brigands. The order of the Knights of St Lazarus was founded in the eastern mediterranean and predate even the Templars, and devoted to care for lepers.

Their principles – to recover for Christianity the Iberian peninsula from its Muslim invaders – could be regarded as an extension of the crusades in the Holy Land. Aspiring knights would be trained and assessed by the Master before they could be initiated into an order. The order of Santiago was said to have been founded by Ferdinand II of León in 1170 at Cáceres: 'To fight under the banner of St James for the honour of the Church and the propagation of the faith.' Rival king Alfonso VIII of Castile also bestowed privileges on the order. They fought variously around Toledo, Valencia and Seville, and held castles in Portugal.

Spiritual backbone was provided by Augustinian canons of the Monastery of San Loyo, near Puente Minho, modern Portomarín – there are scant remains today. In 1172 the papal legate Cardinal Jacinto approved the order, as did Pope Alexander III three years later, granting many of the privileges and exemptions enjoyed by monastic orders. The royal monastery of Las Huelgas, at Burgos, also played an important role from 1219 onwards *(see page 116)*.

The order of Santiago provided a pilgrims' hospital, San Marcos, at León, and one for lepers at Carrión de Los Condes. Frescoes and effigies of some of the knights of Santiago can be seen inside the church of San Salvador, one of the order's outposts, at Vilar de Donas, a couple of miles off the Camino before Palas de Rei *(see p. 230)*. In 1280, the order was almost wiped out in the battle of Moclín, near Granada, against an insurgency by a new Moorish dynasty, the Marinids. They were in turn defeated later that year, and no more raids were attempted. By 1482, *Los Rayos Católicos*, Ferdinand and Isabella, began to complete the reconquest (*reconquista*) by waging a hard fought war on Granada. The order of Santiago was again to the fore, losing its Master and fielding 1000 knights and 2000 infantry.

The symbol of the order is the famous red Cross of St James, which terminates in the blade of a sword. They also use the scallop shell.

Cross of Santiago
Crucs, CC-BY-SA-4.0

The orders gradually declined, while being increasingly drawn into the regional squabbles and politics that they had vowed to avoid. Today, however, the order of Santiago still exists under the Spanish crown and maintains affinity with the Way of St James.

Knight's tombstone at Vilar de Donas (see p. 230)

to add the spoils of Castile and Galicia to his own Leonese inheritance, and later he added La Rioja and Navarra – a northern swathe of lands from east to west. He invited the Cluniacs to establish a chain of religious houses and hospitals along the pilgrimage way, which with its French influence, and increasingly the French origins of many of the pilgrims, became known as the French Way (Camino Francés).

The Bishopric passed from Iria Flavia to Compostela in 1095, under the protection of the Holy See. Five years later, Diego Gelmírez became Bishop. When Guy de Vienne, who knew Gelmírez, became Pope Calixtus II in 1119, privileges were granted to the diocese (1122); elevation of the diocese to metropolitan status, the holding of a Holy Year when the Feast of St James fell on a Sunday, and affording the pilgrimage the same status as Jerusalem and Rome. In 1179 Pope Alexander III confirmed these privileges in the Bull, Regis Aeterni. The Cathedral expanded in magnificent scale and detail. French clerics were also instrumental in the coding of the pilgrimage. In 1130 the Abbey of Cluny commissioned five books on the life of St James and at the same time the clarification of the pilgrimage's status was prefaced by a letter from the Pope. The series became known as the Codex Calixtinus. The fifth book – the first Pilgrims' Guide to the route and the facilities along it – was said to be by Aymeric Picaud, a French monk, though his authenticity as author is nowadays disputed by many. The book describes four routes, across Gascogny, Burgundy and Provence to the Camino Francés, crossing the Pyrenees at Roncesvalles – with an alternative pass at Somport before these two paths converged at Puente la Reina. It divides the Spanish section into just 13 stages. Besides describing the pilgrimages to be made along the way, its lodging and hospitals, its food, the book is very subjective about the various local peoples including dress sense, coarseness of speech, and importantly, their greater or lesser

Bishop Gelmírez

The Pope's letter from the Codex Calixtinus

propensity to exploit, attack, rob and murder pilgrims!

The increase in pilgrim traffic, the organisation and provision for pilgrims along the way, and of course papal blessing and royal patronage, all greatly enhanced the economy

The Way of St James in Europe

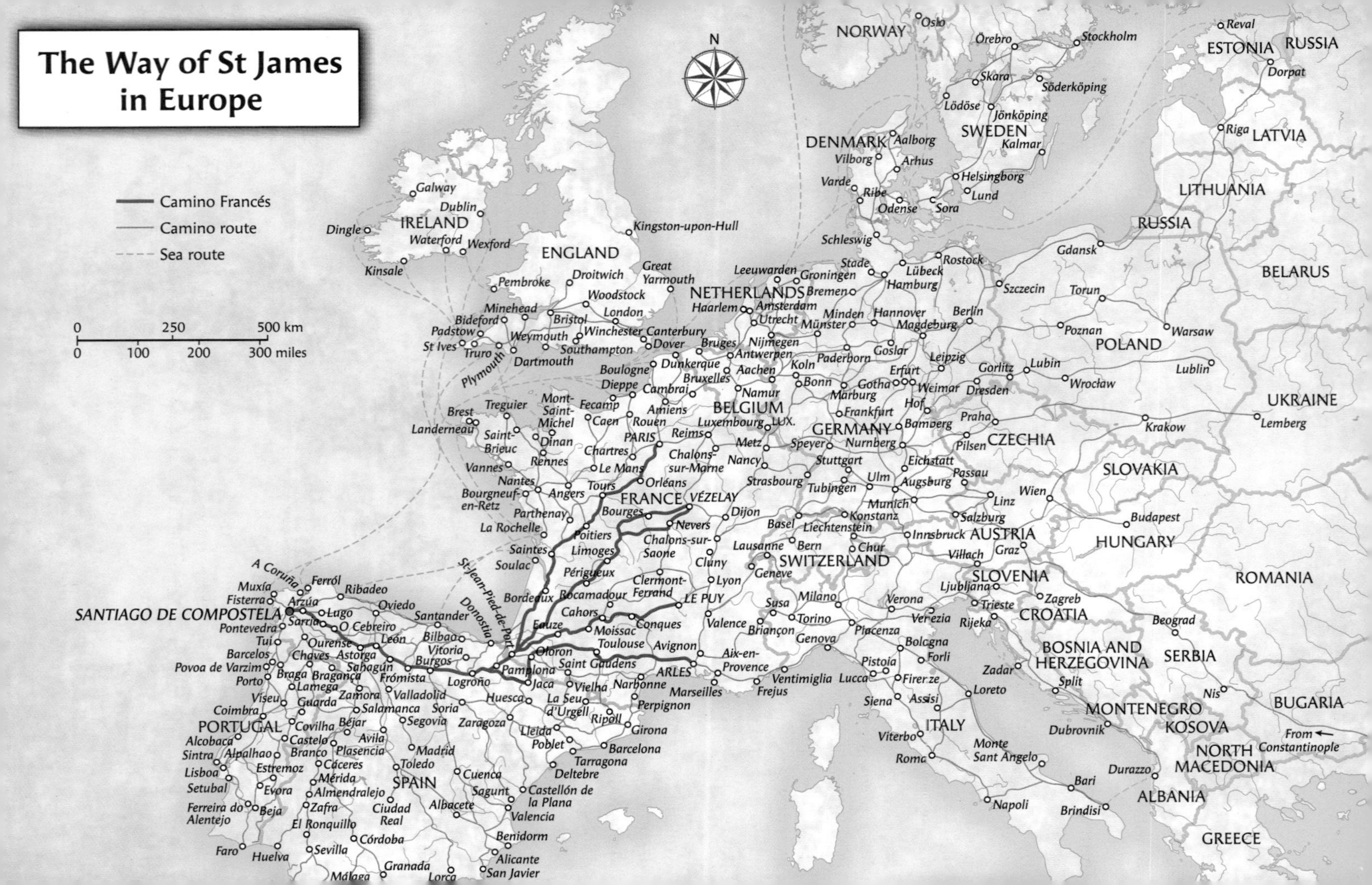

and infrastructure of the region. By the end of the 12th century the monastery of Roncesvalles was reportedly feeding 100 000 pilgrims each year. A network of paths had spread, to Germanic kingdoms, to the Nordic lands, to Italy, the Low countries, and to Britain and Ireland. And with this mix of peoples came their cultures – poetry, music, scholarly findings, and storytelling – and practical techniques such as stone masonry, with the inevitable broadening of horizons and the taking back home new experiences and ideas at the end of one's pilgrimage. Many more routes fed on to the Camino Francés from the northern coast, and up through Portugal and southern Spain, such that several defined routes were established. But given that one's pilgrimage starts from whenever and wherever it starts, perhaps it is instructive not to be too precise about the physical ways.

Picaud described what an individual would gain from making the pilgrimage, as, 'mortification of the body, increase of virtue, forgiveness of sin … and the protection of the Heavens'. But what more do we know of the early medieval pilgrims? Well, we know that whilst they came from a variety of backgrounds, many were poor and many were sick. Their motivation to make a pilgrimage may have been through devotion. It might have been to serve penance by the church; some were convicted criminals sent on pilgrimage by a judge, the dangerous ones were known to make it in chains! Or it might have been simply to fulfil a vow. So often, it was to seek a cure, or to complete their pilgrimage before death, and in somewhat practical terms, to get out of often disease-ridden cities to try and rid themselves of their afflictions. The open path, through countryside, natural water, with the prospect of being fed and watered with basic provisions, and even care in a hospital, could have been motivation enough! Official encouragement for making a pilgrimage came to include exemptions from taxes and tolls, with various regulations to protect pilgrims, such as from commercial exploitation by those who catered for their needs. The pilgrim's certificate – Compostelana – and the stamps picked up along the way, were part of the codification, to verify that your pilgrimage was your own and had not been stolen, that you had completed the path and were entitled to the accommodation, food and indulgences that came with your status as a pilgrim.

DECLINE

It is believed that numbers of pilgrims peaked in the Holy Years in the 14th and 15th centuries. The Protestant Reformation of the 16th century probably put the routes from further across Europe, as well as from Britain, into disuse. And it was the rivalry between England and Spain which is believed to have forced the Archbishop of Santiago, D. Juan de San Clemente, to reopen the tomb of James and rebury his remains for safety. Sir Francis Drake and Sir John Norrys launched a raid on A Coruña in May 1589. It was feared that Drake and his cohorts planned to continue on to Santiago and seize the relics. They appear to have become lost as the result of this exhumation, after which, once this episode became well known, the pilgrimage must have lost much of its draw.

The confiscation of church lands in Spain, secured by the constitution of 1837, again dealt a blow to the influence of the church and the various orders – some of whom were disbanded or expelled – along the pilgrim routes. In 1879, however, the historian D Antonio López Ferreiro guided workmen in the Cathedral to a spot where he thought the relics might have been reburied. A comparison of the skull and jawbone was made with a description given some centuries before to the cathedral at Pistoria in Italy, and in 1884 the relics were authenticated by Pope Leo XIII.

IMAGES OF JAMES AND FEAST DAYS

The image of St James in traditional pilgrim's attire of wide brimmed three-cornered hat, wallet worn over the shoulder, sometimes carrying a book or a scroll, and carrying a staff, adorns many churches along the Caminos, as well as throughout Spain. Pride of place goes to a stone figure of James the Pilgrim – *Santiago Peregrino* – atop the central element of the Obradoiro façade of the Cathedral of Santiago de Compostela. The warrior image – *Santiago Matamoros* – can be seen on many paintings and statues. Of course, the other image of James, apart from those of the pilgrim and of the warrior, is that of the saint in traditional garb – *Santiago Mayor* – usually with a cruciform halo appearing around his head. But this third image without any pilgrim accoutrements is unusually hard to find.

Santiago Peregrino, Roncesvalles

St James has in total three feast days (23 May – the Apparition; 25 July – his martyrdom; and 30 December – the translation of the relics). A Holy Year falls every 6, 5 and 11 years when 25 July is a Sunday. After 2010, therefore, 2021 was the next Holy Year, followed by 2027, and then 2032. The 2021 Holy Year was extended to include 2022 as well, as a response to the reduced opportunities and restrictions of the Covid-19 pandemic.

In addition to St James, the French St Roch frequently appears dressed as a pilgrim in several statues along the Way. He was often invoked against the plague. And so too, St Lazarus, with his propensity to be raised to life, gives his name to many of the pilgrims' hospitals, so many for the care of lepers placed deliberately just outside city walls. Later, St Francis of Assisi who made a pilgrimage to Santiago, is honoured along the Way in churches and monasteries. The Franciscans and the Poor Clares built a network of monasteries and convents, many still operating today. Then there are the 'building saints' who constructed bridges, roads and hospitals, notably Santo Domingo de la Calzada and his mentor San Gregorio Ostiense.

Santiago Matamoros – the warrior

A CONTEMPORARY REVIVAL

By this time, however, the pilgrimage had well and truly lost its place as an essential part of life – and death – in Europe and so, along with civil war and the effects of two world wars, it looked as though it would never be absorbed into the 20th century. The Holy Year of 1948 was the first real attempt for some time to publicise the pilgrimage outside Spain, with special postage stamps and the publication of a major three-volume History. But it was not until two French pilgrims were filmed in the 1960s on their Camino, and a society of friends *(Societe des Amis du Chemin de Saint Jacques)* was founded in France the following year, that things started to change. The Camino began to appear in French television documentaries, and the response was to walk the route as a long distance hike, just as backpacking began to become popular. In 1982 John Paul II became the very first Pope to visit Santiago.

Soon afterwards, the key concepts of international preservation, co-operation and promotion of the post-war contemporary world called on northern Spain. In 1987 the Council of Europe certified the route to Santiago (including all its branches) as a Cultural Route, with a European Federation based at Le Puy-en-Velay (www.saintjamesway.eu).

 The familiar blue and yellow 'milky way' signs appeared. In 1985 UNESCO had declared the Camino Francés the 'foremost cultural route in Europe'. In 1993 it was 'inscribed' onto the World Heritage List, and then in July 2015, the Northern Routes (the Norte, Primitivo, Liebana Santo Toribio, and the Inland / Tunnel route – a.k.a. *Camino Vasco* or Basque Way) all joined as an 'extension' of the 1993 inscription. Modern roads, built in Franco's time, had already appropriated some of the original pathways, given that they both wanted the same thing – the easiest route. Now, therefore, the route runs alongside and criss-crosses some main (still often single carriageway) highways, before disappearing into peaceful open countryside, before re-emerging again to brave the juggernauts. So, it was far from a case of faithfully re-dedicating the old route of the French Way.

Nonetheless, improvements to the paths have been made ever since, often with the assistance of transnational funds. The Way of St James had successfully re-established itself as a modern concept with ancient roots. Further, the growth of ecological tourism is a perfect fit for the Camino. But to what extent is the modern Camino a Christian experience, or to really work in today's world, does it embrace people of all beliefs, and none?

Part 4
THE PILGRIMAGE TODAY

Of course, anyone who requires absolutely the hard evidence of history and archaeology to believe, or reaffirm vanishing belief, will be disappointed, or simply be content to mock the legend (or legends). However, many hundreds of thousands of Christian pilgrims come every year to Compostela because, implicitly, they *believe*. Many of them do not necessarily walk or cycle the route, rather they come directly to venerate the tomb and images of St James, from throughout the Hispanic world especially. Others come not so much as believers in all that is said to have happened, but still to reaffirm their faith. However, we have barely begun to cover the phenomenon that is today's Camino: the search for spirituality, peace and self-reconciliation in today's muddled, stressed world that draws so many.

SO, WHY DO THEY COME, AND WHAT IS IT REALLY LIKE?

In the Christian world, we have seen **disillusionment** with church based worship and fellowship, but also some **new discovery** such as the growth of evangelical 'mega churches', often from the humble beginnings of a simple meeting. There has at the same time been a **revival and huge expansion of pilgrimage** in Europe and across the world, eg. to Lourdes in France and Aparecida in Brazil, and attendance of worship at cathedrals. There is also a clear sense of looking for something different, maybe having never experienced traditional forms of spirituality, or needing a replacement or supplement to what we have been taught.

The **rush of modern living**, with its rampant consumerism, globalisation, competitive corporate working environment with its frequent upheavals, and the relentless march of technology eventually summons the spiritual. It will be necessary to try to understand, or at least to come face to face with the mystery of life in both body and mind. And it is here that the 'belief systems' – in the very broadest sense – of most modern day pilgrims merge. Whether they are devout or lapsed, of no faith but looking to find something, to make sense of their lives, or atone for something, or honour a recently departed loved one or close friend.

Whatever they are looking for, they come, having heeded the call of the Camino. And it is the **rhythm** of the Camino, the routine of daily walking – for the most part through remote peaceful countryside – that is so conducive to the process of unravelling one's knotted and suppressed thoughts. Yes, there is **camaraderie** among pilgrims – everyone from everywhere – and that is a large part of what makes it special. *Buen Camino!* is the parting cry of every encounter, however brief. However, to work, it is and has to be an **individual experience**. Some may think they are not doing it for particularly strong reasons of self-discovery, they may even keep it that way and return year after year, and yet these aspects have an unerring habit of coming to the fore, sometime and somehow. And that may well produce a real emotional challenge, as well as a physical one; in fact for those who find the physicality of the pilgrimage hard it can become impossible to separate the two. These 'moments of reckoning' can take those pilgrims by surprise, including where a group of friends have decided to come to Spain to walk together. Whether it comes, when it comes, it is your experience. It is up to you if you do or don't want to share anything with other pilgrims. Pilgrimage is personal. Suffering and serving penance in order to experience the renewal of the self was the lot of the medieval pilgrim; perhaps ultimately, there is no getting away from it today.

The **hospitality** along the route is one of its essential features. Principally, the network of *Albergues* – pilgrims' dormitory-style hostels – that are provided by the municipalities, holy orders, parishes, and societies of friends, is in its origins and in many of its current places of rest, a Christian **infrastructure**, that was considerably strengthened by the Municipal and Xunta (Galicia) Albergues – the authorities able to obtain government/European Union grants – and latterly a large number of private Albergues. Often you may find yourself staying in a hostel in a monastery, or as part of a diocese, with the opportunity to attend Mass or Vespers and be blessed along your journey – regardless of your faith if any (and you don't have to take communion); at other times there will be no overtly religious theme at all to your accommodation. All who walk, cycle and ride are welcome. All are received with the understanding that the majority are making this journey for spiritual reasons, whatever their belief system, and all are received with the knowledge that they are keeping this remarkable tradition of pilgrimage alive.

There is a wealth of Medieval, Renaissance and Baroque **monuments** to rival anywhere in the world, and just a few from later on. But the modern pilgrimage has also produced a profusion of personal mementoes: small stones left on waymarks, and larger ones at the foot of ancient crosses; personal messages; the odd walking boot; and memorials to pilgrims, some of whom perished on the Way. In these ways, the pilgrimage to Santiago is a remarkable melding of the ancient and the modern. How your life unfolds after your pilgrimage? It should be different, whether that is immediately apparent, or it takes a while. Perhaps you'll need to return, to continue the journey.

WHO GOES?

The Pilgrim's Office of the Archdiocese of Santiago de Compostela keeps records of all pilgrims who register for and receive the Compostela, following all the Caminos, not only the Francés. The figures have been showing a sharp rise. The 2013 figures show over 215 000 registered during the course of the year. The following year, the overall number rose to 237 810 and in 2015 it was 262 436. By 2019 the total had climbed to 347 578 (10 000 up on 2018). However, remember many more are walking stretches of Camino without completing the journey to Santiago – whether in Spain or across borders – and indeed, many do a stretch each year as time, mind and body allows, returning again and again. In 2019, 18.93% of those getting their bit of paper were over 60, 54.52% between 30 and 60, with the remainder under 30.

In terms of who goes, well, we have to bear in mind it is left to the individual pilgrim to describe him/herself.

Religious and others..........169 314 (48.71%)
Religious..........................140 110 (40.31%)
Not religious......................38 154 (10.98%)

The majority used to be from Spain, who in 2019 total 42%, with all the other nationalities far behind. In 2013 it was 49% from Spain but the actual number is fairly consistent. The next highest is Italy with 8.3%, then Germany with 7.5%. English-speaking countries are high up the list. By this time pilgrims from the USA had soared into fourth place with 20 652 – double the number in 2013. The UK brought 9132 and Ireland 6826, Canada and Australia each bringing over 5000. There are 190 countries listed in total (up from 156 in 2013). The two pilgrims who came from Vanuatu, take a bow! An unexpected country high up the list is South Korea with 8224 pilgrims (more than three times the number in 2013). Some of this is down to two pilgrims who wrote about their experiences on the Camino around 2006, inspiring a whole generation of Korean youth and now retirees, determined to follow in their footsteps. Truly today, a gathering of peoples.

THE CREDENCIAL – THE COMPOSTELA – PLENARY INDULGENCE

Today's Compostela (*donation*) is a certificate for spiritual pilgrims, a document in Latin that states that the person has come to the tomb of St James for religious and/or spiritual reasons. The recording of the statistics have changed accordingly to: Religioso y otros; Religioso; No religioso. And that allows a looser description, in part to cater for wider definitions of spirituality, levels of engagement with Christian faith that is these days accepted by the Archdiocese.

There is an alternative certificate – the larger Certificate of Distance – which nowadays is available to everyone, including those who have obtained the Compostela, so not only for those who steadfastly maintain that they have made the journey for, say, cultural reasons, or have treated it like a race! In those examples you don't get the Compostela. Instead you get a Certificate of Welcome (*donation*). So that's

The Compostela PdO, CC BY-SA 4.0

The Certificate of Distance *Oficina de Acogida al Peregrino*

A stamped Credencial (note: without handwritten dates)   Forestman, CC BY-SA 3.0

three different certificates. With the Certificate of Distance your start and distance are written: Price €3.

To gain either, you must present a valid *Credencial.* Your Credencial ('Pilgrim's passport') is valid if you fill up the spaces, each one with a stamp – *sello* – in chronological and geographical order showing a progression from east to west, a date in the square of your first stamp and one in that of your last stamp; but this must include every daily stage if you only walk the minimum distance of 100km (200km by bike) – yes indeed, that means two consecutive stamps in the same location, the first dated the day of arrival and the second dated the day of departure; for those walking longer than 100km it's two stamps a day anywhere once you get to 100km away from Santiago; this includes if you walk one part of the Camino one year and come back another year to walk further (dates and stamps for each part/year, finish and resumption). *See also pages 219, 222.*

Sellos are all of different design according to where they relate to, are available in Albergues, many hotels, monasteries and churches, town halls, some bars and restaurants that are directly on the Camino. This book details painstakingly all the monuments you will see on the Camino and it is stamps from those most closely associated that the Pilgrim's Office looks for the most. For more information see pages 245, 255.

You can go further than obtaining your Compostela. When visiting in a Holy Year, the Plenary Indulgence (or Jubilee) is a reduction of the amount of time spent in purgatory upon death – in fact all the time up to the point of arrival in Santiago, sins absolved, and performing the following duties:

• Visit the Cathedral and Tomb of St James
• Pray, at least the Apostle's Creed, the Our Father, and a prayer for the Pope

Or within 15 days before or after visiting the Cathedral –

• Go to confession – receive the Sacrament of Reconciliation
• Go to communion – receive the Eucharist

THE ROUTE – WHEN TO GO – STAGES – PLANNING – HEALTH – MAKING YOUR WAY

The Camino Francés as understood today is a 765km (475 miles) route from St-Jean-Pied-de-Port in France to Santiago de Compostela. It crosses four of Spain's autonomous communities – Navarra, La Rioja, Castilla y León, and Galicia – over mountains, through vineyards, up and down hills, across high plain, more mountains, and green countryside, to reach one of the Catholic Church's three Holy Cities. There are many religious monuments, several of the finest built in whole or in part for the pilgrimage, including six cathedrals, several monasteries, hundreds of churches and chapels, also some surviving hospitals and many bridges. How much of it you walk and where you start is your choice. The entire route should take up to 36 days approximately, including rest days, with extra days for travelling to starting point, from finishing point, flights. Some of the most common starting points are, in geographical order and with pilgrim numbers recorded for 2019: Saint-Jean (33K); Roncesvalles (5K); Pamplona (3K); León (10.5K); Astorga (4.5K); Ponferrada (6.8K); O Cebreiro (8K); Sarria (96K). Logroño and Burgos would be two further suggestions. The Camino Finisterre to the coast from Santiago and its now officially absorbed extension to Muxía were, specifically, walked by 1548 pilgrims who had their Camino recorded by the Office in Santiago.

The most popular months, and therefore most likely to present issues of overcrowding, are July and August. They are also generally the hottest. May and September are increasingly seen as good choices, October can be dry and sunny especially if the summer has been unsettled. There are nowadays a few pilgrims on the route in November and December, with fewer facilities open, while April (Easter especially) is traditionally the opening month of each season.

The **stages**, as each day's walk, are never set in stone, and where they appear to be, the authors of the stages across various resources including books such as this, do not concur. In this book, we work to the consistently agreed stages among Spanish Camino Friends, who have worked with the Spanish geographical Survey, to describe the paths onto each map set (providing separate .kml Google Earth files). We utilise both in this book. On average, they are broken down into 25–30km segments – sometimes even more for perceived easier terrain and less (where possible!) for those involving harder mountainous climbs and descents – 25km being the *recommended* **average daily distance**. Most will walk at an average 4km per hour, and of course, it will be less when you are tired and on a stage with many climbs and descents. Factor in rest stops, taking in liquid, food, and making

any adjustments to footwear and other gear, and you should be able to estimate your time between accommodations. Some pilgrims will aim to do less as a daily rule, others will see how much energy they have come the afternoon and go further on some days, less further on others. Some will be governed by pre-booked accommodation, and therefore **pre-planning**. It should be noted, however, that most of the Municipal Albergues and many of the Parochial ones say they do not admit reservations.

It is recommended that those walking for two or more weeks plan-in one rest day a week, perhaps in a city with lots to see, like Burgos and León; many also find they need a day longer than planned in Santiago, to recover and finalise their getaway. But it is entirely up to the pilgrim. Generally, there will be more facilities at the common end/start points of stages, however on the Francés in particular the network of accommodation, eating places etc. is nowadays extensive, covering less crowded stops.

You need to be reasonably **physically fit**, but certainly not an athlete. That said, there is no escaping that to walk long distance is physically demanding, and it is essential you are prepared in advance, and make daily checks throughout your Camino. Some of the stages at altitude – involving sharp climbs and then those deceptively punishing descents – are challenging, so it pays to take more regular exercise in the months leading up to your trip, including some trial walks of at least half a day. Even physically fit people can injure themselves, resulting in an unplanned day of rest, medical attention, and perhaps terminating their pilgrimage. And if you already have some problems with toes, feet, knees: well, look after yourself. Everyone who develops them needs to re-check on their **blisters** each day. You'll find especially well-equipped Pharmacies along the Way for these complaints! Do warm-up and cool-down exercises. Drink plenty of **water** on each day's walk – about four Litres, more on warm days and hilly terrain – with places on each stage to refill or buy from a shop. That said, there will be some days where there is only one fountain between your start and finish points. **Fountains** should be signed as to whether the water is *potable* or *no potable*, however, even today along the Camino Francés, there is sometimes no sign at all. Some water purifying tablets are a good idea as a back-up in case of doubt.

Most pilgrims set off early in the day (departure by 8am is mandatory in many Albergues) – after a light breakfast. You do, however, see groups communing at cafés around 9 or 10am – whether before they set off or after walking the first 1–2 hours. Stopping to eat a morning snack, then again for lunch, is a standard daily routine. All this with the aim to be in their night's accommodation by mid afternoon. In peak season on the most popular stages, it can, in truth, be a struggle, despite the growth of private Albergues and small hotels to supplement the main public, Parochial and Association Albergues. Thinking about where to stay can detract from the pilgrimage. Making the early start is one solution, making each reservation a day or two before, another.

ACCOMMODATION – FOOD – ESSENTIALS – PACKING

The vast majority of Albergues now offer coin-op or pay-at-desk machines to wash and dry clothes ready for the next day's walk, and a washing line. Some of the hotels do too. And for those who want to prepare their own food and even carry camping pots and utensils (essential if cooking in the Xunta Albergues all across Galicia) several Albergues do offer some kitchen facilities. Several association/parochial/some private Albergues provide a communal evening meal *(cena comunitaria)*, besides a simple breakfast for those who want it. The Hospitalero will usually prepare the

Pilgrims relax at Refugio Gaucelmo (Rabanal del Camino)   Confraternity of St James

home-cooked meal. A few even encourage all the pilgrims staying there to prepare the meal themselves and contribute food towards it. Private Albergues in rural areas are often part of local Bar/Restaurants and will have meals covered.

The expectation – usually the rule – is you only stay in a single Albergue for one night; the exceptions are in Santiago itself, where most Albergues will let you stay for longer; also if you sustain an injury and/or are looking for an additional rest day; always ask. **Prices** range from at least €6 in a basic Albergue to €18 in the swishest private one with possibly less people to each room; breakfast may be included but usually separate for a few Euros extra. Some albergues ask for a *donativo* – give what you can and think is appropriate for your bed, breakfast, even meal too – and please do not abuse it. A great many private Albergues also offer single, double, also triple **private rooms** with or without en-suite – and these have recently increased to the detriment of dorm beds. Depending on the layout and size it can be possible to accommodate a small group in a single dorm room with own bathroom. There are also many **Pensions, Hostales** and *Casas Rurales* run as hotels; prices start from €25 for a single room with or without en-suite, the better ones typically around €40–50. Prices have risen sharply for many accommodations during the post-Covid recovery. In the larger towns there

Bathroom at Casa Rectoral, Lestedo nr. Palas de Rei

is also the choice of more modern business hotels, often with good deals. And we must not forget the famous *Paradores* – the state run chain of mostly historic properties with some of the most famous being directly associated with the Camino, the former hospitals at Santo Domingo de la Calzada, León and Santiago. Even in these hotels, less than €150 for a room with breakfast is not out of the question and they also offer pilgrims a discount. Increasingly there are also some comfortable/luxury inns in individually restored historic properties, again at the upper price range: €70–80 is typical. Certainly, those who want to be more pampered after each day's exertion, and are prepared to pay, are no longer without choices. Tour companies who carry your baggage ahead to the next pre-booked hotel; many hotels which make a feature of the bathroom, with tired limbs in mind – jacuzzi anybody? multijet shower? or how about a Roman bath? At the other end of the scale, a few pilgrims walk with a ground sheet and sleeping bag, even a tent, fully intending to sleep out under the stars on at least some nights of their Camino. It is, however, illegal in Spain to set up camp away from an authorised site and any suitable piece of ground next to the path is likely to have been used as a toilet. Some Albergues will accommodate campers in their gardens, as a registered guest,

with use of bathing facilities.

Pilgrims are further catered apart from any cena comunitaria. The **Pilgrim's Menu** in a restaurant or bar is an institution of the Camino Francés, usually a three course dinner at a budget price, including wine. Minimum is €8 per person – but with at least one processed food course – while expect to pay €12 for a better one in pleasant surroundings, on the face of it at a fraction of the price of any compatible options on the main menu. However, portions can be small. Many prefer the set *Menú del Día* you can find in restaurants and bar-restaurants all over Spain. The cities and major Pilgrim towns, of course, offer more choice with seemingly every restaurant and café offering the Pilgrim's meal, while at isolated Albergues it will be the hostel itself or the neighbouring bar that does the honours. It is the custom for the Spanish to eat later, from 9PM, when pilgrims have mostly retired for the night, and this could limit choice if you don't want a set meal. Pilgrims are further catered for with wayside bars, some more reasonably priced than others, good places to rest the feet while tucking into a tortilla, sopa or bocadillo sandwich for lunch. Mini markets are more plentiful along the Camino than might otherwise be the case for isolated villages, as pilgrims seek their own supplies and effectively bring a service to the locals. There are many lonely stretches of even the most popular routes, and so it is always advisable to carry a few basic items of food and the odd mini carton of juice.

Like most guides, this book is geared more for walkers than for cyclists. But, especially in León province and Galicia on the final 200km of the Camino Francés (because they have to complete double the distance of walkers to earn their Compostela), there is a pack carrying service operating out of many of the municipal Albergues. The blisters are just as real for cyclists as they are for walkers; it's just that they occur in different places!

EQUIPMENT & CLOTHING

There is a plethora of advice available on what to pack, and all manner of other Camino tips. The following may serve as a packing list:

Packing List

Sunhat – *wide brimmed*
Sunglasses
Shirts – *short and long sleeved – 1 of each*
T-shirts – *cotton or synthetic moisture wicking – 2*
Hiking trousers – *high quality, water repellent/proof (convertible to shorts?)*
Trousers – *for evenings/onward travel*
Shorts – *hiking or outdoor – cotton blend or synthetic moisture wicking*
Waterproof jacket
Fleece top/jumper
Rain jacket – *lightweight*
Underwear – *3 pairs, sports bras*
Socks designed for walking or trekking (double layered or add liner socks) – *merino woollen or special blend - 3 pairs*
Walking boots – *not heavy but with ankle cover/Walking shoes/trail runners/trail sandals*
Sandals – *for evenings, or trail sandals as second option to boots*
Backpack cover or all-over poncho – *waterproof*
Walking poles – *optional but recommended for reducing impact*
Water bottles – *2 x 1 – 1.5 litre or hydration bladder system that fits inside your pack*
This book (or device if using the eBook)
Phone or device, for making reservations, keeping in touch (?), emergencies
Charger – *universal travel type*
Camera – *compact type*
Towel*, face cloth, toilet roll, tissues
Sleeping bag*
Sanitary wear
Toiletries – *soap, shampoo, tooth brush, toothpaste, razor/small shaver, cream (shaving, moisturiser)*
Handwashing laundry powder/liquid
First Aid Kit – *incl. foot care eg. gel, spray & blister plasters, sport tape, antiseptic cream & plasters, painkillers (eg ibuprofen subj. to medical advice), small scissors*
Your medication
Bug repellent, bed bug spray*
Sun block, sun cream, aftersun
Penknife (eg. Swiss Army type)
Sewing Kit (small eg. from hotel)
Earplugs – *high quality*
Torch*
Alarm clock (if not on phone/device)
* *If staying in Albergues*

Do not carry more than 10% of your body weight in your pack, plus water and food, as it is a common cause of injury besides fuelling daily exhaustion. Make sure your backpack is of high quality, lightweight and light-coloured material from one of the specialist brands, and it matches your torso height – they come in different settings. The pack when full should take the weight on your hips, once the cross strap is tightened. A 40 litre pack is an option, 30 litres with everything packed inside/outside and you're doing well. Winter packing: add 10 litres.

Sort out your **footwear** and socks well before you go – bite the bullet if you need new boots/shoes and get good advice on fitting, then break them in. Advice against footwear with waterproof protection is sometimes proffered as a way of preventing blisters, but blisters are caused in the first place by friction and then by moisture, so that comes back to fitting. Upsize to allow for your feet to swell on each day's walk – or alternate socks and liner socks, boots and sandals, but always ensure they will wick away moisture. Some people prefer Trail runners/ sandals as an alternative to walking boots/ shoes, especially in high season and claimed to prevent blisters, but remember they don't offer ankle protection and northern Spain can be wet at any time, with Camino paths covered with water in places.

Mobile **internet/phone** can be had if your phone is unlocked and you purchase a SIM from a Spanish provider like vodafone.es | orange.es or movistar.es This could be a great help in booking ahead and going online to access or download apps or GPS while on the move (rural reception permitting). Pay €10 or the Orange 'tourist package' is €15–25. Many people get by on free apps such as WhatsApp, Facebook and Viber, and of course using the wi-fi in hostels, hotels and cafés.

EMERGENCIES & SAFETY

Dial 112 for Police, Ambulance and Fire.

There is a new app called AlertCops which is advisable to download from the Stores or on https://alertcops.ses.mir.es/alertcops

The Camino is safe, however, there have been isolated incidents that suggest women should take extra care, especially if walking alone. Do not respond to someone trying to divert you off the main path, and be suspicious of homemade signs doing just that. If you feel threatened, uncomfortable, or in any kind of assault, remove yourself from the scene as best you can and contact the police.

See also Glossary on page 292.

TRAVEL INFORMATION TO AND FROM

Getting to your Camino start:

The two international airports in Spain for **intercontinental flights** are Madrid and Barcelona, with Madrid preferred for a **start from Burgos** and further west. Bus and rail for onward transport (see below). Porto or Lisbon (a long 8 hours + from Santiago) could be considered for the return flight. Bilbao, Santander, and Asturias airports might be considered for European arrivals.

If **starting at Saint-Jean-Pied-de-Port**, however, there are low cost flights into Biarritz

Airport which is 12 mins. by local bus to Bayonne for the **train** (1 hr. 20 min.) – change at Bayonne if coming from Paris by TGV and reckon on 6 hours total. Also Pau (domestic in France) and Tarbes-Lourdes airports. Toulouse is another option with flight and train connections. Paris, Barcelona or Madrid are the options for flights from further away. Check the bus and train information below and add www.sncf.com for French trains. Camino-oriented taxi companies operate from here, including https://expressbourricot.com

Starting at Sarria: Santiago is the nearest airport with long 3–4 hour connection via Santiago city (by bus to Lugo and train to Sarria). Consider a Taxi if you have a small group, or change arrival airport. But watch for any improvements. Train from Madrid (3+ hrs. Change at Ourense).

Bus Network:

Spain's bus network is extensive, and reaches many parts that trains don't. The main national motor coach company operating scheduled services is ALSA https://www.alsa.com with itineraries from one country to another available. Try also https://global.flixbus.com for long-distance. www.busradar.com and https://www.omio.com/ are among the comparison sites. Typical one-way from Madrid (Estación Sur) to Ponferrada via Astorga with ALSA €27.50 (4+ hrs.). Jiménez Movilidad (formerly PLM) www.plmautocares.com runs buses from Madrid (Airport and Av. de América bus station) to Logroño (€19+) and Pamplona (€24+). Pamplona to Saint-Jean: See ALSA. Pamplona to Roncesvalles: https://tinyurl.com/2p86xebw

Bus Station:

The impressive new bus station in Santiago is now next to the train station and opened in May 2021. Besides electronic boards for bus services, there is another showing departures from the Airport. Otherwise it is more than a 20-minute walk to the Praza Obradoiro.

To get the **Santiago Airport Bus** look for **Bus 6A** (not Bus 6) of the yellow Tussa city buses. Frequency 20 minutes. Journey time varies 15–20 minutes. So far with the changes still being completed, the bus is caught outside the stations at a covered Stop on the main Rúa Hórreo drag (after Av. de Lugo junction). This may change to inside the bus station in future. Initial price €1 each way. Pay on board. A walkway connects the bus station. There is elevator access to/from the station below if required. See the **Camino Finisterre and Muxía** section for bus services from both finish points.

Train:

The station is off Avenida de Lugo, in the south of the city. There are two to three direct trains from and to Madrid Chamartín (not Atocha – which is used from Madrid to northeast Spain for a Camino start) each day, as well as one from/to Barcelona plus more involving a change. (Madrid = 3–4 hours €35+) Santiago is now connected to the AVE high-speed Madrid–Galicia line which runs to Ourense. One change of train increases the options considerably, as far as Paris and Portugal. Regional trains serve destinations in Galicia roughly every hour. The luxury historic Trans-Cantabrico trains start and terminate here, travelling through northern Spain.

More information and booking (usually not far ahead) at www.renfe.es or download the Rail Europe app (formerly Loco2) or go to https://www.raileurope.com Renfe trains and ALSA buses each have an office at the Pilgrim's Office.

Airport (SCQ):
And once off the bus (or 15–20 minutes by car) pilgrims and visitors can fly direct to and from London Gatwick and Stansted, Edinburgh, Dublin, Amsterdam, Paris, Frankfurt, Geneva, Zurich, Barcelona, Bilbao and Madrid. Low cost and national carriers are represented. Some of the routes only operate in summer, and destinations and schedules are, of course, subject to constant change. In the 2022 Holy Year it handled a record three million passengers. There are a few more options serving the airports at A Coruña and Vigo.

Taxis – Santiago & SCQ Airport & Sarria: *Taxiclick is an app (Playstore only) for Spanish radio taxis.* www.taxitravelscq.com *+34 659 26 22 88 English-born Spanish taxi driver. Pre-bookable for up to 7 people.* https://radiotaxicompostela.com *+34 981 56 92 92 One of the main companies, sedans or*

minivans (MPV). See also https://peregrinotaxi.es https://www.taxigalicia.com
www.uber.com | https://cabify.com and https://free-now.com are ride hailing services – availability in Spain and all cities subject to change.

Road:
Santiago de Compostela is 57km from A Coruña, 413km from Fátima, 569km from Bilbao, 599km from Madrid, and 1094km from Barcelona. The AP-9 links Santiago with Portugal, as well as the Atlantic coastal cities of Galicia; the A-8 continues the journey to Bilbao and towards France (including Lourdes). The A-6 is the main artery linking Santiago with the rest of Spain, via the AP-9. Another way to Madrid is the AP-53 via Lalín, where it becomes the AG-53, then onto the A-52, and finally the A-6. Car hire can be a good option but check the drop-off fees/inclusive prices if thinking of hiring and returning a car at different locations. https://www.rome2rio.com can be used to compare possibilities. See also the omio travel app for buses, trains and flights.

Pilgrims arriving at the railway station in Saint-Jean-Pied-de-Port

USEFUL WEBSITES

Official tourism information:

www.spain.info *The official national tourism site of Spain*

www.Turismo.gal *Galicia Xunta (government)*

www.santiagoturismo.com *The city's official tourism site includes 'real time' accommodation availability*

www.turismo.navarra.es *Kingdom of Navarra*

https://lariojaturismo.com *La Rioja*

www.turismocastillayleon.com *Castile & León*

Cultural information:

https://consejojacobeox21.es/en/ *Programme of events to mark the 2021 & 2022 Holy Year*

https://whc.unesco.org/en/statesparties/es/ *UNESCO list of sites/map in Spain*

www.pitt.edu/~medart/menuglossary/ INDEX.HTM *Glossary of church and cathedral architectural terms*

www.circulo-romanico.com *Dedicated to Romanesque architecture*

https://arteguias.com *Rich site from a publisher and club on all things concerning medieval church architecture*

www.arquivoltas.com *Vast collection of photographs and notes detailing leading monuments*

https://fiestas.net *Comprehensive Guide to Spain's fiestas by region, province and date*

http://semanasanta.galiciadigital.com *Details of Holy Week celebrations in Galicia*

https://www.lavozdegalicia.es/ *Galicia's largest regional newspaper*

Country Confraternities – credencial available to order:

www.csj.org.uk *London based Confraternity of St James. Many resources. Also, how to volunteer as a Hospitallero at one of their two Albergues.*

www.caminosociety.com *Camino Society Ireland*

www.americanpilgrims.org *American Pilgrims on the Camino*

www.afotc.org *Australian Friends of the Camino*

www.santiago.ca *Canadian Company of Pilgrims*

www.csjofsa.za.org *Confraternity of St James South Africa*

https://xircammini.org *Malta*

www.caminosantiago.org *Federation of Spanish friends of the Camino. Big on resources & info in Spanish*

Online forums:

www.caminodesantiago.me/ *The leading forum in English, with some expert contributors, and many threads*

Information:

www.caminodesantiago.gal/en *The Junta's site dedicated to the Caminos*

www.gronze.com *Stage maps showing distances and elevations, albergues, pensions, town facilities, and more. In Spanish.*

https://caminodesantiago.consumer.es *Unexpectedly, the foundation attached to the Eroski chain of supermarkets provides information to pilgrims on routes, terrain, accommodation, and sights. Similar to Gronze.*

https://www.alberguescaminosantiago.com *Albergues listing and much more information (Spanish with translation enabled)*

www.mundicamino.com *Spanish information and blog. Well ordered site.*

www.pellegrinibelluno.it *Italian site with good information, well presented*

www.santiago-compostela.net *Originally a photographic journey, now a planning aid (linked to tours company)*

www.caminoadventures.com *Introduction to the Camino routes, planning tips and comparisons of pilgrims' equipment*

KEY TO MAPS AND SYMBOLS

STAGE MAPS

CNIG road classification

AP–6 ══ Autopista ⎤
           ⎥ referred to as
A–2 ══ Autovía ⎦ Motorway

N–340 ━━ State National road

LR–111 ══ 1st class road

C–634 ══ 2nd class road

CR–326 ══ 3rd class and other road

══ Urban road

══ Track

Camino Francés information

Main camino route

⎤ Alternative
⎦ camino route

O Start / End of stage

◀ Direction of camino route

1 Albergue

1 Hotel

TOWN PLANS

═══ Main road

─── Other road

Main camino route

Alternative camino route

── Railway

～ River

━━ Wall

Built-up area

Park / garden

▭ Place of interest

✝ Place of worship

🏛 Museum

🏛 Gateway

ⓘ Tourist information centre

O Start / End of stage

◀ Direction of camino route

1 Albergue

1 Hotel

Distances are centre-to-centre of the village/
town/city rather than an Albergue. The next
stage therefore resumes where the previous
stage left off.

SERVICES IN CITIES, TOWNS & VILLAGES

Facilities
- Restaurant
- Bar or Café with limited choice of food
- Groceries shop, Supermarket or Mini Mart
- ATM/Bank office
- Pharmacy
- All Services

R|B|S|€|P|∞

These symbols apply to services outside those only available to guests staying in the Albergues and hotels; therefore please refer to them while passing through on your Camino and also where you have checked in and want to visit the services, such as a Pharmacy. The All Services symbol is used where there is at least one restaurant, bar, supermarket/ groceries shop, pharmacy, and cash machine/bank office, so this can be in a large village or small town where there may only be one of each. In villages the Bar and Restaurant symbols may apply to the same premises. Where the Shop symbol does not appear there may be a limited choice of groceries in the Bar or Albergue. It's advisable to check what pots and other utensils there are in the Albergue kitchen before purchasing food items to cook!

Medical help: It is assumed that a Doctor can be called in any location on the Camino. Towns and large villages will also have health centres (centros de salud) open in the daytime, whereas larger towns and cities will have a general hospital, including at least a minor injuries clinic. Get help via your accommodation, fellow pilgrims or dial 112 from any phone.

ACCOMMODATION LISTS

ALBERGUES

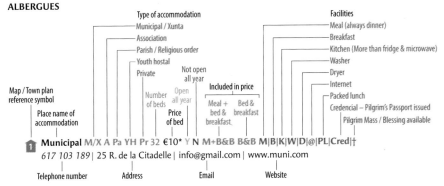

Type of accommodation
- Municipal / Xunta
- Association
- Parish / Religious order
- Youth hostal
- Private

Facilities
- Meal (always dinner)
- Breakfast
- Kitchen (More than fridge & microwave)
- Washer
- Dryer
- Internet
- Packed lunch
- Credencial – Pilgrim's Passport issued
- Pilgrim Mass / Blessing available

Map / Town plan reference symbol

Place name of accommodation

Number of beds

Not open all year

Open all year

Price of bed

Included in price
Meal + / Bed & bed & / breakfast breakfast

Municipal M/X A Pa YH Pr 32 €10* Y N M+B&B B&B M|B|K|W|D|@|PL|Cred|†
617 103 189| 25 R. de la Citadelle | info@gmail.com | www.muni.com

Telephone number | Address | Email | Website

*(+ 2 Priv. €25/30) – private rooms available (not always en-suite) with price for single/double
Year-round Private/Association Albergues out of season (Oct/Nov-Mar) may require prior reservation to open up.

Albergues marked 'Closed during 2022' may have been closed for longer, due mainly to Covid and staffing, are expected to reopen, but the price and other information may change.

HOTELS

Map / Town plan reference symbol

Place name of accommodation | Rating

Price of single/double room
Minimum price that will increase according to season &/or quality of room

Hotel Camino **** €70/90 €70+
610 118 234| 3 R. de la Citadelle | info@gmail.com | www.camino.com

Telephone number | Address | Email | Website

Always mention you are a pilgrim on the Camino when enquiring and booking direct, to obtain the best rate. Booking sites may also contain discounted rates.

Part 5
THE CAMINO FRANCÉS

SAINT-JEAN-PIED-DE-PORT TO PAMPLONA

Many pilgrims choose to begin their Camino at the French Basque town of Saint-Jean-Pied-de-Port (it literally means 'at the foot of the pass') before the climb through the Ibañeta Pass of the Pyrenees into Spain. It begins one of the most arduous stages of the entire French Way, with few facilities for the pilgrim (even though there is also a lower pass), and so others choose the historic Abbey of Roncesvalles as their start. Saint-Jean is symbolic as it is close to where three ancient pilgrim routes – from Paris, Le Puy-en-Velay, and Vézelay – converge and because it marked the resting point for pilgrims from France and further away before tackling the pass. Today, the route from Le Puy, in the Auvergne, is the most travelled, and is marked in red and white as the GR-65, a *Grande Randonnée, Le Chemin de Saint Jacques*. These markings are in addition to the Camino 'Milky Way' blue and yellow star waymarks.

SAINT-JEAN-PIED-DE-PORT (∞)

It is a small medieval town – originally part of the kingdom of Navarra – along the banks of the river Nive, full of character and very much 'Pilgrim Central' in the summer months. Traditionally, pilgrims enter by the **Porte de Saint-Jacques** and depart through the **Porte d'Espagne**, though you should also walk via the **Porte Notre Dame** with its attractive **old bridge**, another of the four medieval gates, where the 14th century **Église Notre Dame** (**Pilgrims' Mass** 7pm Mon, Tues, Thur) can be found. Along the river bank are attractive balconied houses. Atop the hill in the

centre of town is the **Citadel**, built in 1688, affording fine views (weather permitting) of the mountains ahead. Continuing on, the **Maison des Evêques** – Prison of the Bishops – nowadays houses a **museum** of the Camino rather than inmates. The **pilgrims' office** *(Acceuil – Welcome)* (39 Rue de la Citadelle) Tel. +33 559 370 509 www.compostelle.fr is a mine of information on the Francés – it will have the latest weather update, as well as issuing the pilgrim's passport (*Credencial* in Spanish, or *Carnet de Pelerin* in French) and the latest accommodation lists. There are up to seven accommodation options (in full season) on this street alone should you require it before embarking on your Camino. Tel. +33 from outside France.

1 **Municipal** M 32 €12 (+ Priv. €30 Dbl.) Y B&B @|Cred *617 103 189* | 55 R. de la Citadelle www.terresdenavarre.fr

2 **Kaserna** Pa 14 €22 B&B N M|@|Cred *559 376 517* | 43 R. d'Espagne www.en-pays-basque.fr/en/sit/refuge-accueil-paroissial

3 **Izaxulo** Pr 18 €21 (+ Priv.€76+) N B|W|D|@ *524 341 900* | 2 Avenue Renaud | josefernandez58@sfr.fr

4 **Ultreia** Pr 11 €23 (+ Priv.€56+) N B&B K|W|D|@|Cred*680 884 622* | 8 R. de la Citadelle | www.ultreia64.fr

5 **La Vita è Bella** Pr 10 €19 M|B|W|D|@|PL *638 599 183* | 4 Place du Trinquet | lavitaebella.gite@gmail.com

6 **Beilari** Pr 14 €40 N M+B&B PL *559 372 468* 40 R. de la Citadelle | www.beilari.info/en

7 **Le Lièvre et La Tortue** Pr 12 €20+ N M|B|W|D|PL *663 629 235* 30 Rue de la Citadelle

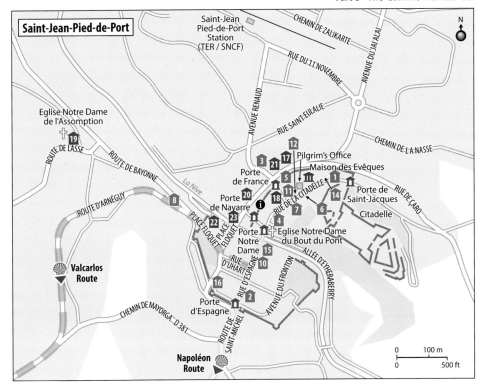

Saint-Jean-Pied-de-Port

---

8 Compostelle Pr 14 €21+(+ Priv. €59+) N B|K
559 370 236 | 6 Route D'Arneguy
gitecompostella@sfr.fr

9 La Coquille Napoléon Pr 10 €18 (+ 2 Priv. €55
Dbl.) Y M|B|W|D|@ *662 259 940* | Uhart-Cize
bixente.eguiazabal@gmail.com (See stage map)

10 Le Chemin Vers L'Etoile Pr 46 €18 (+ Priv. €21+) Y
M|B|W|D|@|PL *559 372 071* | 21 R. d'Espagne
https://tinyurl.com/464n9jmj

11 Esteban Etxea Pr 12 €19 (+ 2 Priv. €55/65)
N M|B|W|D|@ *638 228 005* | 29 R. de la Citadelle
esteban.etxea@yahoo.fr

12 Makila Pr 8 €25–28 (+ 2 Priv. €68+) B&B N W|D|@
663 101 346 | 35 Rue de la Citadelle
https://makila-saintjean.com

13 Zazpiak-Bat Pr 14 €25–26 N M|W|D|PL *631 011
963* | 13b Rue du Maréchal Harispe (approx. 250m
off Route Napoléon) | giteguill.lopepe@gmail.com

14 De la Porte Saint-Jacques Pr 6 €27 B&B N K|@
630 997 561 | 51 Rue de la Citadelle
giteportestjacques@gmail.com

15 Bidean Pr 12 €18 Y M|B *648 980 522*
11 Rue d'Espagne | gite.bidean@gmail.com

16 Zuharpeta Pr 23 €32 (+ Priv. €78/86) B&B N M|@
559 373 588 |5 R. Zuharpeta | gitezuharpeta@laposte.net

17 La Villa Esponda €68+ Dbl. *620 423 763*
9 Place du Trinquet | https://www.villaesponda.com

18 Hôtel Ramuntcho ** €76+ *559 370 391*
1 Rue de France | www.hotel-ramuntcho.com

19 Hôtel Camou €65–68 *559 370 278* | Route de
Lassée (In Urhart-Cize 400m from St-Jean centre)

20 Des Pyrénées **** €110+ *559 370 101*
19 Pl. Charles de Gaulle | www.hotel-les-pyrenees.com

21 Itzalpea ** €65+/85+ *981 883 826* | 5 Pl. du Trinquet
https://itzalpea.com

22 Hôtel des Remparts ** €75+ *676 122 858*
16 Pl. Floquet | www.hoteldesremparts.fr/

23 Hôtel Central *** €85/95 *559 370 022*
1 Pl. Charles de Gaulle

24 Antton Pr 14 €38 M+B&B PL *665 195 073*
Route Napoléon (+2km from start)

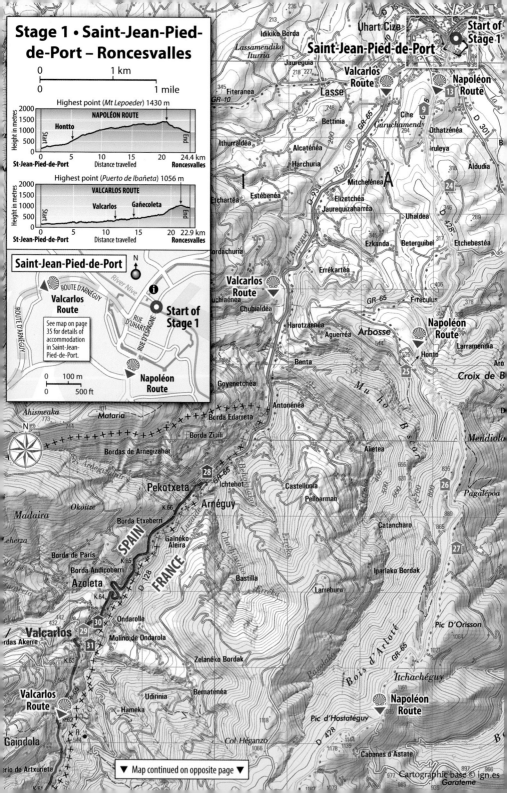

Stage 1 • Saint-Jean-Pied-de-Port – Roncesvalles

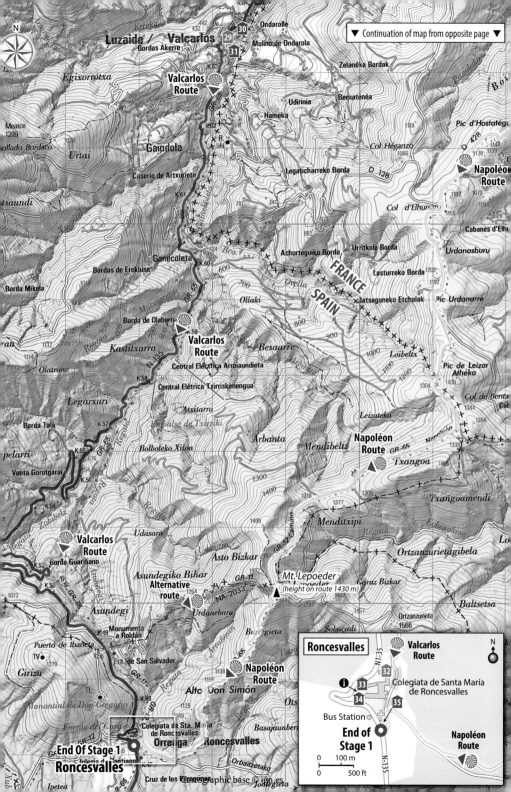

N

Luzaide / **Valcarlos**
Bordas Akerre

30
29
31

Ondarolle
Molino de Ondarola

Zelanéko Bordak

▼ Continuation of map from opposite page ▼

K.63

Valcarlos Route

Udirinia

Bernaténéa

Egixorrotxa

Pic d'Hostateg

Meatce
1209

Gaindola

Hameka

Col. Héganzo
1066

D 428

Napoléon Route

Caserio de Artxurieta

Legaticharreko Borda

D 128

Col d'Elhursa

Cabanes d'Elh

Urdanasburu

K.61

Ganecoleta

K.60

Achurteguiko Borda

Urnitkola Borda

FRANCE

Pic Urdanarre

Bordas de Ereklusa

Ollaki

SPAIN

Jatsaguneko Etcholak

Loibellx

Borda Mikela

Orella

Besaarre

Pic de Leizar
Atheka

Borda de Olaberri

Valcarlos Route

K.59

Kastilxarra

N-135

Central Eléctrica Arroiaundieta

Central Elétrica Txirriskimengua

Col de Benta
Cal

Legarxuri

Atxitarro

Embalse de Txaniki

Arbanta

Leizateka

Napoléon Route

Txangoa

Borda Tala

Bolboteko Xiloa

Mendibeltz

GR-65

Txangoamendi

Venta Gorotgarai

K.56

Menditxipi

Ortzanzurietagibela

Udasaro

Valcarlos Route

K.53

Borda Guardiano

Asundegiko Bihar
Alternative route

Asto Bizkar

GR-11

GR-12 Camino

Garaz Bizkar

Ortzanzurieta
1566

Baltsetsa

Asundegi

Urdanebaro

Mt. Lepoeder
Lepoeder
(height on route 1430 m)

NA-2033

Sobucadi

Puerto de Ibañeta

Monumento a Roldán

Buregieta

Girizu

Eta. de San Salvador

Alto Don Simón

Napoléon Route

Manantial de Don Gregorio

Colegiata de Sta. María de Roncesvalles

Orreaga

Roncesvalles

Basajaunber

End Of Stage 1
Roncesvalles

Iglesia de Santiago

Cruz de los Peregrinos

Orbaitzetako

Jodegiela

Ipetea

Roncesvalles

N

Valcarlos Route

32

i

33

Colegiata de Santa María de Roncesvalles

34

35

Bus Station

End of Stage 1

Napoléon Route

0   100 m
0   500 ft

Graphic base © 100 es

TO RONCESVALLES (24.4Km or 22.9 km according to Option)

For those walking through the pass into Spain, there are two routes to consider. An early start and plenty of provisions are recommended on either route.

The higher level *Route Napoléon* is so-named because this was chosen by the French when they came in to Spain, and were chased out again by Wellington. Napoléon in fact followed the route already favoured by pilgrims for many centuries who found it gave less cover to brigands. This is the more arduous option (closed 1st November to 31st March – longer if bad weather continues) but it is the most scenic, and continues the GR-65. It is essential to check carefully the weather conditions, as high winds and atrocious storms are commonplace at any time of the year – though during the summer, on most days, it has to be said it will be OK. Leave via the Rue d'Espagne and its gateway. Beginning your climb through attractive woodland – and getting very steep – follow the D-428 minor road fairly constantly as you pass through Hontto (5km B)

25 **Ferme Ithurburia** Pr 17 €20 (+ Priv.€70+) N
M|B|W|D|PL 559 371 117
jeanne.ourtiague@orange.fr (check to ensure not whole house rental)

and – with the option of a steep shortcut (left) that cuts out a bend – on to Orisson (7.5km R|B) and its *pic* at over 1000m.

26 **Refuge Orisson** Pr 28 €40 M+B&B N W|D
638 269 738 / 559 491 303 | Route Napoléon
refuge.orisson@wanadoo.fr | www.refuge-orisson.com

27 **Auberge Borda** Pr 12 €42 M+B&B N W|D|@
661 929 743 (1Km on from Orisson)
aubergeborda@gmail.com

Here a statue of the *Vierge d'Orisson* is a good place to pause to admire the views. It was brought here by shepherds from Lourdes – a reminder that perhaps the most famous Marian shrine is not far away. The local D-128 (right) is the first opportunity to switch to the Valcarlos route; otherwise continue on and Quickly branch off (right) onto a path, passing a modern stone **cross**. Pass between two rocky mountains and at *Col de Bentartea* (16km) you walk parallel with the Spanish border, before crossing into Navarra and Spain. Climbing another 300m or so, the highest point at *Col de Lepoeder* (20km; 1430m; Emergency shelter) is reached. From here at the top of the Ibañeta Pass and on all but foggy days, with Roncesvalles in sight, there are two **options**. A steep descending path takes you via a forest of beech trees directly to the Abbey, however, a less taxing *alternative route* is to follow the NA-2033 road (right) down (adds approx. 400m).

The alternative, slightly shorter *Valcarlos Route* takes a lower track and picks up the D-933, although there is a parallel pathway that can be followed away from the road but it is less flat – look out for this just 700m along the main road. Leave Saint-Jean via Rue d'Espagne and its gateway, before turning right down Chemin de Mayorga. The paved parallel path (right) provides a bridge crossing of the river Nive. A service station provides refreshments behind which is the continuation of the path. Crossing the border at the town of Arnéguy (Pekotxeta on the Spanish side) (8.5km R|B|S|€)

28 **Hôtel Clementenia** ** €46/60 +33 524 341 006
Le Bourg D-933 (Temporarily closed in 2022)

follow the river, and you can opt to cross back over the river into France via Ondarolle to avoid again a road stretch. On to Valcarlos (11.5km R|B|S – last facilities before Roncesvalles – Tel. +34 from outside Spain)

29 **Luzaide** M 24 €10 B&B Y K|W|@ 948 790 117
c/ Elizaldea 52 | luzaide-valcarlos@wanadoo.es
Entry code from Tourist Office/Town Hall.

30 **Casa Rural Etxezuria** €50+ 609 436 190
c/ Elizaldea 60 | www.etxezuria.com

31 **Casa Rural Erlanio** €45/55 948 790 218
c/ Elizaldea 58 | https://tinyurl.com/y4rtwttp

Here, the **church** has a Santiago Matamoros. Charlemagne favoured this route, as he marched in and then was chased out of Spain. It was here that his army rested after the death in 778 of his rearguard officer, Roland, he of the famous *Chanson*. Continue on and off the main road, through the quiet Gañecoleta, to Puerto de Ibañeta (21.5km; 1058m). The *alternative route* joins. This was where pilgrims were served by a church and hospital before Roncesvalles took over that role. Nowadays, there is a modern **chapel of San Salvador** and a **monument** to Roland. From this high point there is a short descent directly to the Abbey.

View from Puerto Ibañeta

RONCESVALLES/*Orreaga*
(R|B|€ Tel. +34 from outside Spain)

32 **Refugio de Peregrinos** Pa 183 €14 Y M|B|K|W|D
@|Cred 948 760 000 | Real Colegiata
www.alberguederoncesvalles.com

33 **Hotel Roncesvalles** *** €70/80+ 948 760 105
At the Abbey | www.hotelroncesvalles.com

34 **Hostal Casa Sabina** ** €54+/63+ 948 760 012
Ctra. N-135 | www.casasabina.roncesvalles.es

35 **La Posada de Roncesvalles** €85+ Dbl.
948 790 322 | https://laposada.roncesvalles.es

A very small village – still high up at 948m – where you feel little has changed; it formed part of the Roman road from Bordeaux to Astorga. The Abbey complex is dominated by the **Collegiate Church of Santa María**. As a

college of canons of the Abbey, it was built by King Sancho VII (the Strong) of Navarra in the 12th century, in order to cater for the needs of pilgrims. Tended by the Augustinian order, it was consecrated in 1219 after Sancho's death, and his tomb – together with that of his wife Clemencia – is located here in the chapel of St Augustine. The Abbey's layout and appearance was transformed from Romanesque to French Gothic, and part of its interior to Baroque, and then controversial reforming in the 1930s and '40s tried to turn it all back to Gothic, with mixed results. A statue of Our Lady of Roncesvalles – Virgin with Child and wearing a crown – dates from the 14th century. In the centre of the cloister – replaced in 1600 after the previous one was damaged by snow – is a baptismal font. The **museum** contains several pilgrim artefacts, together with a treasury. Outside, the **chapel of Sancti Spiritus** (the Holy Spirit) is 12th century Romanesque and the reputed burial ground of Charlemagne's rearguard as well as of many pilgrims. Next to it is the simple Gothic **chapel of Santiago**.

The **Abbey was** one of the traditional places where the Credencial was issued; today it can be issued at the Albergue. The **Blessing of pilgrims** in the Collegiate Church takes place at the end of Mass which is from 8pm Monday–Friday and on the eve of festivals; weekends and holidays at 6pm. The Feast Day is September 8th. See www.roncesvalles.es for more information.

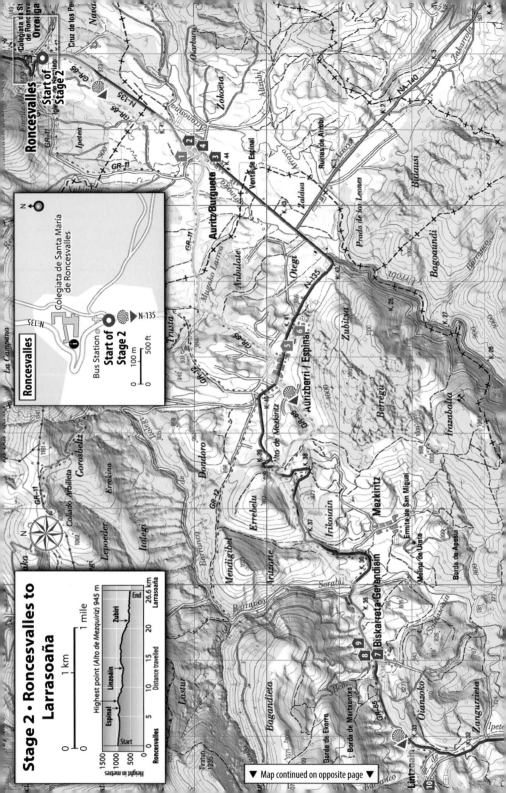

Stage 2 • Roncesvalles to Larrasoaña

Highest point (Alto de Mezquiriz) 945 m

Roncesvalles

Start · Espinal · Lintzoain · Zubiri · End
26.6 km
Larrasoaña

Distance travelled

Height in metres

Roncesvalles
Start of Stage 2
Bus Station
Colegiata de Santa María de Roncesvalles
N-135

Colegiata de Santa María de Roncesvalles
Cruz de los Peregrinos
Start of Stage 2
Roncesvalles

Aurítz/Burguete

Aurizberri / Espinal

Alto de Mezkíritz

Mezkíritz
Ermita de San Miguel
Molino de Urrutia

Biskarreta-Gerendiain

Borda de Martxantxo

▼ Map continued on opposite page ▼

▼ Continuation of map from opposite page

Larrasoaña

End of
Stage 2

Church of
San Nicolás

21 25 23 24 22 26

CALLE ST NICOLÁS

N-135

River Arga

100 m
500 ft

Cartographic base © ign.es

N-135

N-135

Erro

N-133

NA-2333

NA-2332

NA-2330

Orondritz

Mendigain

Paso de Roldán

Narrobide

Puerto de Erro

Borda de Etxeberri

Agoreta

Larrabelts

Borda de Salgots

Salgots

Río Arga

Leranotz

Usertxi

Ibarzulogain

Río

Poblado de Urquiaga/esias

Zubiri

Murelu

Bordalde

Inbuluzketa

Ibañeta

NA-2530

NA-2530

NA-2515

N-138

GR-65

Ossagain

Ildoi

Orradi

Borda Dorrea

Mearscoz

Ollarburu

Osteritz

Magdalena
de Navarra

N-135

GR-65

Ilarratz

Eskirotz

Urdanitz

Barranco

Umakoi

Usmakoi

NA-2335

NA-2337

Ermita de
S.Salvador

Inbuluzketeak

End Of Stage 2
Irurí

Larrasoaña

End Of Stage 2

TO LARRASOAÑA (26.6km)

Following yesterday's exertions, it is an easy and pleasant oak woodland walk of 3km close to the N-135, to the next village, **Burguete** (2.5km ∞)

1 **Lorentx Aterpea** Pr 42 €17 N K|B|W|@
623 286 129 | c/ San Nicolás 56
info@lorentxaterpea.com

2 **Hostal Burguette** ** €40/56 948 760 005
c/ San Nicolás 71 | https://www.hotelburguete.com

3 **Hotel Rural Loizu** *** €60+/71+ 948 760 008
c/ San Nicolás 13 | www.loizu.com

4 **Casa Rural Txiki Polit** €25 (Pilgrim rate) 948 760 019
Av. Roncesvalles (off Camino) | www.txikipolit.es

where there are traditional Basque houses with coats of arms, and a modern-looking **church** dedicated to **San Nicolás de Bari**. This, besides Pamplona, was one of the author Ernest

Hemingway's haunts, where he enjoyed boar hunting. Turn right by a bank and cross the río Urrobi. Cross several streams, passing through cattle pasture. Another well preserved village, **Espinal** (6.5km R|B|S)

5 **Hostal Haizea** Pr 26 €15+ (+ Priv. €63+ Dbl.) Y
M|B|W|D|@ 948 760 379 | c/ Sarroiberri 2
https://www.hostalhaizea.com

6 **Irugoienea** Pr 21 €12 (+ 3 Priv. €45+) N
M|B|K|W|D|@|Cred 622 606 196 | c/ Oihanilun 2
(500m off Camino) | www.irugoienea.com

is next with the 20th century **church of San Bartolomé**. Take a track, left. A climb to **Alto de Mezquiriz** – back up to the height of Roncesvalles – and a **stele** invites prayers to Our Lady of Roncesvalles. After descending through beech woodland to cross the río Erro, and then the N-135, enter **Gerendiain/Bizkarreta** (11.5km R|B|S).

7 **La Posada Nueva** €35–45 Dbl. 948 760 173/699 131
433 | c/ San Pedro 28 | www.laposadanueva.net

8 **Casa Rural Batit** €37+/41+ 616 068 347
c/ San Pedro 18B

9 **Casa Rural Adi y Lastur** €15+ (Pilgrim rate) 679 270
519 | c/ San Pedro | https://www.adilastur.com

The 13th century **church of San Pedro** has a rectangular apse, unusually for that period. Cross the N-135 again before **Linzoáin**

10 **Posada El Camino** €Enquire 622 688 535
Camino de Santiago 46 | https://posadaelcamino.com/

then a steep climb to **Alto de Erro** (16.5km; bar-van) where there is the **ruin** of a former pilgrims' inn.

The *alternative road route* is marked but its hairpins and proximity to traffic can be unnerving. You can keep on it to Urdaniz and Larrasoaña or rejoin the Camino from Zubiri.

Now we make a steep descent to come alongside the **río Arga** by a medieval **bridge**. This river will accompany the pilgrim much of the way into and beyond Pamplona, as it is crossed several times. Here is believed to be the site of a lepers' hospital, originally one of many along the Camino. The bridge is also known as Puente Rabia, as animals were walked around its main pillar to stop them getting rabies – legend has it that the pillar has the power to cure the disease. Some pilgrims choose to end their day at functional **Zubiri** (21km ∞) with many more beds and eating places.

11 **Municipal** M 46 €9 N K|W|D|@ 628 324 186
Av. Zubiri (old School)

12 **El Palo de Avellano** Pr 59 €18–20 (+ 3 Priv €62 Dbl.)
B&B N M|W|D|@ 666 499 175 | Av. de Roncesvalles 16
www.elpalodeavellano.com

13 **Zaldiko** Pr 24 €14 N W|D|@|Cred. 609 736 420
c/ Puenta de la Rabia 1 | www.alberguezaldiko.com

14 **Río Arga Ibaia** Pr 8 €15 (+ 2 Priv. €40+ Dbl.) B&B Y
K|W|D|@ 948 304 243 | c/ Puenta de la Rabia 7
hrioarga@gmail.com

15 **Suseia** Pr 20 €16 (+ 3 Priv. €40-50) N M|B|W|D|@
948 304 353 | c/ Murelu 12
www.alberguesuseia.com/

16 **Segunda Etapa** Pr 12 €16 B&B N W|D|@
697 186 560 | Av. De Roncesvalles 22
info@alberguesegundaetapa.com

17 **Pensión Amets** €45/55 618 636 189 | c/ Gerestegi 25

18 **Pensión Usoa** * €25/34–38 628 058 048
c/ Puente de la Rabia 4

19 **Pensión Zubiaren Etxea** * €45-55 Dbl. 618 014 515
c/ Camino de Santiago 2
www.pensionzubiarenetxea.com/

Turn right to cross the bridge if this is your choice – to make it 20km into Pamplona. It is

another 5.5km – with **Urdaniz** (R) off Camino (cross the river to access a ccommodation – it is directly on the road route)

20 **Hostel Acá y Allá** €20 Bunk B&B 10 beds 615
257 666 c/ San Miguel 18 (500m off Camino, Pool,
Dinner, €) | www.alojamientosacayalla.com

and **Ilarratz** to enter historic **Larrasoaña** (R|B|S) over another medieval bridge.

21 **Municipal** M 10 €10 N K|B|@ 626 718 417
c/ San Nicolas 16 | alberguelarrasoaina@gmail.com

22 **Asteia** Pr 12 €15 B&B N W|D|@ 663 371 513
c/ Errotabidea 24 | (closed during 2022).

23 **San Nicolas** Pr 40 €12 N M|K|W|D|@ 619 559 225
c/ Sorandi 5–7 | www.alberguesannicolas.com

24 **Pensión Casa Elita*** €60+ 629 412 120
c/ Amairu 7 | www.casaelita.es (closed during 2022).

25 **Pensión El Peregrino** €45–55 663 895 411 | c/ San
Nicolás 50 | www.pensionperegrinolarrasoana.com/

26 **Pensión Casa Tau** €60+ Dbl. 622 745 620/948 304 720
c/ Errotabidea 18 | https://tinyurl.com/22yrnpaz

You can continue without crossing this bridge if you stopped the night at Zubiri. The 13th century **church of San Nicolás** has a statue of St James. This village was once the site of a monastery and two hospitals. Rejoining the Camino involves going back over the bridge.

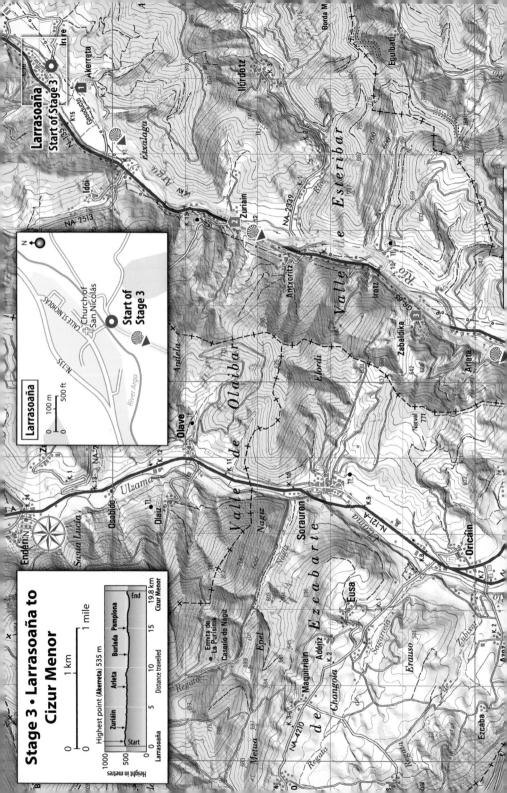

Stage 3 • Larrasoaña to Cizur Menor

Highest point (Akerreta) 535 m

Height in metres

Zuriáin — Arleta — Burlada — Pamplona

Larrasoaña — Start — Ermita de La Purísima — Caserío de Nagiz — End — Cizur Menor

Distance travelled — 19.8 km

Larrasoaña

Church of San Nicolás

Start of Stage 3

CALLE SAN NICHOLAS

NE135

River Arga

N
500 ft
100 m

Larrasoaña · Start of Stage 3

TO CIZUR MENOR VIA PAMPLONA (19.8km)

This stage passes through and beyond Pamplona, though many pilgrims will inevitably want to stay in the city – it is also where several start their Camino – and therefore, much of this section serves to guide you out of the city the next morning. There is also a local bus service from Cizur Menor to the city centre. The suburbs just before the city also provide refuge for pilgrims.

A full city guide is in the next section, with all the accommodation which we list for the city found there.

Pay attention to the San Fermín revels if your Camino is in July.

From Larrasoaña, walk up to the hilltop village of **Akerreta**

1 **Hotel Akerreta** ** €55+/86+ *948 304 572*
c/ Transfiguración 11 | www.hotelakerreta.com

(**church of la Transfiguración**) and then back down to the riverside, crossing the river three times over the next 3km over bridges ancient and modern. At **Zuriáin** (3.7km B)

2 **La Parada de Zuriain** Pr 7 €10 (+3 Priv. €50+) N
M|B|W|D|@ *699 556 741* | c/ Landa 8
laparadadezuriain@yahoo.es

join the N-135 before taking a left and crossing the river again. At **Irotz** (B) the **church of San Pedro** has a 16th century altarpiece; cross a 12th century **bridge**. At **Zabaldika** (7km) the path bypasses close to the hamlet if not intending to visit.

3 **Parroquial** Pa 18 Don N M|B|K|W|D|@|† *948 330 918*
c/ San Esteban de arriba 8
https://malele11.wixsite.com/zabaldika

The 13th century **church of San Esteban** contains a statue of St James; the adjacent Albergue has communal meals and a **pilgrim service** by the Diocese and the Sisters of the Sacred Heart. Continue on for about 1km to rejoin the Camino before **Arleta**.

Further on, a 2.5km slightly longer but flatter *detour* is possible to **Huarte** (∞)

4 **Hotel Don Carlos** ** €52+ *948 330 077*
c/ Dorraburu 1 | www.hdoncarlos.com

which will bring you back on Camino at Villava (see further on).

Otherwise, after passing under one section of Pamplona's ring road, and skirting Monte Miravalles, you cross a Romanesque multi-arched **bridge** over the Ulzama – one of the Arga's tributaries – at **Trinidad de Arre** (10.5km ∞).

5 **Trinidad de Arre** Pa 34 €10 Y K|W|D|@|†
948 332 941 | c/ Puente del Peregrino 2
alberguetrinidadarre@gmail.com

Here, alongside the site of a pilgrims' hospital, is the **Basilica de Sanctísima Trinidad** with its Romanesque origins visible in parts from the outside. Today, the basilica and the Albergue are run by the Padres Maristas – the Society of Mary – and this site has been putting up pilgrims since the 11th century.

For the next 2km, the suburbs of **Villava** (∞)

6 **Municipal Villava** M 54 €15 (+ Priv. €76) Y
M|B|K|W|D|@ *948 517 731* | c/ Pedro de Atarrabia
17–19 (rear) | www.alberguedevillava.com

7 **Pensión Obel** €30/40 *948 126 056* | c/ Las Eras 5
2nd floor (next to Bar)

– **regular bus** to Pamplona – and **Burlada** (12km ∞)

8 **Hotel Burlada** ** €45+/53+ *948 131 300*
c/ de la Fuente 2 | www.hotelburlada.es

have little cultural interest for the pilgrim. The next 3km will take you right into the old town, crossing the Arga once more over the 12th century **Puente de la Magdalena**, skirting the city walls (16th – 18th century) or walking along them, and then through the **Portal de Francia** via a drawbridge. Waymarks are everywhere, but as always in the cities, so are plenty of distractions.

At the last count, there are only six (down

Maribel Roncal Albergue

Inside the Municipal Albergue

from nine) Albergues in the city itself. The impressive Albergue de Peregrinos is in the converted **church of Jesús y María** (c/ Compañía near the Cathedral) with 112 bunks on two levels, power points by each bed, full kitchen and washing facilities, and wi-fi. The German-run Casa Paderborn (c/ Playa de Caparroso – left after Magdalena bridge) is the other low cost option. All the others are said to up their prices during San Fermín [5-15 Jul. incl.].

Leaving Pamplona from the City Hall in Plaza Consistorial, find c/ San Saturnino and then c/ Mayor. Crossing into the **Parque Ciudadela** – alongside the Citadel – and crossing Vuelta del Castillo. Follow Fuente del Hierro all the way down (ahead at the roundabout then later under the ring road) and you are in the well-kept grounds of the **University** (18km). It was founded in 1952 as a corporate work of the apostolate of Opus Dei. From 2015 it houses a prestigious art museum with works by Picasso and Kandinsky, among others. Cross the ríos Sadar via a footbridge and the Elortz, and over the A-15, onto a quiet pathway to Cizur Menor (20km **R|B|P**) with more facilities at neighbouring Zizur Mayor 3 hotels incl. **Hostal Ardoi** €35/45+ *948 185 044* & **Exe Zizur** (ex-Silken)**** that can have deals – 25 mins walk to each).

9 **Orden de Malta** A 27 €7 B&B N K *616 651 330*
Left side of village entrance

10 **Maribel Roncal** Pr 51 €13 N K|W|D|@|Cred.
670 323 271 | Paseo de Lurbeltzeta
www.elalberguedemaribel.com (closed during 2022).

This is a neat and quiet town with much Camino history. Formerly a commanderie of the order of St John, there is an Albergue run by the order adjoining the 12th century Romanesque **church of San Miguel Arcángel** and the former hospital. The **parish church** is dedicated to Emeterius and Celedonius: originally Romanesque it has been adapted over the centuries.

PAMPLONA/*IRUÑA* (∞)

1 **Jesús y María M** 112 €11 Y* B|K|W|D|@|Cred
948 222 644 | c/ Compañía 4
jesusymaria@aspacenavarra.org | *Closed Dec. 23–Jan. 7

2 **Casa Paderborn A** 26 €7 N B|W|D|@|Cred
948 395 423 | Playa de Caparroso 6
https://jakobusfreunde-paderborn.com/

3 **Casa Ibarrola Pr** 20 €19 B&B N K|W|D|@|Cred
692 208 463 | c/ Carmen 31 | www.casaibarrola.com

4 **Aloha Pr** 26 €17–19 B&B Y K|W|D|@ 648 289 403
c/ Sangüesa 2 1st floor | www.alohahostel.es

5 **Iruñako Aterpea Pr** 22 €16 B&B N M|K|W|D|@
678 813 741 | c /Carmen 18
alberguedepamplona@gmail.com

6 **Plaza Catedral Pr** 38 17–20 (+ 2 Priv. €50+) Y
B|K|W|D|@|Cred | 620 913 968 | c/ Navarrería 35
https://www.alberitgueplazacatedral.com/en/

7 **Catedral Hotel** **** €73+/75+ 948 226 688
c/ Dos de Mayo 4 | www.pamplonacatedralhotel.com

8 **Sercotel Hotel Europa** *** €59+/89+ 948 221 800
c/ Espoz y Mina 11 | www.hoteleuropapamplona.com

9 **Hotel Alda Centro** ** €67+ Dbl. 948 030 149
Plaza Virgen de la O 7 | www.hotel-eslava.com

10 **Hostal Navarra** ** €55+/69+ 627 374 878
c/ Tudela 9 | www.hostalnavarra.com

11 **Hostal Rodas Pamplona** ** €50+ 626 838 303
c/ Estella 10 | www.hostalrodaspamplona.com

12 **Pensión Escaray** €25+/50+ 948 227 825 | c/ Nueva 24
(1st left)| www.pensionescaraypamplona.com

With a population of over 190 000 and seemingly expanding ever outwards, Pamplona is a bustling city, all of which can make orientation difficult, especially for those staying away from the ancient centre. It is said to have its origins as a Roman camp for Pompey, the famous general, in the 1st century BC and thereafter, *Pompaelo* became an important stop on the road from Bordeaux. From the troubled roots of Christianity in Spain, Pamplona is associated with two saints, their veneration interwoven with a world-famous festival – about all three more in a moment. For a short while in the 8th century, Abd al-Rahmān used it

as his gateway to France, before being pushed back. The Vascones – the forerunners to the Basques – called it Iruña, or 'the city'. After Charlemagne sacked the city, they drove him out, only for the Moors to return in 918 to do the same. As inheritor of the kingdom of Pamplona (later named Navarra) Sancho III (the Great; 1004–1035) encouraged the French Navarrese to establish two quarters, San Cernín and San Nicolás, but whilst it brought trade, it was not good for the cohesion of the city. The French quarters quickly established a rivalry that often spilled over into armed conflict; a third was occupied by the put upon natives. Centuries of fighting included the struggle between the Navarrese and the Spanish 'Catholic King' Ferdinand who annexed the kingdom, including in 1521 the battle in which Íñigo de Loyola (St Ignatius) was wounded. In between the quarters were stretches of 'no man's land' that were later developed. And, as you might expect, Pamplona saw action in the later wars of the 19th and 20th centuries. Today the city is home to the Navarra government and parliament, two universities, a car plant and renewable energy industries.

WHO WAS SAN FERMÍN?

Pamplona is probably best known for the adrenalin and alcohol-fuelled **San Fermín fiesta**, which involves the *Encierro* – running through the streets in front of six fighting bulls and a number of steers – each day from July 7th to 14th. It was made famous by Ernest Hemingway in his novel *The Sun Also Rises*, and who – naturally – is celebrated in the city. The city is packed out and prices skyrocket. It is important to mention it here as much for pilgrim travellers – and those who don't care for that kind of 'sport' – to plan to avoid being around during those mad two weeks; indeed several Albergues officially no longer open to pilgrims during this time. The atmosphere is unique; one or more deaths are not uncommon. The bulls are released from their corral in Santo Domingo followed by a left fork around the town hall onto Mercaderes, before making a dramatic sharp right turn along the straight Estafeta, finally arriving at the Plaza de Toros where they will take part in the day's bullfighting. The balconies overlooking the route are hired out to revellers, while the runners reserve their places in the doorways below and practice their dodges. Besides the economic benefits of 'the Sanfermínes' perhaps there is also a wider sporting legacy? The world headquarters of Basque *Pelota* is here, they play a lot of football, and the area has produced a five-time Tour de France winner, so maybe running away from ferocious/frightened bulls has its uses after all!

But there still is religious significance in this festival, held to the hearts of the Navarrese, even if to most everyone else it is overshadowed by the secular side of the celebrations. It should be mentioned that the saint is sometimes ascribed to have been martyred by being dragged

through the streets of Pamplona with his feet tied to a bull, during Roman occupation; but this fate is more reliably associated with his mentor, San Cernín, in Toulouse, and it is also said Fermín was beheaded at Amiens. He is understood to have been the son of a Roman senator in Pamplona, born around 272; he

Sanfermines paraphernalia

died in 303. Certain relics were brought back to Pamplona in 1196, following a much earlier discovery of his remains and translation of the relics c.600, and it was decided to celebrate annually, hence the birth of the fiesta. He is co-patron of Navarra along with St Francis Xavier. Prior to each morning's bull run, the runners – dressed in their white shirts and trousers, red waistbands and berets – sing a benediction, asking San Fermín for guidance and protection.

In the northwest corner of the old town, is the **church of San Lorenzo**. It was rebuilt in 1901 in the neoclassical style, but its point of interest is the Baroque **Chapel of San Fermín** inside which contains the bust reliquary of the

CASCO VIEJO

There is much to admire in Pamplona's old town. The grand square is the Plaza del Castillo which contains the *Modernista* **Café Iruña** and **Hemingway's statue** propping up a separate bar. South of the Plaza by Avenida Carlos III, the neoclassical **Palacio de Navarra** features frescoes on its tympanum. Inside there are a number of elaborate rooms, and a painting of Ferdinand VII by Goya. This is the office of the President of Navarra and the regional (styled Kingdom of Navarra) government. In the garden is a more than 37-metre high sequoia tree. While one can continue down Carlos III to find the **Encierro monument**, leading off the southwest of the Plaza is the **Paseo de Sarasate**. Named after the celebrated violinist and composer who was born here (his **museum** is in the **Palacio del Condestable**, on c/ Mayor), it is lined with trees and royal statues, and begins with the elaborate **Monumento a los Fueros** erected after Madrid tried to take away the kingdom's privileges in 1893 – with the figure on top of the plinth brandishing the laws. Navarra is even today one of only two communities in which the principal taxes are paid to the region and not to Madrid.

saint –15th century and placed here in 1717. The statue is silver plated and the face of the saint is darkened – it was once speculated that the saint was dark-skinned, however, recent analysis has determined that the colouring is from candles. The festival starts on July 6th when there is a civic service, and then a procession of the statue on the following day before the first bull run.

There is a lesser known feast on September 25th, the day the saint was martyred, complete with its own church. The **church of San Fermín Aldapa** (c/ Dos de Mayo, opp. Palacio del Virreyes) is built on the site of the Roman complex where he is believed to have been born. The present church is 16th century but with neoclassical façade, and as you would expect, has a statue of Fermín in the altarpiece.

Parallel to the Paseo, along the c/ San Nicolás – amid the lively *pintxos* (Basque *Tapas*) bars – is the **church of San Nicolás**. This was in one of the two French rival quarters of the city, and was used as a fortress when the going got really tough. Today it represents an unusual collection of styles. Of 12th century late Romanesque / Gothic, it is surrounded on two sides by a mostly 19th century porch. The wide medieval crenellated tower is topped with an 18th and 19th century belfry. There are many altarpieces and statues in the interior. Moving north, we come to the rival Gothic **church of San Saturnino**, or **San Cernín**. Also used as a fortress when the action swung this way, its defensive purpose can be seen. The saint – a

Open to the public Mon–Fri, 8AM–3PM.
Moving further north past the Baroque **Casa Consistorial** – the City Hall – we come to the **Museum of Navarra**. Housed in the former hospital of Our Lady of Mercy, with adjoining 16th century church, it comprises exhibits from pre-history, Roman, Moorish, medieval, and contemporary periods. Included is a Roman mosaic, a collection of icons, capitals from the Romanesque cathedral, besides paintings by Goya and Navarrese artists. Nearby are several old palaces, starting with the **Palacio de Virreyes** (Viceroys) with its 12th century origins. It has been a royal and bishop's palace, and nowadays houses the royal and general archives of Navarra.

CATHEDRAL OF SANTA MARÍA LA REAL

Off the east end of the Plaza Castillo, a series of narrow streets characterise the former Jewish quarter, which in turn lead to the Cathedral. Construction was begun by Charles III of Navarra (the Noble) in 1394 in the Gothic style, though remains of earlier churches have been found on site. It was changed again in the 15th century, again in the Gothic style, and then in the 18th century a neoclassical façade was effectively clamped onto the front – not to universal aesthetic approval. Recently there have been extensive restorations. It was the scene of coronations and royal weddings when Navarra was a separate kingdom, and even hosted the royal court and parliament. The alabaster **tombs** of Charles III and his queen, Eleanor of Castile, are in the 28 metre-high nave. Behind a Gothic grille, is a gilded **statue** of the patron under a baldachin, and the Renaissance **choir**.

The highlight is the **cloister**, considered one of the finest examples of Gothic architecture anywhere. Built between 1286 and 1472, the doorway from the cathedral is carved with a beautiful Dormition of the Virgin. Each side

Church of San Nicolás

patron of Pamplona represented by a statue – is said to have baptised the first Christians in the city at a nearby well – as you leave look for a plaque in the ground. One of them was San Fermín. There are two towers, the cockerel atop the weathervane on one being a symbol of the city, and the bell marks the start of each day's bull run during 'the Sanfermínes'. The main portal has scenes from the life of Christ. Inside there is a single nave and – unusually – perpendicular to the church sits the Baroque **Chapel of the Virgen del Camino**, which venerates the patroness of the city (Feast May 24th). It was built over the cloister – the layout can seem something of a double-take. On your way between the two churches, you might pass the **Camara de Comptos** (Counting House; c/ Ansoleaga). It retains some of its original Gothic elements from 1364, and as such is the oldest secular building in the city. It takes its name from its use as a treasury by Charles V from 1524 and today that function has returned in modern form for the government of Navarra.

Rosary 7.30pm.
MUSEUM: Mon–Sat 10.30am–7pm (arrive before 6pm); from October – March 10.30am–5pm (arrive before 4pm). Closed Sundays.

OTHER ATTRACTIONS

Southwest of the Old Town, is the interesting **Citadel**. It is star-shaped and has unusually low walls for a fortification. Philip II commissioned an Italian military engineer in 1571 to build it. Three out of the original five bastions remain; it houses exhibition halls, and forms part of the aforementioned park that includes the Camino.

is lined with six delicate lattice pointed arches. Leading off, the **Barbazán chapel** – guarded at the door by images of Sts. Peter and Paul – contains the tomb of the 14th century bishop below an octagonal vault. Next to the cloister, including in the refectory and kitchen, is the **Diocesan museum** and the **Occidens exhibition**. Besides many works of art, including sculpture from the Romanesqe, Gothic and Baroque, there are two outstanding reliquaries – the 1258 Holy Sepulchre, and the 1401 *Lignum Crucis*. The exhibition also attempts to show the archaeological remains of the city. One other highlight is a collection of 28 statues of the Virgin – adding to those in the Diocesan museum – lined up along four rows. Next door we find the 17th century **Archbishop's Palace**. Ask about all the visiting options when you buy your ticket inside the Cathedral entrance – Pilgrim's discount.

CATHEDRAL Worship: Mon–Sat Lauds & Mass 9.30am, Rosary 7.30pm; Sat evening Mass 8pm; Sun & Hols Traditional Mass 10am, Tierces (organ) 11.30am, Mass 12pm,

Several more churches repay visits as time allows. In the northwest of the Old Town, the **convent de las Agustinas Recoletas** is in its own Plaza off c/ Mayor. It was built in 1624 by order of Don Juan de Ciriza, secretary to Philip II. The sparse façade – in three sections flanked by wide pilasters and topped by a triangular pediment – is considered to be a prototype of Carmelite architecture. There is an image of the Immaculate Conception at the entrance, while the church has a fine Baroque altarpiece and a statue of the Virgin of Maravillas. Up from the convent in its own plaza is the chapel of the **shrine of the Virgen de O**. The church of Discalced Carmelites (c/ Descalzos) at the **Convent of Santa Ana**, has a Baroque façade.

Southwest, the **Basilica of San Ignacio de Loyola** (Av. San Ignacio) and **Monument to St Ignatius** are on the site of Ferdinand's castle Iñigo was defending. Originally built in the late 17th century, the church was rebuilt in 1927 in the Churrigueresque style. The bronze shows the wounded commander tended by soldiers. The 'missing' main altarpiece from the Cathedral is in the modern **church of San Miguel** (c/ San Fermín/c/ De Francisco Bergamin Kalea). The 16th century work is by Pedro González de San Pedro.

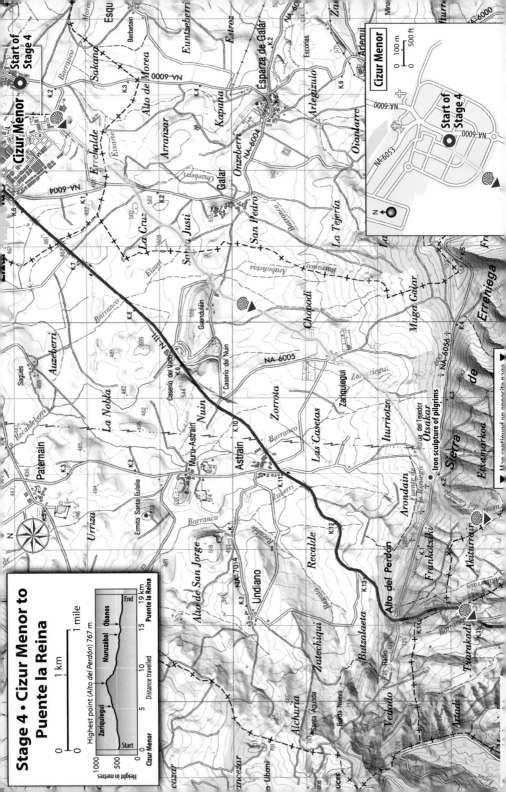

CIZUR MENOR TO LOGROÑO

TO PUENTE LA REINA (19km) WITH EUNATE DETOUR

Leaving Cizur Menor, via a modern urbanization and along a dirt track, you are soon on the open fertile plain. The route continues straight on, with the village of Galar off to the left, and the ruins of the **Palace of Guenduláin** to the right – church and former pilgrims' hospital. At **Zariquiegui** (6km **S**) there is the 13th century **church of San Andrés** with its attractive Romanesque doorway. Now a steep climb begins, as you approach Alto del Perdón and its wind turbines – somewhat ubiquitous in Navarra. Beforehand, it's time for a Camino legend at **Gambellacos**, the *Fuente Reniega* (Fountain of Renouncement). Legend has it that an exhausted and very thirsty pilgrim was confronted by the devil, disguised as a pilgrim, who offered to show him a spring if he would renounce God, the Virgin Mary and St James. The pilgrim refused, upon which St James appeared and led the pilgrim to a hidden spring where he was able to scoop water up with his scallop shell and quench his thirst. Unless the same happens to you, you won't be able to refill your bottle here as the well is dry. On the *Alto del Perdón* (752 m) there is an iron **sculpture** depicting a parade of pilgrims and animals. There are fine views of the way ahead and of Pamplona, behind.

From here it's possible to take a *road option* (right) which leads onto the N-111 and into Puente la Reina, bypassing the rest of the route, but otherwise continue straight.

Your descent will take you to **Uterga** (R|B)

1 **Camino del Perdón** Pr 16 €12 (+ 3 Priv. €60 Dbl.)
N M|W|D|@ 948 344 598 | c/ Mayor 61
http://caminodelperdon.es

2 **Casa Baztán** Pr 24 €13 (+ 2 Priv. €40+) B&B Y
M|K|W|D|@|† 948 344 528 | c/ Mayor 46
albergue@casabaztan.com

3 **Hostal Camino del Perdón** €60+ 690 841 980 for reservation | c/ Iruzpeguia 20
www.caminodelperdon.es (also for albergue)

with its attractive houses and **church of Asunción de María**. At **Muruzábal** (14.5km R|B|S)

4 **El Jardín de Muruzábal** Pr 14 €10 (+ 4 Priv. €40+ Dbl.)
N M|B|K|W|D|@|Pool 696 688 399 | c/ Monteviejo 21
https://tinyurl.com/7uu9x463 (Closed during 2022)

5 **Mendizabal** Pr 12 €15 Y M|K*|W|D|@
678 010 119 | c/ Mayor 7
alberguemendizabal@gmail.com (* No utensils)

6 **Casa Rural Villazón** I [Casa Villazon I] €60+
620 441 467 | c/ El Rebote 5 | www.casavillazon.com

the **church of San Esteban** has a statue of St James, and there is a 17th century **palace** to admire.

It is here that a *detour* (adds 3.2km) departs the route (left) in order to admire one of the finest churches of the north of Spain, **Santa María de Eunate**, and an important focal point for the history of the Camino. Once past the village, the church is visible, as it sits alone on the plain. It will add 3km to the stage, coming in to Óbanos. It is also a great excursion by taxi if you are in Puente la Reina for the night – go as the light begins to

fade. The church is understood to be built by the Knights Templar in the late 12th century. The order protected and ensured the care of pilgrims, and the remains of both the knights and many pilgrims – buried with their scallop shells – were discovered here; this was also the site of a hospital. Templar churches were often octagonal, said to reflect the Holy Sepulchre, though this one's shape is irregular. It is also said that its shape informs its funerary function. Its unique feature is its open porch with 33 double pillared arches with decorative capitals, which completely surrounds the church and follows its shape. The interior is sparse, one of the highlights being the semicircular apse. There is a statue of Santa María, though the original was stolen. The lack of a central keystone supporting the ribbed vaults adds weight to those who suggest that an Arab architect was commissioned to design the church.

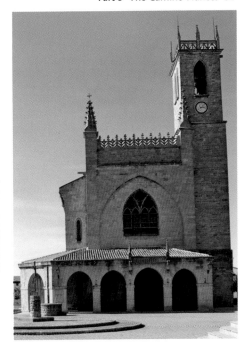

Eunate is on the **Camino Aragonés**, from the Somport Pass – the alternative Pyrenees crossing from France – which joins the Francés here at Óbanos (16.5km R|B|S).

7 **Usda** Pr 42 €9 N B|W|D *676 560 927*
c/ San Lorenzo 6

8 **Hostal Mamerto** €30/45 *948 344 344/649 139 611*
c/ San Lorenzo 7

9 **Casa Rural Villazón II** €60+ *620 441 467*
Travesía San Sebastián 5 | www.casavillazon.com

10 **Casa Rural Raichu** €54/60 *686 679 415*
c/ Larrotagaña 2

The town offers fine houses and squares, with the **shrine of Nuestra Señora de Arnotegui**, where the 14th century legend of San Guillén and Santa Felicia has its origins. They were the children of the Duke of Aquitaine, the brother murdering his sister when she refused to resume her duties after returning from her pilgrimage to Santiago, preferring to live as a hermit. Wracked with remorse, Guillén also went to Santiago, whereupon he vowed to live his life in poverty and penance, residing at a hermitage close to the village.

The story is played out every two years in a 'mystery play' in Óbanos, while the chapel itself is on a remote hill 2.5km south of the village.

The neoclassical **church of St John the Baptist** houses Guillén's skull.

Leave Óbanos through the arched gateway and cross over the road, to follow the valley of the río Robo for 2.5km.

PUENTE LA REINA (∞)

12 **Padres Reparadores Pa** 100 €7 Y K|W|D|@|Cred
948 340 050 | c/ Crucifijo 1 (Seminario)
albergue.p.reparadores@gmail.com

13 **Amalur Pr** 20 €11 N M|B|W|D|@ 696 241 175
c/ Cerco Viejo | www.albergueamalur.com

14 **Estrella Guía Pr** 14 €18 (+ Priv. €46 Dbl.) Y K|W|D|@
622 262 431 c/ Población 2
albergueestrellaguia@gmail.com

15 **Jakue Pr** 40 €20–25 (+ 11 Priv. €48+ Dbl.) N
M|B|K|W|D|@ 948 341 017 | c/ Irunbidea
www.jakue.com (also **Hotel Jakue *** €70 Dbl.)

16 **Puente Pr** 30 €16 (+ 4 Priv. €48) N M|K|W|D|@
661 705 642 | Paseo los Fueros 57
https://alberguepuente.com

17 **Santiago Apóstol Pr** 100 €13 (+ Priv. €25/35 not
en-suite) N M|B|W|D|@ 660 701 246 | 400m before
town at Camping | www.campingelreal.com

18 **Hotel Rural El Cerco *** €52+/78+ 948 341 269
c/ Rodrigo Ximénez de Rada 36 | www.hotelelcerco.es

19 **Hostal Rural Bidean *** €40/58.50 948 341 156
c/ Mayor 20 | www.bidean.com

20 **Hostal Plaza** €40/54+ 948 340 145
c/ Mayor 52 | https://hbrlaplaza.es

While the town itself has several monuments, its highlight is the magnificent 12th century **bridge** over the river Arga, which pilgrims cross on leaving towards Estella. The plaudits to being the town's founder go to a variety of individuals – Doña Mayor, wife of Sancho III is in whose honour the town was renamed – however it is clear that its importance as a meeting point on the Caminos was there from the outset and that this prompted the bridge's construction.

The **church of the Crucifixion** is another associated with the knights Templar, however when they were expelled in 1312, the Hospitallers of St John took over. Having been abandoned for years, following the confiscation of church property and the Carlist wars, the Padres Reparadores (Priests of the Sacred Heart of Jesus) took charge of it in 1919, and remain to this day. The church takes its name from an unusual crucifix left here by a German pilgrim, where Christ is nailed to a Y-shaped tree trunk and branches. The portal and two naves have designs of scallop shells and various images. **Blessing of pilgrims**: 7pm during July and

Santiago Beltxa

August.

All along c/ Mayor, there are fine houses, many with coats of arms. The **church of Santiago** is originally Romanesque, while it was remodelled and extended in the 17th century. The original portal has five carved archivolts fanning impressively inwards and Moorish style lobed decoration over the door. The tall bell tower is topped by an 18th century addition. There are two fine polychrome carvings, one of St James – *Santiago Beltxa* in Basque, meaning 'black' and one of the most distinctive Santiago images on the Camino – and also one of St Bartholomew.

The third church near the bridge – **San Pedro Apóstol** – is also known as Nuestra Señora del Chori (Our Lady of the Bird) after a legend. Originally the bridge had three defensive towers, one of which contained the Renaissance image of the Virgin of Puy, and a bird used to visit the image every day to clean it, brushing away cobwebs and diving into the river to wash the statue's face with water from its beak. The statue is in the 14th century church.

Stage 5 • Puente la Reina to Estella

Height in metres

Highest point 493 m

Puente la Reina	Mañeru	Lorca	Villatuerta	Estella
Start				End

Distance travelled

0   5   10   15   21.6 km

1000

500

Puente la Reina · Estella

0   1 km
0   1 mile

Monument to the Pilgrim

N

Church of the Crucifiction

Church of Santiago

Start of Stage 5

Puente la Reina

0   100 m

River Arga

NA-1110

Start of Stage 5

Puente la Reina

▼ Map continued on opposite page ▼

▼ Continuation of map from opposite page ▼

Estella

End of Stage 5

N

NA-1110

Santo Sepulcro

Church of San Pedro de la Rúa

0   100 m
0   500 ft

Bus Station

Convent of Santa Clara

River Ega

10
13
18 14
1
9
19
11
16
12
15

Cartographic base © ign.es

TO ESTELLA (21.6km)

Much of this next stage is on ancient road now as track – there are Roman stones but it probably predates the Romans as well as the pilgrims. Their modern replacements are too close and too visible on this stretch. Exit Puente la Reina via the old bridge, cross the road and turn left. Once past the **Convent of Comendadoras de Sancti Spiritus** (18ᵗʰ century) follow the course of the river to start with, and begin a climb, past the **ruins** of the 13ᵗʰ century Monasterio Bargota. A descent brings you to the village of Mañeru (B|S|P)

1 El Cantero Pr 26 €12 N M|B|K|@ 948 342 142
c/ Esperanza 2 | www.albergueelcantero.com

with its medieval *cruceiro*. During the 13ᵗʰ century the village belonged to the Hospitallers of St John. The **church of San Pedro** features a baroque altarpiece.

Leave via c/ Forzosa to the cemetery and then a path. Passing through vineyards, climb to the beautiful hilltop village of Cirauqui (7.5km R|B|€|P)

2 Maralotx Pr 20 €15 (+3 Priv.€50+/60+) N M|B|W|D|@ 678 635 208 | Plaza Grande 4
https://alberguecirauqui.com

in which the route will take you through a twisting but interesting radial maze of narrow streets. Central to this town plan is the **church of San Román** with a strikingly similar Romanesque portal to that of Santiago at Puente la Reina – the geometric designs and figures are better preserved here. The **church of Santa Catalina** dates from the 13ᵗʰ century. From September 14ᵗʰ there is a week-long Fiesta, beginning with the Exaltation of the Holy Cross. As you leave under an arch – collect a stamp – you walk on a **paved Roman road**, and then cross the river on a Roman **bridge** (remodelled in the 18ᵗʰ century). The A-12 is in view as you cross under it a couple of times, go under a modern canal before crossing the río Salado via a recently restored medieval

bridge. It was here – warned the *Codex* – that unsuspecting pilgrims watered their horses and themselves, only for them both to die of salt poisoning, with unscrupulous butchers waiting to skin the animals. While the river is salty it is hardly lethal, so perhaps the first guidebook writer was also the first to suffer from hearsay! A further passage under the main roads leads up to Lorca (13km B|S)

3 Albergue de Lorca Pr 12 €12 (+ 2 Priv.€25 Dbl.)
N M|B|K|W|D|@ 948 541 190 | c/ Mayor 40
txerra26@mixmail.com

4 La Bodega del Camino Pr 40 €13+ (+3 Priv.€38+)
N M|B|K|W|D|@ 948 541 327 | c/ Placeta 8
bodegacamino@gmail.com

5 Casa Nahia €59+ Dbl. 660 444 640 | c/ Iturtxiki 1
https://casanahia.es

where the 12ᵗʰ century **church of San Salvador** has a semicircular apse and somewhat eroded decoration. Walk through the main street.

There is more pathway alongside the main road, passing the **ruins** of a pilgrims' hospital. Through an underpass, go through the outskirts of Villatuerta (17.5km R|B|S|P)

6 La Casa Mágica Pr 35 €15 N M|B|W|D|@ 620 281 829 | c/ Rebote 5 | https://alberguelacasamagica.com

7 Etxeurdina Pr 14 €13+ (+ 2 Priv €40+) Y B|K|@
621 267 282 /618 629 351 | Río Iranzu 3
www.etxeurdina.com

8 Casa Rural 643km €49-55 Dbl. 615 003 690
Pl. Rebote 3

and then cross a medieval **bridge**. The 12th century **church of la Asunción** proudly displays outside a **statue** of Saint Veremundo, the 11th century abbot of Iraache, whose birthplace is said to be here; he is the patron saint of the Camino in Navarra.

This is where an *alternative route*, known as the *Camino de Zaraputz* begins. It is on the GR-65 and includes the ruins of a pilgrims' hospital at Zaraputz and comes out at Irache, on the northern outskirts of Estella, adding 3km to your journey. It can also serve as the start of a *quieter route* that misses out half of the next stage – scenic, steeper, with few facilities (see also next stage).

Continuing with the main *Camino route* in Villatuerta, however, look out for the ruins of the **Ermita de San Miguel** which was once part of an extensive monastery and hospital dating back as far as the 10th century. Crossing the río Ega, Estella's procession of monuments begins, though this is also a busy town of some 15 000.

ESTELLA–LIZARRA (∞)

9 **Municipal** M 78 €8 Y K|W|D|@|Cred
948 550 200 | c/ La Rúa 50
caminodesantiagoestella@gmail.com

10 **ANFAS** A 24 €8 N K|W|D|@ 639 011 688
c/ Cordeleros 7 | www.alberguenfas.org

11 **Capuchinos Rocamador** Pa 30 €16–20 (+10 Priv. €40)
N M|B|K|W|D|@ 948 550 549 | c/ Rocamador 6
reservas.estella@alberguescapuchinos.org

12 **Oncineda** YH 150 €11 (+ 2 Priv. €21/30) N
M|B|K|W|D|@ 948 555 022 c/ Monasterio de Irache
11 | www.albergueestella.com

13 **San Miguel** Pa 32 Don B&B N W|D|†
654 480 239 | Mercado Viejo 18
sanmiguelestella0@gmail.com

14 **Hostel Ágora** Pr 20 €18–20 (+ 3 Priv. €70 Triple only)
N B|K|W|D|@ 948 546 574 | c/ Callizo Pelaires 3
www.dormirenestella.com

15 **Hosteria de Curtidores** Pr 30 €15–20 (+ 4 Priv.
€38+/48+) Y B|K|W|D|@ 663 613 642 | c/ Curtidores
https://lahosteriadelcamino.com/

16 **Alda** Pr 12 €13+ (+ Priv. €48+ Dbl.) Y K|W|D|@
948 030 147 | Pl. de Santiago 41
https://aldahotels.es/alojamientos/alda-estella-hostel/

17 **Hostal El Volante** ** €41+/56+ 948 553 957
c/ Merkatondoa 2 | www.hostalelvolante.com

18 **Hospidería Chapitel** **** €77+/99+ 948 551 090
c/ Chapitel 1 | www.hospederia-chapitel.es

19 **Pensión Buen Camino** * €40/55* 948 550 337
c/ San Nicolás 27–1st Floor | * shared bathrooms

20 **Hotel Yerri** ** €55/60 948 546 034 Avda. Yerri 35
www.hotelyerri.es

Originally the small village of *Lizarra* existed on the south bank of the río Ega. The town on the opposite bank was founded on a stellar legend. In 1090 it is said that nightly showers of shooting stars descended on a nearby hill. Among those curious were some shepherds, who climbed up and discovered a cave covered by thorns. When they went inside they found a statue of the Virgin. Returning from the siege of Toledo later that year, King Sancho Ramirez of Aragón and Navarra established the town, and gave it *fueros* which encouraged merchants and artisans to set up business there; as in Pamplona there were Gascones, and a Jewish quarter was established. The pilgrimage began to assume greater importance, and the town's benefactors enriched it with fine buildings. However, in 1512, Cardinal Cisneros and the Inquisition literally cut the town down to size, by demolishing the tops of Estella's tallest towers, mostly on its churches. But don't let that put you off – Estella boasts a fine collection of churches, monasteries, medieval streets, houses and fiestas. With its range of accommodation – including many hundreds of pilgrim beds – and restaurants, Estella makes a good base. The Thursday **market** is also recommended.

On the hill of San Millán, on the Lizarra side of the river, where the Virgin was discovered, the **Basilica de la Virgen del Puy** houses a polychrome wooden Gothic statue, gilded in silver. The figure would have been made at a time when French pilgrims making the journey along the *Chemin de Puy* numbered in their thousands. The old Baroque basilica – which in turn replaced a chapel – was replaced in 1951 with a concrete and glass structure in the shape of a star. This gives the interior the desired effect of intense light. There are also two 17th century images of Christ on the Cross. Her Feast day is May 25th. The Virgin is patroness of the town and, along with its patron St Andrew, is honoured in the main fiesta in the first week of August.

The first of Estella's **churches** to greet the pilgrim is the **Santo Sepulcro**. Construction began in the late 12th century and owes its design to French Romanesque influences. The original ambitious design – incorporating three naves – was left unfinished. It is not possible to go inside this church, however what can be seen from the outside is impressive. Along its late 13th century north façade is one of the finest collections of Gothic sculpture in Navarra. Statues of the Twelve Apostles stand in a frieze

either side of the portal of ribbed archivolts. At ground level the portal is flanked by an image of Santiago on one side and one of St Martin of Tours on the other. The tympanum shows scenes from the Last Supper, the Crucifixion and the Resurrection.

Nearby is the medieval **Puente de Carcel**, which was damaged during the Third Carlist War in 1873, and near the former monastery of Santo Domingo, **the church of Santa María Jus del Castillo** is the former Synagogue which became a church after the Jews were expelled in the 14th century, and now in the guise of the **Interpretation Centre of Romanesque architecture and the Way of St. James**. The c/ de Rúa is the best way to start exploring Estella, with several palaces emblazoned with coats of arms, including the Plateresque **Casa Fray Diego**. The **Governor's Palace** now houses the **museum** of Carlism, of which this town

Palace of the Kings of Navarra

was a stronghold.

The Camino continues along the *Lizarra* side of the river, to the Plaza San Martín with its 16th century fountain and linden trees. On one side is the **Palace of the Kings of Navarra**, said to be the only surviving civil Romanesque building in the autonomous community. There is a depiction on one of the capitals of Roland fighting the giant, Ferragut; inside there is an extensive collection of the works of the painter Gustavo de Maeztú. The tourist office is here, and you could ask about guided tours

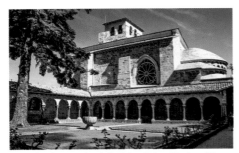

Church of San Pedro de la Rúa   Turismo Kingdom of Navarra

of the next church. A flight of steps lead up to the **church of San Pedro de la Rúa** with its high bell tower; it is built on a steep slope on the site of Sancho's original castle. Here is the third church in the area with the, by now, characteristic Moorish style lobed decoration over the door. The highlight is the cloister, even though only two sides remain. The capitals are richly decorated with the lives of the saints and the Apocalypse, while one of the columns is a cross-legged folly, a copy of the one at Santo Domingo de Silos. There is also direct access to the cloister via an elevator at street level (100m further on from the Tourist Office). Open Mon-Sat 10am-1.30pm & 6-7pm. Mass 7pm Mon-Sat & 12.30 Sun/Hols. St Andrew became patron of Estella after the 13th century bishop of Patras in Greece did his Camino accompanied by a relic of the saint's shoulder blade. Arriving in Estella, he died and was buried in the cloister with his relic, which miraculously made its presence known with a curious light shining above the tomb. Later, in 1626, when Andrew was declared patron, a burning vision of his saltire hovered overhead. The church also houses a black Virgin of O, a cult figure among stone masons. The Camino continues on through the medieval Puerta de Castilla out of town to Irache.

Across the river, the **church of San Miguel** greets you at the top of its flight of steps with the most elaborate of Estella's church portals, though admittedly it's a tough choice. Protected by a modern porch, the tympanum depicts the

Last Judgement, including an image of Christ in Majesty. In the relief, to the left St Michael fights the dragon and weighs souls, and to the right the three Marys look on Christ's empty tomb. Among the treasures inside is the altarpiece of Santa Elena (1406) which shows the saint discovering the True Cross. Connected to the church by a pointed archway, the chapel of St George contains a wooden image of the saint fighting a winged dragon. In the Plaza de los Fueros, is the rather plain-looking **church of San Juan Bautista**; inside is a Renaissance polychrome main altarpiece.

Southwest of the Plazas across several blocks, the bus station is housed in the former narrow gauge train station. Built in 1927, it is worth a look even if you are not arriving by bus. In front of it, on a meander of the river, is the Parque de los Llanos. It is a very pleasant place to relax, and also contains a salt water pool where traditionally pilgrims bathe. The **Convent of Santa Clara** (of the Poor Clares) was founded in the 13th century, although the present building is 17th century. The exterior shows little decoration, while the church is lined with several Baroque altarpieces, including a sizeable main altarpiece. Nearby, the former convent of San Benito is now partially converted into a multiplex cinema.

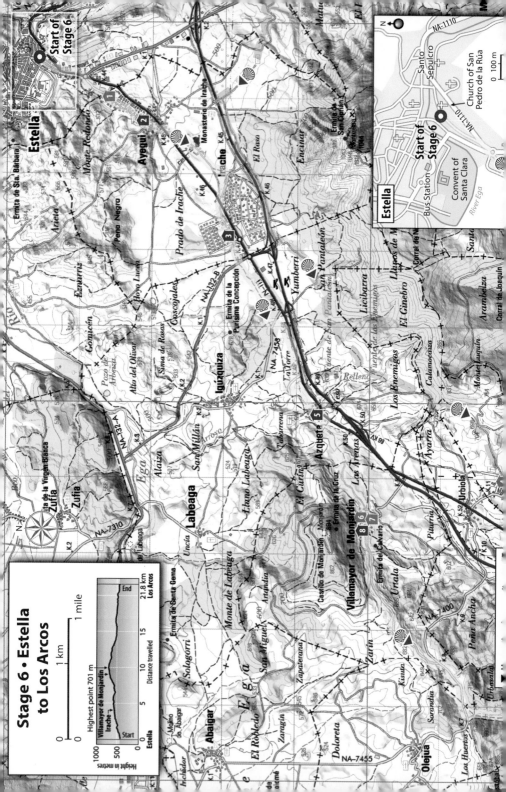

Stage 6 • Estella
to Los Arcos

Highest point 701 m

Villamayor de Monjardin
Irache

Start
Estella

End
21.8 km
Los Arcos

Distance travelled

Height in metres

Estella

Start of
Stage 6

Ayegui

Monasterio de Irache

Ermita de San Gordón

El Raso

Irache

Prado de Irache

Ermita de la Purísima Concepción

San Pantaleón

Yumbeni

Cascojales

Iguzquiza

Sima de Rosas

Atio del Olivar

Pozo de Arbeiza

Comicén

Peña Negra

Monte Redondo

Ermita de Sta. Bárbara

Estella

Ega Rio

Zufia

Ermita de la Virgen Blanca

Labeaga

San Millán

Alaiza

Izko Labeaga

Valdarena

El Curria

Azqueta

Los Arenas

Ermita de la Cruz

Casetío de Monjardín

Monjardín

Ermita de San Pelayo

Relleno

Los Enemigos

Fuente de los Enemigos

Puente de los Enemigos

Calamonozaza

El Ginebro

Licíbarra

Llanos de M

Corral de N

Urbiola

Ayarra

Pituría

Monteljuqui

Arambelza

Monte de Labeaga

Villamayor de Monjardín

Urtala

Ermita del Calvario

Peña Ancha

Zarin

Kisuta

Sorandia

Olejua

Los Huertos

Dolereta

Zaragin

San Miguel

Zapaterana

Ega

Abaigar

Molino de Abaigar

Inchidor

El Robledo

Sologorri

Ermita de Santa Gema

Estella

Bus Station

Convent of
Santa Clara

River Ega

Church of San
Pedro de la Rúa

Santo
Sepulcro

Start of
Stage 6

NA-1110

Continuation of map from opposite page ►

Los Arcos

Cartographic base © ign.es
Ibargun

End of Stage 6

Los Arcos
End of Stage 6

TO LOS ARCOS (21.8km)

Continuing along c/ San Nicolás, pick up the main road (NA-1110 cross the roundabout keeping on the right of it) and straight on, then slight right after the petrol station to the suburb of Ayegui (∞).

1 **San Cipriano** M 42 €12–15 Y K|W|D|@|Cred
948 554 311 | c/ Polideportivo 3
albergue.ayegui@gmail.com

2 **Hotel Casa Luisa** €77+ (Dbl.) 848 460 100
c/ San Lázaro 9 | https://www.hotelcasaluisa.es

After the Albergue it's possible to take an option that saves less than 0.5km but misses out on the following attractions – it rejoins the Camino in the village of Irache (R|B|S).

This is part of the D.O. Navarra wine region, and by the Bodegas Irache, pilgrims can take a few sips of the product at its free **wine fountain**. The inscription next to the tap reads: "Pilgrim, if you wish to arrive at Santiago full of strength and vitality, have a drink of this great wine and make a toast to happiness." There is a wine museum, with tours of the Bodega available.

The adjacent **Monastery of Santa María la Real de Irache** was first recorded as a monastic site in 958 and, through a grant from Sancho III (the Great) the Benedictine foundation saw one of the first pilgrims' hospitals to be established on the Camino. In 1569, Philip II moved Sahagún's university of theology here, where it remained until 1824 with the expropriation of the monasteries. A pleasing mix of architectural styles, there is a Plateresque doorway, leading to a Romanesque church with three apses under a Renaissance dome. The capitals of the Plateresque cloister are decorated with religious and grotesque motifs. The monastery closed in 1985, and its conversion to a *Parador* has been abandoned due to economics and the property returned to the Navarra Government.

3 **Hotel/Camping Irache** €8-12 in multiple room
W|D 948 555 555 | Av. Prado de Irache 14
www.campingiratxe.com

1km on from the fountain and monastery, passing under the motorway, you can take the aforementioned *alternative quieter route* via Luquín (R|B|S)

4 **Casa Tiago** Pr 14 €12 (+ 1 Priv.) N M|B|K|W|@
626 240 862/948 537 159 | c/ San Martín 1
https://www.alberguecasatiago.com

which is only slightly longer, more scenic, but more rigorous, and rejoins the Camino after Villamayor de Monjardín, or can continue on its own path to join up just before Los Arcos. The village contains the 18th Century **Basilica of N.S. de los Remedios del Milagro** (key at Albergue) in which two Virgin statues are venerated by the Navarrese. The fiesta takes place on the closest weekend to September 8th. In addition the parish **church of San Martín Obispo** is 13th Century with Baroque revisions. On either route, Monte Jurra (1045m) is in view.

Slight right to continue on the main route (or straight on to join the alternative route) – cross main road and pass campsite. Passing on through Azqueta (7.5km B)

5 **La Perla Negra** €22/person 627 114 797
c/ Carrera 18 | https://alberguelaperlanegra.business.site

and the **church of San Pedro Apóstol** – worth a look inside if open – you come across the **Fuente de los Moros** ('Fountain of the Moors') a Romanesque cistern of the 12th century with stairs descending to the spring. An impressive vault forms two pointed arches. It was restored in 1991. Continue a steep climb. Villamayor de Monjardín (9km R|B) lies itself at over

6 **Hogar de Monjardín (Oasis Trails)** A 22 €12 (+ 2 Priv. €35/40) N M|B|@|† 623 428 216 | Opposite San Andrés church | https://albergueoasistrails.com

7 **Villamayor de Monjardín** Pr 20 €15 N M|B|K|W|D|@ 677 660 586 | c/ Mayor 1
info@alberguevillamayordemonjardin.com

8 **Casa Rural Montedeio** €Enquire 676 187 473
c/ Mayor 17 | https://www.casaruralmontedeio.com

650m, and looking down on the village is the

ruined **Castillo de San Esteban**. The **church of San Andrés** is Romanesque with some later remodelling, as well as a 17th century tower. Its portal is important for its archivolts, while the apse is decorated with several polychrome statues of the saints. There follows a descent and then 10km of walking, again through fields, vineyards, olive groves and woodland, uninterrupted by settlements. After some 5km there are the **ruins** of a pilgrims' hospital.

Arrive in the small town of **Los Arcos** (21.5km ∞) following the long c/ Mayor.

9 Isaac Santiago M 70 €8 N K|W|D|@ 948 441 091 c/ San Lázaro (on way out of town)

10 Casa de la Abuela Pr 30 €15 (+ 3 Priv. €40-45) N B|K|W|D|@ 948 640 250 | Plaza de la Fruta 8 www.casadelaabuela.com

11 Casa Alberdi Pr 30 €15 Y M|B|K|W|D|@ 650 965 250 | c/ Hortal 3 | www.alberguecasaalberdi.com

12 Fuente Casa de Austria Pr 42 €12 (+5 Priv. €35 Dbl.) N B|K|W|D|@ 948 640 797 | Travesia del Estanco 5 www.lafuentecasadeaustria.com

13 Pensión Los Arcos €45/50 608 585 153 c/ la Carrera 8A

14 Hostal Suetxe €45/55+ 948 441 175 c/ Carramendavia s/n | www.hostalsuetxe.es

15 Pensión Mavi €59 Dbl. 948 640 984 | c/ del Medio 7 www.pensionmavi.es

16 Hostal Mónaco ** €39+/49+ 948 640 000 Pl. del Coso 1 | www.hotelmonaco.es

Originally a Roman mining settlement, the town follows the right bank of the río Odrón, and was once fortified with walls, which when no longer needed, were used as building materials. The street once contained houses for nobles and pilgrims' hospitals, and now very much caters to the modern pilgrim. A lot of the medieval town – once significantly larger – is well preserved. In the centre, the **church of Santa María de los Arcos** was originally constructed in the Romanesque, but was remodelled and decorated between the 16th and 18th centuries. The north door has a fine Plateresque portico – unusual for these parts – with a statue of the Virgin 'inside' an ornamental pediment, while there is a large and beautiful late Gothic cloister. The substantial church itself is primarily Baroque; the choir stalls unusually feature an image of James the Less alongside one of James the Great. A **blessing of pilgrims** is held at the end of Mass here each evening (8pm in summer, 7pm in winter). There are three surviving gates, including the **Portal de Castilla** through which the Camino passes across the road and over the river. Los Arcos contains five **chapels**, one of which, 13th century **San Blas** is on the Camino route out of the town. It was formerly dedicated to San Lázaro, so we can guess that it may have had a hospital attached. Between August 14th and 20th the town's festivities are held in honour of Our Lady of the Assumption and San Roque; besides religious ceremonies there is bull running and bull fighting. On July 25th (feast of St James) there is a special **celebration for pilgrims** by the local confraternity.

Times of the year that pilgrim visitors might want to avoid are when the nearby motorsport track www.circuitodenavarra.com is staging a major event. Isaac and Fuente Albergues are stated to be exclusively for pilgrims.

Portal de Castilla and church of Santa María

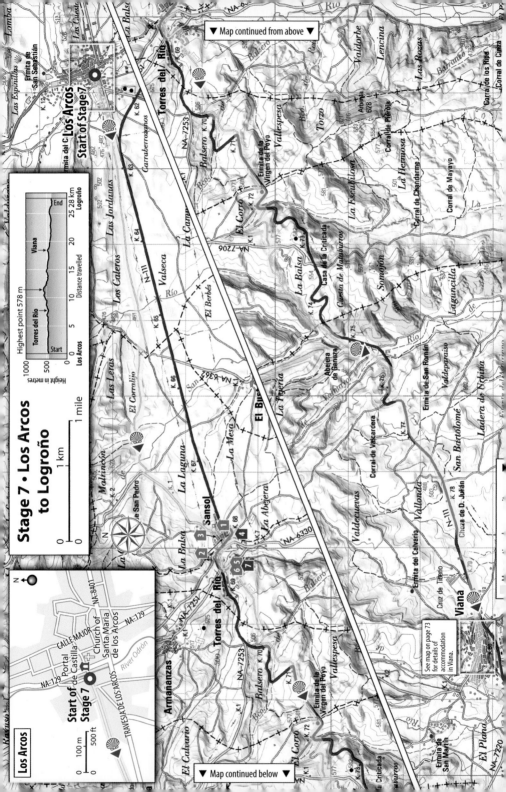

Stage 7 • Los Arcos to Logroño

Highest point 578 m

Height in metres — 1000 / 500

Torres del Río, Viana, End (Logroño)

Start — Los Arcos

Distance travelled (km): 0 5 10 15 20 25 28 km Logroño

Scale: 0 — 1 km / 1 mile

Los Arcos

N

Start of Stage 7

Church of Santa María de los Arcos

Portal de Castilla

CALLE MAYOR

TRAVESÍA DE LOS ARCOS

River Odrón

NA-129 · NA-8401

0 — 100 m / 500 ft

See map on page 73 for details of accommodation in Viana.

▼ Map continued from above ▼

▼ Map continued below ▼

Ermita del C...
Los Arcos
Start of Stage 7
Ermita de San Sebastián
Las Espinillas

Torres del Río

Sansol

Armañanzas

Viana

Torres del Río

Ermita de la Virgen del Poyo

Ermita de San Román

Ermita del Calvario

Cruz de Tiribio

Chaza de D. Julián

Ermita de San Martín

Valdorbe

Lencina

Los Rozas

Las Barrancas

Corral de Cieza

Valdeparaíso

San Bartolomé

Ladera de Urbina

El Planu

Viana

La Pila

NA-632

La Cañada

España

NA-632

Chize

Pamper

NA-632

El Plano

NA-7220

Sequero

Camino

Arroyo

de

Plana de Abajo

Valderas

Ullagosa

El Pago

Ermita de San Vicente

Ermita de las Cuevas

Penzuelas

de

Ayo

El Salobre

La Ratailla

El Roble

Miralobueno

El Roble

El Nabal

El Nabal

Nabal

Papelera del Ebro

El Puntido

El Salobre

Pantano de Salobre y de las Cañas

Polígono Industrial Cantabria-I

Polígono Industrial Cantabria-I

Varea

Río

Río

Cantañis

Yacimiento arqueológico

So. Quintín

Laserna

El Pozo

La Poleja

Oyón / Oion

El Coto

El Plano

San Antonio

Cantabria

San Antonio

Valparaíso

El Corvo

Las Nadas

End of Stage 7

EBRO

OGROÑO

Santa María

Alto del Pozo

El Romeral

EBRO

Camino

LOGROÑO

San Lázaro

Cartographic base © ign.es

See map on page 77 for details of accommodation in Logroño.

Logroño

N

River Ebro

LR-131

Church of Santiago el Real

Church of Santa María de Palacio

Church of San Bartolomé

Cathedral of Santa María de la Redonda

End of Stage 7

0   100 m
0   500 ft

TO LOGROÑO (28km)

Leave Los Arcos via the Portal de Castilla and bridge over the river, joining a track parallel to the NA-1110 alongside wide fields. After 7km of easy walking, you reach the small hilltop village of **Sansol** (B|S|P)

1 **Deshojando** Pr 36 €10 N M|B|W|D|@ *948 648 473*
c/ Barrio Nuevo 4 | info@deshojandoelcamino.com

2 **Karma** Pr 12 €6 Y M|W|D *665 170 116*
c/ Taconera 11 | alberguekarma@gmail.com

3 **Palacio de Sansol** Pr 32 €11–15 (+ 5 Priv. €25/50)
N B|K|W|D|@ *646 334 730* | Pl. del Sindicato 1
josemarialeuza@hotmail.com
https://www.palaciodesansol.com

4 **Casa Rural El Olivo** €25+/40–50+ *948 648 345*
c/ Taconera 9 www.elolivodesansol.com

Named after San Zoilo (Saint Zoilus), its **church** contains frescoes of the Ascension and a Gothic statue of St Peter. There are further examples of Baroque architecture among the houses. Descend to cross the río Linares, to climb up to **Torres del Río** (7.5km B|S|€).

5 **Casa Mariela** Pr 70 €12 (+ 4 Priv. €30 Dbl.) Y
M|B|W|D|@ *603 359 218* | Pl. Padre Valeriano Ordónez
6 fernando_berdeja_7@hotmail.com

6 **Pata de Oca** Pr 32 €12 Y M|B|W|D|@ *948 378 457*
c/ Mayor 5 | https://alberguelapatadeoca.com
(+ Inn €70+ Dbl.)

7 **Hostal San Andrés** €53+/70 /Albergue Bunk €12
948 648 472 | c/ Jesús Ordoñez 6
www.sanandreshostal.com

The highlight here is the 12th century Templar **church of Santo Sepulchro**. Like Eunate, it is an octagonal design, though without the surrounding porch. Its dome is star vaulted, another hint of Arabic involvement in the design. In the apse is a fine 13th century crucifix, also known as the Holy Christ of the Knights of the Sepulchre. This is one of the churches where, if you arrive when it is closed, you might want to try and obtain the key from the custodian – check the notice on or near the door or ask. Again, it is believed many pilgrims are buried in the land surrounding the church.

Continuing out of the village, ascend to the **Ermita de Nuestra Señora del Poyo** where, at an altitude of 579m, you will enjoy far reaching views unless you are unlucky with the weather. Descend to cross the río Cornava and in turn the main road, walking closely alongside it for a kilometre or more, before crossing again to enter the town of **Viana** (18km ∞).

8 **Andrés Muñoz** M 46 €8 Y K|W|D|@|Cred
948 645 530/609 141 798 (Nov-Feb) | c/ Medio de
San Pedro | alberguedeviana@hotmail.com

9 **Parroquial – Santa María** Pa 17 Don N M&B(Don)|†
948 645 037 | Pl. de los Fueros
parroquiaviana@gmail.com

10 **Izar** Pr 38 €15 B&B (+ 2 Priv. €40 Dbl.) N K|W|D|@
660 071 349 | c/ El Cristo 6 www.albergueizar.com

11 **Hotel Palacio de Pujadas** *** €63+/70+ *948 646 464*
c/ Navarro Villoslada 30 | www.palaciodepujadas.com

12 **Hostal Casa Palacio Hernández** €50+/60+
685 836 070 | c/ San Felices 5 (closed during 2022)

13 **Pensión San Pedro** ** €40+/50+ *948 645 927*
c/ Medio de San Pedro 13
www.pensionsanpedro.com

Founded by Sancho VII (the Strong) in 1219 as a defensive fortress against rival Castile and its **walls** are still in evidence on the western side of the town. Becoming a principality of the heir to the throne – a tradition that continues today with the heir to the Spanish throne – nobles from the royal court established themselves and built fine houses. The pilgrimage gave this place a renewed importance – with four hospitals – and then, in 1507, Viana became the 'final' resting place of the remarkable Cesare

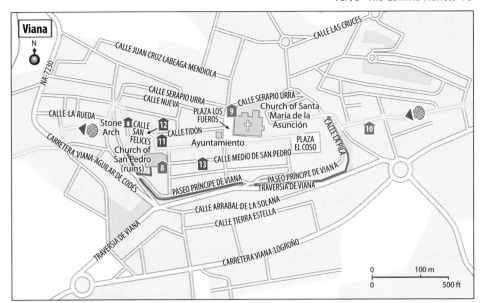

designed and carved by Juan de Goyaz. It is possible to tour the interior via a gallery. There are several altarpieces, the main one being a particularly fine example of Navarrese Baroque. The ruined **church of San Pedro** has an 18th century façade and a park leading from it, with good views of the walls and La Rioja and Basque Álava province beyond.

Exiting Viana through the stone arch on c/ San Felices and descending through the more modern outskirts until picking up the N-111, and then the **Ermita de la Trinidad de las Cuevas** (rest area behind). Continuing on past lakes, a bird reserve and tunnels under the road network, until, some 6km after Viana, you cross into the autonomous community of La Rioja. Immediately, the capital Logroño's ring road and modern industry have to be negotiated – although there are some major **wine producers** near here offering tours – before climbing the **Cerro de Cantabria** hill, site of a prehistoric city and later Roman settlement. Cross one of Spain's major rivers, the **río Ebro** via the **Puente de Piedra**.

Borgia. The illegitimate son of Pope Alexander VI, made a cardinal, commander of the Papal armies, and lionised by Machiavelli as an arch political operator, he had married Charlotte, sister of King John III of Navarra. His power suddenly evaporated when his father died and was succeeded by his enemy Julius II, so he fled to Spain. He was killed defending Viana from Castile, and his tomb lies outside the main door of the **church of Santa María de la Asunción**, having been desecrated when originally inside. This late 13th century church took on a Renaissance façade and tower in the 16th century. The southern portico is a magnificent concave affair resembling a triumphal arch,

LOGROÑO (∞)

14 **Albergue de Peregrinos** M/A 68 €10 Y
K|W|D|@|Cred 941 248 686 c/ Ruavieja 32
www.asantiago.org/albergues | (also in Navarrete)

15 **Iglesia de Santiago** Pa 30 Don Y* M&B(Dons)|K|@|†
941 209 501 | c/ Barriocepo 8 | www.santiagoelreal.org
*Winter location at Barriocepo 58

16 **Santiago Apóstol** Pr 78 €12 (+ 3 Priv. €43+ Dbl.) Y
M|K|W|D@ 635 371 036 | c/ Ruavieja 42
ruavieja42@gmail.com

17 **Albas** Pr 26 €15 (+ Priv. €45) N W|D|@|Cred
688 766 475 | Pl. Martínez Flamarique 4
albasalbergue@gmail.com

18 **Logroño** Pr 30 €15+ Y K|W|D|@ 608 234 723
c/ Capitán Gallarza 10 (2nd left)
info@casaconencanto.net
(also **Pensión La Bilbaina** €45+ Dbl.)

19 **Hostel Entresueños** YH 100 €11+ (+ 3 Priv. €40+ Dbl.)
Y B|K|W|D|@ 941 271 334 | c/ Portales 12
www.hostellogrono.com (closed during 2022)

20 **Winederful Hostel & Café** Pr 30 €16+ N B|K|@
600 904 703 | c/ Herrerías 2–14 | www.winederful.es
[Not only for pilgrims!]

21 **Logroño Centro** Pr 18 €10–18 Y K|@
678 495 109 | Trav. de Palacio 6 (off C. Marqués de
San Nicolás) | www.apartamentoslogronocentro.com

22 **Pensión Logroño** €59+ Dbl. 670 494 129
c/ Canelejas (2nd floor) | www.pensionlogrono.es 7

23 **Pensión El Espolón** €35/45+ 601 021 200
c/ de Juan XXIII

24 **Hostal La Numantina** ** €52+/62+ 941 251 411
c/ Sagasta 4 | www.hostalnumantina.com

25 **Hotel Murrieta** *** €45+/50+ 941 224 150
c/ Marqués de Murrieta 1
www.hotel-murrietalogrono.com

26 **Hotel F&G Logroño** *** €69+/78+ 941 008 900
Avenida de Viana 2–6 | www.fglogrono-hotel.com

27 **Hotel Los Bracos** **** €68+/72+ 941 226 608
c/ Bretón de los Herreros 29
www.hoteles-silken.com/en/hotel-los-bracos-logrono/

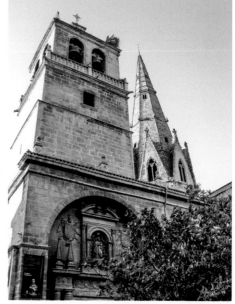

Church of Santa María de Palacio   Miguel Yustes CC BY 2.0

Now the thriving capital of the smallest of Spain's 17 autonomous communities, and the commercial centre of one of the world's most renowned wine regions, Logroño was little more than a village until the onset of the pilgrimage to Santiago, when a stone bridge was built over the Ebro by San Juan de Ortega (St John the Hermit). The bridge crossed by today's pilgrim is a 19th century replacement at the eastern end of the old town, from which there is a series of churches – and towers – to admire. In the 16th century, a network of tunnels and cellars was established in order to transport and store barrels of wine, without the disturbance of carrying it through a bustling town and, above all, to keep it cool.

Instead of progressing along the Camino by turning right (west) down the c/ Ruavieja, you may want to visit the churches in turn, in which case continue south after the bridge, across the wide junction and along c/ el Puente until you reach the **church of San Bartolomé**. The oldest surviving church in the city, it was built probably on the site of an earlier church. Its floor plan retains the Romanesque element of three naves terminating in three apses; however there are Gothic and 16th century additions and modifications. The superbly carved portal differs in several respects from many that we have seen; its Last Judgement tympanum gives the appearance of having been slotted in, with recent restoration revealing a red stone background; there are scenes from the life of St Bartholomew. The Mudéjar tower outside was reconstructed in the 15th century. There is a plaza nearby, and once on c/ Portales you will come to the Cathedral; otherwise, to continue to visit each church in turn retrace steps until the c/ Marqués de San Nicolás, turn left and arrive at the door of the **church of Santa María de Palacio**. Built on the site of a royal palace, its attractive tower features a very tall spire – *La Aguja* or 'needle of the palace' – atop the lantern, but the narrow streets mean you might have to remember to look skywards to see it. Inside, the highly detailed, gilded altarpiece is by Arnao of Bruselas, a Spanish Renaissance sculptor who also produced the choir stalls in

The Annunciation by Gillis Coignet

the cathedral. Opposite is the **chapel of San Gregorio**, and while there used to be a shrine to the influential Cardinal, next door is the entrance to the largest preserved of the city's **wine cellars** which is named after him.

Further along the street on our tour is the **Cathedral of Santa María de la Redonda**, situated in Plaza del Mercado. Its impressive twin towers flanking the Baroque portal are by Martín de Beratúa. Otherwise the cathedral is Gothic, built over a Romanesque plan of the former church. Inside you can view the painting *Tabla de Calvario*, attributed to Michelangelo and encased in a high security box in the ambulatory. There are several more paintings and sculptures of note, including a set of Flemish panels by Gillis Coignet. The plaza is arcaded, and behind it and parallel to c/ Portales are some medieval winding lanes lined

Cathedral of Santa María de la Redonda

The city's stuffed mushroom Matyas Rehak/Shutterstock.com
Tapas

with **bars serving Tapas**. The Riojans insist on calling them *pinchos*, and the mild derision with which that is met in the Basque Country and Navarra is only to be expected! Nevertheless, the quality of the fare on offer is excellent, with no shortage of imagination and skill used to concoct these mini dishes, and besides the best alcoholic accompaniment, you could also try a refreshing Riojan red grape juice frappé.

Further along c/ Portales, we come to the Plaza San Agustín and there in the **Palacio del General Espatero** – former home of one of the city's most influential citizens – is the **Museo Provincial de la Rioja**, with an impressive collection from the Prehitoric to religious and contemporary art. Back on the Camino, before the pilgrim's church is the restored fountain – **fuente peregrines** – and laid out in the adjoining plaza, a game of *Juego del Oca* – a kind of Spanish 'snakes and ladders'– but here

with the theme of the pilgrimage. The original **church of Santiago el Real** is said to have been built by one of St James' disciples, Arcadio. The site of the, probably mythical, battle of Clavijo is not far away, and this church has a large Santiago Matamoros statue above the Renaissance south portal – albeit accompanied by a Santiago Peregrino – and continuing inside with a polychrome Santiago el Mayor – yet dressed as a pilgrim – on the altarpiece. The latter contains more images relating to Santiago, including the translation of his body and his appearance at Clavijo. Building started in 1513, with the 40m high tower completed in 1573. The single nave is no less than 16m wide. Elsewhere in the church stands a statue of Our Lady of Hope (La Virgen de la Esperanza) patroness of Logroño. We are now on c/ Barriocepo, and pass some impressive palaces now converted to educational use.

The Way opens up to the plaza and building of the **Rioja parliament** and the **Cubo del Revellín**, alternatively named the *Puerta del Camino* as this is where pilgrims exit the city. On either side, are preserved the original defensive

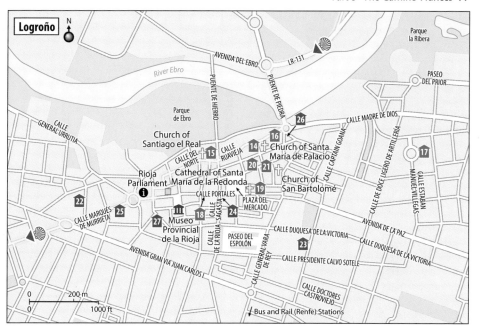

Rioja Parliament   CC0 1.0

Archway for the San Bernabé Festival   Jynus CC BY-SA 4.0

walls, and inside the fort there is a historical exhibition of the city and its fortifications.

Notable **fiestas** in Logroño include **San Bernabé** on June 11th with the 'Fraternity of the Fish' – distribution of grilled fish, bread and wine, next to the ramparts of the Revellín. The Fiestas of **San Mateo** and the Grape Harvest festival take place on St Matthew's Feast day, September 21st. The treading of the grapes takes place in the Paseo del Espolón, with the first grape juice offered to the Virgin of Valvanera, the patroness of La Rioja; there are more festivities for a week around this day. As a regional capital, there is a year-round programme of plays, concerts and film, one highlight being the *Actual* festival of contemporary culture from January 2nd to 7th.

Stage 8 • Logroño to Nájera

Map continued from above

Map continued below

LOGROÑO

Navarrete

See map on page 80 for details of accommodation in Navarrete.

Portada Románica

Ventosa

Highest point 668 m

Height in metres

Start of Stage 8

Logroño

- Church of Santiago el Real
- Church of Santa María de Palacio
- Church of San Bartolomé
- Cathedral of Santa María de la Redonda

Start of Stage 8

Ermita del Buen Suceso

Centro Hípica

Pantano de la Grajera

Alto de San Antón

Monte Paterna

El Palomar

El Cerrillo

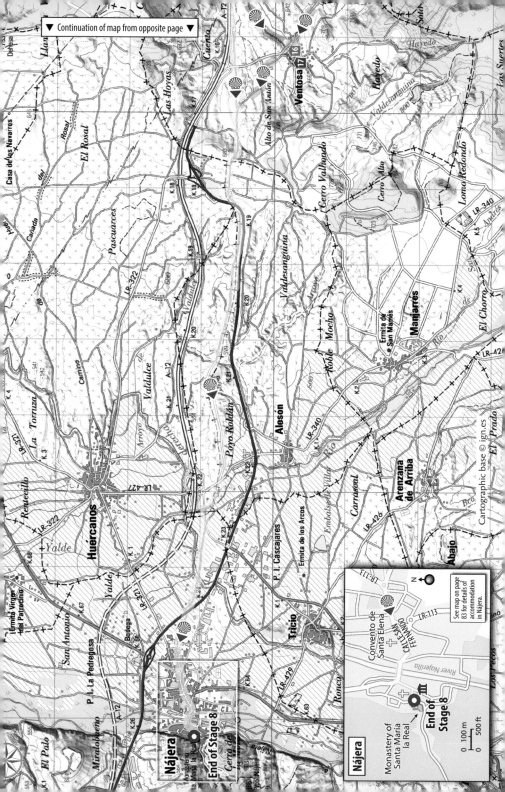

LOGROÑO TO SANTO DOMINGO DE LA CALZADA

TO NÁJERA (28km)

Having passed through the *Puerta* and therefore exiting the old town, the Way follows the route out to Burgos, crossing the railway line and then under the A-12 after which the modern city fades via a purpose-built parkland track. A welcome rest point is by the reservoir, **La Grajera**, with its *Alto* giving a view back to the city. The track runs alongside the main road, then departs it and meets (and crosses over) the AP-68 1km later; nevertheless there is an early opportunity to experience the vineyards and rich reddy soil that make this part of Spain famous. On the other side are the ruins of the 12th century **monastery and hospital of San Juan de Acre** – an order founded to care for pilgrims. Parts of the ruins have been relocated to the cemetery on the opposite side of Navarrete on the Camino – the portal is now its gate – and in all many of the finely carved figures of pilgrims and capitals remain to explore.

In the well-preserved medieval centre of Navarrete (11.8km ∞) the 16th century Renaissance **church of the Asunción de**

1 **Municipal – de Navarrete** M/A 34 €10 N K|W|D|Cred *941 440 722* | c/ San Juan 2 info@asantiago.org

2 **El Camino de las Estrellas** Pr 38 €12 (+ 4 Priv. €35–40 Dbl.) N M|B|@ *695 998 038* Ctra. De Burgos 9 | peregre34@gmail.com

3 **Buen Camino** Pr 6 €12 (+ 2 Priv. €25/35) N B|W *941 440 318* | c/ La Cruz 2 reservas@alberguebuencamino.es

4 **El Cántaro** Pr 17 €12 (+ 5 Priv. €25-35/40-45) Y B|K|W|D|@|Cred *941 441 180* c/ Herrerías 16 | www.albergueelcantaro.com

5 **La Casa del Peregrino Ángel** Pr 18 €12 N M|B|K|W|D|@|Cred *630 982 928* | c/ Las Huertas 3 http://alberguenavarrete.wordpress.com

6 **La Iglesia** Pr 15 €15 Y K|M|B|W|D *621 231 044* c/ Mayor Alta 2 | reservas.alberguelaiglesia@gmail.com

7 **A la Sombra del Laurel** €35/50 *639 861 110* | Ctra. de Burgos 52 | info@alasombradellaurel.com (former Albergue. Only private rooms available)

8 **Casa Peregrinando** €58+ (Dbl. Shared bathroom) *622 164 328* | c/ Mayor Alta 34

9 **Hostal Villa de Navarrete** * €32+/43+ *941 440 318* c/ la Cruz 2 | www.hostalvilladenavarrete.com

10 **Pensión Posada Ignatius** €55+ Dbl. *941 124 094* Pl. de Arco 4 | www.posadaignatius.com

11 **Hotel Rey Sancho** *** €70+ Dbl. *941 441 378* c/ Mayor Alta 5 | www.hotelreysancho.es

María contains a fine altarpiece set into the

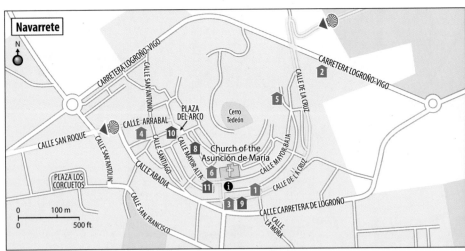

14 Casa Rural El Colorao €40+ *652 432 304*
Ctra. de Hornos 1 | www.casaruralelcolorao.com

15 Casa Rural Señorío de Moncalvillo €35/40
(Groups only) *629 930 169* | c/ La Iglesia 9
www.senoriodemoncalvillo.com/casa-rural-en-la-rioja/

which continues on to Ventosa (19km **R|B**)

16 San Saturnino Pr 42 €13 Y K|W|D|@|Cred
941 441 899 c/ Mayor 33 | ventosa@jacobeos.net

17 Hotel las Águedas ** €60+/66+ *941 441 774*
Pl. de Santa Coloma 11 | www.hotellasaguedas.com

Second choice – ignore turning to Sotés and 2km later take the waymarked Camino option (left) to Ventosa.

Another of La Rioja's hilltop villages, Ventosa's 16th century **church of San Saturnino** stands in pleasant grounds offering a fine view, while inside the main altarpiece is dedicated to the church's patron and the Virgin Mary. The two smaller altarpieces are dedicated to the Virgen del Carmen and the Virgen Blanca. There is a 14th century carving of a recumbent Christ. Having exited the village and the bypass route rejoined, continue to climb.

apse, the elaborate decoration continuing into the dome and out to the flanking walls. Its fiesta in mid August honours San Roque and the Virgin, whose statue is in the church, with a further feast on St Michael's day, September 29th. Besides wine, the town is well known for its pottery – the colour of the soil – which is displayed outside several factories and shops. Leaving the town, past the cemetery, there is 7km of countryside, a wine co-operative and a couple of skirmishes with the road.

The *option to Ventosa* (it used to be on the main Camino) has a sub-option:
First choice (not waymarked at time of writing) turn off the main Route to Sotés (**R|B|S**) by road (left) if you need more accommodation plus dining option

12 San Martín €15+/person *941 441 768/650 962 625* | c/ San Miguel 67 (formerly an Albergue)

13 La Casa de Sotés €35+ Dbl. *606 443 165* | c/ Conde de Garay 45–47 | www.lacasasotesmarijose.com

Past Ventosa   *La Rioja Turismo*

Otherwise stay on the main route, bypassing Ventosa altogether saving 2km and giving a gentler climb; go straight on. The *Alto de San Antón* is the site of a former pilgrims' hospital (Antonine order). Pass through a tunnel under the N-120. Follow the path close to the road for 4km, close to its junction with the motorway, while on the right is another hill, the *Poyo de Roldán*. Here is the spot where Roland is said to have felled the giant Ferragut with a large rock, and then freed the Christian knights of Charlemagne's army from Nájera. The Syrian giant is said to have been related to Goliath, allowing for an unmistakable comparison with David's feat.

Cross the río Yalde via the footbridge and then there is a poem, which asks, *Pilgrim, who calls you?* Through modern outskirts, cross the N-120 and then cross the río Najerilla to the old town of Nájera (∞).

NÁJERA

18 **Municipal** M 48 €6 N K|W|D|@ *941 095 730*
Pl. de Santiago

19 **Nido de Cigüeña** Pr 15 €15 N K|W|D|@
611 095 191 | Calleja Cuarta San Miguel 4
https://alberguenajera.es

20 **Puerta de Nájera** Pr 29 €15–20 (+ 3 Priv. €40–45)
N K|W|D|@ *941 362 317* | c/ Carmen 4 (enter via c/ Ribera del Najerilla) www.alberguedenajera.com

21 **Las Peñas** Pr 10 €15 Y B|W|@ *621 209 432*
c/ Costantilla 56 | alberguelaspenas@gmail.com

22 **Sancho III – La Judería** Pr 16 €12 (+ 4 Priv. €20/30)
N M *630 864 148* | c/ San Marcial 5
https://www.lajuderiasanchoiii.com

23 **El Peregrino** Pr 25 €12–15 Y M B W D *643 323 174*
c/ San Fernando 90

24 **Calle Mayor** €30–40 *941 360 407* | c/ Dicarán 5

25 **Pensión San Lorenzo** €32/40+ *941 363 722*
c/ Constantino Garrán 10 | www.pensionsanlorenzo.es

26 **Hostal Hispano** * €38+/55+ *941 363 615*
c/ La Cepa 2 | https://www.hostalhispanonajera.com

27 **Hostal Ciudad de Nájera** ** €44+/51+ *941 360 660*
Cuarta Calleja San Miguel 14
www.ciudaddenajera.com

28 **Hotel Duques de Nájera** *** €45+/50+ *941 410 421*
c/ Carmen 7 | https://hotelduquesdenajera.com/en/

With a population of 8000 – nowadays home to a furniture industry – Nájera straddles both banks of the río Najerilla. Originally a Roman settlement was established between here and neighbouring Tricio, though later the area came under Muslim rule – the name is derived from Arabic meaning 'between two hills'. The kings of Navarra made Nájera their second home after Pamplona was razed to the ground by the Moors in 918. When Sancho the Great held his court here, he diverted the Camino to bring in trade. When he divided his kingdom between his two sons, one took Pamplona, and the other, García Sánchez III took Nájera. In 1052, García was out hunting and sent his falcon after a dove.

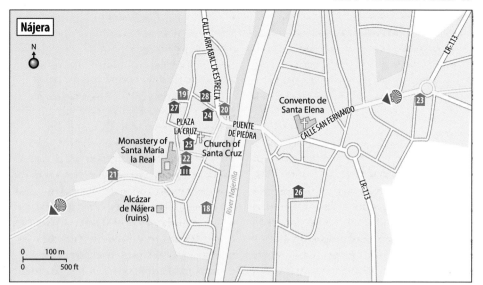

Following the birds' path through woods to a cave, from where a bright light was shining, inside, he found the birds side by side, next to a statue of the Virgin and child, alongside a jar of fresh lilies, together with a lamp and a bell. To honour the miracle, García founded a chivalrous order, the *Caballeros de la Terraza* (order of the pottery jar) – it was also known as the order of the lilies.

The church which was founded at the same time was rebuilt in the 15th century as the **Monastery of Santa María la Real**. Situated on the left bank of the river, built next to the cave and housing the statue, there lies one of the most intricately carved of cloisters with 24 arches. The cloister contains the tombs of royalty and nobility. The church contains many more tombs, including the Dukes of Nájera, who once employed Íñigo de Loyola, and the Royal Pantheon. Only the top remains of the tomb of Sancho the Great's Queen Doña Blanca of Navarra and Castile, who died in childbirth, but it is especially beautifully carved, telling of the king's grief. The choir stalls are a florid Gothic masterpiece, believed to be carved by Jewish *conversos* with Hebrew letters

on chair no. 23. Originally the Virgin wore a large ruby, but this was given away by Pedro the Cruel in 1367 to Edward of England – the Black Prince – who fought at the battle of Nájera to rid the kingdom of the French-backed army of his rival half-brother. After being abandoned as a monastery during secularisation, it was occupied by the Franciscans in 1893, who remain to this day. There is an historical and archaeological **museum** in the Abbot's palace, with artefacts from the Roman settlement, as well as Moorish, Jewish and Christian ceramics.

In the Plaza la Cruz is the 17th century **church of Santa Cruz** while up above the ancient castle survives in ruins. The **Convento de Santa Elena** is home to a community of Poor Clares, the Baroque structure housing a cloister and church. At nearby Tricio, it is well worth seeking out the **Ermita de Los Arcos**, for its origins as a Roman temple, its statue of the Virgin, its stucco vaulting, and its Romanesque frescoes – a remarkable fusion (2km; guided tours).

Here is another place where you can catch the bus to Yuso and Suso Monasteries.

Stage 9 • Nájera to Santo Domingo de la Calzada

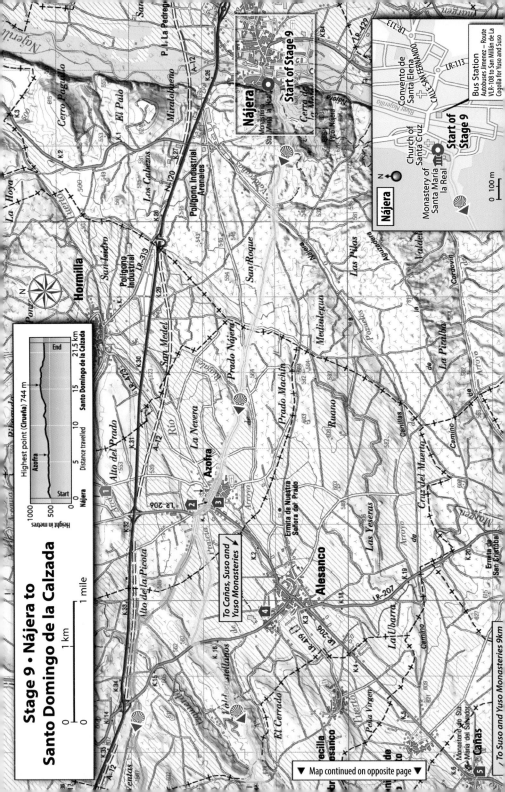

Highest point (Cirueña) 744 m

Azofra → Santo Domingo de la Calzada

Nájera — Start

Distance travelled

Height in metres

Start of Stage 9

Nájera

Bus Station
Autobuses Jiménez – Route
VLR-108 to San Millán de La
Cogolla for Yuso and Suso

Church of Santa Cruz
Convento de Santa Elena
Monastery of Santa María la Real
Start of Stage 9

Hormilla

Azofra

Alesanco

Cañas

To Cañas, Suso and Yuso Monasteries

To Suso and Yuso Monasteries 9km

▼ Map continued on opposite page ▼

▼ Continuation of map from opposite page ▼

Cartographic base © ign.es

From Suso and
Yuso Monasteries

Cirueña

Santo Domingo de la Calzada

End of Stage 9

Hervías

Manzanares de Rioja

Ciriñuela

Santo Domingo de la Calzada

N

Cathedral of
Santo Domingo
de la Calzada

End of
Stage 9

0   100 m
0   500 ft

N120-A

TO SANTO DOMINGO DE LA CALZADA (21.5km)

Exit Nájera by Santa María la Real monastery up c/ Costanilla, turning onto a track, alongside pine trees and climb further. Otherwise this part of the stage is relatively easy, and away from main roads. Join a paved road keeping left and enter Azofra (5.7km R|B|S|P) with its modern all-twin-roomed! Albergue*(alternative arrangements in winter).

1 **Municipal** M 60 €10 N K|W|D|@|Cred *638 261 432* c/ Las Parras 7 | alberguemunicipalazofra@gmail.com

2 **Hotel Real Casona de las Amas** *** €139+ Dbl. *941 416 103* | c/ Mayor 5 www.realcasonadelasamas.com

3 **Pensión La Plaza** €30/45 *941 379 239* Pl. de España 7 | reservasplaza@gmail.com

La Rioja Turismo

Its **church of Nuestra Señora de los Angeles** has a figure of St Martin of Tours and a Santiago Peregrino. There is a **Pilgrims' Mass** at 7pm. From here, after passing the medieval pilgrims' fountain and a *Rollo* – a stone judicial boundary marker from the 16th century – there is a 7.5km climb, skirting the golf club of the Rioja Alta to Cirueña (15.5km).

6 **Virgen de Guadalupe** Pr 10 €15 N M|B|W|D|@ *638 924 069* | c/ Barrio Alto 1 https://albergue-virgendeguadalupe.webnode.es

7 **Victoria** Pr 10 €14 (+ 2 Priv. €42+ Dbl) N M|B|K|W|D|@ *941 426 105* | c/ San Andreas 10 albergue@casavictoriarural.com

8 **Pensión Casa Victoria** €30+/44+ *628 983 351* Pl. del Horno 8 | www.casavictoriarural.com

Here at a turning (left) is one of the *routes to the monasteries* of Yuso and Suso at San Millán de la Cogolla, and before that, the one at Cañas, in all a 15km journey, with return to the Camino via Villar de Torre (facilities) to Cirueña (13km).

Otherwise continue on; it is another 6km on a steady descent to historic Santo Domingo, the last stretch alongside the N-120 before arriving in front of the Cathedral and Parador.

SANTO DOMINGO DE LA CALZADA (∞)

9 **Cofradía del Santo** A 164 (new hostel) €13 Y K (microwave & fridge only, utensils available) W|D|@|Cred|† *941 343 390* | c/ Mayor 38–42 www.alberguecofradiadelsanto.com

10 **Hospedería Cicterciense** ** €40/59 *941 340 700* c/ Pinar 2 | www.cister-lacalzada.com

11 **Hostal Miguel** €24+/34+ *600 212 691* | Paseo de los Molinos 2 (1st floor) | www.pensionmiguel.com

12 **Hostal la Catedral** €43+/55+ *651 948 260* c/ Isidoro Salas 49 | https://hostallacatedral.es

13 **Hostal El Molino de Floren** €50+/64+ *941 342 931* c/ Margubete 5 | http://elmolinodefloren.com

14 **Parador de Sto. Domingo** **** €113+ B&B Pilgrim's rate | *941 340 300* | Pl. del Santo 3 | www.parador.es

THE SAINT, THE BUILDER, THE ROOSTER AND THE CHICKEN

Domingo García (1019–1109) was born into a humble peasant family in Viloria de Rioja – although some accounts point to Vizcaya as his birthplace. He was determined to take Holy orders and tried to get in first at Valvanera,

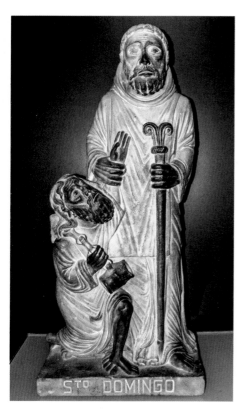

and then at San Millán de la Cogolla, but was turned away, apparently for his illiteracy. The young man became a hermit in a forest near his birthplace, and began to help pilgrims on their way to Santiago de Compostela. In an area infested with bandits, he would clear pathways, and built a refuge and a chapel. San Gregorio Ostiense, that other constructor saint, took Domingo under his wing and ordained him a priest. Together, they built a wooden bridge over the río Oja. After San Gregorio died, Domingo redoubled his efforts, replacing the wooden bridge with one made of stone. His paved causeway – *calzada* – became the principal route on this part of the pilgrim's way, replacing in importance the Roman road. His **hospital** opposite the cathedral in the Plaza del Santo is now a *Parador*. The original church may have been on the site of the **Ermita de Nuestra**

Señora de La Plaza, on the south side of the square. So, the whole town owes its existence to Santo Domingo. His public works, to smooth the way and encourage the tide of pilgrims, have earned him the title patron saint of civil engineers. He in turn took on a disciple, San Juan de Ortega, who continued the good works.

Many miracles have been attributed to St Dominic of the Causeway. But the most famous concerns a German mother and father who were on their way to Santiago in the 14th century with their son, 18-year-old Hugonell. While staying in Santo Domingo de la Calzada, the innkeeper's daughter made advances to the young Hugonell, who being of a pious disposition rejected them. The girl avenged herself by placing a silver goblet in Hugonell's pack, and accused him of stealing it. The penalty for theft, according to the laws of Castile, was death by hanging, and so Hugonell, having been found guilty by the local magistrate, was sent to the gallows. His parents are said to have continued to Santiago, but on their return called in to see their son's body still on the gallows. Miraculously, he called out to them, and said he was alive because of the intercession of Santo Domingo. The parents went straight to the magistrate, who, in the middle of eating, laughed and said, "Your son is as alive as this rooster and chicken that I was feasting on before you interrupted me." Whereupon, the erstwhile roasted rooster and chicken jumped up from the platter and began to crow and coo. The magistrate ran to the gallows, cut Hugonell down and issued a full pardon. To this day, a live cockerel and hen are kept in the cathedral – white feathered, they are said to be descendants of the original birds, of course! Pilgrims would take one of their feathers and place it in their hats as a blessing from Santo Domingo, and were known to try to feed the birds from the top of their staffs, another sign that their pilgrimage would end without ill fate.

THE CATHEDRAL

There is 'Donative' admission charge. Pilgrims get a €1 discount = €3 for the Cathedral; €4 to include the Tower. Guides (groups) and Audioguides are available for extra cost. Open in summer from 9am – 8.30pm Mon.–Fri.; Sat. until 7.10pm; Sun. 9–12.20 & 1.45–7.10pm; reduced hours in winter.

The original church is said to have been founded in 1098, and consecrated in 1106, on land donated by King Alfonso VI of Castile, a promoter of the pilgrimage who wished to consolidate his annexation of La Rioja, who attended to lay the first stone. It was extended in 1158 to incorporate Santo Domingo's tomb and provide more room for a growing number of pilgrims seeking to venerate him, and in 1232 its status was elevated to a cathedral and the seat of a bishop. While there are Romanesque elements in the apse and ambulatory, the rest is mostly Gothic, with some Plateresque decoration. The **tower** was rebuilt in 1762 away from the church after the original and its successor had both been damaged.

The main **altarpiece** was begun by Damián Forment, one of the finest Renaissance sculptors in Spain, in 1537 and continued two years later by Andres de Melgar. There are interactive displays to help understanding of the incredible detail in this massive installation. The **tomb** of Santo Domingo is covered by an alabaster baldachin by Juan de Rasines, dating from 1513. The recumbent two metre-long statue is 13th century, and was restored in 2009. There is also a standing statue of the bearded saint. A **crypt** below the tomb displays another statue of him. Opposite is the curiosity, the **henhouse**. It is very elaborate, considering its basic function, with grille and carved stone surround. For those worried about animal welfare, the birds are changed fortnightly, if indeed that is reassuring! Of the beautiful features of the chapels, the screen of the **Capilla de la Magdalena**, and

the **Capilla de Santa Teresa** for its altarpiece and tombs, are all worthy of note. The **museum** is in the cloister, and displays three Flemish triptychs, an altarpiece and several sculptures. The Chapter House leads off, and continues the collection of cathedral treasure, including Mexican silver.

OTHER SIGHTS

The west-east c/ Mayor, which runs in and out of the Plaza del Santo, contains several palaces displaying their coats of arms. The **Casa Consistorial** (Town Hall) off in the Plaza Mayor is an arcaded 16th century affair. The **Casa del Santo** (confusingly on c/ Mayor) is the Pilgrims' information office, and in the garden of its Albergue is the chicken coop where the cathedral reserves are kept. Remains of the defensive **walls** are in evidence, especially to the west, and to the southwest is the Renaissance **Convento de San Francisco**, recently converted into the town's second Parador ***. It was built by King Philip II for his confessor, Fray Bernardo de Fresneda; the church was built in 1569 by Juan de Herrera. There is a **pilgrim's monument** outside.

FIESTAS

In December, a large Medieval fair, La Concepción, takes place. King Alfonso X (the Wise) granted the town a royal charter allowing it to hold a fair, and nowadays it attracts 100 000 people. The town's patroness, the Virgin of the Plaza, has her feast day on August 5th, and is celebrated again with a parade on a 'Thanksgiving Day' on September 18th. The Feast Day of Santo Domingo is May 12th with several other rites and festivities taking place around this date, usually from 10th to the 15th.

YUSO & SUSO AND CAÑAS MONASTERIES

CRADLE OF THE SPANISH LANGUAGE – AND BASQUE

Castilian has developed into what most people regard as Spanish, though there are other languages indigenous to modern Spain, such as Gallego (Galician), Basque and Catalan, besides Latin American variants. It emerged as the pre-eminent language during the long *Reconquista*, due to the power of the kingdom of Castile, and perhaps due also to the recognisable simplicity of its phonetics.

Emilian of Cogolla, patron of Castile and La Rioja, was an early Iberic saint, born around 472. He is said to have had a vision while still a young man, and went to live and study with San Felices at Bilibio (modern Haro). He then lived as a hermit in caves, and attracted a following of anchorites, who built a small monastery, which was rebuilt after his death (at over 100 years old) as the Visigothic Suso in the 7th century. One of the monks, San Baudelio, wrote the *Life of San Millán* which was part of a growing reputation the community was acquiring for academic works. In 1053, King García Sánchez III decided that San Millán's relics should move to Nájera, however once the oxen pulling the cart reached the bottom of the hill, they refused to go any further. This was taken as a sign that the saint did not want to leave, and so the king built the more elaborate Yuso monastery. What had apparently already taken place here was the writing down of the first 43 words of Castilian by an anonymous 10th century monk. The written word of the time was, of course, Latin, but the monk strayed while writing a commentary in the margin of the text he was studying. The same thing happened twice more – only this time the language was Basque, another spoken in these parts at the time. Later, a local lad from the village of Berceo, Gonzalo (b.1198) joined the monastery as a choirboy, and began writing poetry in Castilian. Nowadays, the monastery houses an international institute for the study of the Spanish language, with a library. The Benedictine community has since been replaced by Augustinian friars, while the original annotated 'Emilian Glosses' are in Madrid.

PRACTICALITIES

San Millán de la Cogolla (R|B|S|P) is located in hills 18km southwest of Nájera, one of the points on the Camino from where it is suggested pilgrims make an excursion. There are buses here from Logroño, via Nájera (Estollo service) allowing for a return day trip. The monasteries are closed Mondays, except August.

Suso monastery, a hike up the hill, is smaller and can be explored on your own, however there is a bus that takes you up there with a short tour on most days; Admission €4 – buy at Yuso.

At Yuso, long compulsory guided tours are included with the Admission €7, and mainly available in Spanish and you have to follow the group; there is also a siesta until 4pm. All this can be frustrating, though it is common in a working monastery not to be allowed to wander about on your own.

Cañas (R) [*NOTE: Monastery closed to visitors due to the pandemic, with hopes it will be reopened.*] It can be visited separately or together: a shorter 6km from Azofra or 12.5km southeast of Santo Domingo de la Calzada and 9km from Yuso monastery. Closed on Mondays, except a Holiday when they close next day. Admission €4.

🔲4 **Pensión Jauja** €50/60+ *609 304 149/941 379 139*
c/ Mayor 38 Alesanco (2.5km from Azofra)

🔲5 **Casa Rural La Posada del Santo** €25+ *686 068 520*
c/ Real No. 2, Cañas | www.laposadadelsanto.com

🔲Ⓐ **Hostería del Monasterio de San Millán** ****
€93+/104+ *941 373 277* | Plaza del Monasterio de Yuso
www.hosteriasanmillan.com

🔲Ⓑ **La Posada de San Millán** ** €43/55 *941 743 402*
c/ Prestiño 5 San Millán de la Cogolla
https://casasruralessanmillan.es

YUSO MONASTERY

Yuso: Retro choir

The original Romanesque monastery was rebuilt in the 16th century Renaissance style. The entrance features a relief of San Millán in the guise of *Santiago Matamoros*, a reminder that the Camino originally passed through here and the saint was one of those venerated by pilgrims making their way to Santiago. The image is repeated in a canvas by Juan Ricci – from the school of El Greco – on the main altarpiece along with others depicting the saint's life. The first room to visit, however, is the **Salón de los Reyes** with more paintings by Ricci of counts and kings of Castile. The 43 words of the Codex are engraved in stone. Through the processional **cloister** with its Gothic style vaulting, we enter the **church** via a superb Plateresque door. In the retro choir, the pulpit is decorated with carvings of the Evangelists and the Passion. There are statues of San Millán's disciples in French Rococo style decoration. One of the highlights is the **sacristy**, with its beautifully decorated barrel vaults, walnut chests with 24 oils painted on copper, and a statue of Our Lady from 1700.

The guide will hopefully include the **library**, and should open one of the huge medieval music volumes; you can also handle copies of other texts. Upstairs, the **museum** contains the reliquary chests of both San Millán and San Felices. Made of wood and inlaid with ivory plates, they originally also had precious jewels and gold, but these were stripped by Napoléon's troops.

SUSO MONASTERY

The caves in which San Millán and his anchorites lived, the Visigothic monastery, its Mozarabic enlargement, and Romanesque embellishments are all here to see. At the entrance, a cloister has the tombs of three queens of Navarra, along with the seven infantes (princes) de Lara and their tutor, who all perished in a tragic act of revenge. The portico opens into the church of horseshoe arches. The nave is built into the cliff. A burial cave contains a 'tomb' of the founder from the 12th century, built of black alabaster and decorated with a recumbent statue.

CAÑAS – ABBEY OF SANTA MARÍA DE SAN SALVADOR

The convent was founded in 1170 from a donation by Felipe Díaz de Haro, ninth Lord of Biscay and his wife, Doña Aldonza Ruiz de Castro, to nuns of the Cistercian order, who have an uninterrupted history of occupation of the site. There are trace elements of the Romanesque, as construction slowly progressed through the architectural periods. There is much more of the Gothic through the 13th to 15th centuries, and finally, in the 16th century when the nave of the **church** was finished. There are two levels of alabaster windows, which fill the church with light. The colourful Renaissance **altarpiece** is the work of Andrés de Melgar and Guillén de Holanda,

commissioned by the Abbess, Doña Leonor de Osorio around 1523 as a triptych. The **Chapter House** contains the beautifully decorated 14th century **tomb** of Doña Urraca López de Haro (d.1262) daughter of the founders who took orders at a very early age and became the fourth abbess of the community. There are two **museums**, one displaying relics from the time of the convent's founding, and the other housing several altarpieces from churches in the area, together with paintings and sculpture.

Yuso and Suso Monasteries

Stage 10 • Santo Domingo de la Calzada to Belorado

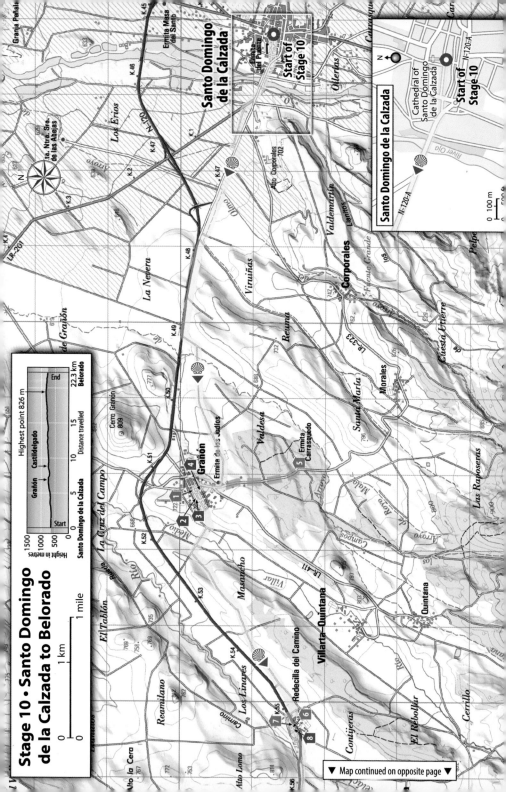

Highest point 826 m

Santo Domingo de la Calzada

Belorado

Map continued on opposite page ▼

Santo Domingo de la Calzada

Start of Stage 10

Cathedral of Santo Domingo de la Calzada

N-120-A

River Oja

0 — 100 m

N

Santo Domingo de la Calzada

Start of Stage 10

Ermita del Puente

Ermita Masa del Santo

Ta. Ntra. Sra. de las Abejas

Granja Peñales

Los Eriales

La Nevera

del Grañón

Cerro Grañón
809

Grañón

Ermita de los Judíos

La Cruz del Campo

El Tablón

Reamilano

Alto la Cera

Corporales

Alto Corporales
702

Valdemarín

Viruñas

Valdesa

Ermita Carrasquedo

Santa María

Morales

Reama

LR-323

Cuesta Grande

Fuente Grande

Las Raposeras

Arroyo

de Rojo

Campos

Mala

de los

Masancho

Villar

Villarta–Quintana

LR-411

Quintana

Redecilla del Camino

Los Linares

Camino

El Rebollar

Contijeras

Cerrillo

Quintana

▼ Continuation of map from opposite page ▼

Cartographic base © ign.es

Belorado

End of Stage 10

Church of Santa María

Church of San Pedro

AVENIDA DE BURGOS

0   100 m
0   500 ft

CALZADA TO BURGOS
TO BELORADO (22.3km)

We are still in La Rioja a short while (some 8km) before entering the northern part of the region that contains more of the Camino Francés than any other – about 450km. Exit Calzada along the wide bridge over the río Oja, paying your respects to the builder of its original predecessor, Santo Domingo. Having crossed the road onto a parallel track, you will pass a modern version of the *La Cruz de los Valientes*, which recalls an ancient land dispute between Calzada and Grañón and its settling by a fierce fight, in favour of Grañón; a procession to the spot takes place in August. Then the easiest way to reach Grañón (7km ∞) is to

1 San Juan Bautista Pa 40 Don Y B&M(Don) K|† 633 915 800 | Church of San Juan Bautista

2 Casas Rural Jacobea €45/50 941 420 684 | c/ Mayor 34

3 Casa Rural Cerro de Mirabel €50 Dbl. 660 166 090 c/ Mayor 40 | www.casacerrodemirabel.es

4 Hotel Casa Grande **** €74+ Dbl. 654 141 936 c/ Caño 13 | https://www.casagrandehotel.net

turn left off the Camino and continue past

Parochial Albergue

the cemetery. The village was caught up in the battles between King Sancho VI of Navarra and Alfonso VIII of Castile in the late 12th century, and then prospered with the opening up of the Camino. The **church of San Juan Bautista** is on the site of a monastery. There is a recently restored altarpiece; a **pilgrims' Mass** is held usually at 7pm. The 16th century **Ermita de los Judios** features a Mannerist altarpiece from 1540 depicting Jesus being beaten by 'Jews' before being crucified. Whatever the highly dubious sentiment behind the piece, it is very interesting, if you can get in to see it.

About 1.5km off Camino to the south of the village (to Corporales) amidst woodland lies the **Ermita de Carrasquedo**.

5 Nuestra Señora de Carrasquedo Pa 24 €15 B&B (+ Priv €42 Dbl.) Y M|B|W|D|@ 638 977 022/941 743 984 Camino Ermita 45 https://alberguecarrasquedo.com

On the site of a hospital, the restored late 17th century chapel contains the Virgin of Carrasquedo – Grañón's patron – on the gilded altarpiece set into the apse. This youth and family-oriented hostel also has private rooms; reserve in advance. Otherwise;

Straight through the village, descend on tracks and cross a stream. **Cross into Castilla y León**; then cross the N-120 and into Redecilla del Camino (R|B).

6 San Lázaro M 52 €6 Y M|B|K|W|D|@ 947 580 283/947 585 221 | c/ Mayor 24

7 Essentia Pr 10 €12 Y M|B|W|D|@ 606 046 298 c/ Mayor 34 | manuramirez6@hotmail.es

8 Hotel Redecilla del Camino * €45/50 947 585 256 c/ Mayor 12 | www.hotelredecilladelcamino.com

Several houses bear the coats of arms of the *hidalgos*, families who resettled Castile during the *reconquista*. The highlight of the 17th century **church of Nuestra Señora de la Calle** is a superb Romanesque baptismal font, carved with scenes of Jerusalem. Leave the village, cross the main road to join a parallel track. At

Castildelgado (12.5km R|B) the church

9 **Bideluze** Pr 16 €13 N M|B|W|D|@ 616 647 115 c/ Mayor 8 | www.alberguebideluze.com

of San Pedro has the tomb of Don Francisco Delgado, Bishop of Lugo and later Archbishop of Burgos. A 13th century carving of the Virgin and Child (Feast day September 16th) is here, whereas the adjacent **church of Santa María del Campo Real** has fewer furnishings but an interesting 18th century façade. The ruins of the palace of the Counts of Berberana, and the pilgrims' hospital are next door. The village once had a monastery as well, founded by Alfonso VII of León and Castile.

There is an *option* to stay alongside the main road and bypass the next village.

However; a distance of 2km *via track and local road* brings us to **Viloria de Rioja** (14km) where Santo Domingo was born and

10 **Acacio y Orietta** A 10 €8 Y B&M(Don) W|D|@|Cred 679 941 123 | c/ Nueva 6 | acaciodapaz@gmail.com

11 **Parada Viloria** Pr 16 €8 N B&M(Don) K|W|D|@ 610 625 065 | c/ Bajera 27 albergueparadaviloria@gmail.com

12 **Hotel Mihotelito** ** €70+/73+ 947 585 225 Pl. Mayor 16 | www.mihotelito.es

baptised; the **church of Nuestra Señora de la Asunción** has images of him. Note the interesting exterior construction of the apse. Alongside is at least the site of the **house** of his birth; it stood until very recently demolished! A fiesta on May 12th and 13th commemorates the saint's death. Another 3.5km, on a path alongside the N-120, leads us to **Villamayor del Río** (R|B|S), a hamlet whose **church of**

13 **San Luís de Francia** Pr 26 €5 N M|B|W|D|@ 947 580 566 | Carretera de Quintanilla (closed during 2022) alberguesanluisdefrancia@hotmail.com (300m off Camino near Quintanilla)

San Gil was rebuilt in the 18th century using materials from the adjoining pilgrims' hospital. More of the same uneventful roadside walking brings us across this busy main road into

Belorado (∞).

14 **El Corro** M 45 €12 Y M|K|W|D|@ 636 634 459 c/ Mayor 68 | albergueelcorro@gmail.com

15 **Parochial** Pa 20 Don N B&B(Don) K 947 580 085 Pl. San Francisco 7

16 **A Santiago** Pr 98 €10–15 N M|B|W|D|@|Pool 677 811 847 Camino Los Paúles | www.a-santiago.es (also **Hotel** €32/42)

17 **Cuatro Cantones** Pr 65 €12–16 N M|B|K|W|D|@|Cred|Pool 947 580 591 | c/ Hipólito López Bernal 10 | info@cuatrocantones.com www.cuatrocantones.com

18 **Caminante** Pr 22 €6–10 + Pensión €25–35/€35–45 N M|B|W|D|@ 656 873 927 | c/ Mayor 36 www.alberguecaminobelorado.es

19 **Hostelpuntob.B** 8 €18 (+16 priv. €38+/48+) M|B|K|W|D|@ 699 538 565 | c/ Cuatro Cantones 4 www.hostelpuntob.com

20 **Pensión Toñi** €38+/44+ 947 580 525 | c/ Redecilla del Campo 7 (next to Post Office) | www.pensiontoni.com

21 **Hotel La Huella del Camino** €35+/49+ 947 564 748 c/ Mayor 49 | turismoburgos.es/lahuelladelcamino/

22 **Hotel Rural Verdeancho** *** €59+/63+ 659 484 584 c/ El Corro 11 | www.casaverdeancho.com

With Roman origins, King Alfonso I of Aragón and Navarra (r. 1104–34) granted the town privileges, making it an important medieval trading centre, and there are buildings today that are understood to be the Jewish Quarter. It also has a defensive past, as it was on the border with Castile, and the **ruins** of its castle remain. Nowadays, this leather-making town attracts shoppers to its factory outlets. The **church of Santa María** includes a Santiago chapel, with a 16th century altarpiece and images of the saint. In the cliffs behind are **caves**, where it is said San Capraiso sought refuge, along with fellow hermits San Pía and San Valentín, under persecution from the Emperor Maximinus in the third century. The **church of San Pedro** was remodelled in the 17th century and has some fine statues. The ruined **church of San Nicolás** can also be seen. The **Ermita de Nuestra Señora de Belén** had a pilgrims' hospital was donated by King Alfonso VIII in 1171.

Grañón: Ermita de los Judios

Belorado: church of San Pedro

Rejoining the roadside track

Belorado: church of San Pedro

Ermita de la Virgen de la Peña

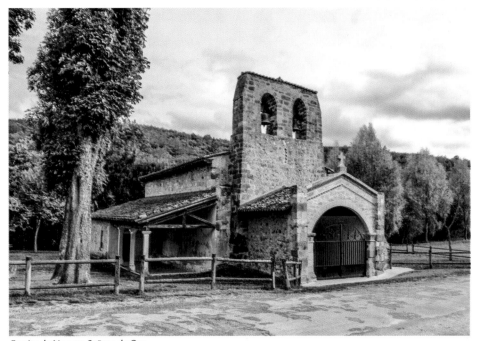

Ermita de Nuestra Señora de Oca

San Juan de Ortega

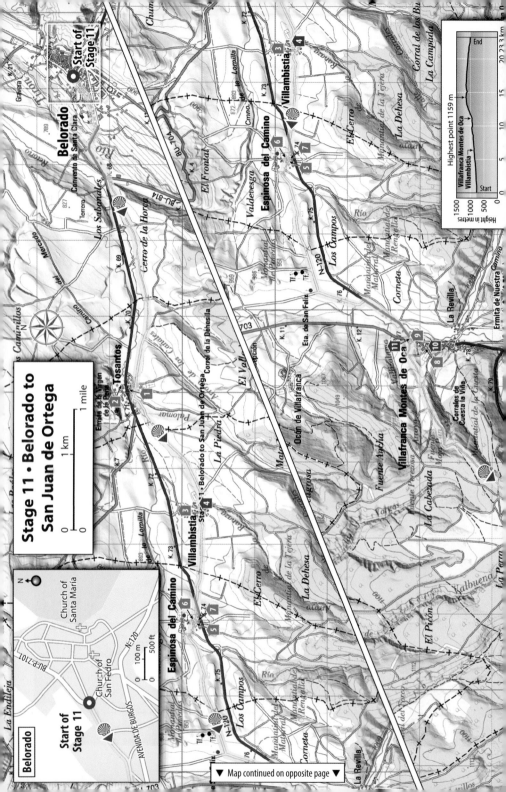

Stage 11 • Belorado to San Juan de Ortega

Belorado

Start of Stage 11

Church of Santa María

Church of San Pedro

AVENIDA DE BURGOS

N-120

BU-P-2101

La Endrina

Start of Stage 11

Belorado

Convento de Santa Clara

Tosantos

Ermita de la Virgen de la Peña

Villambistia

Espinosa del Camino

Villafranca Montes de Oca

Corrales de Cuesta la Viña

La Revilla

Ermita de Nuestra

N-120

Los Campos

Ocón de Villafranca

El Valle

Map continued on opposite page

Highest point 1159 m

Villafranca Montes de Oca
Villambistia

Height in metres

Start

End

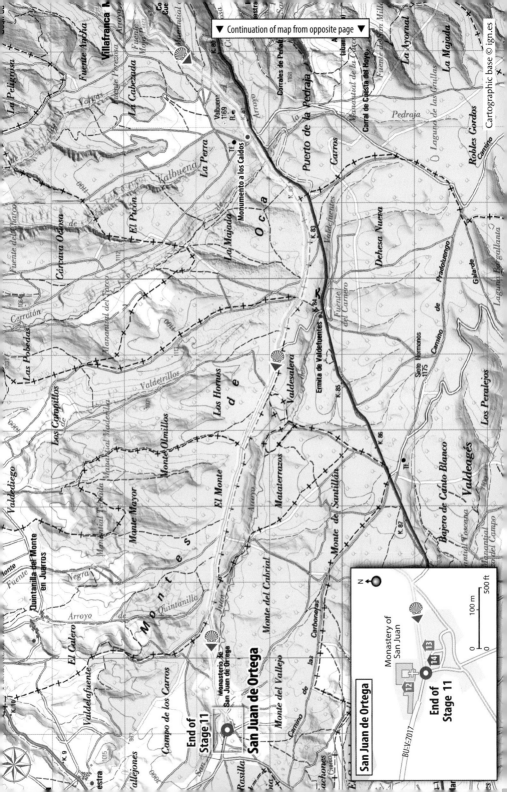

Cartographic base © ign.es

▼ Continuation of map from opposite page ▼

End of
Stage 11

San Juan de Ortega

San Juan de Ortega

N

Monastery of
San Juan

End of
Stage 11

0   100 m
0   500 ft

TO SAN JUAN DE ORTEGA (23.3km)

This stage description ends at the Monastery Albergue; however, there is more accommodation 3.5km further on at Agés (see next stage) or at Santovenia.

Exiting Belorado, pass the **Convent of Nuestra Señora de la Bretonera** (16th century) run by nuns of the order of St Clare. Cross the río Tirón – the original bridge was built by Santo Domingo – and brush with the N-120, before the path puts a more comfortable buffer between you and it. The terrain here is still relatively flat, but later in this stage there are three Montes de Oca peaks to surmount and skirt. After nearly 5km, arrive in the hamlet of Tosantos (4.8km B) whose **church of San**

1 **San Francisco de Asis** Pa 30 Don N M&B(Don) †
947 580 371 | c/ Santa Marina (next to N-120)

2 **Los Arancones** Pr 16 €15 Y M|B|W|D|@ 693 299 063
c/ de la Iglesia | carloseguiluz@outlook.es

Esteban is modest, though there was also a hospital on the site. To the north, a matter of 1km off Camino but a climb, the **Ermita de la Virgen de la Peña** is built into a cave in the rock. If it is open, then your visit is enhanced, however the setting is special enough. A small altarpiece houses a 12th century image of the Virgin and Child. There is a procession on September 8th, the Feast of the Nativity of Mary. Mid August sees a Feast of locals and pilgrims who have stayed at the Parochial Albergue.

Arriving at Villambistia (R|B), pass the

3 **San Roque** M 12 €10 B&B Y* M|W|D|@ 687 669 734
c/ Cayetano Ortiz 39 | * Closed Weds & Feb. 7–28

4 **Hotel Rural Casa de los Deseos** €35/45 653 326 020
c/ Las Eras 16 | www.casadelosdeseos.es

17th century parish **church of San Esteban**, which houses a painting of St Sebastian from the Italian school and several Renaissance altarpieces. The **chapel of San Roque** is set in a small plaza with pilgrims' fountain, while inside is a Rococo altarpiece (Turn right for Albergue and bar/restaurant; otherwise continue

straight). It is another short distance crossing the N-120 to Espinosa del Camino (7.8km R|B) after which climb and descend a hill to

5 **La Campana** Pr 10 €17 M+B&B Y 678 479 361
c/ Villafranca | lacampanadeespinosa@gmail.com
https://lacampanadepepe.blogspot.com/

6 **Casa Las Almas** Pr 5 €12 Y M|B|K|W|D|@
618 568 845 | c/ Barruelo 23 | www.las-almas.es

7 **La Taberna** Pr 22 €12 Y M|B|K|W|D|@ 660 916 937
c/ Barruelo 17 | https://tinyurl.com/ynjhbx72

pass the ruins of the 9th century **monastery of San Félix de Oca** in the Mozarab style. Diego Rodríguez Porcelos, founder of Burgos, was buried here. As you cross the río Oca, you begin to climb and reach the heavily-clued Villafranca Montes de Oca (11.2km R|B|S|€).

8 **San Anton Abad** Pr 49 €15 (+ 3 Priv. €40+) N
M|B|@ 947 582 150/613 147 747 | c/ Hospital 4
www.hotelsanantonabad.com (+ **Hotel *** €63/75)

9 **Montes de Oca** M 60 €7 K|W|D|@ 691 801 211
c/ Mayor 17 (closed during 2022)
alberguemunicipalvillafrancamo@gmail.com

10 **Pensión Jomer** €20/40+ 947 582 146 | c/ Mayor 52
pension.jomer@hotmail.com

11 **Casa Rural La Alpargatería** €30/40 686 040 884
c/ Mayor 2 | www.casarurallalpargateria.es

Roman and Bronze Age remains have been found here, indicating important settlements. This village was once a Bishop's see, but the other clue in its name is that it was one of several stops on the Camino settled by the Franks, who brought their skills as builders and craftsmen. The pilgrims' **Hospital of St Anthony the Abbot** has undergone restoration, and now serves as both the Albergue and a more comfortable hotel. Founded by Juana Manuel, Queen of Castile, in 1380, what we see today is 15th century. The **church of Santiago** is visible for its dome atop its tower, while inside is a Baroque sculpture of St James. The **Ermita de Nuestra Señora de Oca** is over 2km southwest of the village –alongside the river – so for walking pilgrims has to be considered as an excursion (pleasant in the evening if staying here) with return recommended by the same route – 4.5km in total. On the way, there is another chapel, the **Ermita de Nuestra Señora de Alba**, before reaching the site associated with the martyred San Indalecio, the first Bishop of Oca, who is said to be a disciple of St James. There is a **fountain** across the bridge where Indalecio is believed to have died, whereupon a spring flowed on the spot.

Returning to the village, from here it is a hilly/mountainous forested trek of 12km – with **no villages/services** in between, mostly split from the twisting main road – before San Juan de Ortega, which itself is remote and has limited facilities. Medieval pilgrims used to prepare as best they could for this journey, as the mountains were infested with bandits. **Fuente de Mojapán** recalls, literally, where pilgrims moistened their bread in the fountain. *Monumento a los Caidos* is a Civil War memorial, after which there is a steep descent to a stream, before a steep climb to *Alto Pedraja* (1100m). After this there is a short path – leading off Camino – to the **Ermita Valdefuentes and fountain**, by the stream of the same name.

Back on track, it's a more measured descent to San Juan de Ortega (R|B).

🏠 **Monasterio San Juan** Pa 60 €15 N M|B|W|D|@|†
947 569 913 | c/ Iglesia 9
www.alberguesanjuandeortega.es

🏠 **Alojamento El descanso de San Juan** Pr 7 €15
M|B|@ 690 398 024 | Camino Transformador
eldescansodesanjuan@gmail.com

🏠 **Hotel Rural La Henera** ** €45+/55+ 606 198 734
c/ Iglesia 4 | www.sanjuandeortega.es

This village was founded by Juan Velázquez (1080–1163) a disciple of Santo Domingo, who returned from a pilgrimage to Jerusalem, determined to build more facilities for pilgrims to Santiago, and try to free areas like this from mortal peril. Naturally, the bandits reviled him and frequently attacked the settlement, but patronage from Doña Urraca and Alfonso VII facilitated an unbowed construction mission here and further along the Way. His hostel still serves pilgrims today, with the tradition of feeding them re-established by one of the Camino's modern defenders, parish priest José María, continuing after his death in 2008.

The **monastery** and **pilgrim church of San Nicolás de Bari** – who is said to have interceded to save Juan from drowning on his return from the Holy Land – sit together. San Juan's 1142 Romanesque design survived with the apse and alabaster windows. In the crypt there is a magnificent tomb with canopy and recumbent statue of the saint, donated by Queen Isabella of Castile (later the 'Catholic' monarch), who in 1475 believed San Juan could intercede so that she could bear a child; she later conceived twice. His original tomb – much less elaborate – is in the monastery church. San Juan is credited as patron of fertility, and this is further witnessed in a 'miracle of light' on a carved capital in the church, which at the spring and autumn equinoxes – March 21st and September 22nd (besides two days before and two after) illuminates with setting sunlight the figure of the Virgin Mary in a scene of the Annunciation, passing briefly on to the Nativity and finally the Adoration of the Magi. Originally Augustinian, the monastery was transferred to the Hieronymite order (Los Jerónimos) in the 15th century. The cloister is among the 16th century additions, while a second in ruins is from the neoclassical period.

Stage 12 • San Juan de Ortega to Burgos

San Juan de Ortega
Monte del Vallejo

Start of Stage 12

Monasterio de San Juan de Ortega

1 Santovenia – 3.3 km from San Juan de Ortega

Monastery of San Juan

San Juan de Ortega

Start of Stage 12

▼ Map continued below ▼

▼ Map continued from above ▼

▼ Map continued on opposite page ▼

Atapuerca

La Dehesilla

Cruz de Atapuerca

Villalval

Riopico

Cardeñuela Riopico

Orbaneja Riopico

Quintanilla Riopico

Villafría

Ximos de Atapuerca

Quintanar

Agés

San Román

Mercadillo

Atapuerca

Cruz de Atapuerca

1 km

1 mile

▼ Continuation of map from opposite page ▼

Cartographic base © ign.es

Height in metres

1500
1000
500

San Juan de Ortega

Atapuerca

Start

Orbaneja Riopico

End

Burgos
25.3 km

0   5   10   15   20

Distance travelled

BURGOS

Villimar

Villafría

Castañares

Cardeñajimeno

San Mede

Polígono Industrial
Gamonal-Villimar

Campos de Tubo de Pallafría

Convento de las Calatravas

Convento de San Estéban

Aeropuerto de Villafría

El Campo

La Horca

Novillas

Cótar

Las Muñecas

Capillejas

Valdeloánez

Fuente Pascual

Valmenor

Fuente Candeleja

Santinsio

El Crujo

Vilhayeda o la Ventilla

El Soto

Fte. de la Salud

Los Cauces

Cartuja de Miraflores

Campo Lukula

End of
Stage 12

See map on page 114 & Stage 13 map for details of accommodation in Burgos.

0   100 m
0   500 ft

Burgos

Cathedral of
Santa María

of San
Lesmes

AVENIDA·LA·Y...
CALLE·LAS·CALZADAS

CALLE·VITORIA

BULEVAR·DEL·FERROCARRIL

CALLE·MADRID

Cathedral of
de la Asunción

La Muñeca

Cementerio de San José

Burgos
Castle

End of
Stage 12

TO BURGOS (25.3 km)

Leave the village and continue through the woodland and meadow, remaining at altitude. At **Agés** (3.6km R|B)

1 **El Camino de Santovenia** M 24 €14+ (€16–21in winter) Y M|B|W|D 650 733 150
elcaminodesantovenia@gmail.com
3.3km off Camino left after San Juan de Ortega; rejoin Camino at Agés; difference of 1.6km.

2 **Municipal – La Taberna** M 36 €12 Y* M|B|W|D|@ 624 635 008 | c/ del Medio 21
silvia_bgs89@hotmail.com | *Closed November

3 **El Pajar de Agés** Pr 34 €14 (+ 2 Priv. €45 Dbl.) N M|B|W|D|@ 686 273 322 | c/ Ochabro 12
www.elpajardeages.es

4 **Fagus** Pr 22 €15 N M|B|W|D|@ 600 506 115 c. Adobera 14–16 | www.alberguefagus.com

before walking over one of San Juan's bridges, **Puente Canto**, perhaps with a song in your heart, the Gothic **church of Santa Eulalia de Mérida** claims to hold in a tomb the entrails of King García Sánchez III of Navarra, while his body was removed to the monsatery at Nájera. **Atapuerca** (6km from San Juan to turn-off – see below R|B|S)

5 **El Peregrino** Pr 30 €11 N K|W|D|@ 661 580 882 c/ Camino de Santiago 25
www.alberguedeatapuerca.com

6 **La Hutte** Pr 18 €10 (+ **Hotel Rural** *** €49/71) Y K|@ 947 430 320 | Papasol (c/ Enmedio 36)
www.burgosturismorural.com

7 **Hostel La Plazuela Verde** Pr 10 €14 Y B|K|W|@ 658 647 720/654 301 152 | c/ San Polo 41
https://laplazuelaverde.es/

8 **Hostal El Palomar** €30+/60+ 947 400 601 c/ Revilla 22 | elpalomardeatapuerca@gmail.com

is the site of the battle between the rival brother kings: García Sánchez was slain by Ferdinand I of Castile in 1054. The prehistoric **caves** are a UNESCO World Heritage site, where the earliest remains were discovered of *Homo antecessor*, an extinct species that may have been a common ancestor to both humans and neanderthals, thought to date back around 800 000 years. Remains of animals, and later implements

and pottery, have also been found. **Visitor centres**, including audio-visual representations, await on site and in the village, along with the **archaeological park** (about 3km off Camino) itself. The **church of San Martín** combines Gothic and Renaissance elements.

Some pilgrims keep on the road for the municipal Albergue at **Olmos de Atapuerca**

9 **Olmos de Atapuerca** M 21 €10 Y K 947 430 524 c/ de la Iglesia 9

(R|B); with a reconnection to the Camino (adds approx. 3km); otherwise turn left onto a track and ascend the *sierra Atapuerca*, where there is a **cross** at the peak (1080m) and a fine view of Burgos on a clear day.

You have the *option* to continue walking up high (with some waymarking) bypassing Cardeñuela and coming into the centre of Orbaneja (saves 0.5km approx.). Otherwise;

Go left to begin a descent to isolated **Villalval**. Continue by local road to **Cardeñuela Riopico** (R|B).

10 **Municipal La Parada** M 12 €7 Y M|B|W|D|@ 660 050 594/661 438 093 | c/ Real 28
laparadacardenuelariopico@gmail.com

11 **Santa Fé** Pr 15 €10–12 (+ Priv. €30-40 Dbl.) Y M|B|W|D|@ 626 352 269 | c/ Los Huertos 2
alberguesantafe@hotmail.com
https://www.baralberguesantafe.com

12 **Via Minera** Pr 38 €8+ (+ 2 Priv. €50 Dbl. B&B) N M|B|W|D|@ 652 941 647 | c/ la Iglesia 1
albergueviaminera@gmail.com

13 **Casa Rural La Cardeñuela** €25 610 652 560 /620 385 008 | c/ Via Minera – on way out of the village

Orbaneja Riopico (14km R|B) has the

14 **Casa Rural Fortaleza** €60 (Dbl.) 678 116 570 c/ Principal 31 | www.casaruralfortaleza.com

church of San Millán Abad containing a statue of San Roque dressed as a pilgrim, and a **chapel** nearby. Cross bridge over the motorway.

There are then two main alternatives. Both routes are waymarked but see below for riverside sub-option.

The **Villafría option** (26km to Burgos from San Juan) is the traditional route, however it involves – after crossing over the railway bridge – following alongside the busy N-1 all the way to the old town. There is, however, an hourly bus service (Bus 8 – may be reduced Sundays) to the old town from Villafría (B|S)

15 Hotel Buenos Aires ** €40/52 947 483 740
c/ Vitoria 349 (Ctra. N-1)

16 Hostal Iruñako ** €39/49 947 484 126
c/ Vitoria 343 (Ctra. N-1) | www.irunako.es

17 Hotel Las Vegas ** €42+/59+ 947 484 453
c/ Vitoria 319 (Ctra. N-1) | www.hotelasvegas.es

The **church of San Esteban** was rebuilt in the 16th century and features a Baroque altarpiece. Gamonal (∞) is a large suburb, and amid the modernity is the 14th century Gothic **church of Santa María La Real y Antigua**. It has been a major landmark on the Camino, since its Romanesque predecessor. The stone **cross** has been placed nearby in more recent times. Inside, there is a Santiago Peregrino image.

The Castañares (R|B) **option** (26.5km to Burgos from San Juan) is a slightly longer

18 Hotel Versus *** €55+/60+ 947 474 977 | c/ Iglesia 8

19 Camping Fuentes Blancas €43+ bungalow. Ask re. Albergue option | 947 486 016 | Along the river www.campingburgos.com

20 Pensión Santiago €40+ Dbl. 947 046 230
c/ Santiago Apóstol 8 | https://tinyurl.com/yc2n3mty

but somewhat quieter route, and also provides a bus option (Bus 4) into the city should you wish.

There is an even quieter *sub-option* that follows the **río Arlanzón** on the opposite bank, having reached Castañares and crossed the N-120. Limited waymarking but easy to follow, it can take you all the way, past the Cartuja de Miraflores monastery to the **puente Santa María**, crossing back over, under the arch to the cathedral. It is also the most direct way to get to the Emaús Albergue.

With the fully waymarked option, follow a track alongside the N-120, and under the A-1 motorway spur. Cross over the main road after a petrol station, with the river to the left. Rejoin the main road, and the large junction is where the two main options meet.

Pass by the **military museum** – boasting one of the largest collections of arms in Spain – and along c/ San Roque, crossing before a large shopping centre. Emerge briefly onto the Av. Cantabria (the busy N-623) then turn onto c/ Calzadas, then onto the Pl. San Juan. Here, the richly decorated interior of the Gothic **church of San Lesmes** contains a fine main altarpiece. Among the tombs is the sepulchre of the church's and the city's patron. **San Lesmes Abad** (d. 1097) (a.k.a. Adelelmus) was born in Loudun in France, into a wealthy family. Pious from a young age, he divided his property among the poor and made a pilgrimage to Rome – later entering the Benedictine abbey at La Chaise-Dieu as a scholar. Queen Constance of Burgundy, wife of King Alfonso VI, called for him to replace the Mozarabic liturgy with the Roman, and established him in Burgos at the **monastery of St John the Evangelist** – ruins of which are in the Plaza and form part of the **Museo Marceliano Santa María** (dedicated to the artist from Burgos). The Abbot also devoted himself to the care of pilgrims. There is a **statue** of the city's founder Diego Rodriguez Porcelos mounted on a horse. Cross the río Vena, pass through the **Arco de San Juan**, along the c/ de San Juan, into c/ de Avellanos, then slightly into c/ San Gil. Once onto and further down c/ Fernán González, you will begin to walk alongside the north elevation of the cathedral (left). The central Albergue is off this street (right) before the cathedral. Emerge into the **Plaza Santa María**, down the steps by the **church of San Nicolás**, to appreciate the splendour of this Gothic masterpiece – one of the momentous points of arrival along the Camino.

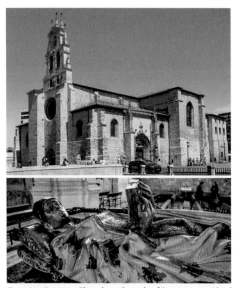

Entering Burgos: Church and tomb of San Lesmes Abad

Burgos: Altarpiece in the church of San Nicolás de Bari

Burgos: Statue of El Cid

Exiting Burgos: Ermita de San Amaro Peregrino

BURGOS (∞)

1 **Casa de Cubos** M 150 €10 Y W|D|Cred
947 460 922 | c/ Fernán González 28 www.
caminosantiagoburgos.com

2 **Emaús** Pa 20 €10 N B&M(Don) @|†
c/ San Pedro de Cardeña 31a
peregrinosemaus@gmail.com

3 **Santiago y Catalina (Divina Pastora chapel)** A 16
€6 N W|D|@|† 947 207 952 c/ Laín Calvo 10
(closed during 2022)

4 **Catedral Burgos** Pr 136 €22–24 B&B Y
K|M|W|D|@ 623 115 887/947 718 435
Pl. Huerto del Rey 5
https://hostelcatedralburgos.es/

5 **Hostal Lar** ** €45+/65+ 947 209 655
c/ Cardenal Benlloch 1 | reservas@hostallar.es

6 **Pensión Boutique Doña Urraca** €52+ Dbl.
689 223 182 | c/ San Gil 16, 1st left
www.pensiondonaurraca.com

7 **Hostal rimBomBin** ** €46+ Dbl. 947 261 200
c/ Sombrerería 6 | reservas@rimbombin.com

8 **Hotel Cordón** *** €49+/54+ 947 265 000
c/ La Puebla 6 | www.hotelcordon.com

9 **Hotel Meson del Cid** *** €62+ Dbl. 947 208 715
Pl. Santa María 8
www.eurostarshotels.com/crisol-meson-del-cid.html

10 **Hotel Abba Burgos** **** €70+ 935 153 075
c/ Fernán González 72 | www.abbaburgoshotel.com

11 **Hotel NH Palacio de Burgos** **** €95+ Dbl.
947 479 900 | c/ Merced 13
nhcollectionpalaciodeburgos@nh-hotels.com

There is a further collection of affordable hotels, shops and places to eat on Camino on the way out of Burgos at the end of the Parque del Parral, near the Hospital del Rey and San Amaro campus of the University. See Stage 13 map.

A **Hotel Puerta Romeros** ** €Enquire 947 462 012
c/ San Amaro 2 | www.puertaromeros.com

B **Hotel Azofra** *** €57+Dbl. 947 461 050 | c/ Don
Juan de Austria 22–24 | www.hotelazofra.com

C **Hotel Abadía** *** €36+/44+ 947 040 404
c/ Villadiego 10 | https://hotelabadiaburgos.com

D **Hostal Vía Láctea** ** €40+ 947 463 211
c/ Villadiego 16 | http://www.hostalvíaláctea.com/

Lying at an altitude of some 850 metres, Burgos began life as a complex of defensive castles, built by Alfonso III to consolidate the reconquest of this part of Spain from brief occupation by the Moors. The wide and deep region became known as the land of Castles, or Castile. Some 40 years later, in 884, Porcelos, as Count of Castile, was charged by the king with the task of increasing the Christian presence in the north of this area. In 926, the town elected its first judges and in 950 one of the judges, Fernán González, declared himself as Count of Castile in an act of independence from León. His descendant, Ferdinand I, declared himself the first king of Castile. After the capital of the kingdom moved to Toledo in 1087, the city developed as one of Spain's religious centres – becoming an archbishopric in 1574 – with numerous monasteries and seminaries, many of which survive today. Later, Burgos was the scene of battles in the Peninsular War – where Wellington laid siege and suffered a rare defeat – the Carlist wars, and during the Spanish Civil War it was Franco's headquarters. The *Caudillo* rewarded the city with state-directed industrialisation – it is home to one of Spain's largest breweries and several automotive manufacturers – and it became a transport hub. Population is now about 180 000. But its favourite son remains Rodrigo Díaz de Vivar (d. 1099), El Cid, who was born just outside the city, and is the most celebrated warlord of the *reconquista*. Even after the superb cathedral, there remains a lot to see, with a two-night stay fully justified. Easter sees one of the most impressive series of Holy Week processions in Spain.

THE CATHEDRAL OF SANTA MARÍA DE LA ASUNCIÓN

Declared a UNESCO World Heritage site in 1984, French visitors are often heard to remark that this is such a fine example of French cathedral architecture, and the proud natives

Burgos Cathedral: West façade

Burgos Cathedral

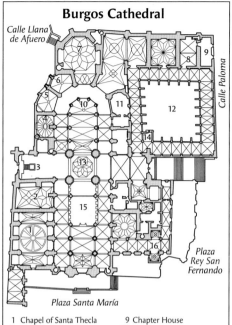

Calle Llana de Afuero

Calle Paloma

Plaza Rey San Fernando

Plaza Santa María

1 Chapel of Santa Thecla
2 Chapel of Santa Ana
3 Escalada Dorada
4 Chapel of the Nativity
5 Chapel of the Annunciation
6 Chapel of San Gregorio
7 Chapel of the Condestables
8 Chapel of Jean Cuchiller
9 Chapter House
10 Altar
11 Sacristy
12 Cloister and Museum
13 Tomb of El Cid
14 Chapel of San Jerónimo
15 Coro
16 Chapel of Santismo Cristo

can react adversely to that – but they shouldn't because, apart from being a huge compliment, it is accurate. Built on the site of the former Romanesque cathedral, construction was ordered by King Ferdinand III of Castile – in honour of his marriage to Beatrice of Swabia – who together with the English-born bishop Maurice, laid the first stone in 1221. The first architects were, indeed, French – the master Enrique also working on that other jewel, León cathedral – and the first part of the building to be completed was the chevet (a choir in the shape of a hemicycle) also a distinctly French Gothic feature. While being consecrated early on (in 1260) building resumed two centuries later, with the addition of the two flamboyant spires, the grand cloister, and more chapels, including the most ambitious of all, the Chapel

of the Condestables. This time, the principal architect was German, John of Cologne, upon whose death in 1481, his son Simon succeeded him as master builder. During this time, another father and son team, Gil and Diego de Siloé, were responsible for some of the most notable sculpture in the interior. The cathedral was finally completed in 1567, with the addition of the lantern over the central nave, yet still to come some internal Renaissance and Baroque decoration, and the replacement of the west façade.

Only the far western portion – with its two chapels used for daily worship – is free to enter, however the standard admission price of €7 and €4.50 for pilgrims (includes audioguide) to see everything is worth every cent – notwithstanding one's view of charging to enter a place of worship. The ticket office is located under the south door.

Starting in the Plaza Santa María, at the **west façade**, the twin spires – they seem to be so light and airy – catch the eye, with the bells clearly visible in the towers below. The earlier Gothic portals were replaced with more simple affairs. There are two Stars of David, one in the central portal and the other incorporated into the large rose window, above which are statues of eight kings. Inside, either side of the narthex are the two chapels. However, before exploring further, look up left, to see a most curious adornment: The ***Papamoscas* clock** (16th century) features a grotesque 'fly catcher' doll who, with mouth opening and closing, pops out above the clock face when the hour is struck. The **chapel of Santa Thecla** was formed out of four smaller Gothic chapels. The plastered dome is flanked by the Evangelists. The altarpiece is by another famous craftsman José de Churriguera. Here, there is a **Pilgrims' Mass** at 7.30pm. Across the narthex, through the glass doors, is the **chapel of Santísimo Cristo**. The 13th century figure of the Holy Christ of Burgos makes this the most revered shrine in the city, and is made out

Burgos Cathedral: South façade

Above is, literally, one of the cathedral's star attractions. The beautiful Plateresque, gold-trimmed, star vaulted **lantern** was begun in the late 15th century by Felipe de Borgoña and completed by Juan de Vallejo. One can discern strong Moorish influence in the design. The stone carving of the vaults, also, is exquisite. The **choir**, carved by Felipe de Bigarny, features the splaying horizontal organ pipes characteristic of many Spanish cathedrals and monasteries; here there is one set on each side of the stalls. Carved into the walnut, there are representations of the Old Testament, followed by the New Testament in the row below. The tomb here is that of Bishop Maurice. The **main altar** and altarpiece date from 1562 and are by the brothers Rodrigo and Martín de la Haya. There are carvings of the life of the Virgin, with a Gothic Maria Maggiore (patroness of Burgos) enthroned in the middle.

Crossing over to the north transept, we admire the beautiful **Escalada Dorada**. Diego de Siloé's Plateresque masterpiece dates from 1523. This side of the cathedral is over seven metres higher than its floor, and the twin staircase bridges that gap perfectly, as it leads up to the north Puerta Alta de la Coronería. At the foot of the staircase is stored the **carriage** and silver tabernacle used in a Corpus Christi procession. To the left, the **chapel of Santa Ana** dates from 1488 and it is the filigree altarpiece by Gil de Siloé and Diego de la Cruz, with its central representation of the Tree of

of animal skin with real human hair and nails, and articulated arms and legs. The veneration has spread widely throughout Spain and Latin America.

The rest of the cathedral is accessible from the **south façade**. Having purchased your ticket, stand and admire the **Puerta del Sarmental** before climbing the steps and entering. The very finely carved tympanum shows Christ directing the four Evangelists (seated at desks) to write the Gospels. Below, the twelve Apostles are lined up – texts in hand – each in animated discussion with his neighbour. Above, another large rose window, which bears greater comparison with the cathedral at Chartres. Inside, we move directly to the main crossing and the **tombs** of El Cid *El Campeador* and his wife, Doña Jimena, which were moved here from the nearby monastery of San Pedro de Cardeña in 1921.

Jesse, which catches the eye. In a niche, there are statues of Santiago Peregrino, and the Virgin of the Pillar – the patron and patroness of Spain. To the right is the oldest chapel in the cathedral, **San Nicolás**. The canon, Pedro Díaz de Villahoz (d. 1230) is buried here. It contains two panels from an older Romanesque retablo. From that relative simplicity, it is back to the elaborate with the **chapel of the Nativity** (late 16th century) the funerary chapel of the widow of a wealthy merchant. Note a buttress of the cathedral inside this chapel, as it was built on to the original structure. We move on to the **chapel of the Annunciation**, its irregular shape reminding us that we are at the start of the ambulatory. While it dates back to 1274, it was re-dedicated, and the altarpiece is from 1540. The **chapel of San Gregorio** contains another of the several tombs of former bishops, Gonzalo de Hinojosa.

Now we come to that undoubted highlight, the **chapel of the Condestables**. This striking example of German Gothic is composed of an octagonal openwork dome on a square ground plan. Begun by Simon of Cologne shortly after his father's death, together with his son Francis – continuing the family line of three generations of dedication to this place – it is formally known as the chapel of the Purification of the Virgin. It was commissioned by Pedro Hernández de Velasco, the High Constable of Castile and his wife, Doña Mencía de Mendoza.

With its own choir and organ, and small sacristy, it is in effect, a church within a cathedral. Gil de Siloé and Diego de la Cruz are responsible for the Gothic altarpiece, while Diego de Siloé, Bigarny and León Picardo made the two in the Renaissance style. In front of one of these are the Italian marble tombs of the Constable and his wife. He is clutching his sword, while she has a small dog resting at her feet, a symbol of fidelity. As head of the army of Castile, Velasco served at the time of the conquest of Granada from the Moors, and there is Moorish influence again in the star vaulted dome above. The stained glass windows are by Arnao of Flanders, the elder. The painting of Mary Magdalene is by Rizzoli (Giampetrino) a pupil of Leonardo da Vinci, although after restoration, the hands and face have been attributed to the master himself. As you leave, note the fine grille by Andino (1523) and the triptych attributed to the Flemish school of Memling and van der Weyden.

Of the five stone **reredoses** in the ambulatory, the three in the centre are attributed to Bigarny (1498–1503) and the other two to Pedro Alonso de los Ríos (1679). Together, they represent the Paschal mystery. We now take a circular route which will come out at the next doorway, so ignore that and enter the main **sacristy**. This was built in 1765, on the site of a former chapel, in the Baroque-Rococo style. Its painted plaster-covered dome is dedicated to the Annunciation and Coronation of the Virgin. We pass through to the **upper cloister**, built from 1260 by Enrique. Here we find several more tombs of bishops and cathedral canons, as well as the **chapel of San Jerónimo** built by Juan de Vallejo in 1545, with an altarpiece by Diego Guillén. Of the cloister sculptures, the group with Ferdinand III and Beatrice is especially noteworthy. Before descending to the lower cloister, there are several chapels leading off the upper cloister, which make up the **Cathedral museum**. Gold, enamel, ivory and precious stones were donated by the wealthy women of Burgos from their jewellery. There are artefacts from the Condestables chapel, including a processional cross with representations of the Passion in polychrome and ivory. In the Chapter Room, there are several more Flemish paintings, including a Virgin and Child by Memling. In the chapels of Corpus Christi and St Catherine, El Cid's chest and his Pledge are displayed. The largest collection is reserved for the conjoined chapels of St John the Baptist and St James. The **lower cloister** is partly given over to interpreting the cathedral and its decorative styles.

This next section begins in the south arm of the transept. The cloister door, the so-called **Paradise doorway** is dedicated to Christ as Man, with the Baptism, entry into Jerusalem and the descent into the Limbo of the Just. In the **chapel of San Enrique** there is a representation of Christ seated, in pain, awaiting crucifixion. Opposite, the **chapel of the Visitation** was built in 1440. Bishop Alonso de Cartagena's tomb is probably a joint effort, with the figure bearing the style of Gil de Siloé, while below it is thought John of Cologne is responsible. Moving round to the left, the **chapel of San Juan de Sahagún** was re-dedicated after a canon of the cathedral, later made a saint. Connecting, the **chapel of the Relics** was built by a barefoot Carmelite monk, Fray José de San Juan de la

Cruz, in the Baroque style. Lastly, the **chapel of the Presentation** was completed in 1524 by Juan de Matienzo, at the request of Don Gonzalo Díaz de Lerma, whose tomb was carved by Bigarny. Based on the chapel of the Condestables, likewise it features an openwork stellar vault.

The two doors on the north side of the cathedral can be explored separately, as they are not usually open. The **Puerta Alta de la Coronería** (1250) depicts the Last Judgement. Christ, seated, shows his wounds, flanked by Mary and St John the Evangelist, while below St Michael separates the good men from the bad. The Apostles are on hand in the door jambs. Around the corner, the Plateresque **Puerta de la Pellejería** (Door of the Fur Room) is by Francis of Cologne and was completed in 1530. Bishop Juan Rodríguez de Fonseca (d. 1524) who commissioned this work is represented here along with images of Sts. Peter and Paul, and the martyrdom of both John the Baptist and John the Evangelist.

And that is not everything! Nor could it possibly be, as there is so much more to take in, or to try to.

AROUND THE CATHEDRAL

At the end of c/ Fernán Gonzalez, adjacent to the cathedral at the top of the Plaza Santa María steps, is the **church of San Nicolás de Bari**. The Colonia family were also responsible for this Gothic structure, whose tympanum features a statue of the saint, by John, together with depictions of the lives of several more. However, it is the huge monumental altarpiece inside – designed by Simon and carved from alabaster by Francis (c.1505) – which really stands out. In total, 36 Biblical scenes are depicted. Above the image of the saint and depictions of some of his miracles, is a circular Coronation of the Virgin surrounded by choirs of angels. The notable works of art in the annexe include several Flemish tapestries, and a Last Supper painting.

– shaded in part by plane trees. Again, there are cafés, leading to the main theatre, beyond which is the Plaza de Mío Cid. Here, you meet the city traffic, the centrepiece being a huge **statue of El Cid** mounted on his trusty charger, Babieca, in full flow. From here you have two or three alternatives.

SOUTH OF THE RIVER

Cross the bridge – embellished with figures from the Cid's life – to visit two of the city's impressive museums. First, we come to the spacious, modern **Museo de la Evolución Humana** (to the left at the Plaza del Conde de Castro) which links in with nearby Atapuerca, to the extent that a special bus connects the two. Here there are life-sized models of our early antecedents, as well as real specimens and artefacts recovered from the site. Continuing south, and turning right into c/ de Miranda, the **Museo de Burgos** is set in the beautiful Casa de Miranda, a former convent (c.1545) with a notable courtyard and Renaissance staircase. The main façade is in c/ de la Calera.

On the south side of the cathedral, the **Plaza del Rey San Fernando** contains cafés at which to sit and admire the structure and commune with a **statue** of a weary pilgrim seated on a bench. In the southwest corner of the square is the **Arco de Santa María**, but you need to pass through and turn around to appreciate the most elaborate of the city's surviving medieval gates. It was in fact redesigned in the 16th century by Francis of Cologne and his father Simon, and Juan de Vallejo, as a triumphal arch, to flatter Charles V, Holy Roman Emperor (Charles I of Spain). Set into the limestone façade above the doorway are six statues, including Charles, Porcelos (bottom centre) and Fernán González (top left), the Cid, and two of the early judges. Above them, a guardian angel holds a model of the city – flanked by two mace bearers – and above them are the Virgin and Child. All in their own ways are defenders of the city, and the crenellated decoration reinforces the theme. Inside, stairs give access to a room with a mural depicting the founding of Castile, with the former council chamber showing paintings of the historical figures under a decorated domed ceiling. On the top floor, the **Pharmacy Museum** recalls the city's prominence in early medicine.

Off to the right (while still facing the Arco) instead of crossing the Puente de Santa María, walk by the river Arlanzón along the **Paseo del Espolón** – one of Spain's most attractive

Casa de Miranda   *Jose Luis Filpo Cabana CC BY 3.0*

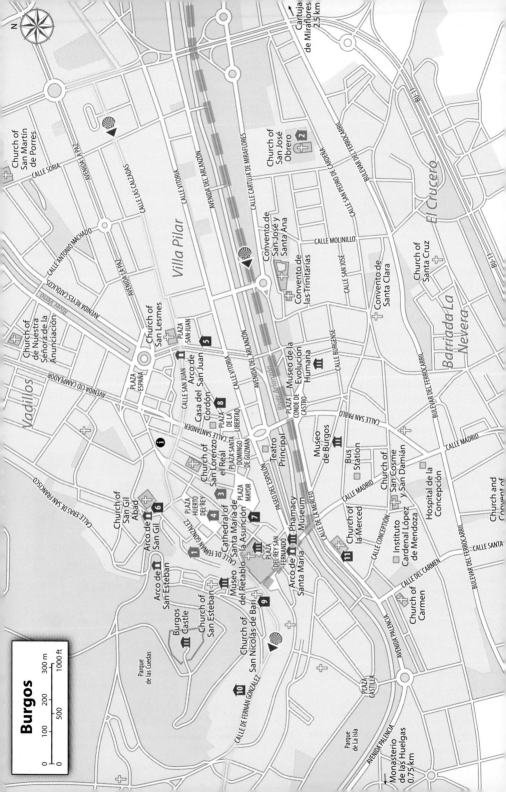

Burgos

N

Cartuja de Miraflores 2.5 km

Church of San Martín de Porres

CALLE SORIA

AVENIDA LA PAZ

CALLE LAS CALZADAS

Church of Nuestra Señora de la Anunciación

Villa Pilar

CALLE VITORIA

AVENIDA DEL ARLANZÓN

CALLE CARTUJA DE MIRAFLORES

Church of San José Obrero

2

BULEVAR DEL FERROCARRIL

BU-11

El Crucero

Church of Santa Cruz

Barriada La Nevera

CALLE MOLINILLO

Convento de San José y Santa Ana

Convento de las Trinitarias

CALLE SAN JOSÉ

Convento de Santa Clara

CALLE ANTONIO MACHADO

AVENIDA LA PAZ

AVENIDA REYES CATÓLICOS

RIVER VENA

Vadillos

Church of Nuestra Señora de la Anunciación

AVENIDA CID CAMPEADOR

PLAZA ESPAÑA

Church of San Lesmes

PLAZA SAN JUAN

Arco de San Juan

Casa del Cordón

5

CALLE SAN JUAN

8

PLAZA DE LA LIBERTAD

CALLE SANTANDER

CALLE VITORIA

AVENIDA DEL ARLANZÓN

River Arlanzón

Museo de la Evolución Humana

PLAZA CONDE DE CASTRO

CALLE BURGENSE

CALLE SAN PABLO

CALLE SAN PEDRO DE CARDEÑA

CALLE SAN FERROCARRIL

Church of San Gil Abad

Arco de San Gil

6

Church of San Lorenzo el Real

3

Cathedral of Santa María de la Asunción

4

PLAZA SANTA MARÍA

PLAZA HUERTO DEL REY

PLAZA SANTO DOMINGO DE GUZMÁN

PLAZA MAYOR

7

Teatro Principal

Museo de Burgos

Bus Station

Church of San Cosme y San Damián

CALLE MADRID

CALLE MADRID

Hospital de la Concepción

Church and Convent of

CALLE ERAS DE SAN FRANCISCO

Arco de San Esteban

1

Church of San Esteban

Museo del Retablo

Church of San Nicolás de Bari

9

PLAZA DEL REY SAN FERNANDO

Arco de Santa María

Phamacy Museum

PASEO DEL ESPOLÓN

Church of la Merced

CALLE DE LA MERCED

Instituto Cardenal López de Mendoza

CALLE CONCEPCIÓN

Church of Carmen

CALLE DEL CARMEN

BULEVAR DEL FERROCARRIL

CALLE SANTA

Burgos Castle

Parque de las Uedas

CALLE DE FERNÁN GONZÁLEZ

10

AVENIDA PALENCIA

AVENIDA PALENCIA

PLAZA CASTILLA

Parque de La Isla

Monasterio de las Huelgas 0.75 km

300 m
1000 ft

0   100   200
0   500

Its collections include archaeology, a medieval section, and an art gallery. Back along the riverbank, beyond the Puente de Santa María, the late Gothic **church of la Merced** (Our Lady of Mercy) is attributed to the Colonia family and Diego de Siloé, with fine vaulted stonework. Behind, the old monastery building of the Mercedarians is now the Palacio hotel.

Along from la Merced, fronted by formal gardens, is the **Instituto Cardenal López de Mendoza**. A Renaissance mansion, it is one of the secondary schools of Burgos, and so a visit to the interior has to be arranged in advance. Tel. 947 257 701. The 16th century **church of San Cosme & San Damián** (c/ San Cosme) features a Plateresque portal by Juan de Vallejo – whose tomb is here – and Baroque and Renaissance altarpieces. In c/ de Madrid, the substantial **Hospital de la Concepción** was built in 1561 by order of Diego de Bermuy, to house pilgrims. It has two façades, one Plateresque, and the other Renaissance. It is used by the University of Burgos. If you can spare the time and effort, another five minutes' walk further south brings you to the working **Convento de Santa Dorotea** (c/ Santa Dorotea), with its 15th century Gothic façade displaying the coat of arms of Ferdinand and Isabella. Inside, there are several fine tombs.

NORTH OF THE RIVER

Moving north of Plaza de Mío Cid along c/ Santander brings you to the Plaza de La Libertad and the **Casa del Cordón**, a palace built by order of the Condestable de Velasco in 1485, by John and Simon of Cologne. Named after the cord of a Franciscan monk's habit, which can be seen in stone framing the portal, Ferdinand and Isabella received Christopher Columbus here after his second voyage. Nowadays the headquarters of the city's savings bank, it is worth a look inside during office hours. Continue up the same road, and turn left to join the Camino on c/ de

San Juan. Turning left down c/ de San Lorenzo, leads to the **church of San Lorenzo el Real**. A Baroque church, it originally belonged to the Jesuits. A large cupola stands above the centre of the nave, illuminating the fine plasterwork of the dome and the surrounding vaults. The gilded main altarpiece (1725) is originally by José Valdán.

Back on the Camino, turn right onto c/ de San Gil and climb the steps of the 14th century Gothic **church of San Gil Abad**. With a fairly plain exterior – it was part of the city walls – its interior marks it out as perhaps the most interesting of the city's churches. There are works by many of the master carvers with whom you have become familiar – though the history of this church is not so definitive, so the names have become interchangeable. A series of chapels include: the **Good Morning**, so named because St Teresa of Ávila is said to have attended Mass here early in the morning; the **Magi**, believed to be the work of Diego de Siloé and Bigarny; the **Nativity**, with its octagonal starred vaulting and Renaissance altarpiece; and the **Holy Christ**, housing an older carved image of Christ at whose feet are drops of blood, said to have been caused when struck by a stone. The main altarpiece is Baroque, and contains a painting of the life of San Gil. There are some important processions associated with the church, during Holy Week and on May 3rd (Feast of the Holy Drops of blood).

A walk further west, beyond the **Arco de San Gil** – whose towers once housed a prison – will reveal a section of the old walls that is more intact, and includes another of the gates, the **Arco de San Esteban**. Moving south below the castle, the late 13th century **church of San Esteban** houses the **Museo del Retablo**, a collection of altarpieces from across the diocese. Inside, there is much to see, including the choir by Simon of Cologne and Nicolás Vergara. From here the remains of the **castle** can be reached, a bit of a climb through the park, but good views of the cathedral and city are the reward. There is little left above ground after it was blown up by the French in 1813 – a year after Wellington's siege – shattering glass in the cathedral below. However, for a slightly higher entrance fee, you can take a tour of the defensive tunnels, donning a hard hat.

MONASTERIO DE LAS HUELGAS

The royal convent is one of the highlights of a visit to Burgos. Its forbidding, plain exterior disguises a stunning interior. It is located in the southwest of the city at c/ Alfonso VIII, not far from the park that runs alongside the river. The convent is overseen by Patrimonial Nacional, who look after the royal palaces, art collections, monasteries and parks. Incl. price €6 (Free May 18th & Oct. 12th & last 3 hours Wed. & Thurs. for EU citizens, residents & workers, Latin American nationals). Open Tues–Sat. 10am–2pm & 4–6pm; Sun. & hols. 10.30am–3pm). The guide should make an effort to explain each part of the tour in English, but only after a much more lengthy explanation in Spanish. As a working Cistercian convent – there are 30 sisters here – containing many priceless treasures, you are not permitted to wander around on your own, photography is prohibited, and bags need to be stored in lockers.

The Friday following Corpus Christi, the *Curpillos* celebration takes place in the courtyard, during which a copy of the Moorish standard from the battle of Navas de Tolosa is paraded with the Blessed Sacrament, and following Mass, there are traditional festivities.

Full of symbols of the *reconquista* this architectural history book was founded by King Alfonso VIII at the request of his queen, Eleanor (daughter of Henry II of England) in 1187. The convent would receive noble and wealthy pilgrims. Alfonso also founded the **Hospital del Rey** – across from the convent via the **Parque del Parral** (see next Stage) to

cater for the needs of the poor and sick pilgrims. The daughters of nobility were attracted to take orders here, as well as it becoming a place where kings were crowned, and princesses and queens were married, and buried.

CARTUJA DE MIRAFLORES

The second great monastery of Burgos is located on the southeast side of the city. Again, this is a working monastery, this time with a community of 20 Carthusian monks (a Charterhouse, without an abbot) but you are free to guide yourself, while inevitably there are parts that are closed to visitors. Open daily 10.15am–3pm; 4–6pm. There is much less to see than at Las Huelgas, however, what you will see comes to rival the works of the cathedral in terms of quality. Founded in 1442 by King John II of Castile and León, the monastery really developed under the patronage of his daughter, Queen Isabella, the 'Catholic' monarch. The **church** was built by the Colonia family (John and Simon) in a typical Carthusian layout with a single nave in three sections.

The **main door** is a Gothic arch with a sculpture of the Pietà in the tympanum; above are the coats of arms of John II (right) and of Castile and León (left). The **atrium** features fine vaulting and carved starry ceiling; note the unusual high window. Through into the **vestibule**, there is a statue of St Bruno of Cologne, the founder of the order (may be moved to a side chapel in future). His Feast day is October 6th. The **Lay Brothers' choir** contains carved Renaissance stalls and a small door with high reliefs. Above the door is a statue of The Virgin Mary in the mystery of the Immaculate Conception. The stained glass windows, brought here from Flanders, have scenes from the Passion, Resurrection and Ascension. The third section comprises the **Fathers' choir** with stalls by Martin Sánchez de Valladolid. Above the cloister door is a statue of the Virgin and Child, attributed to Gil de Siloé;

She balances a choir book on one knee.

The superb **main altarpiece** is carved by Gil de Siloé, with the polychrome work by Diego de la Cruz; the gold is said to be the same as that presented by Columbus at the Casa del Cordón. It is one of the most descriptive that you will see. A circular host-like representation is formed by carved angels, inside which is a crucifix being held by God the Father and the Holy Spirit (represented here in human form). Four scenes from the Passion are on either sides of the Cross. A pelican gives blood to its young from its heart, symbolising Jesus' sacrifice to our souls. At the foot of the Cross are the Blessed Mother and St John the Beloved Disciple. Other carvings include Sts Peter and Paul, and the Four Evangelists, each of whom is accompanied by one of the 'Church Doctors', Sts Ambrose, Gregory, Augustine and Jerome. Above the tabernacle is a set of representations of the six main feasts of the Church calendar, which revolves according to the time of year –

so you will only see one on your visit. Either side are St John the Baptist and Mary Magdalene. Further out are St Catherine of Alexandria (left) and St James. The remaining carvings are various Biblical scenes, and John and Isabella protected by Saints.

In front of the altar, the **tombs of John II and Isabella of Portugal** are also by Gil de Siloé. He was clearly at his peak, the alabaster effigies of the king and queen are so delicately carved, he leaning to one side, and she reading a book. Mounted on a slab in the form of an eight-pointed star, there are Biblical and allegorical figures surrounding. The master continued his work with the **tomb of the Infante Don Alfonso,** Isabella's brother, whose death gave her the succession, and shows the young prince kneeling in prayer. Of the three **side chapels,** the first now houses an art collection, including the Annunciation by Pedro Berruguete. The second is dedicated to the monastery's patroness, with 17th century frescoes. The third displays manuscripts and books from the monastery library.

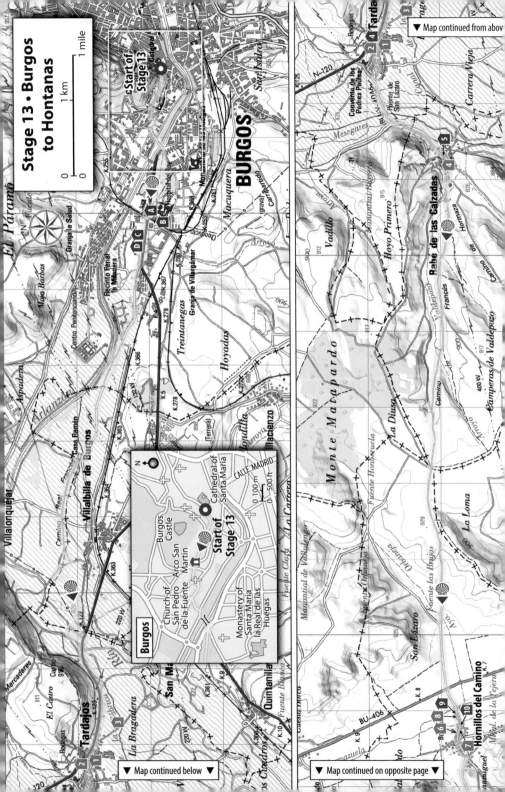

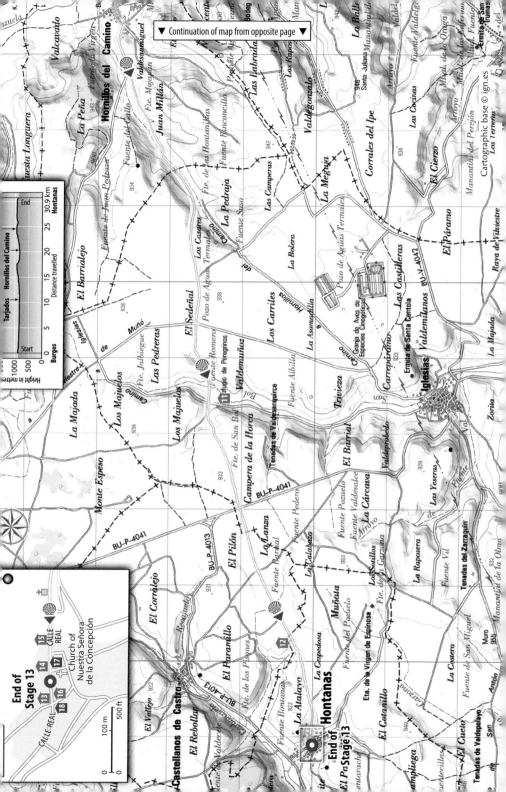

▼ Continuation of map from opposite page ▼

Cartographic base © ign.es

Hornillos del Camino

Iglesias

Hontanas

End of Stage 13

End of Stage 13

Castellanos de Castro

Church of Nuestra Señora de la Concepción

CALLE REAL

CALLE REAL

100 m

500 ft

Height in metres

Distance travelled

Start

End

Burgos

Tarjados

Hornillos del Camino

Hontanas

30.9 km

BURGOS TO LEÓN
TO HONTANAS (30.9km)

Passing the north side of the cathedral and church of San Nicolás, proceed alongside the 16th century **Arco Fernán González** and memorial to Juan Martín Díez – a hero of the Peninsular War. The next monument, the **Solar del Cid**, marks the spot where his house once stood. Pass through the **Arco San Martín** alongside further remains of the medieval walls. Outside the walls we pass the sites of several pilgrims' hospitals. Turn onto c/ Emperador and pass the **church of San Pedro de la Fuente**; the Gothic structure was destroyed by French troops in 1813. Turning left to find c/ Vilalón, at the end of the street is the river, and **Puente Malatos**. There was a bridge here in the 12th century, and its name means, in old Spanish, sick people. Cross the N-120.

You can **detour** to visit the Monastery of Las Huelgas by going straight on along Paseo de los Comendadores, then turning left along c/ Bernardino Obregón – see above for introduction and allow at least an hour for the compulsory tour. **To continue on Camino**, however, turn right and through the Parque del Parral. You will pass the **Hospital del Rey** (courtyard off left, church may be open), now part of the Unversity of Burgos. Exit the park and in front of you is the **Ermita de San Amaro Peregrino** (17th century). The chapel, dedicated to a French saint who devoted his life here to the care of sick pilgrims, contains his tomb and a Santiago Peregrino statue above the altar – and one above the main gate. Open at Mass times, which are well attended. Turn right and follow the main N-120 and the **pilgrim statue**. After the next set of university buildings, turn right opp. Bella Vista (restaurant with rooms www.bella-vista.es). Continue straight with the prison complex distant right, then alongside a rest area and onto a new road layout; pass the suburb of ▪️Villalbilla▪️ (∞) on your left,

before traversing the motorway junction (A-231 and BU-30) and then cross over the N-120. Cross the Arlanzón for the last time via the **Archbishop's Bridge** (rebuilt in 17th century) which is where Alfonso VI is said to have fallen from his horse while pursuing enemy troops, and a stone **cross**.

The path continues alongside the main road into ▪️Tardajos▪️ (11.5km ∞).

1 ■ **Municipal** M 18 Don N B *947 451 189/ 676 141 025* c/ Asunción, s/n

2 ■ **La Casa de Beli** Pr 34 €10 (+ 7 Priv. €45/55) Y M|B|W|D|@ *947 451 234/629 351 675* | Av. General Yagüe 16 | www.lacasadebeli.com

3 ■ **La Fábrica** Pr 14 €13 (+ 6 Priv. €38+/41+) Y M|B|W|D|@ *620 111 939* | c/ de La Fábrica 27 www.alberguelafabrica.com

On the site of a Roman settlement and road, the village has the **church of Nuestra Señora de la Asunción** (13th – 16th centuries but with 18th century façade) and the Apostolic School of the Fathers of St Vincent de Paul contains the remains of the façade of a 16th century palace of the descendants of Santo Domingo. Follow local road over the río Úrbel into the next village. ▪️Rabé de las Calzadas▪️ (13.4km R|B)

4 ■ **Liberanos Domine** Pr 24 €10 Y M|B|W|D|@ *695 116 901* | Pl. Francisco Riberas 10 clementinadelatorre@gmail.com www.liberanosdomine.com

5 ■ **Hostal La Fuente de Rabé** €42/52 *947 451 191* c/ Santa Marina 17 | www.hostalfuentederabe.com

has a 17th century palace, a square with the **church of Santa Mariña** and an old hospital now offering accommodation. Continuing, the **Ermita de Nuestra Señora de Monasterio** refers to the local name at the time of the discovery of an image of the Virgin, and it is the last remaining of three shrines in the village that were documented in the 18th century. For the next 7.5km there are no more facilities save rest area & fountain. Continue the ascent of a hill to 950m. We are at the start of over 150km of largely open, but not always flat, *Meseta*,

where each isolated hamlet and village feels like an oasis, before reaching León. Finally, after descending the hill, we cross a local road to reach **Hornillos del Camino** (21km R|B|S).

6 Municipal M 30 €10–12 Y B|K|W|@|Cred
689 784 681 | c/ San Román 3
hornillos.alberguemunicipal@gmail.com

7 El Alfar de Hornillo Pr 20 €12 N M|B|K|W|D|@
654 263 857 | c/ Cantarranas 8
www.elalfardehornillos.es

8 Meeting Point Pr 32 €12 (+ 5 Priv. 38/42) N
M|B|K|W|D 608 113 599 | c/ Cantarranas 3
info@hornillosmeetingpoint.com

9 Casa Rural De Sol a Sol €15 Bed €44/55
649 876 091 | c/ Cantarranas 7

10 Casa Rural del Abuelo €45/55 661 869 618
c/ Real 44 | www.lacasadelabuelohornillos.webnode.es

Before fully appreciating the special nature of this peaceful pilgrim village, at the entrance is the **Sancti Spiritus Hospital**, the last surviving of three that were here; note the cross keys and chalice relief on the lintel. **The Ermita de Santa María** originally formed part of a Priory, Nuestra Señora de Rocamador. The Parish **church of San Román** is late Gothic.

Follow the village street, then it's back out onto the *meseta* for six kilometres, crossing the small river to and past the turn-off to the Albergue at **San Bol**.

11 Arroyo de San Bol M 10 €10 N M|B|K|W|D 606
893 407 Arroyo de San Bol
reservas@alberguesanbol.com | Details of this and other Albergue accommodation in Hontanas can be found at https://alberguessantabrigida.com

An isolated riverside spot where once was a colony for people with skin poisoning from the ergot fungi – often referred to as 'St Anthony's fire' – there stood the first of two hospitals – see also next stage – tended by the Hospital Brothers of St Anthony. Otherwise, continue for another 5km, passing café/restaurant and Albergue

12 Fuente Sidres Pr 12 €18–23 N M|B|W|D|@
686 908 486 | Cam. Santiago Francés
https://alberguefuentesidres.es

before a quick 100m-plus descent and arrival below in **Hontanas** (R|B).

13 Antiguo Hospital San Juan M 42 €10* Y
M|B|W|D|@ 653 532 647 | c/ Real 26
alberguemunicipalhontanas@gmail.com (* €15 in winter, reserve)

14 El Puntido Pr 40 €9 (+ 8 Priv. €37/39) N
M|B|K|W|D|@ 947 378 597 | c/ Iglesia 6
www.puntido.com

15 Juan de Yepes-Santa Brígida Pr 34 €12 (+ 4 Priv. €55 Dbl.) N M|B|K|W|D|@ 638 938 546 | c/ Real 1
reservas@alberguejuandeyepes.com

15 Santa Brígida Pr 16 €12 N M|B|K|W|D|@ 628 927
317 | c/ Real 19 | reservas@alberguesantabrigida.com

16 Hostal Fuentestrella €39/49 646 612 530
c/ Iglesia 6 | https://fuentestrella.es

17 Hotel Rural Villa Fontanas *** €61/80
680 296 238 | c/ Real 23 | www.hotelvillafontanas.com

NOTE: At busy times the old School and old Town Hall will open for basic accommodation.

This is one of the spots that pilgrims feel is theirs – nobody else has reason to go there. An area of springs – as its name implies – there is a **fountain** by the 14th century **church of Nuestra Señora de la Concepción**. Next to the church was the palace of a Prelate of the Bishop of Burgos – a Gothic arch remains. The former **Hospital of San Juan** is but one of the lodging possibilities. There are **ruins** of the Convent of San Miguel and also of the shrine of San Vicente. In addition, there is a **fortified tower**. It is 7km to the outskirts of Castrojeriz, so pilgrims who stay in Hontanas will walk through its 2km main street in the morning.

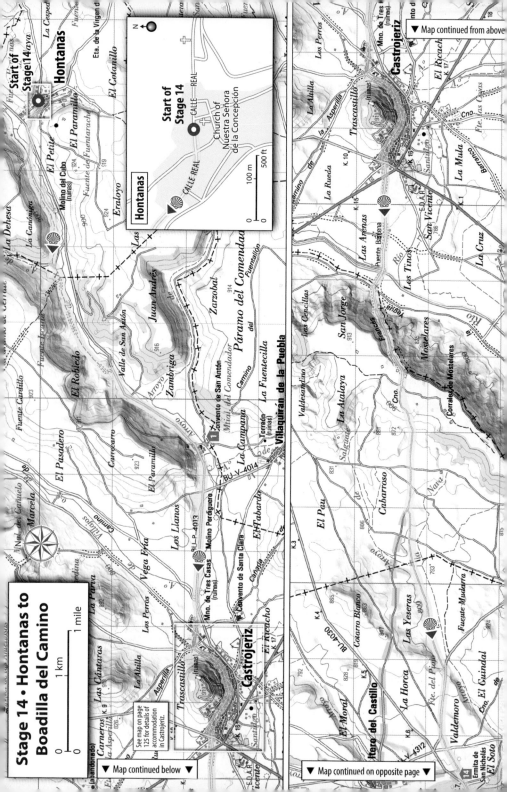

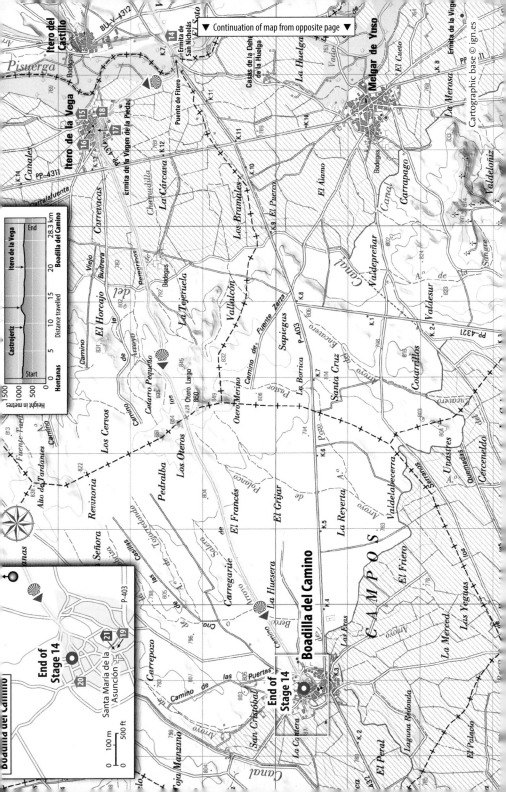

Cartographic base © ign.es

Itero del Castillo

Pisuerga

BU-V-1312

Ermita de San Nicholás
K.7

Melgar de Yuso

Ermita de la Virgen

La Huelga

Casas de la Dehesa
de la Huelga

El Cueto

K.8

Itero de la Vega

16 18
17

Puente de Fitero

La Huerga

La Merosa

Ermita de la Virgen de la Piedad

Bodegas

Ermita de la Virgen de la Piedad
K.12

PR-BU-7
K.13

Chenadilla

La Cárcava
K.11

K.11

Valdeloniz

Valdesur

PP-4311

Contralfuente

Carrevacas

Los Brambles

K.9 El Puerco

K.10

El Alamo

Carrapago

Canal

Canal

Valdepreñar

Height in metres

1500		
1000		
500		

Itero de la Vega
End
Boadilla del Camino
28.3 km
20

Castrojeriz

Start
Hontanas

0 5 10 15 20
Distance travelled

El Horcajo

Butrera

Viejo

peregrinos

Bodegas

La Tejeruela

Vallalcón

Fuente de Zarza

Sapiegas
P-A03

K.8

K.1

K.2

Valdesur

PP-4321

del

Arroyo

de

Camino

Catarro Pequeño

Otero Largo
860

Otero Merino

Camino de

La Borrica

Santa Cruz
814
K.7

Pastor

Pozo

606

Encañero

Cotarrillos

Los Cervos

Los Oteros

Pedralba

El Francés

El Grijar

K.6

Valdelabecerra

Unastres

Cerceneldo

Cerceneldo

Alto de Tardantes

Fuente-Tardes

Revinoria

822

Polanco

de

La Reyerta

A.°

El Friero

Serranos

Quemadas

A.°

Encañero

del

Camino

Camino

Castillas

Tojo-Tepedo

Subera

Carregarite

La Huesera

Berco

Camino de

C A M P O S

Las Eras

K.5

K.4

K.3

La Merced

Las Vegas

Las Vegas

End of Stage 14

Santa María de la Asunción

21 19

20

P-403

Carrepozo

Camino

San Cristóbal

Arroyo

de

las

Puertas

Tojal/Manzano

Boadilla del Camino

La Huesera

Boadilla del Camino

End of Stage 14

100 m
0

500 ft
0

La Cantera

El Peral

Laguna Redonda

El Palacio

Canal

TO BOADILLA DEL CAMINO (28.3km)

You can follow the tree-lined road on exiting the village rather than the unshaded waymarked path, until after 5km the two meet up before the Gothic ruins of the **monastery of San Antón**.

1 **Hospital de Peregrinos** A 12 Don N M&B(Don)
No electricity! | Convento San Antón
www.fundacionsananton.org

The other posting for the brothers of St Anthony – the Abbot/of Egypt – it included a hospital. The confusion is that the 'fire' is said to be the cause of death of the other St Anthony – of Padua. The since disbanded order's symbol is a black cross in the shape of the Greek letter **Tau T**, which embodied the healing power of the order, and these can now be bought as souvenirs, an additional pilgrim's symbol to the Cross of St James. The remains include the rose window, portal, and the porch where bread would be left in niches for pilgrims who arrived late – nowadays pilgrims leave messages here. The basic Albergue inside the ruins is the Camino in its humble and hospitable essence. Pass under the arches of the porch and it's a further 4.25km to the end of Castrojeriz.

CASTROJERIZ (9.7km ∞)

2 **San Esteban** M 35 €7 Y B (Don)|K|D(Free Spindryer)|@ 679 147 056 | Plaza Mayor 16
sanestebancastrojeriz@gmail.com

3 **La Rinconada** Pr 18 €14+ (+ 4 Priv. €45+) M|B|W D|@ 698 942 323 | Av. Virgen del Manzano 4
https://rinconada.net

4 **Casa Nostra** Pr 26 €7.50 N K|W|D|@ 947 377 493 c/ Real de Oriente 52 | encastrojeriz@hotmail.com

5 **Rosalía** Pr 30 €13 N M|B|W|D|@|Cred 947 373 714/637 765 779 | c/ Cordón 2
https://alberguerosalia.com

6 **Ultreia** Pr 28 €12 (+ 3 Priv €38/50) N M|B|W|D|@|Cred 947 378 640/640 298 817
c/ Real de Oriente 77
www.albergueultreiacastrojeriz.com

7 **Camping Camino** Pr 30 €6 (+Bungalow €75+) N M|B|W|D|@ 947 377 255 | c/ Virgen del Manzano info@campingcamino.com

8 **Orión** Pr 22 €13 (+ 3 Priv. €45/55) N M|B|K|W|D|@ 649 481 609/672 580 959 | Av. Colegiata 28 albergueorion2016@hotmail.com

9 **A Cien Leguas** Pr 24 €13 (+ 6 Priv. €40/60) Y* M|B|W|D|@ 947 562 305/619 289 476 | c/ Real de Oriente 78 info@acienleguas.es | www.acienleguas.es
*Closed Tuesdays

10 **Hostal El Mesón de Castrojeriz** ** €36 Dbl. 947 378 610 | c/ Cordón 1
https://www.laposadadecastrojeriz.es
Includes **Posada** *** €43+/64+

11 **Hostal El Manzano** * €40/50 659 581 345 Av. Colegiata s/n (entrance to the town)
https://www.hostalelmanzano.com

12 **Hotel Iacobus** ** €46/60 947 568 952 Paseo Puerta del Monte 3 (down steps from Pl. Mayor) | https://www.iacobuscastrojeriz.es

13 **Posada Emebed** *** €50+/70+ 947 377 268 Pl. Mayor 5 | www.emebedposada.com

There have been fortifications here since Celtiberian times, and then through Roman, Visigothic and *reconquista* periods. The town began its rise to prominence when, as part of the repopulation of the *meseta*, it was granted a *fuero* and French and Jewish merchants joined the Castilians, who aspired to minor nobility. There were as many as seven pilgrims' hospitals at one time, as it became a significant stop on the road to Santiago. In 1521 during the time of the Catholic Monarchs, the General Council of Castile set up residence. As you would expect, there are several palaces – many of them from the later periods – displaying coats of arms.

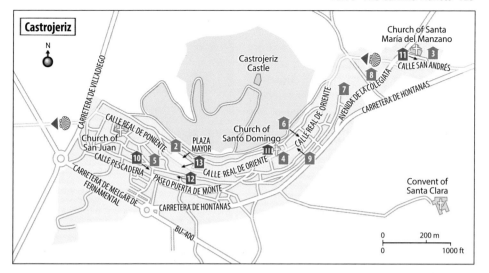

Church of Santa María
del Manzano

Florencio Benítez-Cano CC BY-SA 4.0

Today with a population of only 1000 its hilltop **castle** still dominates.

Albergue San Esteban

Tiberioclaudio99 CC BY 2.5 ES

At the entrance to the town is the former collegiate **church of Santa María del Manzano**. Origins are in the Romanesque/ Gothic transition, with several subsequent additions and remodelling. Legend has it that Santiago on his white horse was observing this spot from the castle, when he saw a vision of the Virgin, and leapt landing heavily – note the horses hooves imprinted onto a rock by the south door. Features include a rose window with 15th century German glass, a Rococo altarpiece with a painting of the Annunciation by Anton Raphael Mengs, and a fine choir and

grille. The polychrome statue of the Virgin (13th century) has early miracles attributed to Her. These are mentioned in a collection of Canticles – *Cantigas de Santa María* – by Alfonso X (the Wise). The tombs include Eleanor of Castile, Queen of Aragón (though disputed with two other sites), and the counts of Castro.

A short (500m) detour on the left, at the entrance to the town, will take you to working **Convent of Santa Clara**. Founded by Alfonso X, the Clares moved here later, in the 14th century, when the Franciscan brothers moved to another monastery (ruins visible in the town). The nuns sell souvenirs, including their traditionally baked pastries, and the Tau crosses, and invite visitors to participate in services. Back in town, a **museum** is incorporated into the **church of Santo Domingo**, and includes six fine Flemish tapestries. Further, towards the end of this linear layout, the **church of San Juan** spans the 13th (tower) to 16th centuries. Its chapel de los Gallos features an altarpiece with Hispano-Flemish board paintings by Ambrosius Benson, and a baptismal font attributed to Diego de Siloé. Three sides of the cloister survive, with Mudejar coffered ceiling. Elsewhere, there is a Franciscan-inspired **Casa del Cordón** and an **ethnographic museum** displaying utensils, tools and farm implements.

Ermita de San Nicolás

After the church of San Juan, leave the town by the crossroads, and you are back out in the open, alongside the **Roman causeway**, crossing the río Odrilla. There is a steady ascent to *Alto de Mostelares* (900m), its rest area and its far reaching views.

Some pilgrims will now make a *detour* – right – of some two kilometres to the pilgrim village and back onto the main Camino (adds 1km). **Itero del Castillo** (B) is no longer on the official route. However, there is less reason to do so following the recent closure of its Municipal Albergue. There is a pleasant rest area alongside the village Bar.

There are fiestas on May 3rd and 15th and on July 25th. The restored **tower** is practically all that remains of the border castle between the kingdoms of Castile and León, its walls used to construct the **church of San Cristóbal** in the 18th century, which has several Baroque and Rococo altarpieces. Continue straight on to return to the Camino by Puente de Fitero with San Nicolás just a little further back.

Otherwise, continue along the high *meseta*. Descend to **Fuente del Piojo** then follow a road to the **Ermita de San Nicolás** (13th

century) (18km). A former pilgrims' hospital, it is now a small Albergue run by the Italian *Confraternita dei San Jacopo*.

14 ⌂ A 12 Don N M&B(Don) † *+39 3664 496 584*
Ermita de San Nicolás de Puente Fitero (No electricity)

A monastery and shrine were also present on this site.

Cross the **Puente de Fitero** whose 11 arches carry us from Burgos province over the río Pisuerga into Palencia province. It was originally built by Alfonso VI in the 11th century for pilgrims, and to unite the two kingdoms, and reconstructed in the 16th century. Follow a path, right, alongside the river.

The village of **Itero de la Vega** (18km B|S)

15 **Municipal** M 13 €5 Y K|@ *605 034 347*
Pl. del Ayuntamiento s/n (closed after August 2022; awaiting update).

Puente de Fitero

16 **Hogar del Peregrino** Pr 8 €12 Y M|B|K|W|D|@
979 151 866 | c/ Santa María 17
alberguehogardelperegrino@hotmail.com

17 **La Mochila** Pr 28 €10 Y M|B|K|W|@ 979 151 781 |
c/ Santa Ana 3 | lamochilaitero@gmail.com

18 **Puente de Fitero** Pr 22 €11 (+ 8 Priv. €30/40) Y
M|B|W|D|@ 979 151 822 | c/Santa María 3
(closed during 2022) hostelpuentefitero@hotmail.com

is located alongside both the river and the
Ermita de Nuestra Señora de la Piedad (13th
century) – with its statue of Santiago Peregrino
and capitals decorated with plant motifs. The
church of San Pedro Apóstol is 16th century,
but includes remains of a 13th century Gothic
portal and a sculpture of St Anne with the
Christ Child. Here we see a tall Gothic *Rollo* or
jurisdictional column – a sign that the village
had autonomy from feudal rule granted by the
king. Continue on c/ Sta Ana, cross the road
junction and join a track straight ahead. We
are at the beginning of the high plains known
as the Tierra de Campos, which are cultivated
and irrigated, as we cross the Canal Pisuerga;
it is also wine country, with cellars set into the
hills. Ascend and descend a small hill. We arrive
in **Boadilla del Camino** (B).

19 **En el Camino** Pr 70 €10 N M|B|W|D|@|Pool
619 105 168 | c/ Francos 3
albergue@boadilladelcamino.com

20 **Juntos** Pr 12 €12 N M|B|W|D|@ 682 181 175
c/ Mayor 7 | www.juntos-albergue.com

21 **Hotel Rural En El Camino** *** €45/55 979 810 999
c/ Rosario 8 | www.boadilladelcamino.com
also for Albergue opp.

This village also has a *Rollo*, finely decorated
with scallop shell motifs. Its tip was added later
in the 16th century, about the same time as the
church of Santa María de la Asunción was
rebuilt. Inside, there is a Romanesque baptismal
font of high quality and interest, a Renaissance
altarpiece, and a Gothic Calvary.

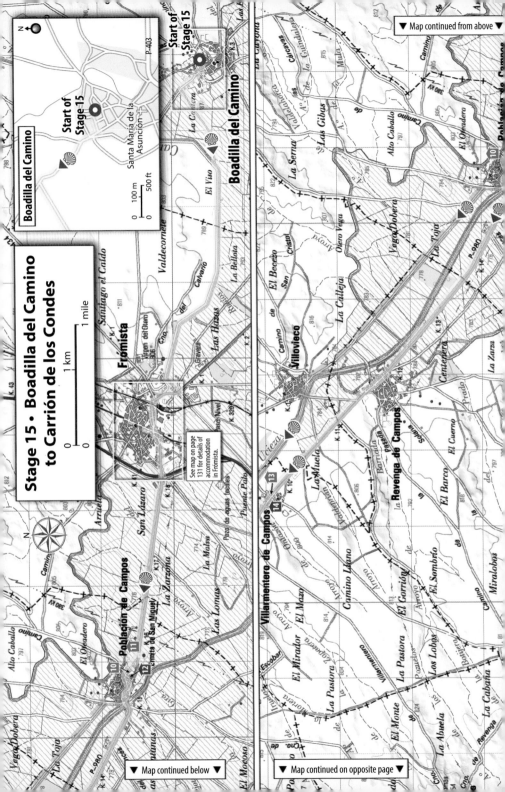

Stage 15 • Boadilla del Camino to Carrión de los Condes

Start of Stage 15

Santa María de la Asunción

Boadilla del Camino

Start of Stage 15

Boadilla del Camino

N

100 m
0
500 ft
0

See map on page 131 for details of accommodation in Frómista.

Santiago el Guido

Frómista

Virgen del Otero

Las Hazas

San Lázaro

La Zarzona

La Malva

Puente Palo

Pozo de aguas fecales

Población de Campos

Ermita de San Miguel

Villarmentero de Campos

Villovieco

La Muela

Revenga de Campos

El Mirador

El Mazo

El Gorrión

Camino Llano

La Pastora

El Sombrío

El Barca

El Cuerno

Miralobos

El Monte

La Abuela

La Cabaña

Revenga

Las Gibas

Alto Caballo

El Oteadero

Población de Campos

La Serra

Valdelaboca

Otero Vega

La Calleja

La Toja

Vega Dobera

La Zarza

Centenera

El Prado

N

1 km
0
1 mile
0

▼ Map continued from above ▼

▼ Map continued below ▼

▼ Map continued on opposite page ▼

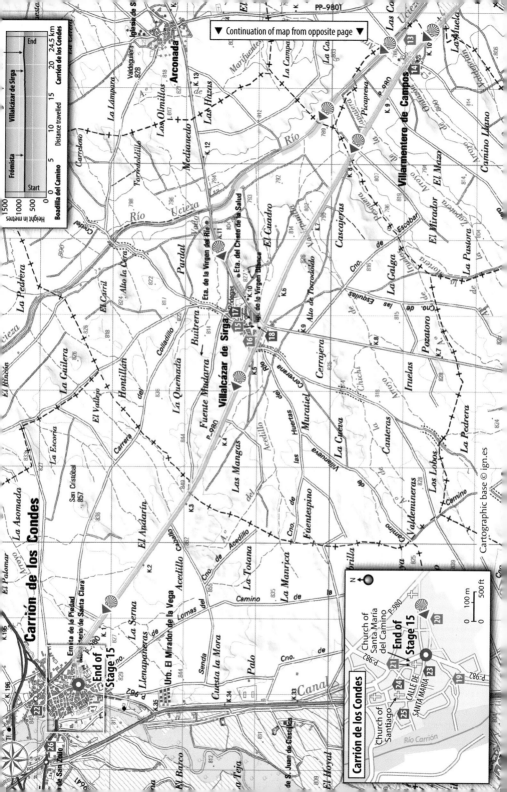

PP-9801

▼ Continuation of map from opposite page ▼

Arconada

Height in metres

1500 1000 500

End

Villalcázar de Sirga

Frómista

Start

0 5 10 15 20 24.5 km

Distance travelled

Boadilla del Camino

Carrión de los Condes

Río Ucieza

Villalcázar de Sirga

Villarmentero de Campos

Carrión de los Condes

End of Stage 15

Ermita de la Piedad

Monasterio de Santa Clara

Cartographic base © ign.es

Carrión de los Condes

N

0 100 m 500 ft

Church of Santa María del Camino

Church of Santiago

Church of Santa María

CALLE DE

SANTA MARÍA

End of Stage 15

Río Carrión

TO CARRIÓN DE LOS CONDES (24.5km)

Continue out of Boadilla; join a track to another canal, the much older **Canal de Castilla**. It was begun in the late 18th century, not only for irrigation, but also to transport produce by water. After walking alongside the canal, cross the lock system – said to have inspired Ferdinand de Lesseps, designer of the Suez and Panama canals – and continue into Frómista alongside the road and under the railway (6km from Boadilla).

FRÓMISTA (∞)

1 **Municipal M** 56 €12 Y M|B|W|D *979 811 089*
Pl. San Martín | carmen-hospitalera@live.com

2 **Luz de Frómista Pr** 26 €12 Y B|K|W|D|@
635 140 169 | Av. del Ejército Español 10
www.albergueluzdefromista.com

3 **Vicus Pr** 6 €10 Y K|W|D|@
617 483 264 | Av. Ingeniero Rivera 25
angelgallegoesteban@hotmail.com

4 **Estrella del Camino Pr** 32 €16–17 N M|B|W|D|@
653 751 582 | Av. del Ejército Español s/n
albergueestrelladelcamino@hotmail.com

5 **Betania Pr** 9 Don N *638 846 043* Av. del Ejército
Español 26 | Open mainly in Low Season (Nov–Mar)
betaniafromista@gmail.com

6 **Hostal Camino de Santiago** * €59+ Dbl.
979 810 282 | c/ Francesa 26

7 **Hotel San Martín** * €45/60 *979 810 000*
Pl. San Martín 7 | www.hotelsanmartin.es

8 **Hostal San Pedro** ** €45/60+ *979 810 016*
Av. del Ejército Español 8

9 **Hotel Doña Mayor** *** €110+/135+ *630 224 369*
c/Francesca 31 | www.hoteldonamayor.com

Apart from those seeking accommodation, visitors will want to head straight for the famous **church of San Martín de Tours**, one of the best examples of Romanesque architecture in Spain. The 11th century church, of mellow golden stone, was ordered by the wife of Sancho III of Navarra (the Great, or *Mayor*), but was deconsecrated in 1893, when much needed restoration was undertaken. Although the interpretive quality of the restoration has been called into question, and you won't be alone when you visit, these are relatively minor quibbles when you see the perfection of form and craftsmanship. It probably helps towards that end that, apart from some benches, all that remains of the fittings is a 13th century crucifix in the central apse.

Two cylindrical towers flank the main portal, with a wider octagonal dome over the crossing, which continues either side with tiled roofing. The roof covering the nave is in three sections. The windows are mostly typically Romanesque; while there is a central and two side apses, the latter appearing to flow from the former. The many hundreds of **carvings** are a mixture of pagan, Christian and the mystical, and here there is a potential link to the church's patron and the **Priscillianists**, whom the 4th century

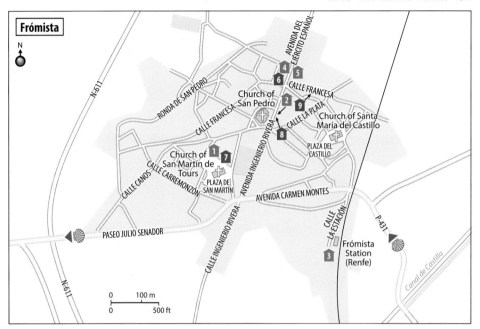

French bishop defended from persecution. This sect had its origins in Gnostic Egyptian doctrines, whereby its adherents walked barefoot, its monks and nuns lived in the same monasteries, and even venerated the elements such as the sun. Martin failed to prevent Prisciliano, who was from Galicia, from being beheaded by the Church in 385, the first to be executed for heresy, although the civil charges were for sorcery. Martin did appear to put a stop to Church councils and legal proceedings combining to persecute more alleged freaks. Priscillianism continued to be practised for another two centuries.

Elsewhere, the **church of Santa María del Castillo** is notable for its Hispano-Flemish retablo panels and other works of art, and otherwise hosts a media presentation, 'Legend of the Camino'. So, amid all this, there also has to be a church for quiet contemplation. The parish **church of San Pedro** is unmistakably Gothic, and has a wide welcoming portal. There is a small **ethnographic museum** next door.

The **Ermita del Otero** contains a Romanesque statue of the Virgin and Child. The town's **Fiesta** is dedicated to San Telmo (Peter González b. 1190) who was from here, and takes place on the Monday evening following Easter Monday, with traditional procession, dances and songs.

Leave Frómista firstly over the N-611, and then the motorway junction.

At **Población de Campos** (9.4km R|B)

10 **Municipal** M 18 €5 Y K 979 811 099 | Paseo del Cementerio (closed during 2022) (Reception & other facilities in **Amanecer en Campos** hotel next door)

11 **La Finca** Pr 20 €13 Y M|B|W|@ 979 067 028 Crta P-980 16km | info@alberguelafinca.es

12 **Hotel Amanecer en Campos** €40/55 979 811 099/685 510 020 | c/ Fuente Nueva s/n www.hotelamanecerencampos.com

the former association with the order of Malta with its hospital has all but disappeared; however, there remains the Romanesque **Ermita de San Miguel**, and the **shrine of Our Lady of Socorro** of similar vintage, which houses a seated image of the Virgin. The

Church of San Martín de Tours, Frómista

Church of Santa María la Virgen Blanca, Villalcázar de Sirga

parish **church of la Magdalena** is 16th century Baroque.

It is just before the bridge over the río Ucieza, still in this village that the scenic riverside *Villovieco variant* begins. It is quieter, offers shade, but does add 1km. Fork right if you want it; cross the bridge if you don't. At Villovieco (13km **B**) the **church of Santa María** is Renaissance in style. A little further on there is a chance to cut short the variant and return to the main route at Villarmentero de Campos (save 0.5km of the additional 1km). Otherwise, continue to enjoy the break from the monotony with a further near 5km of shaded walking before reaching a bridge and the **Ermita de la Virgen del Río**. This chapel features a statue of Santiago Peregrino. After a further 2km enter Villalcázar de Sirga.

The main route passes through Revenga de Campos (**B**), whose **church of San Lorenzo** features a main altarpiece from the 18th century; several noble houses bear coats of arms, and there is a modern sculpture dedicated to pilgrims. At Villarmentero de Campos

🛏 **Amanecer** Pr 20 €7 N M|B|K|@ *629 178 543*
c/ Francesca 2
albergueamanecervillarmentero@gmail.com

🛏 **Casa Rural La Casona de Doña Petra** €45/55
979 065 978 | c/ Ramón y Cajal s/n
www.lacasonadepetra.com

the small – yet quite imposing – **church of San Martín de Tours** (15th century) features a Moorish coffered ceiling and a Plateresque altarpiece.

Villalcázar de Sirga (18.6km R|B|S),

🛏 **Casa del Peregrino** M 20 Don N B|K|W|D|@
979 888 041 | Pl. del Peregrino
https://tinyurl.com/ycyyhhwc

🛏 **Don Camino** Pr 26 €12 N M|B|W|D|@ *620 399 040* | c/ Real 23 | aureafederico@hotmail.com

🛏 **Hostal Las Cantigas** * €30/40 *979 888 027*
c/ Doctor Durango 2 | www.hostallascantigas.es

🛏 **Hostal Infanta Doña Leonor** * €35/45–50
979 888 118 | Av. Condes de Toreno s/n

the home of the other Mary to the one at Castrojeriz mentioned more than once by Alfonso X (the Wise) in his *Cantigas de Santa María*, has long been a significant stop on the route, and was a Commanderie of the Knights Templar.

Their **church**, the 13th century **Santa María la Virgen Blanca**, is one of the most notable on the route. Next to a rose window, its strikingly tall porch shelters an unusual double portal – a trio of architectural features. The statue of the miraculous Virgin is located here, and in side chapels are six altarpieces, each of which recalls a healing. The main altarpiece is mostly 16th century and contains a series of board paintings; however the central Calvary dates from the 1300s; the Virgin is housed under a spire canopy. There are some beautifully carved royal tombs, of the Infante Don Felipe – son of Ferdinand III (the Saint) – and his second wife, Doña Leonor Ruiz de Castro, together with that of a knight of the order of Santiago. They retain some of the original colouring. Alfonso X is said to have murdered Don Felipe, his brother, after the latter stole and married his intended bride, adding more than a touch of irony to the sung piety associated with this place. A further altarpiece depicts the life of St James, and has coin-operated illumination. There is a small entrance fee. Elsewhere, the **town hall** is a former 18th century palace, and the remains of the pilgrims' hospital can be seen. Continue out of the town and then on for 5km.

Church of Santa María del Camino, Carrión de los Condes

CARRIÓN DE LOS CONDES (∞)

19 **Espíritu Santo Pa** 96 €10 Y K|W|D|@|† *979 880 052*
c/ San Juan 4 | espiritusanto@hijasdelacaridad.org

20 **Monasterio de Santa Clara Pa** 30 €8–10 (+9 Priv.
€25/44+) N K *979 880 837* | c/ Santa Clara 1

21 **Santa María Pa** 58 €7 N K|W|D|@|Cred|† *650 575
185* | c/ Clérigo Pastor 2 | viastellarum@gmail.com

22 **Casa Espiritualidad Nuestra Señora de Belén** €25
Bed/58 Dbl. B&B (Half Board available) *979 880
031* c/ Leopoldo María de Castro 6
cdadcarrion@rfilipenses.com

23 **Hostal La Corte** * €40/48 *979 880 138*
c/ Santa María 36 | www.hostallacorte.com

24 **Hostal Santiago** * €37/48 *629 935 034*
Pl. de los Regentes 8 | www.hostalsantiago.es

25 **Hostal Plaza Mayor** €39+/50+ *669 340 131*
c/ Aldolfo Suárez 1 | www.hostalplazamayorcarrion.com

26 **Hotel Real Monasterio de San Zoilo** **** €67+/87+
979 880 049 | c/ Obispo Souto Vizoso
www.sanzoilo.com

Church of Santiago

A town that boasts royal heritage – including two monasteries – one of Spain's oldest dated churches, and the remains of two Roman villas cannot be overlooked. Besides pilgrims travelling east-west, Carrión de los Condes was a stop along one of the kingdom of Castile's important north-south roads. At one stage, the town had to give up 100 daughters every year to the Moorish sultan as Tribute; this is commemorated on a capital of the portal of the **church of Santa María del Camino** (12ᵗʰ century) towards the middle of town. A sizable Jewish community inhabited the town in Medieval times, and besides some sadly predictable persecution, a leading scholar, Rabbi Shem Tov Ardutiel (Shem Tob d.1370) produced the major works, *Proverbios Morales* and a Dance of Death, *Danza General de la Muerte*. Additionally the town produced the poet Iñigo López de Mendoza, the 1ˢᵗ Marqués de Santillana (d.1458).

The first historic place of worship one comes to on the Camino here is the **Convent of Santa Clara** (13ᵗʰ century), with an adjoining church,

Ermita de la Piedad, and **museum** which displays sculpture and ornaments, with a Pietà by Gregorio Fernández. Founded by two of St Clare's companions, this is the site of one of St Francis' supposed stops on his way to Santiago. The remains of the **church of Santiago** have preserved perhaps the highlight of the town, the superb image of Christ Pantocrator, together with a frieze showing the 12 Apostles. The two capitals depict the triumph and the damnation of the soul, while the archivolts show 22 figures of the brotherhood of Guilds. Inside, there is a small museum, including a Santiago Matamoros. There are yet more **churches**, including San Andrés, San Julián and the town shrine, Nuestra Señora de Belén, all of which have Baroque altarpieces.

On the way out of town, after the bridge, the originally Benedictine **Monastery of San Zoilo** dates from the 11ᵗʰ century. It was at different times tended by the Cluniacs and the Jesuits. Buried in the lavishly carved Renaissance cloister are the two wicked sons of the Count of Carrión, who married El Cid's daughters, but seemingly only for money, as they beat them and left them for dead, having collected their dowries. Not a wise move, for the Cid and his followers killed them and found new husbands for his rescued daughters. It is nowadays an upmarket hotel. Visits to the church and cloister can be made during summer months for a small fee.

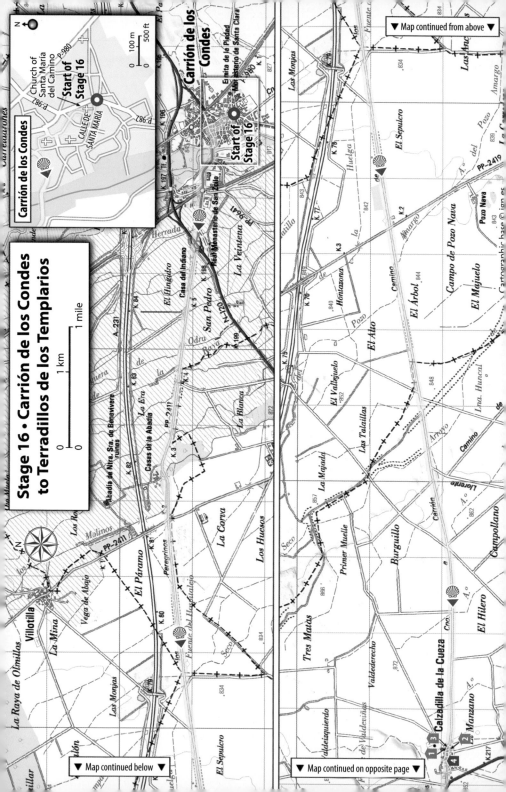

Carrión de los Condes

Church of Santa María del Camino

Start of Stage 16

CALLE DE SANTA MARÍA

Carrión de los Condes

Ermita de la Piedad
Monasterio de Santa Clara
Start of Stage 16

Stage 16 • Carrión de los Condes to Terradillos de los Templarios

Real Monasterio de San Zoilo

Carreruones

La Veintena

Herrada

Casa del Indiano

El Hinguiro

San Pedro

Casas de la Abadía

Abadía de Ntra. Sra. de Benevívere (ruins)

La Era

La Abadía

La Blanca

La Corva

Odra

Roya

El Sepulcro

El Arbol

El Majuelo

Campo de Pozo Nava

Pozo Nava

Las Monjas

Huelga

Amargo

El Alto

Las Talaillas

El Vallejuelo

Hontazona

Peregrinos

Fuente del Hospitalejo

Molinos

El Páramo

Vega de Abajo

La Mina

Villotilla

Las Monjas

La Raya de Olmillos

Los Huesos

Seco

La Majada

Primer Muelle

Tres Matas

Burguillo

El Hilero

Valdederecho

Campollano

Llorente

Valdeizquierdo

Valdeviñas

Calzadilla de la Cueza

Manzano

El Hilero

Calzadilla de la Cueza

La Camperona

Manzano

K-217

1·3
2
4

Bodegas

Vado

Laderas de San Miguel

La Nota

Fuen

Río

El Pico

A-231

k.72

K.1

Oriental

El Matón

El Rayón

Dehesa de Bust

Tres Matas

Valdederecho

Valdeizquierdo

Fuente de Valderiñas

Valdecalabazas

La Rapoeras

K.70

K.69

Cabañas

Valle Grande

Las Cabañas

Valdejea

K.68

San Zorrín

Camperona

La Malena

La Veguilla
Ermita de la Dehesa

Fuente-Arriba

Arroyo
Cueza

N-120

K.219

K.220

N-120

Cno. de las Tiendas

Los Cajones

Costa Molar

El Tomellar

San Cristóbal

Arroyo de Tascanso

K.221

K.222

K.223

K.224

Paramillo

Ledigos

5
6

Los Prados

K.65

K.120

Terradillos de los
Templarios

Arroyo de la

Cueza

Río Valdejinate

P-970

K.25

K.24

Los Charcos

Paramillo

K.69

K.63

K.64

K.235

Los Herrenes

K.26 8

End of
Stage 16

Población de Arroyo

El Bosque

Carretraviesa

Casa Palacio de
la Dehesa de Bustocirio

Cartographic base © ign.es

Terradillos de los Templarios

End of
Stage 16

Church of
San Pedro

CALLE IGLESIA

TR

N-120

7

0   100 m
0   500 ft

N

Chart (left side):

Height in metres

500
1000
1500

Carrión de los Condes

Calzadilla de la Cueza

Terradillos de los Templarios

Ledigos

End

Start

Distance travelled

0   5   10   15   20   26.7 km

TO TERRADILLOS DE LOS TEMPLARIOS (26.7km)

Temporary bars have previously provided much needed options in summer on this lonely stretch. From the centre turn left onto c/ Piña Blasco and cross the bridge over the Río Carrión. After San Zoilo, we go straight on at the roundabout and cross the N-120.

There is an alternative stage from here (left) the *Antiguo Camino Francés* that follows this road to Cervatos de la Cueza, then on to Villada (33km ∞ incl. Albergue Tel. *669 906 172/ 666 501 410*) https://tinyurl.com/bdexnsz5 before heading north. Utilising the last few km of the Camino de Madrid and, if required, its Albergue at Grajal de Campos (€10 *987 784 506*) the route finishes back on the Francés at Sahagún (15.5km from Villada). The tourist offices should provide information to help weigh up your options.

Continuing on, however, we come past the ruined **Abbey of Benevívere**, now part of a private dwelling, and cross a river. From here, we pick up the *via Aquitania*, the old Roman road that went to León and Astorga and a cue to the area's strong links with earlier occupants. It's a long, straight walk, before reaching Calzadilla de la Cueza (17.2km R|B) and its facilities,

1 **Municipal** M 34 €8 Y W|D *670 558 954*
c/ Mayor 1 | municipalcalzadilla@outlook.es

2 **Camino Real** Pr 80 €11–14 Y M (in Hostal)
W|D|@|Pool *979 883 187* | c/ Trasera Mayor
rikcardo64@gmail.com

3 **Los Canarios** Pr 11 €15–19 N|M|B *659 976 894*
c/ Mayor 2 | llcm8@hotmail.com

4 **Hostal Camino Real** €41/52 *616 483 517*
c/ Trasera Mayor 8 – As above

a welcome sight. The **church of San Martín** features a rescued Renaissance altarpiece from the now ruined abbey up ahead.

One kilometre past the village, we come to the *variant* that offers the same distance as the main route. Either choice crosses the Arroyo Cueza but at different points. To take this, turn left and cross a bridge to begin a small climb through woodland, before descending to join the main route and highway again.

The main route also involves a climb, and allows you to see that there are enough remains of the **Monasterio de Santa María de las Tiendas** to spark hopes that it will be restored to cater for pilgrims (however well heeled). It was, essentially, an important pilgrims' hospital provided by the knights of Santiago.

It is possible to take another small *variant* (opp. El Palomar) that by-passes some of Ledigos and comes out in the centre of Terradillos, saving at least 500m.

Otherwise, the route now enters Ledigos (23.4km R|B) whose **church of Santiago** (13th

5 **El Palomar** Pr 47 €8 (+ 5 Priv. €20 Dbl.) N
M|B|K|W|@ *979 883 605* | c/ Ronda de Abajo s/n
info@albergueelpalomar.com

6 **La Morena** Pr 18 €15–20 (+ 9 Priv. €45+/57+) Y
M|B|W|D|@|Cred *626 972 118* | c/ Carretera 3
www.alberguelamorena.com

century) contains images of St James in all three of his guises, Peregrino, Matamoros, and the Apostle.

A further three kilometres brings us to **Terradillos de los Templarios** (R|B)

7 **Jacques de Molay** Pr 50 €10–12 N M|B|W|D|@
979 883 679/657 165 011 | c/ Iglesia, 18
yacquesdemolay@hotmail.com

8 **Los Templarios** Pr 52 €10–12 (+ 9 Priv. €28+/38+)
N M|B|W|D|@|Pool *667 252 279* | Camino de Santiago s/n | www.alberguelostemplarios.com

longest such stretch – the monotony can be tiring or it can aid meditation. So, if that sounds all too familiar, then the *Via Romana* has earth tracks that follow more Roman road, is more scenic, and mostly feels very remote.

The two routes almost touch at Reliegos – some 7km before Mansilla by the *Romana* route, up to 1.5km less via the *Real Camino Francés*. For those tempted to stay overnight in Sahagún (some 12–13km on from Terradillos) and try the *Romana* the most logical is to stay here and our Romana distances are from Terradillos in case you agree. But for those who start at Sahagún and want to follow the *Real* then the choice of stop is either El Burgo Ranero (17.5km) or Reliegos (30.5km). See after Sahagún to follow either option. Mansilla to León is a shorter stage.

As its name suggests, this is another former seat of the Knights Templar, under the Commanderie of Villalcázar de Sirga. Today, it is a peaceful village with just the small, 18th century **church of San Pedro** and its Gothic crucifix. It is 13km further to Sahagún where there are more accommodation and walking options.

PLANNING: SAHAGÚN AND ONWARD OPTIONS

From some 5km west of historic Sahagún at Calzada del Coto, there is a distinct alternative to the official route which takes in different villages, and continues on in parallel for a further 32km before joining at Mansilla de las Mulas. Both have facilities, though the alternative less frequently. The main route – *Real Camino Francés* – offers shaded, wide, roadside gravel track. The stage from El Burgo Ranero is the

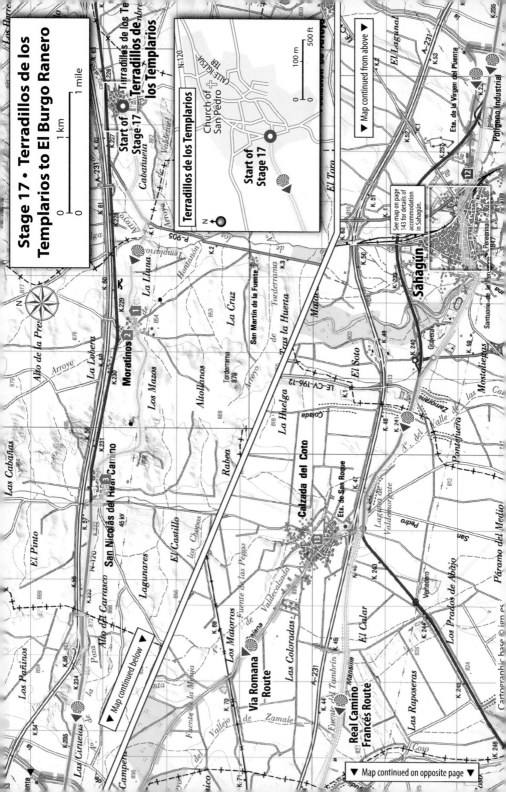

Stage 17 • Terradillos de los Templarios to El Burgo Ranero

0 — 1 km
0 — 1 mile

Terradillos de los Templarios

Start of Stage 17

N-120

CALLE IGLESIA

Church of San Pedro

Start of Stage 17

N

0 — 100 m
0 — 500 ft

► Map continued from above ▼

See map on page 143 for details of accommodation in Sahagún.

Terradillos de los Templarios

Terradillos de los Te...

K 63

K 62

A-231

K 61

K 228

K 227

Cabañuela

Arroyo de Valdezate

P-905

K 2

Arroyo de los ...nabre

El Laguna

A-231

K.53

Eta. de la Virgen del Puente

Polígono Industrial

Sahagún

K.50

K.51

K.52

El Toro

N 120

K.49

K 240

Gravera

Santuario de la Pere...

Peregrina

K 60

La Llana

Hontanón

La Cruz

San Martín de la Fuente

Tras la Huerta

de Torderrama

El Soto

K.1

LE-CV-196-12

K.48

K.241

Moratinos

K 229

El Ternplario

La Lobera

Arroyo

Alto de la Pre...

Los Mazos

Altollanos

Torderrama

Arroyo

La Huelga

Colada

K.47

N

Las Cabañas

El Pinto

La Lobera

K 230

K 58

K 231

San Nicolás del Real Camino

El Castillo

los Chopos

Rabea

La Colada

Calzada del Coto

Eta. de San Roque

Laguna de Valdemorquete

San Pedro

Alto del Carrasco

Poza de la M...

K 57

N-120

K 232

45 KV

Lagunares

El Pinto

K.56

K 233

K.59

K 69

Los Matorros

Fuente de las Pegas

de

Salana

Valdecalzado

Las Coloradas

K 40

K 243

Los Prados de Abajo

Páramo del Medio

► Map continued below ▼

K.55

K 224

K 54

K 235

Los Peñinos

Los Ciruelos

Campos

Fuente de la Mocha

Vallejo

Zamale

de

Via Romana Route

Real Camino Francés Route

K 70

K 71

K.45

Mansilla

K.44

Fuente del Tamburo

K 244

K 245

El Calar

Las Raposeras

K 246

El Vertedero

813

▼ Map continued on opposite page ▼

Cartographic base © ign.es

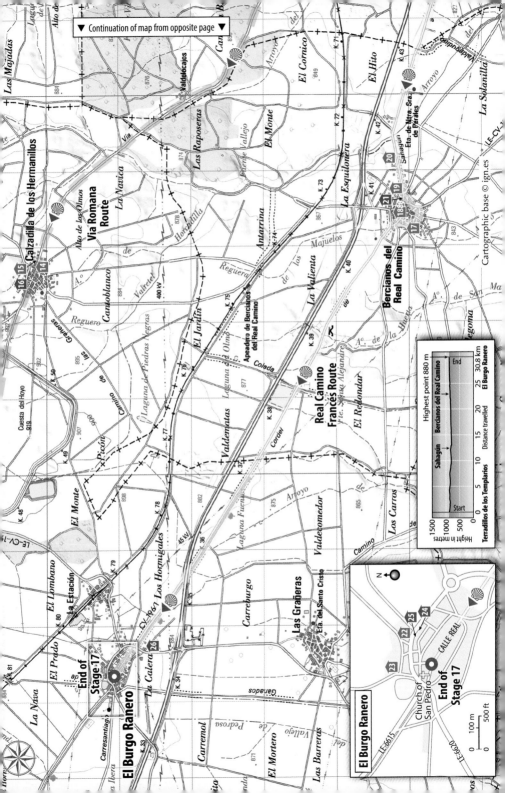

▼ Continuation of map from opposite page ▼

Cartographic base © ign.es

Las Majadas

Alto de

Laguna de

Calzadilla de los Hermanillos

Via Romana Route

Alto de los Olmos

Valdelocajos

Las Raposeras

El Cornico

El Hito

La Solanilla

El Monte

Puente Vallejo

Ermita. de Ntra. Sra. de Perales

Sahagún

LE-CV-1

La Navica

Horcadilla

Antarrina

La Esquilonera

Bercianos del Real Camino

de

Canoblanco

Valretel

El Jardín

Reguera

Majuelos

La Valienta

de San Ma

Cuesta del Hoyo

Reguero

Laguna de Piedras Negras

Laguna del Olmo

Apeadero de Bercianos del Real Camino

Colada

Real Camino Francés Route

Ermita. Santa Alejandra

El Redondar

Aº de la Huerga

de la Huerga

El Monte

Picón

Valdematas

Corasel

Arroyo

Valdetomedor

Los Carros

Camino

El Lombano

La Estación

Los Hormigales

Laguna Fuente

Valdetomedor

Carreburgo

Las Grañeras

Ermita. del Santo Cristo

Ganados

El Prado

La Calera

Carresantiago

El Burgo Ranero

End of Stage 17

Carremol

de Pedrosa

Las Barreras

Vallejo

Highest point 880 m

End

30.8 km

El Burgo Ranero

Bercianos del Real Camino

Distance travelled

Sahagún

Terradillos de los Templarios

Start

Height in metres

El Burgo Ranero

End of Stage 17

Church of San Pedro

CALLE REAL

N

100 m

500 ft

TO EL BURGO RANERO (30.8km)

For now, we leave Terradillos, crossing the river after a short stretch of local road, and enter the tiny hamlet of **Moratinos** (3km R)

1 **San Bruno** A 30 €14 (+ 2 Priv. €45 Dbl.) N
M|B|W|D|@ 979 061 465 | c/ Ontanón 9
brunobernoni@gmail.com
https://estanciasespana.top/albergue-san-bruno

2 **Hostal Moratinos** Pr 16 €10–13 (also Hostal €48+/65) Y M|B|W|D|@|Cred 979 061 466
c/ Real 12 www.hostalmoratinos.es

with its single-nave **church of Santo Tomás**: turn right here to exit the village. It is just three kilometres to the next village, **San Nicolás del Real Camino** (5.6km R|B).

3 **Laganares** Pr 20 €10 N M|B|W|D|@ 979 188 142
Plaza del Pueblo | laganares@yahoo.es

There was a pilgrims' hospital run by Augustinian canons, caring mainly for lepers. The **church of San Nicolás Obispo** is another unimposing structure, but this time it houses a very good Baroque altarpiece. We now enter the province of León. While the *official path* continues alongside the main road into Sahagún, there is a **parallel path** (left) described here

that allows a short *detour* back to the main route. Cross the N-120 to follow the río Valderaduey to bring us across the bridge and alongside the **Ermita Virgen del Puente**. This site of a former pilgrims' hospital, with Romanesque origins, houses a framed image of the Virgin, who is venerated every April 25th in a procession. Enter Sahagún, after passing under the N-120 and heading towards grain silos (13km).

SAHAGÚN (12.5km ∞)

4 **Cluny** M 64 €6 Y K|W|D|@|Cred 987 781 015
At the Iglesia de la Trinidad, c/ Arco 87
https://www.turismosahagun.com/albergue-municipal

5 **Santa Cruz** Pa 58 €6 (+ Priv.) N M(Don–food)
B(Don)|K|W|D|†|@ 650 696 023 | Monasterio de Santa Cruz | c/ Antonio Nicolás 40
alberguesantacruzsahagun@gmail.com
www.alberguesensahagun.es

6 **Domus Viatoris** Pr 50 €5–7 (+ Priv. €18+/25) N
M|B|W|D|@ 987 780 975/679 977 828
Travesía El Arco 25

7 **Hostal Escarcha** ** €25/35–42 987 781 856
c/ Regina Franco 12

8 **Hostal Alfonso VI** ** €30/37 987 781 144
c/ Antonio Nicolás 4

9 **Hostal El Ruedo II** ** €32+/52+ 987 781 834
Pl. Mayor 1 | www.restauranteelruedo.com

10 **Casa Rural Los Balcones del Camino** €35+/52+
646 838 242 | c/ Juan Guaza 2
www.losbalconesdelcamino.es

11 **Hostal Domus Viatoris** ** €45/55 679 977 828
Ctra. Arriondas 1 | www.domusviatoris.com

12 **Hostal La Codorniz** ** €43/55 987 780 276
Avda. de la Constución 97
http://www.hostallacodorniz.com

This town was, in common with much of the province, resettled in the 10th century during the *reconquista* by Benedictine Mozarabs, in this case from Córdoba, at the request of King Alfonso III. The early parts of their monasteries date from this period, and are among the most prized architecture on the Camino Francés. The monuments are mainly constructed of Mudéjar brick, due to the lack of available stone, and while it has given them a distinctive look, it has not made their preservation easy. Prior to this, there was a Roman settlement, and an early Christian basilica dedicated to San Facundo (*San Fagún* from whom the town derives its name) who, along with his brother San Primitivo, were martyred during the 3rd century.

The **arch of the abbey of San Benito** will not be the first monument you come to, but the story of this once illustrious institution is intertwined with the 11th century struggle between brothers Sancho and Alfonso for the thrones of Castile and León. It had been established earlier by Alfonso III for the aforementioned monks. The town marked the end of the seventh stage of the *Codex Calixtinus*, and so was well established when Sancho II (the Strong) of Castile – with the help of El

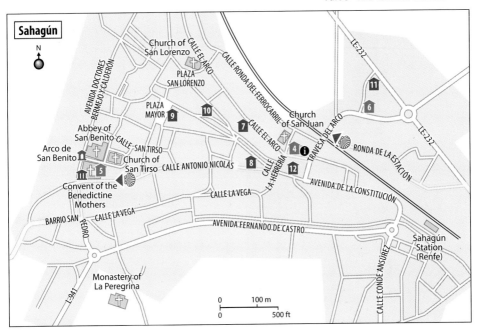

Cid – took León from Alfonso in 1072, and imprisoned him in the abbey. He escaped to Toledo, with the help and support of the abbot and his sister, Urraca (of Zamora), and lived among the Moors. Sancho was assassinated, and Alfonso assumed his titles to become King Alfonso VI (the Brave) of León and Castile. He lavished privileges and riches on the monastery in gratitude, handing it to the influential Cluniac monks, and built a large pilgrims' hospital. Its star faded from the late 16th century, and many of the crumbling buildings were destroyed by fire a century and a half later. However, the nearby **Convent of the Benedictine Mothers** (Monastery of Santa Cruz) and its **museum** house Alfonso's **tomb**, as well as a statue of the Virgin removed from the **monastery of La Peregrina**, which lies to the south of the town, and is undergoing at least partial restoration to its substantial structure.

The first monument in the town proper that pilgrims will come across, is the **church of La Trinidad**. It is nowadays the tourist office and

municipal Albergue, but it dates from the 13th century, with 16th and 17th century additions and modifications.

Next, and beginning a departure off Camino, is the **church of San Juan** (17th century) where you can find the tombs of San Facundo and San Primitivo. Next is the **church of San Lorenzo**, one of the town's outstanding Mudéjar brick structures. With a visible 13th century structure, this Romanesque church has a huge tower split into four differently designed arcades. The interior was remodelled in the 18th century, while the neighbouring **chapel of Jesus** features Renaissance Bas-reliefs by Juan de Juni. Sahagún's Plaza Mayor is a worthwhile stop, and this connects with the Plaza Santiago – back on Camino. Continue alongside the town hall and head generally west until you reach another of the town's Mudéjar structures, the **church of San Tirso** (12th century). In its own plaza, across from San Benito, again, there is a striking high tower with arcades, this time rising from three apses of differing heights, although

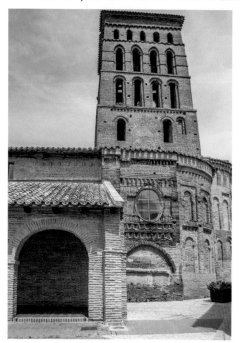

Church of San Tirso

bridge. Note the poplar trees on the other side: legend has it that when a Christian force led by Charlemagne made camp for the night, the men stuck their lances into the ground; the next morning they had become trees, a sign of the bearers' impending martyrdom, and they were among those slaughtered by the Moors. The town is also the site of a Peninsular War battle of 1808 between British Hussars and French cavalry.

Follow alongside the N-120 then cross it at the roundabout junction where the options appear by **Calzada del Coto** (17.3km); take the variant to stay at the Calzada del Coto Albergue (0.5km) – see below – even if you plan to walk the *Real Camino* next day. On the way out of the village as though you are continuing on the *Via Romana* there is an optional left turn to rejoin the *Real Camino Francés*.

it was questionably restored after collapsing in 1948. There are a number of artefacts in this deconsecrated church, some from San Benito arch. Pick up c/ Antonio Nicolás to head out of town on the Camino. The **Puente Canto** (14.5km) across the Cea has five arches, and was reconstructed from an earlier Roman

Arch of San Benito

Bercianos del Real Camino (23km R|B|S)

17 **Parish Casa Rectoral** Pa 44 Don N M&B(Don) @|†
692 858 498 | c/ Santa Rita 11

18 Santa Clara Pr 10 €15 (+6 Priv €25+/30+) Y*
B|K|W|D|@ 605 839 993 | c/ Iglesia 3
alberguesantaclara@hotmail.com
* Closed every Thursday

19 Bercianos 1900 Pr 20 €15+ N M|W|D|@
669 282 824 | c/ Mayor 49
hello@bercianos1900.com | www.bercianos1900.com

20 La Perala Pr 56 €12 Y M|W|D|@ 685 817 699
Camino Sahagún s/n | alberguelaperala@hotmail.com

21 Hostal Rivero €40–45 Dbl. 987 784 287 | c/ Mayor 12
Search hostalrivero Bercianos

also has accommodation choices. Before arriving, the **shrine of la Virgen de Perales** is the site of an annual pilgrimage on September 8th. Follow the roadside track, under the motorway and over the small río Fuente. **El Burgo Ranero** (R|B|S) has the **remains**

22 Domenico Laffi M 30 Don Y K|W|D|@
987 330 023 Pl. Mayor | elburgoranero@gmail.com

23 La Laguna Pr 20 €12-15 (+5 Priv. €40) N K|W|D|@
648 824 258 | c/ La Laguna 24
piedrasblancaselburgoranero@gmail.com

24 Hostal El Peregrino * €30/45 987 330 069
c/ Fray Pedro del Burgo 36 | jumeca07@hotmail.com

25 Hotel Rural Piedras Blancas €35/45 987 330 094
c/ Fray Pedro del Burgo 32

26 Hotel Castillo El Burgo ** €32/55 987 330 403
A231 34km (by Services, left before the village)
https://tinyurl.com/y9nd5wcv

of the shrine of El Santo Cristo de la Vera Cruz before entering, plus the **church of San Pedro**, which contains a silver processional cross and Renaissance altarpiece.

To commence the *Via Romana option,* leave Sahagún and turn off right at the roundabout (18km from Terradillos; 3–4km from Puente Canto leaving Sahagún). The villages are named Calzada after the Roman road – first at **Calzada del Coto** (R|B)

13 San Roque M 36 Don Y B|K|@ 987 781 233
c/ la Era | roblemirador@hotmail.com

where, just after the motorway bridge, the **Ermita de San Roque** is to be found. In the

village proper, the 17th century **church of San Esteban** contains a Baroque altarpiece. After leaving the village, cross rail tracks and continue through scrub and woodland. The next village is **Calzadilla de los Hermanillos** (26.5km R|B|S).

14 Municipal M 34 Don Y K|W|D|@
987 330 013 | c/ Mayor 28

15 Vía Trajana Pr 10 €20 B&B (+ 5 Priv. €50) N
M|W|D|@ 600 220 104 | c/ Mayor 57
www.albergueviatrajana.com

16 Hotel Rural El Cura €65/80 987 337 647
c/ la Carretera 13 | reservascasaelcura@yahoo.es

The **shrine of Nuestra Señora de los Dolores** is housed in a single-nave church where the 15th – 16th century image of the Virgin is contained in a Baroque altarpiece.

Ermita de NS de los Dolores, ©Stanislava stock.adobe.com
Calzadilla de los Hermanillos

The parish **church of San Bartolomé** features a large image of the saint overcoming the devil, as well as a 16th century Calvary.

See next section for continuation and options at Reliegos.

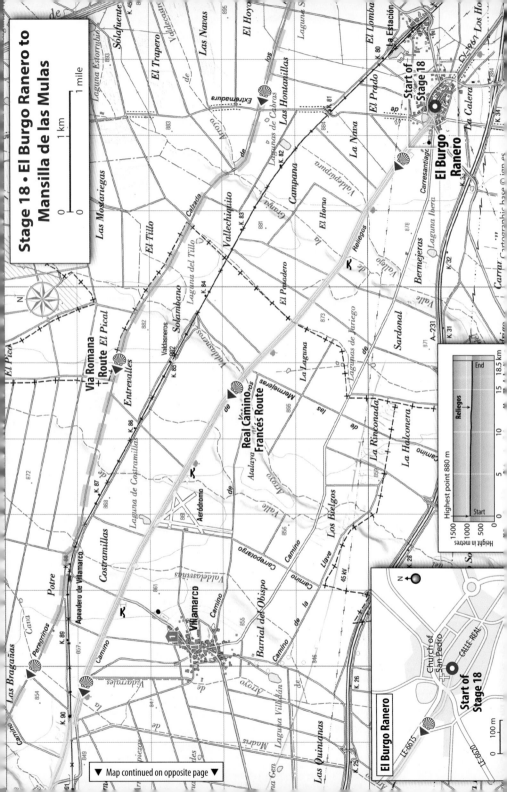

Stage 18 · El Burgo Ranero to Mansilla de las Mulas

0 1 km
0 1 mile

N

Start of Stage 18

El Burgo Ranero

Via Romana Route
El Pical

Real Camino Francés Route

Villamarco

Apeadero de Villamarco

El Burgo Ranero

N

Church of San Pedro

CALLE REAL

Start of Stage 18

0 100 m

LE-6615

LE-6620

Height in metres

Highest point 880 m

Start · Reliegos · End

0 5 10 15 18.5 km

▼ Map continued on opposite page ▼

▼ Continuation of map from opposite page ▼

Cartographic base © ign.es

Stage 18

Mansilla de las Mulas

Vía Romana Route

Real Camino Francés Route

Reliegos

Valdearcos

Est. de Santas Martas

Centro Penitenciario

El Páramo

El Pajuelo

Los Castros

Los Regueros

Fraecillas

Malillos

Mansilla de las Mulas

N

0   100 m

0   500 ft

Vía Romana Route

Real Camino Francés Route

Arco de Santa María

Bus Station

8 End of Stage 18

13 Church of Santa María

9

11

12

10 Puerta Castillo

14 León Provincial Ethnographic Museum

TO MANSILLA DE LAS MULAS (18.5km)

Continuing the *Real Camino option.*

We have the longest stretch of parallel path. Leave El Burgo Ranero. Pass an airfield and under the rail track via a tunnel.

Before the rail track by a rest stop is a left turn to the Albergue at Villamarco (B)

🏠 **La Vieja Escuela** M 8 €5 Y K|W(free) *657 958 092*
c/ Carremonte 31 | juntavillamarco@hotmail.com
Contact to reserve. Bar serves tapas only. 1 km from the Real Camino – ask about return route.

At Reliegos (13km R|B|S)

2 **Municipal (Don Gaiferos)** M 44 €8 Y K|@
658 686 860/619 591 396 | c/ Escuela 24

3 **Las Hadas** Pr 20 €13+–17+ (+ 2 Priv. €40+/60+) N
M|B|W|@ *620 547 454* | c / Real 42
https://alberguelashadas.com/

4 **Gil** Pr 14 €13 (+ 4 Priv.) N M|W|D|@
987 317 804 | c/ Cantas 28
alberguegil@outlook.es

5 **La Parada** Pr 36 €12 (+ 2 Priv. €40) N M|K|W|D|@
987 317 880 | c/ Escuela 7
alberguelaparada@gmail.com

6 **Vive tu Camino** Pr 20 €13 N M|B|W|D|@|PL
610 293 986 | c/ Real 56 | carmenmagin@gmail.com
www.alberguevivetucamino.com

7 **La Cantina de Teddy** €50/60 *622 206 128*
Camino Real s/n | monteciber@hotmail.com

where there are scant remains of defensive walls, the **church of San Cornelio and San Cipriano** has several carvings, including of the two patrons.

Finally, through the village, resume the roadside track, and then a rest area heralds the end of the gravel and a woodland path. Cross over the N-601 and an irrigation channel and through the walls of the **old castle gate** (Puerta Castillo) into Mansilla .

MANSILLA DE LAS MULAS (∞)

8 **Municipal** M 74 €5 Y* K|W|D|@ *661 977 305*
c/ del Puente 5 | alberguemansilla@gmail.com
* Closed during 2022 and before.

9 **El Jardin del Camino** Pr 40 €13.50 Y M|B|W|D|@
987 310 232 | c/ Camino de Santiago 1
olgabrez@yahoo.es | https://tinyurl.com/2v32cm5c

10 **Gaia** Pr 16 €12 Y B(Don)|K|W|D|@ *699 911 311*
Av. de la Constitución 28 | alberguedegaia@hotmail.com
www.alberguedegaia.wordpress.com

11 **La Pensión de Blanca** €25–35/40
626 003 177 | Av. Picos de Europa 4
www.lapensiondeblanca.com

12 **Hotel Rural La Casa de los Soportales** ** €35+/50+
600 471 597 | Pl. Arrabal 9
www.albergueeljardindelcamino.com

13 **Alberguería del Camino** €38/56 *987 311 193*
c/ Concepción 12 | www.albergueriadelcamino.com

14 **Casa Rural El Puente** €35/46–66 *987 310 762*
c/ Los Mesones 3

Nowadays a town of less than 2000 inhabitants, this was an important stop on the Medieval Camino, having been repopulated and fortified in the 12th century, and granted its charter by Ferdinand II of León in 1181. There are Roman origins as well, but the nearby battlefield at **Lancia** (on the way out out of town towards León) is where the Romans fought to capture the settlement of the ancient Astures. The river was where 1500 Spanish troops were cut down by Soult's French cavalry in 1808 in the Peninsular War. The town's **defensive walls** are the most intact in the province of León, having towers where they do not flank the river. But much of the pilgrim monuments have disappeared, including the three hospitals.

Church of Santa María and Santiago Peregrino statue

The two routes converge at the 18th century **church of Santa María** (built on the site of an earlier church) whose Baroque altarpiece is supplemented by a collection from the churches that are no longer standing. Close by, the older **church of San Martín's** (13th century with later additions) capitals around the portal are decorated with lion motifs, and some of the *Mudéjar* coffered ceiling has been preserved. Deconsecrated, it is home to a Cultural Centre. The **León Provincial Ethnographic Museum** https://tinyurl.com/4zdbw6t8 is located in the restored Convent of San Agustín to the northwest. To the southwest, near the bus station, is the shrine of **Nuestra Señora de la Virgen de Gracia** which houses an exquisite image of the Virgin and Child. The pilgrimage takes place on the first Sunday in September, with festivities the following weekend. Other fiestas include a tomato fair in the last weekend of August, and medieval fairs are held around the Feast of St James (July 25th).

Arco Santa María

Miguel Angel Pescador Santirso
CC BY-SA 3.0

To continue along the **Via Romana option.** From Calzadilla de los Hermanillos, it is another 16.5km approx. to the sight of a radio mast that cues you up to a choice: either the short turn to Reliegos in order to lodge, eat/drink and/or to join the Real Camino or continuation into Mansilla. Keeping right begins the descent into Mansilla crossing the N-625 and sight of the río Esla (32.5km). Head left and enter the old town through another of its **gates**, Arco Santa María. Turn right by the church up c/ del Puente to reach the Municipal Albergue (Distances are to the Town Hall/Centre as ever).

Stage 19 • Mansilla de las Mulas to León

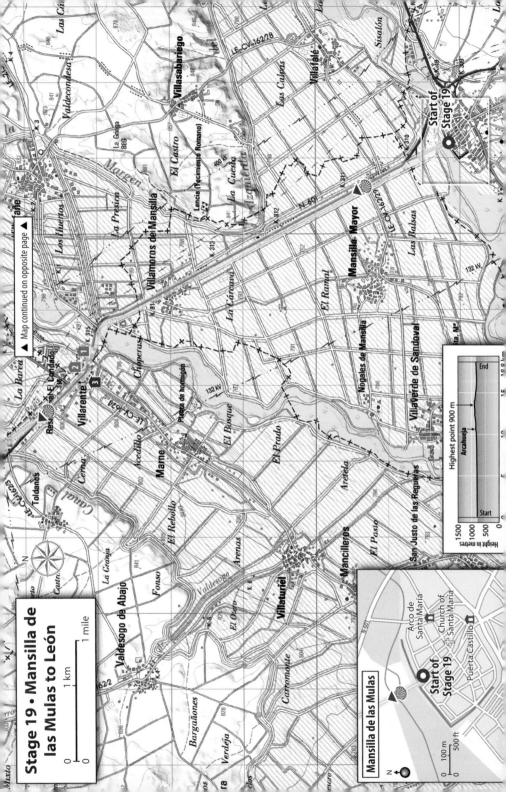

Map continued on opposite page ▲

Mansilla de las Mulas

- Arco de Santa María
- Church of Santa María
- Puerta Castillo
- Start of Stage 19

N

0   100 m
0   500 ft

Highest point 900 m

Height in metres

1500
1000
500
0

Start   Arcahueja   End

N

0   1 km
0   1 mile

Place names

Villasabariego
Villafalé
Villamoros del Mansilla
El Castro
Lencia (Yacimiento Romano)
La Cuesta
La Izquierdo
Mansilla Mayor
Villamoros del Mansilla
La Córcana
El Ramal
Nogales de Mansilla
Villaverde de Sandoval
El Prado
El Bosque
Marne
Acedillo
El Rebollo
El Reguero
Villarente
Villamoros
San Justo de las Regueras
Mancilleros
Villaturiel
Valdesogo de Abajo
Toldanos
Las Cuestas
Canal
La Barca
Start of Stage 19
Mansilla de las Mulas

TO LEÓN (18.8km)

There is just one, shorter stage after Mansilla, with a 100m climb to Valdelafuente, before the descent to the city proper. Because of the peace and desolation of the *meseta*, the contrast with the bustle of the city could hardly be greater. Many of the positive distractions – the city sights – are officially part of this stage, but can be explored fully once you have found your lodgings; it's also another popular place to include a rest day as you are about a week on from Burgos.

Leave Mansilla via the bridge over the Esla, and pass Lancia on a hill the other side of the main road, which you are following closely. Cross the canal to Villamoros de Mansilla (R|B) and its **church of San Esteban**. Cross the río Porma via the modern footbridge, alongside the 200m long **Puente de Villarente** (6km) with its 20 arches; then into the village of Puente de Villarente (∞).

1 **El Delfín Verde** Pr* 20 €5 N M|B|@ 987 312 065
Ctra N601 15km | http://complejoeldelfinverde.es/
Also Hostal €30/50 | *Albergue may still be closed

2 **San Pelayo** Pr 57 €15 (+ 10 Priv. €43/56) Y
M|B|W|D|@ 650 918 281 | c/ Romero 9
www.alberguesanpelayo.com

3 **Hostal La Montaña** * €35/40 690 355 603
c/ Camino de Santiago 17 | https://tinyurl.com/yvwrnt3f

The building on the left is the former **hospital** which is reputed to have operated a donkey 'ambulance' to transport sick pilgrims into León. The **church of San Pelayo** contains a 16th century image of the saint, together with a Baroque altarpiece and Gothic panel paintings. Continue with several café options, crossing the main road with care at the petrol station. Over the canal and under the motorway to Arcahueja (10.4km R|B)

4 **La Torre** Pr 22 €10+ (+ 4 Priv. €30+/35+) Y
M|B|W|D|@ 987 205 896 | c/ Juan Carlos I 19D
info@alberguetorre.es

5 **Hotel Camino Real** *** €49 Dbl. 987 218 134
Ctra. N601 320km (200m behind main road)

and its strikingly modern **church of Santa María**. Rejoin the main road at Valdelafuente (R|B|S) and then cross it via a footbridge. Cross over the motorway on another high bridge (often in high winds) and pass the hospital, before crossing the río Torío at Puente del Castro (∞). *For accommodation, see albergues 6 and 7 on page 154.*

Puente del Castro   LOBO QUIRCE CC BY-SA 3.0

There was a medieval Jewish quarter here, and before that, a Roman fort. Follow the Camino over the large roundabout.

Further along, the Av. Alcalde Miguel Castaño takes the oncoming traffic that goes onto the Av. de Europa but look ahead left; cross over and then right into the Pl. Santa Ana (but continue on if going to Albergue No. 2). The **church** is the first of many to be seen in the city, however, there is speculation this may originally have been a synagogue. Follow c/ Barahona all the way down; it goes straight into c/ Puertamoneda, passing through the gate of the same name; and the medieval city walls. To reach the central Albergue, you can turn right before the Mercado church onto c/ Escurial. Here is the cobbled Plaza Santa María, its trees and fountain, and the **church of Santa María del Camino** (or del Mercado). It retains much of its 12th century Romanesque origin, while its tower is late 16th century. The image of the Virgin is 15th century, as is a Pietà. The Albergue run by Benedictine nuns – who sing Gregorian chant every day – is just off the square. If not visiting the Albergue and to arrive at the magnificent cathedral, pass the church and its lion statues, continue along the Camino up c/ Rúa, and the Pl. San Marcelo, turning right into c/ Ancha.

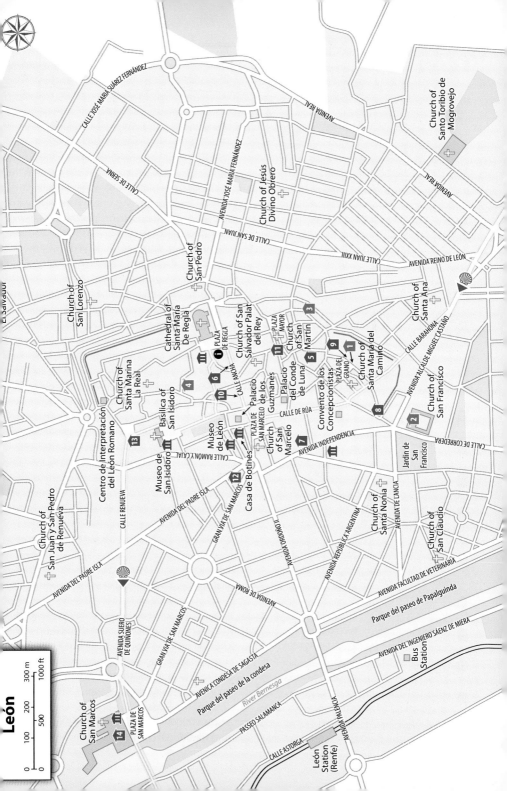

León

Scale:
0 — 100 — 200 — 300 m
0 — 500 — 1000 ft

Church of Santo Toribio de Mogrovejo

Church of Jesús Divino Obrero

Church of San Pedro

Church of San Lorenzo

El Salvador

Cathedral of Santa María De Regla

Church of San Salvador Palat del Rey

PLAZA DE REGLA

PLAZA MAYOR

Church of San Martín

Church of Santa Ana

Church of Santa María del Camino

Church of San Francisco

PLAZA DEL GRANO

Palacio del Conde de Luna

Convento de los Concepcionistas

Church of Santa Marina La Real

Basílica of San Isidoro

Centro de Interpretación del León Romano

Museo de San Isidoro

Palacio de los Guzmanes

Church of San Marcelo

PLAZA DE SAN MARCELO

Casa de Botines

Museo de León

Jardin de San Francisco

Church of Santa Nonia

Church of San Claudio

Church of San Juan y San Pedro de Renueva

Church of San Marcos

PLAZA DE SAN MARCOS

León Station (Renfe)

Bus Station

River Bernesga

Parque del paseo de Papalguinda

Parque del paseo de la condesa

Streets:
CALLE JOSÉ MARÍA SUÁREZ FERNÁNDEZ
CALLE DE SERNA
AVENIDA JOSÉ MARÍA FERNÁNDEZ
AVENIDA REAL
AVENIDA REAL
CALLE DE SAN JUAN
CALLE JUAN XXIII
AVENIDA REINO DE LEÓN
CALLE BARAHONA
AVENIDA ALCALDE MIGUEL CASTAÑO
CALLE ANCHA
CALLE DE RÚA
AVENIDA INDEPENDENCIA
CALLE DE CORREDERA
AVENIDA DE LANCIA
AVENIDA REPÚBLICA ARGENTINA
AVENIDA FACULTAD DE VETERINARIA
CALLE RAMÓN Y CAJAL
CALLE RENUEVA
AVENIDA DEL PADRE ISLA
AVENIDA DEL PADRE ISLA
GRAN VÍA DE SAN MARCOS
GRAN VÍA DE SAN MARCOS
AVENIDA ORDOÑO II
AVENIDA DE ROMA
AVENIDA SUERO DE QUIÑONES
AVENICA CONDESA DE SAGASTA
AVENIDA DEL INGENIERO SÁENZ DE MIERA
PASEO SALAMANCA
CALLE ASTORGA
AVENIDA PALENCIA

Numbered locations: 1, 2, 3, 4, 5, 6, 7, 8, 9, 10, 11, 12, 13, 14

LEÓN (∞)

At Puente del Castro on the way to León

6 **Santo Tomás de Canterbury Pr** 48 €12 (+ 3 Priv. €45+ Dbl.) **N M|K|W|D|@|Cred** 987 392 626 Av. la Lastra 53 (Lower) | https://tinyurl.com/53hr24sv Detour left after Hospital

7 **Check in León Pr** 40 €11 **Y K|W|D|@|Cred** 987 498 793 | Av. Alcalde Miguel Castaño 88 www.checkinleon.es

1 **Monasterio de Benedictinas (Carbajalas) Pa** 134 €8 **Y M|B(Don)|W|D|@|Cred|†** 680 649 289 Pl. de Sta. María del Camino 3 sorperegrina@hotmail.com | www.alberguesleon.com

2 **San Francisco de Asis A** 70 €12–17 (+ 11 Priv. €45/50) **Y M|B|@|Cred** 987 215 060 | Av. Alcalde Miguel Castaño 4 | www.alberguescapuchinos.org

3 **Muralla Leonesa Pr** 65 €16+ (+ 6 Priv. €50+ Dbl.) **Y K|W|D|@** 987 177 873 | c/ Tarifa 5 www.alberguemurallaleonesa.com

4 **Unamuno Pr** 86 €13–18 **N* M|B|W|D|@|Cred** 987 233 010 | Pl. San Pelayo 15 | *July-Sept only albergue@residenciaunamuno.com

5 **Hostel Quartier León** €15–17 Bunk/€40+ Dbl. 620 428 758 | c/ Juan de Arfe 2 | https://quartierleon.com

6 **León Hostel** €18–20+ Bunk/45+ Dbl. 987 079 907 c/ Ancha 8, 3rd Fl. | www.leonhostel.es

7 **Hostel Rúa** €15+ Bunk/40+ Dbl. 666 139 873 | c/ Rúa 35

8 **Pensión Sandoval** €29+/48+ 987 212 041 c/ del Hospicio 11, 2nd Fl. www.pensionsandovalleon.com

9 **Hospedería Monástica Pax** *** €57+ Dbl. 987 344 493 | Pl. de Sta. María del Camino 11 www.hospederiapax.com

10 **Hotel Spa Paris** *** €44+/54+ 987 238 600 c/ Ancha18 | www.hotelparisleon.com

11 **Hospedería Rincón de León** €43+/49+ 987 033 282/625 419 046 | c/ Plegarias 14

12 **Hotel Occidental Alfonso V** **** €67+/80+ 987 220 900 | Av. Padre Isla 1 | https://tinyurl.com/ynt434vu

13 **Hotel Real Colegiata de San Isidoro** *** €85+/112+ 987 875 088 | Pl. de Santo Martino 5 opp. Basilica www.hotelrealcolegiata.com

14 **Parador de León** ***** €155/175 987 237 300 Pl. San Marcos 7 | www.parador.es

Meaning 'Legion', León was founded by the Romans in AD68, initially to protect the road leading to the gold mines at El Bierzo to the west, and the road to Zaragoza (*Caesaraugusta*) in the east. The Legion in question was the seventh *Gemina*, sent by the Emperor Galba, although the sixth *Vitrix* made an encampment here much earlier, around 29BC under the leadership of Octavian, who later became Caesar Augustus. The enemy initially were the Cantabrians, during the final stage of the Roman conquest of Hispania, and the Astures. But the seventh stayed until the 4th century. The reconquest of Spain spread here from Asturias in the 850s, when the city was recaptured from the Moors. However, it changed hands several times more, including occupation by Al-Mansur in 981, and it was not until Alfonso V's legendary victory at the Battle of Calatañazor in 1002 that the city and the Kingdom of León began to prosper. In 1188 Alfonso IX founded here what is said to have been the first democratic parliament in Europe, with commoners represented alongside the nobility and clergy. The eventual union with the Kingdom of Castile spelt partial decline, as the royal court moved away from the city, but it was its place at the end of the eighth stage in Picaud's guide, and its importance as a crossroads of major trade routes, that kept it going. Lying along the banks of the río Bernesga, nowadays a city at the centre of a 200 000 strong metro area, León has an elegant, prosperous feel about it. As with Burgos, there are several processions with floats during Holy Week, for which the city is renowned. The San Juan and San Pedro fiestas take place in the last week in June, with many attractions. The Sunday before October 5th the Las Cantaderas fiesta gives thanks to the ending of the tribute of the 100 maidens that the kings of León had to give annually to the Caliphs. This is at the time of the Feast of San Froilán, when there is also an interesting procession of decorated carts and traditional costume.

CATHEDRAL OF SANTA MARÍA DE REGLA

www.catedraldeleon.org

Mass is celebrated at 9am, 12pm and 6pm Monday to Saturday, and at 11am, 12pm, 1pm and 6pm on Sundays and holidays. It takes place in the Blessed Sacrament chapel (entry free of charge via the cloister). Additional Masses are held during festivals, during Advent and Lent.

Standing on the site of the Roman baths, a previous cathedral and palace had been built by King Ordoño II around 916, but was twice destroyed. The present cathedral was begun around 1205 during the reign of Alfonso IX – a massive statement that his kingdom was there to stay. Work began slowly, but was well underway by the middle of the 13th century, and completed by the 15th century. It was constructed in the pure Gothic style, of yellow sandstone, and bears strong similarities with the cathedrals of Reims and Amiens in France. Master architect Enrique – he also of Burgos cathedral – and later, Joosken of Utrecht, who built the openwork west tower, are those most associated with the structure. The cathedral's most memorable feature is its mass of vivid stained glass – 1800 square metres of it – so much so that its alternative names are *La Pulchra Leonina* (Beauty) or House of Light. Because it is said to cost €3500 per square metre to clean the glass, it is hardly surprising that there is an entrance fee, €7 and €5 each respectively for the cathedral and the museum, reduced combined ticket and concessions available.

The **west façade** features three portals – San Juan, Final Judgement, and San Francisco – with two towers and an enormous rose window. The scale of ambition is there for all to see. Unusually, the two towers – both belfries – are free standing, supported into the central nave by buttresses. The central column of the middle portal features a carving of Nuestra Señora la Blanca, and is flanked by saints on each side

of the doorway, however the originals were in a delicate condition (they were in the cloister at time of writing, but may be moved to the workshop to be restored) and copies are likely to be there in their place. The tympanum is a Christ Pantocrator, with particularly gruesome punishment being meted out to sinners. The left portal shows the Childhood of Jesus, while the right is dedicated to St Francis. In between the portals, a pillar with a statue of Solomon is where the king would sit in judgement. Before going inside, the **south façade** also has a tripartite portico and a huge rose window above – known collectively as San Froilán's

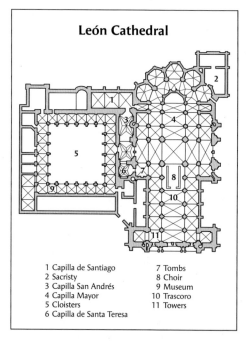

León Cathedral

1 Capilla de Santiago
2 Sacristy
3 Capilla San Andrés
4 Capilla Mayor
5 Cloisters
6 Capilla de Santa Teresa
7 Tombs
8 Choir
9 Museum
10 Trascoro
11 Towers

doorway. The decorated archivolts and jambs remind one of the southern portal of Burgos cathedral. There are the Twelve Apostles and depictions of Christ and the Tetramorph.

Now, entering the **interior**, the effect of the 125 **stained glass windows** immediately starts to become apparent. This is especially the case in late afternoon, and rewarding to catch coloured reflections on the floor. The cathedral

was stripped of much of its later Baroque decoration, leaving a vast space of stone and glass. Much of the glass is original, some of it added as late as the 19th century. The oldest is in the north transept, and the Capilla Mayor. Of the central windows, there is a depiction of the Tree of Jesse. The **choir** and **trascoro** is set behind an ornate façade, and features 15th century Renaissance alabaster carvings by Juan de Badajoz the Elder. There are Old and New Testament depictions on the oak stalls – and a seat for the king and the bishop.

Of the chapels, **St Joseph's** font is still in use. There is a 16th century Calvary. In the apse (starting anti-clockwise) **St Anthony's** has a dedication to Anthony of Padua and a number of wall paintings. The **Virgen Blanca** in the centre has a justly well-known image of the Virgin, and 16th century stained glass depicting the Nativity. **Our Lady of Hope (Esperanza)** features a statue of the Virgin with the Child in her womb. The **Nativity** features a Flemish crib from the 15th century with a charming relief of the Holy City and out-of-perspective Holy Family. **Blessed Sacrament/Santiago** features a statue of Our Lady of the Camino and some of the best of the stained glass. **Santa Teresa** has a Baroque statue of the saint. Wall paintings by Nicolás Francés have been rediscovered. **San Andrés** has an excellent portal, and a 17th century painting of the saint. By the western doorways and under the towers: **San Juan de Regla** includes paintings of the life St John the Baptist, as well as those depicting St John the Evangelist and the Assumption of the Virgin; **Santa Lucia** has an interestingly carved font by Juan de Badajoz the Younger, and a Baroque altarpiece.

The **Capilla Mayor's** altarpiece has Francés' fine 16th century painting of Christ's Burial, among other panels that include a few on the life of San Froilán, and the transfer of the remains of St James. A silver urn by Enrique de Arfe contains the relics of San Froilán. The

tombs are of exceptional quality, including that of Ordoño II, behind the main altar.

It is through the Plateresque doors of the **Puerta del Dado** – with remains of medieval colouring and images of the Pantocrator, the Visitation, the Tetramorph, and the Virgen del Dado – that you reach the **cloister** which also houses the **museum**. The cloister was added in the 13th century but has 16th century characteristics after it was remodelled. Here, apart from the statues of the saints, we can admire the Cistercian form of the courtyard, the ceiling, the carved capitals, and the surviving wall paintings by Francés. The museum's section on Romanesque art includes many sculptures of the Virgin from churches across the diocese, and a crucifix by Juan de Juni. There is Hispano-Flemish art, including a triptych. The **library** holds several Visigothic codices, a Bible and a Mozarabic antiphonary from 1069 (copied from a 7th century document) said to be a precursor of Gregorian chant. Back outside in the Plaza de la Regla, opposite the cathedral and next to the Bishop's palace, the **workshops** are housed in a former seminary. They include a shop restoring the prized stained glass. It may be possible to tour the workshops: ask at the tourist office in the same square.

AROUND THE CATHEDRAL

The cathedral should serve as your focal point during your stay in the city. The Roman walls were pressed into service on many occasions after the seventh finally departed, before being built over in the 14th century during the reign of Alfonso XI. It is these **walls**, by and large, that you can see today, including sections by the east of the cathedral. In the opposite direction, to the southeast of Plaza de la Regla, the so-called **Barrio Húmedo** – 'wet' quarter – is the district of narrow lanes where the Leonese tapas is served. For just over €1 you say what colour wine you want, and the accompaniment comes with it, usually meat with your red and fish with your white. Restaurants are harder to spot but are all around; *morcilla* here is served as a hot stew, usually on its own, and as such may be a bit much to the uninitiated; other delicacies include *cecina de vacuno*, which is beef either cured, dried or smoked, and a wide variety of cheeses. Further south, the typically colonnaded **Plaza Mayor** hosts a market on Wednesdays and Saturdays. The early Baroque **Consistorio**, or Town Hall, was hardly used as such, and has been just about every other kind of public building besides. It is currently used as a handicrafts workshop for the Holy Week processions. The **church of San Martín** retains its Romanesque apse, but is visibly attributable to the 18th century. Inside there is a Pietà by Luis Salvador Carmona from 1750. The portal is 15th century. Head west to see what remains of the **Palacio del Conde de Luna** and a later **tower**, the seat of the Count of Luna, which preserves a Gothic portal. The **church of San Salvador de Palat del Rey** is easily missed, but

Plaza Mayor   *María Teresa García Montes CC BY-SA 4.0*

is the city's oldest surviving church. Built in the 10th century by King Ramiro II, it was originally part of a royal convent and pantheon. Altered in the 16th century, its Mozarabic origins have been uncovered during restoration; it has a Renaissance altarpiece. The **Convento de las Concepcionistas** was founded in 1512 by Doña Leonor de Quiñones, daughter of the Count of Luna, in the palace inherited from her mother. Inside, when open, the Baroque main altarpiece is by Juan de Ribero, with several painted panels; nearby is a statue of the founder of the order, St Beatriz da Silva. We are almost back at the church of Santa María del Camino, and close to the next sight on this tour if instead you turn north up c/ Cid.

As you entered the city, you may have caught a glimpse on the other side of the very busy **Plaza San Marcelo**, of an unusual neo Gothic building. The **Casa de Botines** (1891) is one of very few buildings designed by Barcelona's Antoni Gaudí that we will come across in all of northern Spain; the next is not

far away in Astorga. As we may know, Gaudí took a theme from each piece of architecture he designed. Built as the headquarters of the city's textile trade – with private residences on the upper floors – here, so close to the French Gothic cathedral, the influence seems to be a French château, although, for Gaudí it is fairly understated. Check www.casabotines.es for visiting. There is a statue of the master sitting on a bench in front of his creation. A number of interesting buildings ring the Plaza and the huge roundabout on the end of Avenida Ordoño II. The **Palacio de los Guzmanes** dates from the 16th century, when it was commissioned by a member of this powerful family, who at the time was bishop of Calahorra. With its façade by Rodrigo de Hontañón, and an equally fine courtyard, it nowadays houses the provincial government, and so is accessible. The **church of San Marcelo** is dedicated to the city's and province's patron saint, another Roman legionary – Marcellus. Martyred as a Christian, but this time in Tangiers, he is

accepted by the Leonese as a local man; his Feast day is October 30th. The church is mainly 17th century, but has a Gothic tympanum inset into a wall. The **Ayuntamiento** (Town Hall) is from the Renaissance period (1585). Art Nouveau houses line the Avenida (from the west up towards the Plaza), which serves as the main commercial area. Now heading north along c/ Ramón y Cajal, the **Museo de León** houses an archaeological collection from the Paleolithic to modern times. The top floor has a great view of the city.

BASILICA OF SAN ISIDORO AND ROYAL PANTHEON

Further up the same road, we arrive at the second of León's three 'graces' (or the third of four if you count Casa de Botines), justly famed for its Romanesque frescoes. The original church, built on the site of a Roman temple, was dedicated first to St John the Baptist, and then to St Pelagius (San Pelayo) of Córdoba. It was razed to the ground in 988 by Al-Mansur,

The Pantheon

Fernando Ruiz Tomé © Museo
San Isidoro de León-Derechos reservados. Prohibida la reproducción total o parcial

though Alfonso V restored it. Rebuilt by Ferdinand I in 1037 as a church and monastery, it came to house the relics of one Isidoro. A 7th century bishop of Seville, Isidore was a noted scholar (*see p. 12*) and much revered by Mozarabs during the Moorish rule of that city; he was canonised in 1598. As the *reconquista* made inroads into Spain, Ferdinand was able to demand tribute, and included Isidore's remains, having them reinterred in the church. It was re-consecrated in 1063, five days after which Ferdinand died here. Remodelled and enlarged in 1149, it is largely this Gothic plan that we see today, with one or two Baroque embellishments. It remains a collegiate church; a small Augustinian community of about nine devote themselves to intellectual study as well as prayer. It was here that the first parliament – *Cortes* – was held. A **Pilgrims' Mass** is held at 7.30pm each day when there are pilgrims about.

The two south portals are 12th century. The **Puerta del Perdón** is by Master Esteban, who would later work on the Cathedral of Santiago. It is one of the doors at which pilgrims who were too sick to complete the journey to Santiago received absolution, the same as if they had completed their journey to the Saint's tomb. Above are depictions of the Descent from the Cross with the Three Marys, and the Ascension. Enter the Basilica through here. The **Puerta del Cordero** – or door of the Lamb – is more richly decorated. There are images of San Isidoro and San Pelayo and animal friezes, while the tympanum depicts Abraham sacrificing Isaac, and a Lamb of God flanked by Angels. Enter the Pantheon through here. A substantial Romanesque **tower** stands above the Pantheon. There is also a north portal, to the original Sala Capitular, now the **Los Quiñones chapel**, above which is a **statue** of San Isidoro on horseback, slaying the Moor. Like St James, Isidore was adopted as a saintly warrior in the *reconquista*, and specifically his spirit was invoked in the capture of Baeza in Andalucía.

In the **Basilica**, you can see at least some

of the Romanesque origins, along with later features from many of the architectural and decorative periods. The capitals in the nave – itself remodelled by Juan de Badajoz the Elder – are all decorated with Biblical, floral and burlesque designs. Originally there were three apses, but one was removed when Gothic modifications were made. The 16th century altarpiece, featuring 24 Renaissance panels, contains a silver casket with Isidore's relics. The Blessed Sacrament is permanently exposed, and so the Leonese come and go at all times of the day and night.

The **Pantheon** is a **museum** containing the frescoes, a separate museum, and a library. In the low six barrel vaulted chamber, in the dry air, the original frescoes greet you unrestored. They are from the Romanesque period, so there is no perspective. Most are from Ferdinand II's reign, the second half of the 12th century. One of the principal paintings is of Christ Pantocrator, sitting inside a rainbow, surrounded by the Four Evangelists, and saying, 'I am the Light of the World'. Other paintings are New Testament scenes such as the Nativity, Last Supper, Passion, and a Tetramorph. There is also an interesting agricultural calendar which shows the tasks to be performed during the year. The capitals are of exceptional quality, as befitting a royal pantheon. Here are buried 11 kings, 12 queens, many princes and nobles.

With photography not allowed, unlike the Basilica, there is a €5 entrance fee including downloadable audio guide, or €7 including guided tour (Open 10am–2pm Tue–Sun & 5–8pm Tue–Sat. Closed Mondays & selected other days – April–Sept.; times change slightly other parts of the year).

https://www.museosanisidorodeleon.com

The Pantheon leads into the **cloister**, part Romanesque and part Renaissance. The museum houses the chest of San Isidoro, and the chalice of Doña Urraca (of Zamora, sister of Alfonso VI). The library contains an illuminated Mozarabic Bible, and codices of Visigothic law.

SAN MARCOS

The third must-see monument is the former pilgrims' hospital and convent of San Marcos. It is located to the west, some distance (15–20 minutes' walk) from the cathedral and other sights, on a huge square next to the river – but you pass it on the Camino exiting the city. It was originally built in 1173 as the western headquarters of the order of Santiago. Much later, in 1514, with their once prized independence well and truly compromised, they rebuilt it in magnificent style, with a donation from Ferdinand the 'Catholic' who they had elected Grand Master of the order; thereafter the position was inherited by the monarch. Originally designed by Pedro de

San Marcos

Larrea, it was completed under Juan de Badajoz the Younger in 1549; however additions were made up to the 18th century. Later, it had a succession of uses, including as a barracks, and was used as a concentration camp to many thousands of Republican prisoners during the Civil War. Having more than once faced the unthinkable fate of demolition, nowadays, much of the Plateresque rebuild is Spain's finest *Parador*, freshly renovated and worth a stroll around.

The **convent façade** is the longest of this architectural style in Spain, and as you are likely to approach it from the opposite side of the Plaza San Marcos, you get the widest eyeful. The Plaza is mercifully traffic free these days, with a relatively quiet road in front of it. Once up close, the richness and extent of the decoration can only be admired; pilasters and medallions, with scenes from the Camino, and scallop shells at the doorway to the church. The portal of the convent is Baroque and features a Santiago Matamoros relief, and the coat of arms of Charles V. Inside, pass through the opulent hotel, where many works of art are displayed, observe the grand **staircase**, and enter the **cloister**. Two sides are by de Badajoz the Younger, with a relief of the Nativity by Juan de Juni, while two sides are later, from the 17th and 18th centuries. There is a frieze of scallop shell decoration before the gallery, among other fine embellishments. You can access the church this way or from outside.

The **church** was consecrated in 1541 and is still in use. It is actually late Gothic in style and origin. It consists of a wide nave with star vaults. The lower carving is the work of Guillermo Doncel, while the remainder is by de Juni. The church doorway has a wide arched porch, before a portal with depictions of the Crucifixion by Juan de Orozco, and the Descent from the Cross by de Juni.

The **Museum** leads off the church, an annexe of the Museo de León. Recently revamped with new layout and information, a superb collection includes steles, mosaics, sculptures by de Juni, a 12th century Calvary, and an ivory Christ by Carrizo de Ribera. Badajoz' sacristy and chapterhouse are here.

OTHER ATTRACTIONS

MUSAC   Drow male CC BY-SA 4.0

The **Museum of Contemporary Art** (MUSAC) is along the Avenida de los Reyes Leoneses that leads off the Plaza San Marcos, but it is worth the short hop on one of the frequent buses to save your feet. The façade of multi-coloured glass is a striking – if rather obvious – nod to the glass of the Cathedral. The interior space is impressive also. If the exhibits, both permanent and changing, are not to your taste, the modern Spanish take on the hamburger at the restaurant may well be.

North of San Isidoro Basilica, at Plaza de Puerta Castillo, the **Centro de Interpretación del León Romano** includes a re-creation of a barracks of the seventh Legion, and their armour, what is known at the time (more discoveries are being made) about the settlement here, and tours conducted by knowledgeable guides. It closes after 2pm Monday to Thursday, but on other days reopens from 5 to 8pm. Just off the Plaza de la Regla, on c/ Sierra Pambley, is a perfectly preserved late 19th century house, the **Casa Museo Sierra Pambley**, home of one of the pioneers of public education in the province.

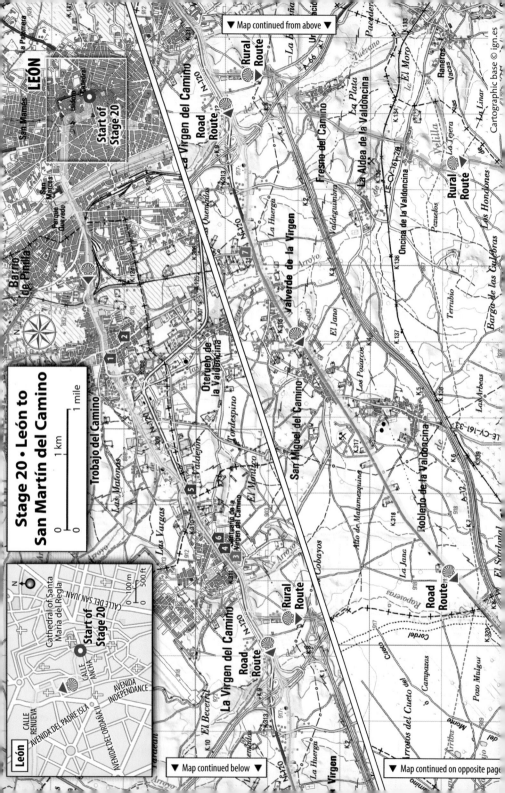

▼ Map continued from above ▼

LEÓN

Start of Stage 20

Rural Route

Road Route

Barrio de Pinilla

Stage 20 • León to San Martín del Camino

1 km
0
1 mile
0

Trobajo del Camino

Oteruelo de la Valdoncina

Tordespino

El Montico

5

4 6 3 Santuario de la Virgen del Camino

La Virgen del Camino
Road Route

Rural Route

Valverde de la Virgen

San Miguel del Camino

Fresno del Camino

La Aldea de la Valdoncina

Oncina de la Valdoncina

Rural Route

Barga de las Culebras

Roblado de la Valdoncina

Road Route

León

Cathedral of Santa María de Regla

Start of Stage 20

100 m
0
500 ft
0

AVENIDA INDEPENDANCE

▼ Map continued below ▼

▼ Map continued on opposite page

Cartographic base © ign.es

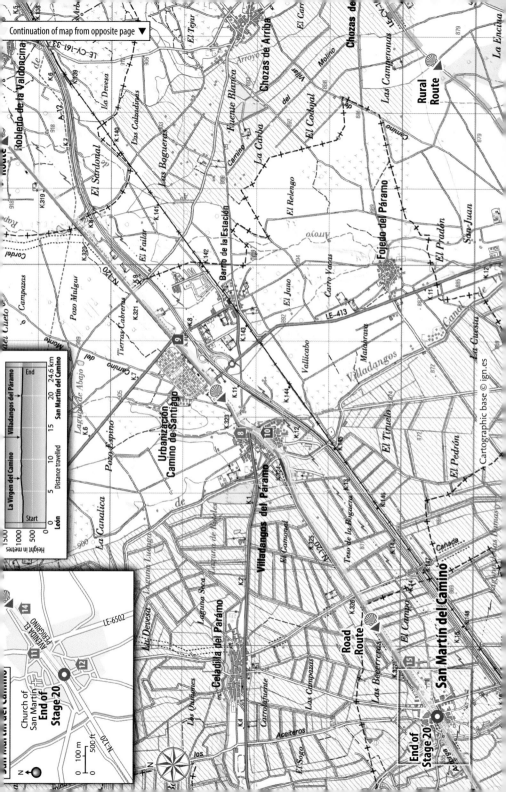

Continuation of map from opposite page ▼

Rural
Route

Robledo de la Valdoncina

Chozas de Arriba

Fuente Blanca

Fojedo del Páramo

Barrio de la Estación

Villadangos

Urbanización
Camino de Santiago

Villadangos del Páramo

Celadilla del Páramo

Road
Route

San Martín del Camino

End of
Stage 20

Church of San Martín
End of
Stage 20

ATENCIÓN EL
PEREGRINO

LE-6502

N-120

Height in metres

La Virgen del Camino | Villadangos del Páramo | San Martín del Camino

Start | Distance travelled | End

León

Cartographic base © ign.es

LEÓN TO ASTORGA

ALTERNATIVES WEST OF LEÓN

A choice of routes is available having reached the shrine and suburban town of La Virgen del Camino, 7km from the city centre. The main *Road Route* – mostly on parallel paths rather than right beside it – is shorter by 3.5km, but is less scenic. This so-called 'alternative' is the official Camino and it does have two churches with plenty of St James motifs. Clearly it is up to you which one you take, but it should be pointed out that the Rural Route is popular; the church at pilgrim-oriented Villar de Mazarife also has Santiago motifs, together with an art gallery. The rural route continues on rather than converging at San Martín del Camino – the official stage end – before crossing to join the road route at Puente de Órbigo, past the start of Stage 21. Both ways cross the *páramo*, an elevated section of high *meseta* (900m). A similar choice is available once more after Hospital de Órbigo, again with the chance to hug the N-120 and save about 1km, or leave it for more pastoral surroundings (option recommended); so you also have the opportunity to swap over before carrying on towards Astorga. These latter options converge about 5km from Astorga.

TO SAN MARTÍN DEL CAMINO (24.6km) / ALTERNATIVE ROUTE TO PUENTE DE ÓRBIGO (35km)

The waymarks are mostly in the pavements. From the Cathedral, the Camino will take you to the other two main monuments: to San Isidoro via c/ Cervantes and joining c/ Cid; then west via c/ Abadía, c/ Renueva, and Avenida Suero de Quiñones to the Plaza San Marcos. Make your way past the magnificent convent, and cross the río Bernesega via the attractive 16th century **bridge** and gardens.

Cross over the railway line and main road, rejoining it at Trobajo del Camino (∞).

1 Hostal El Abuelo * €55 Dbl. 987 801 044
c/de los Mesones 6–8 www.hostalelabuelo.es

2 Hotel Alfageme ** €52+ Dbl. 987 840 490
c/ Alfageme 350m down (left) from Camino

We are in the industrial western suburbs of León, however the **Ermita Santiago** (rebuilt in the 18th century; a Santiago Matamoros inside) serves as a reminder of the four chapels and hospital that tended to the needs of medieval pilgrims; also, the authorities have constructed a pilgrim monument. From the Plaza, there is a short break from the busy road, before crossing it again and heading uphill, away again from the road, to pass some Bodegas. Continue past the industrial buildings, joining the main road (N-120 and you are parallel with the city's airport) until you reach a significant shrine on the route, and the small town of the same name, La Virgen del Camino (7km ∞).

3 Don Antonio y Doña Cinia M 40 €7* N K|W|D|@
615 217 335 | Av. Padre Eustoquio 16 (behind the seminary opp. the shrine) | alberguevirgen@gmail.com
https://tinyurl.com/2p8heyhy | * Closed during 2022

4 Hostal Central * €30/52 987 302 041
Av. Astorga 85 | www.hostalrestaurantecentral.com

5 Hostal Soto ** €35+/53+ 987 802 925
Ctra. León-Astorga 5km | hostalsoto@gmail.com
www.hostalsoto.es

6 Hotel VillaPaloma ** €40/55+ 987 300 990
Av. Astorga 47 | www.villapaloma.com.es

SANCTUARY OF LA VIRGEN DEL CAMINO

Tended by the Dominican friars, the modern architecture contains an ancient image of much local veneration. According to tradition, on July 2nd 1505 the Virgin appeared to a shepherd, Alvar Simón Fernández; a stone was thrown to the precise spot where the sanctuary is today – it became a boulder when it landed. To serve as a focal point of the veneration, some short time afterwards, a metre tall image of the Virgin, cradling the body of Christ looking down, was carved in walnut. It is, of course, unusual not to

see the Virgin and Child; Her Son is wearing a loin cloth and invokes the taking down from the Cross; it is also unusual not to see in a representation of Mercy, Christ looking up. In 1715 a silver crown and canopy to house the image were made. Although the artistic merit of the image does not say top quality, note the expression of pain on the Virgin's face. It is housed on the altarpiece, which dates back to 1730. The Virgin has been a patron of the kingdom of León since 1738 and of the province of León since 1914. In 2009, Pope Benedict XVI granted the title of Minor Basilica. The church is dedicated to San Froilán. Pilgrims have asked the Virgin for help throughout. The most famous miracle was the release of the prisoner of Algiers, Alonso de Ribera, who in 1522 is said to have invoked Her spirit. As he did so, his chains broke, and both prisoner and captor came here and served at the sanctuary, where the chains, and box in which he was imprisoned, are displayed.

The old Baroque sanctuary – where previously there had been a chapel – was replaced by the present structure in 1961. It was built by Francisco Coello de Portugal, a Dominican friar who had originally trained as an architect, and who continued successfully to combine both callings, with many religious projects as far afield as Africa and Taiwan; he died in 2013. At the time, the façade of this modern structure sparked a national

controversy. Even now, the plain hangar-like building and the contrasting statues are not to everyone's taste. However, as with the sanctuary at Arantzazu deep in the Basque Country, and the Basilica de la Virgen del Puy at Estella, there is a powerful combined sense of renewal of faith and tradition, all the more stark because, naturally, the vast majority of monuments we see in northern Spain are much older. For that reason alone, the importance of this place on the Camino is hard to dismiss.

The huge bronze statues stand against a lattice and stained glass background, with heavy doors below. In Modernista style, by José Maria Subirach, they depict the 12 Apostles and the Virgin, the group a representation of the Descent of the Holy Spirit; the statue of St James points the way along the Camino. The glass was made in Chartres. There is a thin, 53-metre-high bell tower, tapering to a Cross.

PILGRIMAGE INFORMATION

Feast day: September 15th; San Froilán fiesta October 5th. Contact: Avda. de Astorga 87, E-24198, Virgen del Camino (LEÓN) Tel: *987 300 001* Fax *987 302 031* email: vcamino.es@dominicos.org https://virgendelcamino.dominicos.es/ Spirituality Centre: vcaminod.es@dominicos.org **Pilgrims' facilities** include a large souvenir shop in the courtyard of the sanctuary. The Dominican seminary across the road has a **Retreat house** and **Spirituality Centre** with its own programme of activities. On rare occasions, the image is processed from the sanctuary the 7km to the Cathedral in the city.

Crossing over the main road from the shrine, there is information on the two routes available, both converging at Puente de Órbigo. A parallel road then takes us down to the divergence.

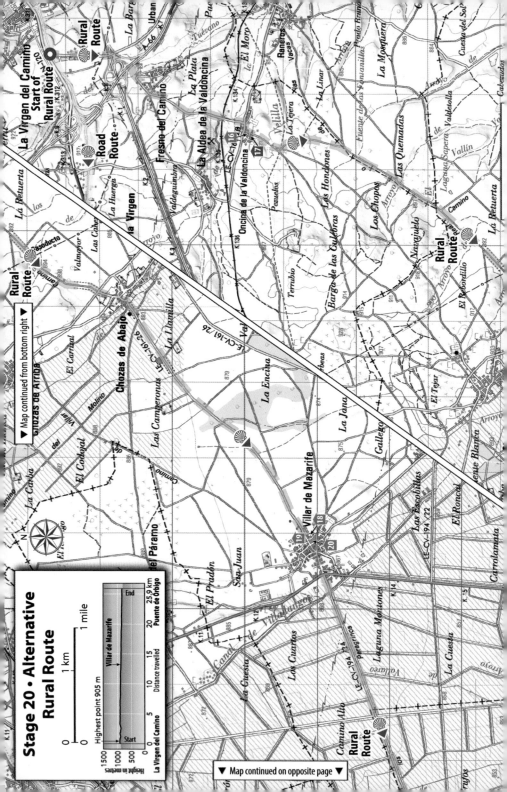

Stage 20 • Alternative Rural Route

Highest point 905 m

Elevation profile (left to right):
- Height in metres: 1500, 1000, 500
- La Virgen del Camino — Start
- Villar de Mazarife
- End
- Distance travelled: 0, 5, 10, 15, 20, 25.9 km
- Puente de Órbigo

Scale: 0 — 1 km — 1 mile

▼ Map continued from bottom right ▼

▼ Map continued on opposite page ▼

Start of Rural Route

La Virgen del Camino

Rural Route

Road Route

Fresne del Camino

La Aldea de la Valdoncina

Raneros

Velilla

La Tejera

El Moro

Oncina de la Valdoncina

Los Hondones

Los Chopos

Naviguelo

Los Quemadas

La Retuerta

Rural Route

El Redondillo

El Tejar

Rural Route

La Huerga

La Virgen

Valdeguimbra

Chozas de Abajo

La Mazilla

Las Camperonas

El Carrizal

El Codojal

La Carba

Páramo

San Juan

El Pradón

La Encina

La Jana

Gallego

Villar de Mazarife

Las Escobillas

El Roncal

La Cuesta

Villabalter

Los Cuartos

Laguna Mortiones

Camino Alto

Rural Route

N

Cartographic base © ign.es

On the **Road Route** , (*see map on page 164 incl. locations of accommodation*) continue uphill, past the cemetery. Now above the road, next a complex road junction with tunnel under the A-66 motorway, and there is actually a track that connects with the alternative route if you have an early change of mind.

At **Valverde de la Virgen** (R|S) the bell

7 **La Casa del Camino** Pr 20 €12 Y M|B|W|D
649 620 168/649 645 820 | Camino El Jano 2
https://alberguelacasadelcamino.es

tower is all that remains of the original **church of Santa Engracia** that was rebuilt in 1961. A further 2km, **San Miguel del Camino** (12.9km R|B|S) retains its 12th century **church of El Arcángel San Miguel**. There is an allegorical **Cross of Santiago**, made out of boulders and farm implements, including railings of Roman origin making the Cross itself. It is over 7km to, **Villadangos del Páramo** (∞).

8 **Municipal** M 48 Don Y K|W|D|@|Cred
Ctra. de León s/n

9 **Hotel Avenida III** ** €52/65+ 630 250 882
Ctra. de León 17km | www.hotelavenidaiii.com

10 **Hostal Libertad** ** €35/50 987 390 123
c/ Padre Angel Martínez Fuertes 25

Iglesia de Santiago Apóstol, Villadangos del Páramo   Rodelar CC BY-SA 4.0

The town is dedicated to St James, and celebrates his Feast day with its own fiesta. The **church of Santiago** is late 17th century and has a Santiago Matamoros statue charging head-on, above the altarpiece. There are also bas-reliefs

of the legendary Battle of Clavijo, showing King Ramiro I's victory. The town has a Roman past, and is also the site of a battle in 1111 between Queen Urraca and Alfonso I of Aragón, some time after their marriage had hit the rocks.

Follow a path out of the town. Rejoin the track parallel to the main road. **San Martín del Camino** (R|B|S) has good facilities for

11 **San Martín del Camino** M 46 €6 Y
M|B(Dons) 676 020 388 | Ctra. de León–Astorga 56
martinez_sonia@hotmail.com

12 **La Casa Verde** Pr 10 €10 N K|W|D|@
646 879 437 | Travesía de la Estación 8
alberguelacasaverde@gmail.com

13 **La Huella** Pr 30 €12+ (+ 10 Priv. €48 Dbl.) Y
640 846 063 | Av. el Peregrino 42
https://alberguelahuella.com

14 **Santa Ana** Pr 40 €8 (+12 Priv. €25+)
Y M|B|W|D|@ 654 381 646 | Av. Peregrino 12
martinez_sonia@hotmail.com
https://tinyurl.com/cxmwhvw

15 **Vieira** Pr 36 €10 Y M|B|W|D|@|Pool 987 378 565
Av. Peregrinos 38 | amelianievesalbergue@gmail.com

pilgrims, and a modern church with statues of protectors of the Camino, Sts Martin of Tours, Anthony the Abbot, Michael, and Roch.

On the **Rural Route** (*see map on page 168*) initially leave the N-120 left onto a track, only to cross both motorways, the A-71 (over) and A-66 (under and follow track). After **Fresno del Camino** (B), cross the railway line and river, and enter **Oncina de la Valdoncina** (3.9km R|B).

16 **El Pajar de Oncina** Pr 9 €10 B&B Y M|K|@
677 567 309 | c/ Arriba 4
elpajardeoncina@gmail.com

17 **Domus Oncinae** €47.50/57 606 803 957
c/ Real 7 | https://oncinaebygescaho.com

The **church of San Bartolomé**, subject of recent renovation, has a belfry characteristic of many in the area. From here, the uphill wide path opens out onto an attractive plateau for 5km to reach **Chozas de Abajo** (B). A further 4.5km brings us to **Villar de**

Villar de Mazarife   Jorge Anastacio stock.adobe.com

Puente de Órbigo   Ikonya stock.adobe.com

Mazarife (14km R|B|S) and the **church of**

18 **Casa de Jesús** Pr 50 €9 Y M|B|K|W|D|@|Pool 987
390 697 | c/ Corujo 11 | refugiojesus@hotmail.com

19 **San Antonio de Padua** Pr 50 €12 (+ 5 Priv. €50
Dbl.) Y M|B|W|D|@|Cred 987 390 192 | c/ León 33
alberguesanantoniodepadua@hotmail.com

20 **Tío Pepe** Pr 22 €12 (+6 Priv. €50 Dbl.) N
M|B|W|D|@987 390 517 | c/ Teso de la Iglesia 2
www.alberguetiopepe.es

Santiago, and its altarpiece, with paintings from the legend of the Saint.

Continuing straight on, a 9.5km stretch takes us out of Villar de Mazarife, on the track continuing straight at the crossroads (Bustillo to San Martín del Camino 3.5km right **Road Route** road – *see map on page 169*) and over the small río de la Mata, and three irrigation canals, to **Villavante** (23.8km R|B).

21 **Santa Lucía** Pr 22 €11(+ 3 Priv. €30+) N
M|B|W|D|@ 669 378 234 | c/ Doctor Vélez 17
www.alberguesantalucia.es

22 **Casa Rural Molino Galochas** €40/55
629 963 870 | Molino Galochas
www.molinogalochas.com

Turn right to access the town, otherwise continue straight.

The **church of las Candelas** is famous for its festival of bell ringers on the first Saturday in August. The interior includes representations of Our Lady of the Candles, Christ at the Column, and St Isidore the farm labourer. A further 4.5km, after crossing the railway (bridge) and another canal – where there is an ancient earth dam and renovated

mill – cross the N-120 near the roundabout and follow the road to where the **two routes join** at **Puente de Órbigo** (R|B), with a red

23 **B&B Puente de Órbigo** €59+-78+ Dbl. 630 149 922
Calle Reguerón, 2 | https://tinyurl.com/38mn5etn

brick water tower acting as the marker.

At 204 metres, this is the longest bridge on the Camino Francés. Built in the 13th century, there was an earlier Roman structure. It is known as the *Paso Honroso* – passage of honour – after a chivalrous challenge laid down by Suero de Quiñones, a knight of León. In 1434, he declared his unrequited love for Leonor de Tovar by wearing an iron collar round his neck as a symbol of enslavement; he further challenged all comers to a joust, claiming he would break 300 lances, each one a declaration that Doña Leonor was the fairest in the land, whereupon he would break the collar. According to one version, in the 13 days prior to the Feast of Santiago, Don Suero and his nine companions broke 200 lances, killing only one knight among those who came from all over Spain, from Portugal, Germany and Britain. The judges of the tournament decided that 200 was enough. Another version has the companions retiring undefeated, setting off for Santiago to offer their weapons to St James, and the collar of iron has become one of gold. The story was at least one inspiration behind Miguel de Cervantes' *Don Quixote*. A plaque on the bridge marks the occasion, as does an annual fiesta held in June.

Stage 21 • San Martín del Camino to Astorga

0
1 km
0
1 mile

Start of Stage 21

San Martín del Camino

Puente de Órbigo

Hospital de Órbigo

Villares de Órbigo

Rural Route

Road Route

Villarejo de Órbigo

Estébanez de la Calzada

Santibáñez de Valdeiglesias

Valdeiglesias

Cruz del Valle

Villamor de Órbigo

Road Route

Rural Route

Puente de Órbigo

▼ Map continued from below ▼

▲ N

San Martín del Camino

AVENIDA EL PEREGRINO

Start of Stage 21

Church of San Martín

0   100 m
0   500 ft

Cartographic base © ign.es

▼ Map continued on opposite page ▼

Continuation of map from opposite page ▼

Cartographic base © ign.es

Roderic Rural Route

Road Route

Santibáñez

N-120

N-VI

El Grillo

El Raso

El Collar

La Reguera

Nistal

San Justo de la Vega

San Román de la Vega

Barrio de Abajo

Barrio de Arriba

Tuerto

Astorga

End of Stage 21

Vía de la Plata

Convento Santa Clara

Astorga

End of Stage 21

Cathedral of Santa María

Church of Santa Marta

CALLE PERPETUO SORCORTO

N-VI

Vía de la Plata

See map on page 179 for details of accommodation in Astorga.

0   100 m
0   500 ft

0   500 ft

San Martín del Camino

Height in metres

Start   Distance travelled   End

5   10   15   20   23.4 km

Astorga

TO ASTORGA (23.4km)

First, we continue with the *Road Route* from San Martín del Camino. Continue on through the village, rejoining the parallel track for a further 6km. The *Road Route* and *Rural Route* combine at Puente de Órbigo.
See Puente de Órbigo in previous stage for description.

Having crossed the bridge over the río Órbigo, you enter Hospital de Órbigo (∞).

1 **Karl Leisner** Pa 92 €8 N K|@ 987 388 444
c/ Álvarez Vega 32 | info@alberguekarlleisner.com

2 **San Miguel** Pr 30 €10–12 N B|K|W|D|@
987 388 285 | c/ Álvarez Vega 35
www.alberguesanmiguel.com

3 **La Encina** Pr 16 €12 (+ 3 Priv. €44 Dbl.) Y
M|B|W|D|@ 987 361 087 | Av. Suero de Quiñones
s/n | segunramos@hotmail.com

4 **Casa de los Hidalgos** Pr 18 €14–16 (+ 3 Priv.
€40–55 Dbl.) N B|K|W|D|@ 699 198 755
c/ Álvarez Vega 36 | https://casadeloshidalgos.com

5 **Verde** Pr 24 €13 N M&B(Dons)|W|D|@
689 927 926 | Av. Fueros de León 76
albergueverde@gmail.com

6 **Hostal Don Suero de Quiñones** ** €55/80
987 388 238 | c/ Álvarez Vega 1 | www.donsuero.es

7 **Hotel Rural Nuestra Señora de Lourdes** **
€Enquire 987 388 253 | c/ Sierra Pambley 40
https://tinyurl.com/273v843p

8 **Hotel El Paso Honroso** *** €44/56+ 987 361 010
Ctra. N-120 335km (by CEPSA Petrol Stn.)
www.elpasohonroso.com

Named after the pilgrims' hospital run by the Knights Hospitallers of St John, the building is now in ruins. The **church of San Juan Bautista** has been rebuilt (18th century) and preserves references to the order.

Continuing on through the town, you come to an *option*, (right) to take the *Rural Route* for part of the way (about 12km out of approx. 16.5km) remaining to Astorga, or follow the traditional, *Road Route* (straight on) along the N-120 roadside (with the AP-71 motorway off to the left), that misses out two villages. The

routes converge at a **Cross** at an altitude of over 900m.

The *Rural Route* soon passes through Villares de Órbigo (R|B|S) and its **church of Santiago** with its Santiago Matamoros image and several altarpieces.

Iglesia Santiago Apóstol,   Rodelar CC BY-SA 4.0
Villares de Órbigo

9 **Villares de Órbigo** Pr 19 €13 (+ 3 Priv. €40+– 45+)
N M|B|K|W|D|@|PL 987 132 935 | c/ Arnal 21
www.alberguevillaresdeorbigo.com

10 **el Encanto** Pr 10 €14+ (+6 Priv. €40/50+) N
K|B|W|D|@ 682 860 210 | Camino de Santiago 23
www.albergueelencanto.es

Then, as the path ahead changes from light brown to gold/red, following a short climb and onto the road a gentle descent, we come to Santibáñez de Valdeiglesias (B).

11 **Parroquial** Pa 20 €8 N M|B|W|D|† 987 377 698
Trav. Carromonte 3

12 **Camino Francés** Pr 24 €12 N M|B|W|D|@
987 361 014 | c/ Real 68
alberguecaminofrances@gmail.com

13 **L'Abilleiru** Pr 6 €27 (+ 3 Priv €54 Dbl.) N
M|B|W|D|@ 615 269 057 | c/Real 44
www.labilleirualberguerural.com

Its **church of La Trinidad** also has a Santiago Matamoros, as well as a statue of San Roch as a pilgrim. From now on, this option comes into its own for natural beauty, with modest ascending and descending woodland hills, and wetland to admire.

At the **convergence** – the **Cross** marking the spot where Santo Toribio of Astorga fell to his knees after being banished – we can get a good view of the bishopric and the slightly more distant Montes de León that await on the stages out of Astorga. There is a steep descent as the path leads to San Justo de la Vega (B|S|P)

🏠 **14** Hostal Juli * €30/50 *987 617 632* | c/ Real 56

which nowadays acts as a dormitory village to Astorga. The 16ᵗʰ century **church of Los Santos Justo y Pastor** contains an image of the patron, besides a Gothic chalice. After walking through the valley, and crossing the río Tuerto (metal footbridge), and then another ancient bridge over a canal, rejoin the main road and cross over the railway. Here, after a roundabout, another Camino, the *Via de la Plata* all the way from Seville joins. You enter Astorga up a steep street that passes through the **Puerta del Sol**, then onto Plaza San Francisco. The large local Association Albergue is here while the San Javier is near the Cathedral.

ASTORGA (∞)

🏠 **15** Siervas de María A 156 €7 Y K|W|D|@|Cred
987 616 034 | Pl. San Francisco 3
www.caminodesantiagoastorga.com

🏠 **16** San Javier Pr 110 €14 N K|W|D|@ *987 618 532* c/ Portería 6 | alberguesanjavier@hotmail.com

🏠 **17** My Way Pr 13 €12 (+ 5 Priv. €40-60 Dbl.) N
M|B|W|D|@ *640 176 338* | c/ San Marcos 7
alberguemyway@gmail.com

🏠 **18** Só Por Hoje Pr 10 €25 B&B N M|B|W|D|@|Cred
690 749 853 | c/ Rodríguez de Cela 30
https://alberguesoporhoje.com

🏠 **19** Hotel El Descanso de Wendy €65+/75+
987 617 854 | c/ Matadero Viejo 11
www.eldescansodewendy.com

🏠 **20** Hotel Imprenta Musical ** €55+/69+ *987 045 704*
c/ del Arzobispo López Peláez 6
https://hotelimprentamusical.com

🏠 **21** Hotel Astur Plaza *** €70+ Dbl. *913 342 196*
Pl. España 2-3 | www.hotelasturplaza.es

🏠 **22** Gaudí Hotel *** €62+/75+ *987 615 654*
Pl. Eduardo de Castro 6 | https://gaudihotel.es

🏠 **23** Posada Real Casa de Tepa **** €75+/84+
987 603 299 | c/ Santiago 2 | www.casadetepa.com

🏠 **24** Hotel Spa Ciudad de Astorga **** €57+/76+
971 897 430 | c/ de los Citios 7
www.hotelciudaddeastorga.com

There are two distinct areas for the visitor, the Plaza Catedral and the district between the Plaza Mayor and Plaza San Francisco. The Camino stage ends at the former. It's an easy visit considering Astorga is a 'town' with a population of just over 12 000 that has some of the historic architecture one might expect of a larger city. A recently discovered fort indicates it was one of Caesar Augustus' main bases during the Cantabrian war (26–22 BC) and afterwards became a *muncipium*. Substantial lengths of the **walls** have been preserved, and other finds include the forum, baths, a temple, and mosaics, though it is clear the town was scaled down in the latter part of Roman occupation, as was the case in other parts of Spain. For the Romans, *Asturica Augusta* was the centre that was closest to the gold mines of the Bierzo, but guarded the road that also transported silver from Galicia and copper from Asturias.

It seems to be a smaller but strangely equal twin to nearby León, not only for its Roman past, but also because of its bishopric (three of the bishops have been made saints) and its importance on the Medieval pilgrims' roads – note the plural – where the Via de la Plata (silver route) converges with the Camino Francés, and where there were as many as 22 hospitals. One legend has both St James and St Paul preaching here; if they came to Spain, then it is very likely, such was the place's importance. Having been fought over by the Visigothic and Suebic peoples in the 5ᵗʰ century, it was part of the repopulation carried out by Ordoño I in the 9ᵗʰ century, following withdrawal by the Moors.

It was later besieged during the Peninsular War. Astorga is the centre of the area of the Maragatos, another small community of Spain whose isolation and spirit was such that they developed their own traditions and architectural style. Today, their architecture is present in the villages to the west.

The Cathedral west portal

CATHEDRAL OF SANTA MARÍA AND DIOCESAN MUSEUM

For pilgrims, it is respectively €5.50 and €5 each for separate tickets to the cathedral and the Bishop's Palace. Standing next to the **Church of Santa Marta** (worth a look for its decorated ceilings) and built over a previous Romanesque church, construction of the present building began in 1471. It was completed in the 18th century, and so displays more than one architectural style, and even quite a variation in composition and colour of materials. Depending on one's point of view, the result can appear anything from a delight to a nightmare. The two towers have flying buttresses propping up a (Baroque) **central façade** as per León cathedral. The **west portal** is superbly florid in the Plateresque/Baroque styles, with so much detail that includes – among all the cherubs and the plants – a Descent from the Cross.

The interior is mainly Gothic. The **main altarpiece** (1558–62) sculptures are by Gaspar Becerra, who trained in Rome, and may have spent at least some time as a student of Michelangelo. The 16th century **choir stalls** are particularly noteworthy, and are attributed to a number of artists. The **sacristy doors** are by Gil de Hontañón, to whom the two larger **chapels** are also attributed. There are sculptures of the Virgen de Majestad, patron of the cathedral, and of the Immaculate Conception by Gregorio Fernández.

The **Diocesan Museum** that leads off the **cloister** is extensive, and can also be visited when the cathedral is closed. Its highlights are a gold casket gifted by Alfonso III to the bishop San Genadio, and a reliquary of the True Cross in filigree gold, silver and jewels, topped with a Lamb of God. There is also a 12th century painted tomb, a figure of Santo Toribio by Becerra, and a Santiago Matamoros painting, besides several altarpieces, and a display of vestments.

THE BISHOP'S PALACE AND MUSEUM OF THE CAMINOS

Juan Bautista Grau Vallepinós was installed as Bishop of Astorga in 1886. Before the year was out, his palace had burned down. That afforded him the opportunity to appoint his friend, Antoni Gaudí, to design a new one, and so considerably liven up the rather crusty diocese. It was begun in 1889, and was completed in 1913; but in 1893 the master's patron died and soon afterwards, the locals attempted to tone down the ambition of the building. As such, Gaudí did not preside over its completion, but some of the interior decoration is, nonetheless striking, as well as the highly distinctive granite exterior. Much of the credit must go to Ricardo García Guereta, the architect who took over the project, and the Catalan Julià Castelltort, who undertook restoration from 1956, although we can still speculate on how much more flamboyant and colourful the result might have been had the master stayed the course. For most of its life, this grandiose building has not served its original purpose, as the bishops have resided elsewhere.

There are Gothic and Moorish influences in the structure, which has French-style **turrets**, a dramatic flared arched **porch** around the portal, and a more classic Latin cross plan. This 'castle/church' is surrounded by a moat.

Inside, in the **central hall**, there is beautiful stained glass, tiled decoration and gold bands round the ribbed vaulting. The **Museum of the Caminos** is incorporated into various rooms in the building, and celebrates the converging of the two Caminos in the town, besides displaying more art from the churches of the diocese, as a continuation of the museum in the Cathedral. In the **basement** there is a collection of mainly Roman artefacts. In the **throne room**, the stained glass is more understated, while two wise owls look down on the bishop's seat. The **banqueting hall** is impressive. The **main chapel** features stained glass narrating the life

The Bishop's Palace

of the Virgin Mary, and an altarpiece of stone and marble. In the **garden**, there are three sculptures of angels – in zinc and mounted on pedestals – designed by Gaudí.

AROUND THE CATHEDRAL

Adjoining the church of Santa Marta, the **chapel of San Esteban** belongs to one of the town's confraternities, and was originally built in the 14th century. There is a cell where women would, according to one account, confine themselves as a penance. In front of the cathedral, the **hospital of San Juan Bautista** dates back to the 12th century, and was reconstructed in the 18th century. Its original purpose, the care of pilgrims, has been faithfully transformed into that of a nursing home run by the Daughters of Charity. Its portal conserves an image of the saint; it may be possible to visit the church. The **house of the Sacristan**

was built in the 17th century. The **convent of Sancti Spiritu** dates from the 16th century, and features Baroque altarpieces; of additional note are the decorative medallions on the cross-vaulted ceiling. All of these sights are passed by on the Camino as it continues through the town.

THE EAST SIDE OF THE TOWN

Pilgrims who follow the Camino will first come to the Plaza San Francisco and its **monastery and church of San Francisco**, and **chapel of Vera Cruz**. The monastery is tended by the Redemptorist fathers, and it is on this site that St Francis of Assisi is believed to have stayed on his pilgrimage to Santiago. Dating from the 13th century, the current structure is attributable more to the 17th. The coats of arms and tombs of several noble families are to be found. Across the plaza is the **Garden of the Synagogue**, a

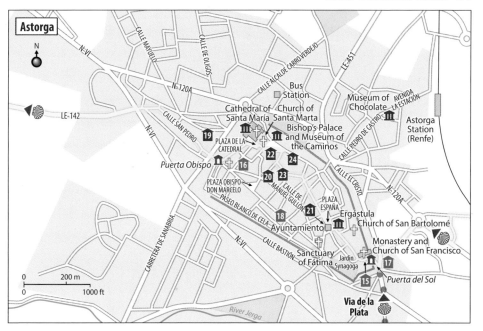

very pleasant park on the site of the place of worship for the old Jewish quarter. The Camino continues back by the monastery, past the **Roman house**, which houses the famous 'bear and the birds' mosaic, to the **church of San Bartolomé**. Founded in the 11th century, making it the oldest in the town today, the church has a Gothic portal and Romanesque tower. In the Plaza Mayor, the **Ayuntamiento** is an attractive late 17th century building, and the clock features two Maragato figures. In front of it is the **Ergástula** or Roman Museum, named after prisoners who were forced to work in the gold mines. On the other side of the square, c/ Bañeza leads to the **sanctuary of Fátima**, on Plaza San Julián. It has Romanesque capitals, but otherwise Baroque renovations, and decorated plasterwork vaulting. The altarpiece is by Churriguerra, with a statue of San Julián. Returning to Pl. Mayor, keep right to make a small detour to **Plaza Santocildes**, and its statue. Afterwards, the Camino continues to Plaza de la Catedral.

The **Museum of Chocolate** celebrates the leading role the town had in this industry during the 18th and 19th centuries. The inclusive sampling will be a welcome treat. It is located before the rail station: south of the Bishop's Palace and gardens, cross Av. de las Murallas and onto Pl. de Pofirio López, then continue on along c/ Pedro de Castro.

Apart from the chocolate, the signature cuisine is the traditional *Cocido Maragato* back-to-front meal, which starts with a meat stew, continues with vegetables, and ends with the soup. The **wines of the Bierzo**, produced to the west of Ponferrada, are well worth seeking out – especially the reds.

Stage 22 • Astorga to Rabanal del Camino

Astorga

Start of Stage 22

CALLE PERPETUO SORCORTO

Church of Santa Marta

Santa Marta

AVENIDA DE LAS MURALLAS

Cathedral of Santa María

Start of Stage 22

0   100 m
0   500 ft

N

▼ Map continued on opposite page ▼

▼ Continuation of map from opposite page ▼

Height in metres

1500
1000
500

Astorga | Start
El Ganso
Murias de Rechivaldo
End
Rabanal del Camino

Distance travelled

0 5 10 15 19.7 km

Gans

Trel

Tue

El La

Laguna

Prado de
la Villa

Las Cuevas

LE-CV-193/1

San Martín
del Agostedo

Santa Cruz

Los Arrotos

Agueveros

LE-192

El Fontinal

Campián

El Cuerno
1114
Cueto

Valle Caión

K-9

K-0

Las Valles

K-11

Alto de la Corona
371

Pedredo

K-12

Barraca

Muras de Pedredo

El Cuerno

Carriluego
Oro

La Prueba

La Fontanosa

La Cuadilla

Bodebajo

El Chano

Teso Peruelo

Los Geijos

K-13

Los Testeos

K-14 LE-142

Grava

Iglesia de San Pedro

Santa Colomba de Somoza

El Ganso
Oro

El Cugallón

Los Estancos

El Castro

Arroyo de la Veiga
Oro

Valdeabrigo

Valseco

El Ganso

El Ganso
Oro

Peña Casada

Piedra Findida

El Urceo

Las Regherinas

Las Febreras

Los Fortús

Almayor

Los Saltaderos

K-15

Cartographic base © ign.es

La Fontanosa

Peña de la Cábaña

Enurepeñas

Las Fuentes

Las Fucaronas
Oro

Minas Romanas
Oro

Laguna de Rubyinal

Las Tornas

La Silva

Santa Colomba
Oro

La Muela

K-17

Laguna Cornada

Rabanal Viejo

Cerro del Cuerno

Los Arroines

La Obidera

LE-CV-192/2

Quintanilla

LE-CV-192

Rabanal

K-18
Oro

K-19
Oro

LE-CV-192/5

Casarino

Rabanal del Camino

San Martino

Peña Mearea

LE-142

Mata Redonda

K-21

El Foryacal

Puente de Pancho

Río

Santa Marina de Somoza

K-20

Río

Prau de la Peña
Oro

Jaluenga

La Trapella

End of
Stage 22

El Culete

Prado de Botas

Ip. Huérida

Río

Piau de la Peña

LE-CV-192/13

Urceo

22 Rabanal del Camino

Rabanal del Camino

N

End of
Stage 22

Monastery of
San Salvador

21

LE-142

16

20

19 17

18

LE-CV-192/13

0 100 m
0 500 ft

ASTORGA TO O'CEBREIRO
TO RABANAL DEL CAMINO
(19.7km)

The Montes de León swing into view

Today sees a dramatic change of scenery, and then terrain, as the Montes de León become part of our journey before the descent into Ponferrada – and that just a brief respite before the mountainous arrival in Galicia. To exit Astorga, pass in front of the cathedral and left, past the Sacristan's house and alongside the convent of Sancti Spiritus, turning right through **Puerta Obispo**, which then becomes c/ San Pedro. Cross the busy N-VI main road, in the direction of Santa Colomba de Somoza. Pass the 16th century **Ermita del Ecce Homo**, scene of a pilgrim miracle, and part of the village of Valdeviejas.

🔟 **Ecce Homo M** 10 €5 N K*|W|D *620 960 060/618 445 910* | 150m on the right after Hermitage morrolas@hotmail.es | *No utensils. No heating.

At the A-6 motorway footbridge, there begins a dedicated parallel pilgrims' path that follows the road to Rabanal del Camino. At Murias de Rechivaldo (4.7km R|B),

2️⃣ **Municipal M** 18 €10 Y W *638 433 716* Ctra. Santa Colomba https://alberguemurias.wixsite.com/home

3️⃣ **Las Águedas Pr** 30 €15 Y M|B|K|W|D|@|Cred *636 067 840* | c/ Camino de Santiago 52 www.lasaguedas.com (+ Casa Rural)

4️⃣ **Casa Flor Pr** 20 €15 + (+ 2 Priv. €35/50) N M|B|W|D|@ *644 695 872* | c/ Traslosportales s/n alberguecasaflor@gmail.com

5️⃣ **Hostería Casa Flor** ** €55+ Dbl. *609 478 323* Ctra. Santa Colomba 54 (different management from Albergue)

6️⃣ **Hotel Rural La Veleta** *** €60 Dbl. *616 598 133* Pl. Mayor 1 | www.laveleta.net

the **church of San Esteban** (18th century) has its belfry accessed by outside steps; beyond the entrance porch, there is a statue of the Virgen del Pilar; inside, is a statue of San Roch the Pilgrim.

Off the official Camino, but accessible via a 5km *variant* is the restored tourist village of Castrillo de los Polvazares (Adds 1km R|B).

7️⃣ **Municipal M** 8 €5 N M|B|K *691 221 058* c/ Jardín 5 | bg@floresdelcamino.com (closed during 2022)

8️⃣ **Hotel Cuca la Vaina** ** €55/70 *987 691 078* c/ Jardín | www.cucalavaina.es

9️⃣ **Hostería Casa Coscolo** €50+ *987 691 984* hola@restaurantecoscolo.com

This is one chance to see the architecture of the Maragato people; life here was depicted by the Spanish novelist Concha Espina in '*La Esfinge Maragata*'. Restaurants specialise in *Cocido Maragato*.

Castrillo de los Polvazares   Anual CC BY-SA 4.0

The Camino otherwise continues straight, the variant rejoining before Santa Catalina de Somoza (9.2km R|B), a climb of 100m.

🔟 **Hospedería San Blas Pr** 20 €10 (+8 Priv. €30/40) Y M|B|W|D|@ *637 464 833* | c/ Real 11 (extra for heating)

11 El Caminante Pr 22 €10 (+12 Priv. €30/45) Y M|B|W
D|@ 987 691 098 | c/ Real 2 | www.elcaminante.es

12 La Bohéme Pr 10 Don M|B|W 722 233 486
c/ El Pozo 11 | dcottereau37@gmail.com

13 Hotel Rural Vía Avis €63+/72+ 670 988 995
c/ El Sol 21 | info@viaavis.com

The village grew up around a pilgrims' hospital, the ruins of which can still be seen. The **church of Santa María** contains a relic of San Blas, the fourth century Byzantine bishop and patron saint of throat diseases. Another 5km brings us to **El Ganso**, (13.3km **R|B|S**) the first in a series

14 El Gabino Pr 26 €10 (+Apts. €40+) N B|K|W|D|@
660 912 823/625 318 585 | c/ Real 9
gabinoelganso@gmail.com

15 Indian Way Pr 27* €10 M|B 691 545 004 | c/ los
Peregrinos | indianway@outlook.es | * Single beds
in tipis.

of half abandoned Maragato villages, with some thatched roof houses. The **church of Santiago** has its **chapel of El Cristo de los Peregrinos** in the atrium and a Santiago Matamoros image. There once was both a monastery and hospital here. Continue to climb, entering a wooded area, and about 3km ahead, there is the opportunity to branch off and visit some of the original Roman **gold mines of La Fucarona**; you will almost certainly have to double back to return to the Camino, a round trip of 3km. Continuing on at **Puente de Pañote**, continue the climb after crossing the bridge. There is a large oak tree, known as the **Pilgrim's tree**. Pass the 18th century **Ermita del Bendito Cristo de la Vera Cruz**. Caution while road walking.

RABANAL DEL CAMINO (R|B|S)

16 Gaucelmo A 36 Don B&B Don N B|K
987 631 751 | c/ Calvario 4 | www.csj.org.uk

17 Municipal M 36 €10 Y K|W|@
678 433 962 | Pl. de Jerónimo Morán Alonso
municipalrabanalbergue@gmail.com

18 La Senda Pr 24 €10 N M|K|W|D|@ 620 542 247
c/ Real | alberguelasenda@hotmail.com

Refugio Gaucelmo   © Michael Krier

19 Nuestra Señora del Pilar Pr 76 €10 (+ 4 Priv. €40
Dbl.) Y M|B|K|W|D|@|Cred 987 631 621 | Pl. de
Jerónimo Morán Alonso | www.albergueelpilar.com
(closed Jan. & Feb.)

20 Hotel Rural Casa Indie *** €45/55 625 470 392
c/ Medio 4A | www.casaindie.com

21 Hotel Rural La Posada de Gaspar €69 Dbl. 987
631 629 | c/ Real 27–29 | www.laposadadegaspar.com

22 Hostal La Candela €42/60
987 691 810 | Ctra. de Rabanal del Camino s/n
info@hostallacandela.com

The **church of San José** (18th century) has a Santiago Matamoros. Rabanal was the end of the ninth stage in Aymeric Picaud's Codex Calixtinus and remains an historic and welcoming, if sparsely populated, place for the modern day pilgrim. It is also a resting place before the ascent of Monte Irago and the Montes de León during the next stage. The Knights Templar were stationed here, and may have built the **church of Santa María La Asunción**, which apart from its apse, is much altered since the 12th century. There is a much more recent presence – since 2001 – in the form of a Benedictine order at the **monastery of San Salvador del Monte Irago**, who hold four daily services in the church, all sung in Gregorian chant. Compline and **blessing of Pilgrims** is at 9.30pm. They also welcome people to stay for a retreat for a minimum of three days; contact in advance. www.monteirago.org Among the Albergues, is one maintained jointly by the British-based Confraternity of St James and the local Bierzo Friends society, next to the monastery.

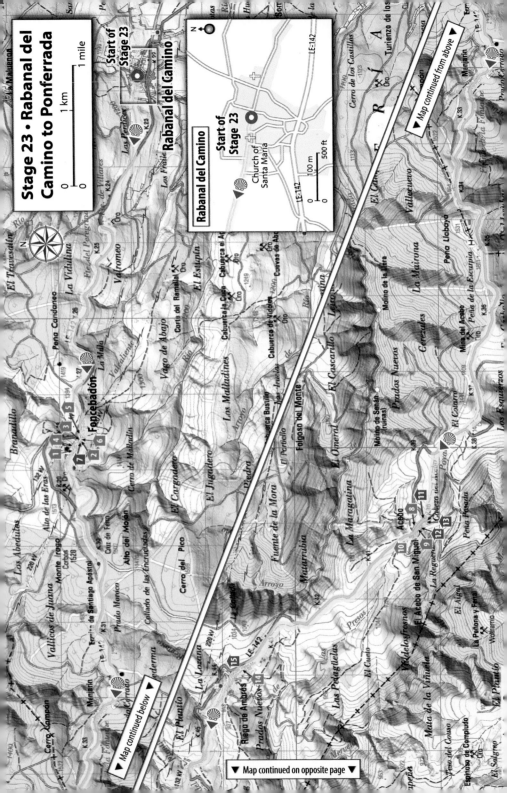

Stage 23 · Rabanal del Camino to Ponferrada

Start of Stage 23

Rabanal del Camino

1 mile
0
0
1 km

Rabanal del Camino

N

Start of
Stage 23

Church of
Santa María

LE-142

LE-142

500 ft
100 m
0

▼ Map continued from above ▼

▼ Map continued below ▼

▼ Map continued on opposite page ▼

▼ Continuation of map from opposite page ▼

Molinaseca

See map on page 188 for details of accommodation in Molinaseca.

Cartographic base © ign.es

Profile chart:

Height in metres

Highest point on Camino 1500 m

Rabanal del Camino — Start

Foncebadón

Molinaseca

End — Ponferrada

Distance travelled

2000 / 1500 / 1000 / 500

0   5   10   15   20   25   32.2 km

Lombillo de los Barrios

Salas de los Barrios

Campo

San Lorenzo

Ponferrada

Santo Tomás de las Ollas

Church of Santo Tomás de las Ollas

End of Stage 23

La Borreca

Otero

Iglesia de Santa María de Vizbayo

Ponferrada inset map:

See map on page 193 for details of accommodation in Ponferrada.

Ponferrada

N

Basílica de Nuestra Señora de la Encina

Ponferrada Castle

End of Stage 23

LE-5228

0   100 m
0   500 ft

TO PONFERRADA (32.2km)

This stage involves a climb to the highest point of the whole Camino Francés. Starting the stage at 1200m, Monte Irago, with two peaks at 1500m +, is more than 50m higher than the Col de Lepoeder on the way to Roncesvalles. The path out of Rabanal crosses the road several times, and continues to climb. However, a 'new' wide path 'for the pilgrim' was built for forestry use, sparking uproar. A **Cross** signals that you have reached **Foncebadón** (R|B) some 6km

Cruz de Ferro   Marques/shutterstock.com

1 **Domus Dei Pa** 18 Don **N** K|W | c/ Real s/n
alberguesparroquiales@gmail.com

2 **Monte Irago Pr** 16 €6 **Y** M|B|K|W|D
655 329 667 | c/ Real s/n
alberguemonteirago1@gmail.com

3 **La Posada del Druida Pr** 20 €12 **N** M|B|W|D|@
696 820 136 | c/ Rea s/n
laposadadeldruida@gmail.com | Also Hotel €35+/55+

4 **La Cruz de Fierro Pr** 34 €15 B&B **N*** W|D|@
699 752 144 /600 715 446 | c/ Real s/n | * Reserve Dec.–Feb. | alberguelacruzdefierro77@hotmail.com

5 **El Convento de Foncebadón Pr** 24 €12 **N** M|B|W|D|@ *644 521 808* | c/ Real s/n
elconventodefoncebadon@gmail.com
Also Hostal €36+/56+

6 **Casa Chelo Pr** 8 €15–20 **Y** W|D|@ *641 023 636* c/ Real 63 | https://tinyurl.com/2cp3asau | Also Casa Rural

7 **Hostal El Trasgu** €41+/58+ *987 053 877* | c/ Real s/n https://eltrasgudefoncebad.wixsite.com/eltrasgu

later. The best views are early on and behind you, back towards Rabanal and beyond. The **former church** of Santa María is now the parish Albergue. The 12th century hermit Gaucelmo built a hospital and church, the remains of which can be seen when exiting the village. At one point, there were only two people left living here, but that has recently changed with the modern revival of the Camino. It is a further climb of less than 2km to reach the first peak, and its iron Cross, **Cruz de Ferro**.

The original cross is said to have been placed here by Gaucelmo. This replica of one

that is kept in the Museum of the Caminos in Astorga stands on top of a tall pole, while all around the base are many rocks left by pilgrims. Traditionally, they drop a rock each with their backs to the cross, to bring them luck on the remainder of their journey. There is a small modern **chapel** nearby. The tall mountain to the south is *Monte Teleno* at 2188m.

From the Cruz, there is a descent to **Manjarín** (9.8km **B**). This tiny hamlet previously had a very basic yet iconic Albergue, with not much else, bar a military communications post further on. However, there was a Templar hospital here once, and the former church of San Roque. 2.5km later, climbing again, you come to the **Camino's highest point**, at 1500m. The mast and nearby cairn are some 20m higher. From here, it is a steep descent of nearly 900m to Molinaseca, so take it easy! On the way down, there are two hamlets. **El Acebo de San Miguel** (16.8km **R|B|S**) is an atmospheric street of balconied

8 Santiago Apóstol Pa 22 Don N M|B|K|@
Pl. de la Iglesia | peregrinosflue@terra.es

9 Mesón El Acebo Pr 16 €10 (+ 2 Priv. €30 Dbl.) N
M|W|D|@ 987 695 074 /616 802 840 | c/ Real 16
mesonelacebo@hotmail.com

10 La Casa del Peregrino Pr 80 €12+ (+ 7 Priv. €45–50
Dbl.) N M|B|W|D|@|Pool 987 057 793 | Ctra. de
Compludo s/n | www.alberguelacasadelperegrino.es

11 Hostal Rural La Casa del Peregrino €35/50
987 057 875 | c/ Real 67–69
www.lacasadelperegrino.es

12 Casa Rural La Trucha del Arco Iris €47+/56+
987 695 548 | c/ la Cruz 10

13 Casa Rural La Rosa del Agua €40+/45+
616 849 738 | c/ Real 52

houses, with a change of architectural style
from red pantile to slate roofs – one that will
stay with us for much of the onward journey.
The **church of San Miguel** has a Santiago
Peregrino; there are several facilities here for
pilgrims; from here there is a possible detour
to Molinaseca. The second hamlet is Riego de
Ambrós (R|B). An attractive place, it includes

14 Municipal M 26 €8 N M|K|W 640 376 118
c/ Real s/n (near hermitage)
valdcarrizo@gmail.com

15 Pensión Riego de Ambrós €25/40 616 123 557
Ctra. de Astorga 3 | www.casaelsusurro.com

the **Ermita de San Sebastián**, and the **church
of Santa María Magdalena**, with its beautiful
Baroque altarpiece.

The descent to Molinaseca includes some
slippery rock face (take extra care when really
wet) and the beautiful valley of the río Maruelo.
The 18th century **Santuario de Nuestra Señora
de la Quinta Angustia** is partly built into the
cliff. The major fiesta takes place on August 15th.

MOLINASECA (21.4km R|B|S|P)

16 San Roque Pr 19 €10 Y M|B|W|@ 600 501 030
Traversía Manuel Fraga (in the chapel)
alberguesanroque2022@gmail.com

17 Santa Marina Pr 38 €10-12 (+ 4 Priv. €40 Dbl.) N
M|B|W|D|@ 653 375 727 | Traversía Manuel Fraga
alfredomolinaseca@hotmail.com

18 Compostela Pr 32 €11 Y M|B|W|D|@
987 453 057/622 317 525 | c/ La Callega 3
alberguecompostela@hotmail.com

19 Señor Oso Pr 16 €14 Y K|W|D|@
661 761 970 | c/ Real 43

20 Hostal Rural Casa San Nicolás €45+/55+
645 562 008 | c/ La Iglesia 43
www.hostalcasasannicolas.com

21 B&B The Way Hotel €41+/45+ 637 941 017
c/ Palacio 10

22 Hotel Molina Real * €40/50 652 871 848
c/ Real 27 | www.hotelmolinareal.com

23 Hostal El Palacio ** €55 Dbl. 987 453 094
c/ El Palacio 19 | www.casaelpalacio.com

24 Hotel Rural Pajarapinta €45+/55+ 987 453 040
c/ Real 30

One of the memorable pilgrim arrivals continues, as we come to the attractive riverside with its plane trees, its swimming area, and its **Puente de los Peregrinos**. The cobble stoned, medieval (though originally Roman) bridge is pedestrian/cyclist only, with the narrow streets of the village on the other side. The river is fed by the mountain snow melt, so it follows that from midsummer there is not as much water in which to bathe – and it is cold – but access is staggered. The village claims royal affiliation, with Doña Urraca, later Queen of León and Castile, said to have lived here. Many of the houses are emblazoned with coats of arms. Today, there are reasonable facilities, and very little traffic, making it a popular stop for pilgrims and tourists alike.

The **church of San Nicolás de Bari**, off to the left, dates from the 17th century. It has a very good altarpiece by Pedro Nuñez de Losada, with an earlier, beautiful sculpture of Christ on the Cross.

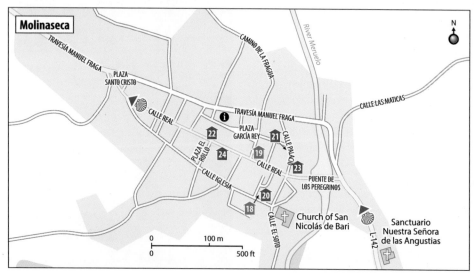

roadside pavement, and passes the main San Nicolás de Flüe and the Alea Albergues – though you can still cross to them on the official route [see below – but take road route for Alea].

The official *Rural Route* (turn left at the hilltop, and then down before up again) takes us first to the village of **Campo** (R|S). Another village with noble and royal affiliations, c/ Real is lined with emblazoned houses; this was also Ponferrada's Jewish quarter, prior to the Inquisition. The **Roman fountain** is testament to its earlier past, while the **church of San Blas**, with its attractive west façade, is 17th century. The **Capilla de la Escuela** (18th century) was built under the patronage of the Marquesa de Campo Alegre. Before crossing the río Boeza, it is worth taking a small detour, some 300m, to the **church of Santa María de Vizbayo**, despite the fact that you normally cannot go inside without pre-arranging a tour at the Tourist Office. This national monument displays the original 11th century Romanesque structure in its pure form, to the extent that the porch and belfry that were built later using local materials, are not intrusive; the same cannot be said about the concrete wall enclosing an adjoining courtyard. It has a single nave with semi-circular apse, and there are some horseshoe arched windows of the Mozarabic style. Inside, there is whitewash covering much of the stone, with mainly 16th and 17th century statues, and a baptismal font.

Leave Molinaseca via the main street, c/ Real, and climb to the top of a hill. Here, there is an *option*, to follow the main **Road Route** rather than the quieter *Rural Route* .

The **Road Route** (turn right) will save about 1km and will come past the castle, if those are the priorities, or arrive beforehand at the Alea or Parochial Albergues, the latter part of a convent that includes the separate **Capilla de Nuestra Señora del Carmen**. Cross the río Boeza, walk alongside and and then cross the railway line, enter or pass the Albergue and chapel. Cross the Avenida del Castillo, and walk along c/ Peregrinos to the **church of San Andrés** and **castle**, [where the other route joins.]

The **Road Route** continues by the

Back on the route, cross the river at medieval **Puente Mascarón**, and if heading for the Parochial Albergue continue up c/ Cruz Miranda, or if heading for the castle, go left along Camino Bajo San Andres, turning right up c/ Hospital to pass the **Hospital La Reina** (c.1498; these days a medical centre).

PONFERRADA (∞)

29 **San Nicolás de Flüe Pa** 186 Don **Y** K|W|D|@|Cred|†*
987 413 381 | c/ Obispo Camilo Lorenzo 2
peregrinosflue@terra.es | https://sannicolasdeflue.com
* Blessing of pilgrims 7.30pm weekdays; Mass 8pm
Sun. & Hols. Priest available.

30 **Guiana Pr** 90 €15 (+ 6 Priv €51+ Dbl.) **N**
M|W|D|@|Sauna 987 409 327 | Av. del Castillo 112
info@albergueguiana.com | https://albergueguiana.com

31 **Alea Pr** 18 €15 **N** M|B|W|D|@ 987 404 133/660
416 251 | c/ Teleno 33 | www.albergealea.com

32 **Hostal San Miguel** €35+/49+ 987 426 700
c/ Juan de Lama 14 | www.hostalsanmiguelponferrada.es

33 **Hostal Nirvana** ** €46+ Dbl. 987 410 761 c/ Largo
de Carucedo 12 | info-reservas@hostalnirvana.com

34 **Hotel El Castillo** *** €44+/52+ 987 456 227
Av. del Castillo 115 | https://hotel-elcastillo.com

35 **Hotel Aroi Bierzo Plaza** *** €60+
987 409 001 | Pl. del Ayuntamiento 4
bierzoplaza@aroihoteles.com

36 **Hotel Temple Ponferrada** **** €54+/65+
987 410 058 | Av. De Portugal 2 (nr. Rail stn.)
www.hoteltempleponferrada.com

37 **Hostal Río Selmo** ** €35+/40+ 987 402 665
c/ Río Selmo 22 (exit the city on the Camino)
http://hostalrioselmo.com/

Standing at the confluence of the rivers Sil and Boeza, and a growing city of 66 000 with industry, Ponferrada grew up on mining. Firstly, the Romans exploited gold and other metals, then, much later, tungsten and coal were extracted right up to the 1980s. Hydroelectricity production escalated with the Bárcena Dam, and latterly the area has tried to exploit wind power, as evidenced by the turbines on top of many of the hills and mountains. Wine production started with the Romans, and after phylloxera wiped out the vines in the late 19th century, it has revived on a significant scale. The name derives from an 11th century iron bridge, erected for pilgrims by order of Osmundo, bishop of Astorga.

There is no cathedral; however, as we have already seen in the environs of the city, there are some jewels of church architecture. But first: the major monument of the city, the magnificent 12th century **Templar castle**. Erected to defend pilgrims from the Moors, it stands today as an historic symbol of how the *reconquista* and the pilgrimage melded. King Ferdinand II of León decreed Ponferrada a protectorate of the Templar order in 1178. The knights responded with a triple ramparted structure, on an irregular polygonal plan, but the dramatic towers, gate and upper part were added both by the Conde de Lemos in 1340 – after the order were expelled by a Church wary of their power and excesses – and later in the 16th and 17th centuries. Originally, there were fortifications on the site that pre-dated the Romans. You enter via the drawbridge; inside the vast complex, there is a modern exhibition area, and a Templar library with more than 1400 volumes, with further plans to utilise the available space. Across the busy road, the 17th century **church of San Andrés** has a 14th century statue of Christ of the Castle, and a Baroque altarpiece.

When the knights were building the castle, legend has it that an image of the Virgin appeared in the heart of a holm oak (*encina*) tree; a forester felling trees found it, guided by a bright light. The fullest version of the legend states that this was the same image that had been brought back from Jerusalem by Santo Toribio, and had become lost when hiding it from Moorish invaders. The **Basilica de Nuestra Señora de la Encina** is located past the castle, on the way in to the old town. The current church – late 16th century, with the tower added from 1614 – houses a 15th century statue of the Virgin, in the 1950s declared the patroness of the Bierzo. The image stands in a dedicated 18th century chapel inside the Basilica. The noteworthy main altarpiece is from the school of Gregorio Fernández. The sacristy was added in the late 17th century. Feast day is September 8th following which there are up to 10 days of various festivities. One of

Ponferrada: Templar castle

Ponferrada: Ayuntamiento   *juantiagues CC BY-SA 2.0*

Ponferrada: c/ del Reloj

Ponferrada: Church of   *José Luis Filpo Cabana CC BY-SA 3.0*
Santo Tomás de las Ollas

Ponferrada: Basilica de Nuestra Señora de la Encina   *Ponferrada: Church of San Andrés*   *Zarateman*

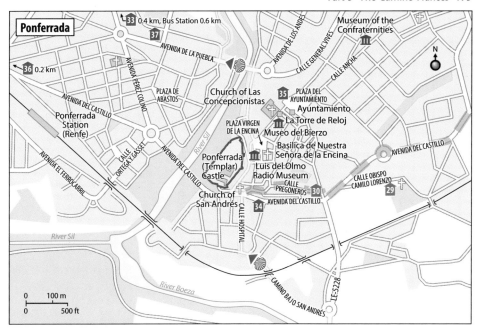

the city's noble houses, the Baroque Casa de Los Escudos, houses a collection dedicated to a more modern phenomenon, the **Luis del Olmo Radio Museum.**

Moving through the old town along c/ de Reloj, the **church of Las Concepcionistas** dates from 1524 and features a Mudéjar roof and single nave. It is part of the convent of the Franciscan Conceptionists of Santiago. Walk through the arch of the clock tower, **La Torre de Reloj,** which is 16th /17th century, and forms the only remaining medieval gate to the city. The **Museo del Bierzo** is housed in the restored 16th century former royal prison. It offers a history of the area from the Paleolithic to the 20th century. The Plaza del Ayuntamiento houses the Baroque **Ayuntamiento** (c.1692).

Accessed along c/ Ancha, the **Museum of the Confraternities** gives some insight into the processions of Holy Week in the city. But the other jewel in the city's ecclesiatical crown is the **church of Santo Tomás de las Ollas.** An excursion along c/ Ancha, then Av. Astorga, and then left by the university onto c/ el Medio, it can be walked in 25 minutes, but check first to ensure it is open. The simple 12th century Romanesque façade and belfry disguises its 10th century Mozarabic structure and interior, supported by nine horseshoe arches. The church formerly belonged to the monastery of San Pedro de Montes at Peñalba.

The **Railway Museum** pays special attention to the role of rail in the transportation of the area's raw materials, and is in a former station, not far from the existing one, in Via Nueva, on the other side of the Sil. Acknowledging Ponferrada's historic role as one of Spain's most important energy centres, the recently opened **National Energy Museum** (Av. Libertad) is housed in the first coal fired power station in Spain; the Camino goes past it. **Las Médulas** are located 25km southwest of the city, at Carucedo. Designated a UNESCO World Heritage site, the former Roman gold mines are a spectacular man (for that read slave) made red clay phenomenon.

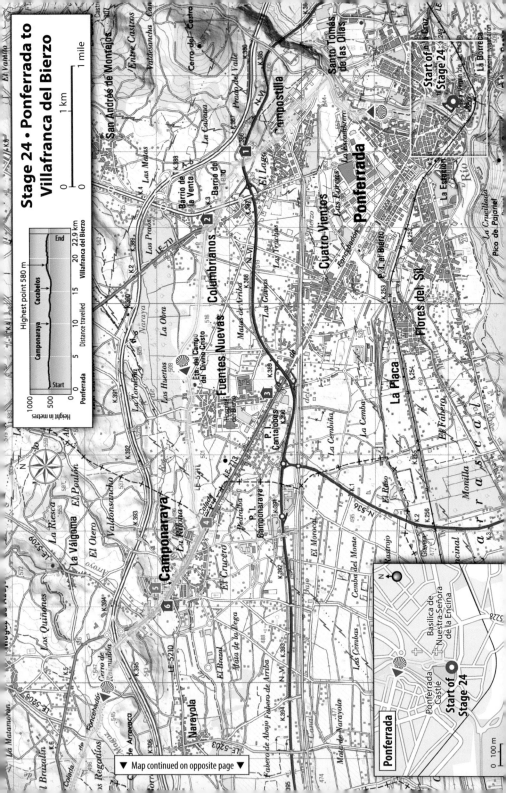

Stage 24 · Ponferrada to Villafranca del Bierzo

Highest point 580 m

Height in metres

1000
500

Ponferrada — Start
Camponaraya
Cacabelos
Villafranca del Bierzo — End

Distance travelled

0 5 10 15 20 22.9 km

0 1 km
0 1 mile

Ponferrada

N

Basílica de Nuestra Señora de la Encina

Ponferrada Castle

Start of Stage 24

0 100 m

▼ Map continued on opposite page ▼

Start of Stage 24

Cartographic base © ign.es

Cacabelos

San Bartolo

Carracedo del Monasterio

Monastery of Carracedo

San Juan

Pieros

Iglesia del Campo

Road Route

Valtuille de Abajo

Villadecanes

Valtuille de Arriba

Parandones

Otero

Corullón

End of Stage 24
Villafranca del Bierzo

Villafranca del Bierzo

0   100 m
0   500 ft

Convento de la Divina Pastora

Church of San Francisco

End of Stage 24
Church of Santiago

Church of Santa María

Convento de San José

Convento de la Anunciada

Villafranca del Bierzo Castle

TO VILLAFRANCA DEL BIERZO (22.9km)

The official Camino and city exit traverses Plaza Virgen de la Encina, down a flight of steps, and a further descent down c/ Rañadero. A left turn at the bottom takes us over the **bridge**, with the río Sil far below. We enter the extensive, modern left bank of the city and its suburbs, turning right into c/ Río Urdiales and through a square used as a car park; turn right at the junction up Av. Huertas del Sacramento until a right onto Av. de la Libertad, then straight onto Compostilla and the Energy museum. The roundabouts with their various sculptures are a feature, providing some respite from the tedium, and the waymarked route opens up into Bierzo wine country with the signature Mencia red grape.

At **Compostilla**, (R|B|S|P) the **church of Santa María** has modern imurals in the entrance portico, and later, the modern **Ermita de Nuestra Señora de Santa María** has its own mural. These and the mural on the later **Ermita de San Blas y San Roque** at **Columbrianos** (R|B|P) were painted for the Holy Year of 1993.

1 **Hotel Novo** *** €50/55 *987 610 630*
Ctra. N-VI km 386 | https://hotelnovo.info

2 **Casa Rural El Amendro de María** €65+
633 481 100 | c/ Real 56 (closed during 2022)
www.elalmendrodemaria.com

Before the entrance to this next 'village' we pass another church, **San Esteban** (c.1778). Continue on through **Fuentes Nuevas** (7.3km ∞) with its **church of Santa María**

3 **Hostal Monteclaro** €27+/42+ *987 455 982*
Av. Antonio Cortés 24

– worth a look inside if open – and **Ermita del Divino Cristo** to **Camponaraya** (∞),

4 **Naraya** Pr 26 €9 N M|B|W|D|@|Cred *987 459 159*
Av. de Galicia 506 | www.alberguenaraya.es

5 **La Medina** Pr 18 €12 (+ Priv. €38+/48+) Y
M|W|D|@ *987 463 962* | Av. Francisco Sobrín 177
alberguelamedina@gmail.com

6 **Hostal Camponaraya** ** €40/48 *619 279 931*
Av. Francisco Sobrín 50 | www.hostalcamponaraya.com

which straddles the road and provides facilities for rest. Here, we find the small **Ermita de Nuestra Señora de la Soledad**. Cross over the A-6 motorway. Another 4km brings us to the outskirts of the town of **Cacabelos** (15.5km ∞). A significant stop on the Camino,

7 **Municipal** M 70 €6 N W|D|@ *987 547 167*
Plaza del Santuario s/n

8 **La Gallega** Pr 29 €15+ (also Hostal €39/49) Y
M|B|W|D|@ *987 549 476* | c/ Santa María 23
hostalgallega@gmail.com

9 **El Molino** Pr 16 €15 (also 4 Priv. €22)Y* M|B|W|D|@
987 546 979 | c/ Santa María 10 | * Closed Tues. & part Sept. | www.elmolinoalbergue.com

10 **Hostal Saint James Way** €20 Bunk/30+/50 *987 037 871* | c/ Santa María 60-62

11 **Hostal Santa María** ** €38/45+ *987 549 588*
c/ Santa María 20-A [Hotel Moncloa ownership]

12 **Hostal Siglo XIX** €46/58+ *633 422 661*
c/ Santa María 2 | www.hostalsigloxix.com

13 **Hotel Moncloa de San Lázaro** *** €79+ Dbl. *987 546 101* | c/ Cimadevilla 97 | https://tinyurl.com/3b9u42b9

there were several hospitals and today there are **museums** of archaeology and wine; the **church of Santa María** is mostly 16th century, but its original Romanesque apse is preserved. Cross the río Cúa by an old mill, the route taken in 1809 by Sir John Moore and his troops in their retreat to La Coruña. The **Santuario de las Angustias** (18th century) on the exit of the town near the Municipal Albergue, is on the site of an earlier chapel and hospital. Its claim to fame is a very unusual relief of the Boy Jesus playing cards with St Anthony of Padua.

Before continuing on the Camino, there is an important site 3km (Or: take local road (signposted left) after Camponaraya and rejoin at Cacebelos – total *detour* 3km) to the south of the town. The **Monastery of Carracedo** (R|B)

14 **Ubaldo Nieto de Alba** Pr 20 €10 (Also Casa Rural €45) Y M|K|@ *608 888 211* | c/ La Roda 1
info@begatur.com | https://tinyurl.com/ywew3h4y

Chapter House, Monastery of Carracedo Angel M Felícisimo CC BY 2.0

enjoyed great political and economic power, yet has a chequered history. It was founded in 990 by King Bermudo II of León and Galicia, as the monastery of San Salvador, at a time of frequent threat from Moorish raids. Then, following decline and abandonment, it was rebuilt in 1138 by Doña Sancha, sister of Alfonso VII. In 1203 the monastery changed from one of the Benedictine to the Cistercian order, and was re-dedicated, Santa María de Carracedo. In the 13th century, Alfonso IX built a small palace in the grounds for his queen (and first cousin) Theresa and two daughters, after papal legate Cardinal Gregory annulled their marriage. In the 18th century, a neoclassical replacement was begun, but only partly completed, when in 1811 the French army occupied the area. As such, there is a succession of architectural styles on view. The museum includes a number of recovered texts. This is a fascinating complex, with much fine carving to admire, in a lovely location. Closed Monday.

Back on the route, after crossing the **bridge** over the Cúa and passing Angustias, the track goes alongside the main road for 2km before reaching Pieros (17.5km B). The small

15 El Serbal y la Luna Pr 20 €10 Y M|B|W|D|@ 639 888 924 | c/ Pozo 13 alberguedepieros@gmail.com

village has scant reminders of its importance to

medieval pilgrims, as a station for the Knights Templar (with Ponferrada and Rabanal) but for its **church of San Martín**, which was consecrated by Osmundo, Bishop of Astorga, in 1086, and partly rebuilt from the 17th century. Inside, there is a figure of St Martin. On the hill are the ruins of **Castrum Bergidum**, the Celtic-Asturian settlement, the conquest of which proved decisive in the Roman occupation of the Bierzo, and therefore Iberia as a whole. They established their own hilltop settlement of **Castro Ventosa** in the same area, the remains of the wall signifying its importance as a guard for the Médulas mines. From here, there is an *option to continue to   follow the road* , before coming off onto a track, which saves about 1km. For the official route, turn right onto a track and pass through the hamlet of Valtuille de Arriba (19.5km), set in rolling

16 Acogida La Biznaga Pr 6 Don B&B Y M|W|D 682 187 093 | c/ Platería 33 | alberguelabiznaga@gmail.com

countryside with vineyards, and some of the best views of the Bierzo.

VILLAFRANCA DEL BIERZO (∞)

17 Municipal M 60 €7 N K|W|D|@|Cred 987 542 356 | c/ Camino de Santiago s/n info@villafrancadelbierzo.org

18 Ave Fénix Pr 80 €10 B&B Y M|W|D|@|Cred 987 542 655 | c/ Santiago 10 albergueavefenix@gmail.com

19 De la Piedra Pr 12 €12 (+4 Priv. €25/32) N M|B|K|W|D|@ 987 540 260 | c/ Espíritu Santo 14 www.alberguedelapiedra.com

20 Leo Pr 24 €12 N B|K|W|D|@ 987 542 658 /658 049 244 | c/ Ribadeo (c/ del Agua) 10 | www.albergueleo.com

21 San Nicolás El Real Pr 75 €10 (Hospadería €30+/50+) Y M|B|W|D|@ 696 978 653 Travesía de San Nicolás 4 | www.sannicolaselreal.com

22 La Yedra Pr 18 €10 N K|W|D|@ 636 586 872 c/ La Yedra 9 | alberguelayedra@gmail.com

23 E Castillo Pr 16 €12 N B|K|@ 622 674 676 c/ del Castillo 8 | https://elcastillovillafranca.es

24 Venecia €14 (Bunk)/30/46+ B&B 629 206 074 c/ Pena Picón | http://www.alojamientovillafranca.es

25 **Hostal Tres Campanas** ** €51+/58+ *670 359 692*
Av. Paradaseca 27 | www.hostaltrescampanas.com

26 **Posada Plaza Mayor** *** €57+/66+ *987 540 620*
Pl. Mayor 4 | www.villafrancaplaza.com

27 **Hotel Las Doñas de Portazgo** *** €60+/70+
987 542 742 | c/ Ribadeo 2 | www.elportazgo.es

28 **Parador de Villafranca del Bierzo** **** €76+ Dbl. *987
540 175* | Av. Calvo Sotelo 28 | villafranca@parador.es

At the end of the 10th stage of the Codex Calixtinus, and founded in the 11th century by French monks from Cluny, hilly Villafranca lies at an altitude of 510m at the confluence of the rivers Burbia and Valcarce. It is today, a quiet town of 2900 permanent residents, with several fine monuments, and historic streets, which would have bustled with activity during the heyday of the pilgrimage, such was its importance. Links with Galicia form part of its heritage, and they include the speaking of the language.

The single nave, 12th century Romanesque **church of Santiago** is the first of those monuments pilgrims come across, and for some, it was the last place they called at. Its finely carved but eroded north Puerta del Pardon, is another of the doors at which pilgrims who were too sick to complete the journey to Santiago received absolution, which perhaps tells its own story – along with the church's cemetery – given that we are less than 200km away. The town is often referred to as 'Little Compostela' in honour of this status. Inside the simple church, there is a Santiago Peregrino statue. The **Castillo Palacio de los Marqueses de Villafranca** was built by the second Marquis in the 15th–16th centuries, occupies an elevated position, and has distinctive round towers.

From the church of Santiago, it is possible to walk – going away from the Camino – up a path and steps to the **church of San Francisco**. Founded originally in 1213 as a monastery by order of Doña Urraca (who had been Queen Consort of Ferdinand II of León), it is said that St Francis of Assisi adopted the site, as he made his way on his own pilgrimage. It was transferred to its present location in 1285, and now owes more to the Gothic and Baroque (the towers) than the Romanesque. Inside, the church is noted for its fine Mudéjar coffered ceiling; otherwise the decoration is mostly Baroque. Although it is now a parish church, the locals have maintained links with the Franciscan order. From here, you can continue to the Plaza Mayor, with its **theatre** (c.1905) and to the **church of San Nicolás el Real** (17th century). Founded by Gabriel de Robles, and built and finished in typical Jesuit style, this was originally a theological college of the order. After the expulsion of the Jesuits, it became a school again in 1899 run by a community of Paulist fathers. It is now home to the town's **museum** of natural sciences. Next to the Tourist Office, the **Convento de la Divina Pastora** was originally one of an estimated eight pilgrims' hospitals, and now adapted successfully for municipal use. Finally, on this section of the tour, we arrive at a public park by the Burbia, in front of one of the most impressive of Villafranca's monuments, the **Collegiate church of Santa María**. The Cluniac order originally established their monastery on this site, but it fell into ruins and was rebuilt in 1544, with some additions up to the 18th century, but if it looks somewhat incomplete, that is because the grandiose plans proved just too much. The interior, with late Gothic, Renaissance and Baroque elements, is upscale. Rejoin the Camino, and either cross the bridge, or head down c/ del Agua.

Villafranca del Bierzo: Church of San Francisco

Staying instead on the Camino will take you down c/ Libertad and through the centre of town, and in particular along the historic **c/ del Agua** – named after the river floods which fill the street – with its palaces and noble houses. It is the birthplace of the Benedictine scholar Fray Martín Sarmiento (1695–1772) and the 19th century novelist Gil y Carrasco. Half way down, the **Convento San José** (17th century) was founded by Don Luis de Castro, canon of the Cathedral of Santiago de Compostela; the interior includes a Baroque altarpiece.

To see the other major sight, you will have to hive off along c/ Rua Nueva, to the **Convento de la Anunciada**. Built on the site of a pilgrims' hospital, it was founded in 1606 by Don Pedro Alvarez de Toledo y Osorio, Marquis of Villafranca, for his daughter, who had chosen to become a nun. The Marquis placed here the remains of San Lorenzo de Brindis, a Capuchin Friar who died in Lisbon in 1619. This is where the Marqueses are buried, and their pantheon is particularly noteworthy. The convent is home to a community of Poor Clares. Between the two bridges, at the confluence, the **Convento de la Concepción** has neo-Gothic altarpieces and a Baroque interior. Finally, on the road to Corullón, southwest of the town, is another Romanesque church, that of **San Juan or San Fiz de Viso**. It is a small church built over a Roman cistern. It is worth continuing to the small town, if time allows, to view its **two Romanesque churches** and **castle**. The major fiesta of Villafranca is Cristo de la Esperanza between September 12th and 15th which includes a procession of floats. The image of Christ of Hope is on the altarpiece in the church of San Nicolás el Real.

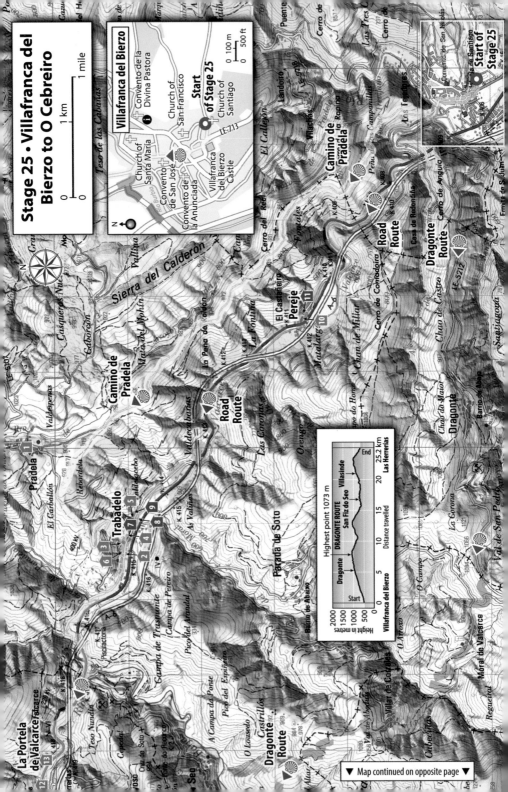

Stage 25 · Villafranca del Bierzo to O Cebreiro

Villafranca del Bierzo

- Convento de la Divina Pastora
- Church of San-Francisco
- Start of Stage 25
- Church of Santiago
- Church of Santa María
- Convento de San José
- Villafranca del Bierzo Castle
- Convento de la Anunciada

0 100 m
0 500 ft

LE-713

Start of Stage 25

Teso de las Cabañas

Sierra del Calderon

Camino de Pradela

Road Route

Camino de Pradela

Road Route

Dragonte Route

Pereje

El Castañeiro

Trabadelo

Parada de Soto

Pradela

La Portela de Valcarce

Dragonte Route

Dragonte

Barrio de Abajo

Villar de Corrales

Moral de Valcarce

Elevation profile

Highest point 1073 m

DRAGONTE ROUTE
San Fiz do Seo

Dragonte · Villasinde · End

Villafranca del Bierzo · Las Herrerías

Height in metres: 2000 / 1500 / 1000 / 500

Distance travelled

Start · 5 · 10 · 15 · 20 · 25.2 km

▼ Map continued on opposite page ▼

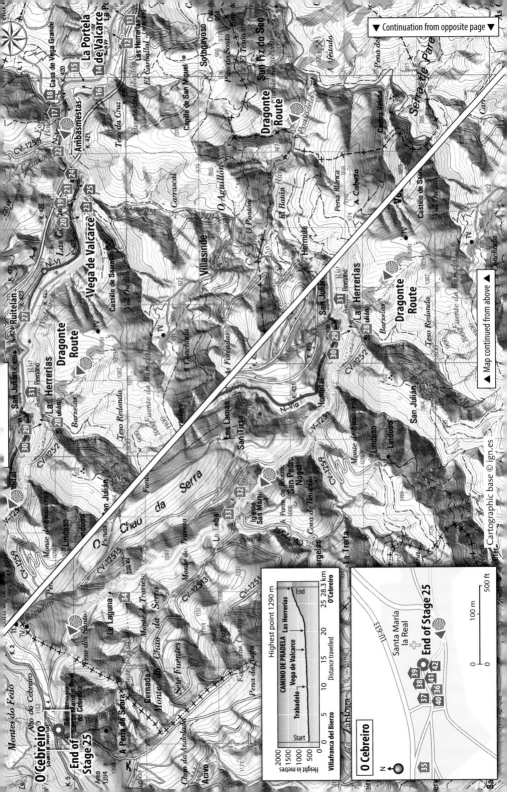

▼ Continuation from opposite page ▼

▲ Map continued from above ▲

Cartographic base © ign.es

Dragonte Route

Dragonte Route

Dragonte Route

La Herrerías

La Herrerías

Vega de Valcarce

O'Cebreiro
(Alto do Cebreiro)
End of Stage 25

End of Stage 25

O Cebreiro

End of Stage 25

Santa María la Real

Santa María la Real

CAMINO DE PRADELA
Highest point 1290 m

Height in metres

Distance travelled

Villafranca del Bierzo
Trabadelo
Vega de Valcarce
Las Herrerías
O'Cebreiro
25 28.3 km

TO O'CEBREIRO (28.3km)

Turn off for Pradela Route   Ikonya/shutterstock.com

Today's 'stage' of 28km represents one of the most arduous climbs of the Camino Francés, and entry to the autonomous community of Galicia, whose capital is Santiago de Compostela itself. The mountain-top settlement of O'Cebreiro is full of significance for the pilgrim. The climb itself can be completed by an even more remote, longer, and more arduous (though, yet more beautiful) route, the green-signed Camino Dragonte. Also called Camino de Los Franceses, this is one for the fittest pilgrims, and then only when the weather permits, travelling if not side by side, then at least within sight of eachother. Those choosing the official route – which is also high level – do have a much lower option to hug the road and river on exit from Villafranca, to rejoin the Camino at Trabadelo (after approx. 9km – a saving of nearly 2km) where it follows the road up to Las Herrerías, where the options converge, and then you head for the 1300m summit for the last 8km. Rain and mountain fog are common, but on better days the views are fantastic. Unsurprisingly, there are several accommodation choices on the two 'sensible' routes while Dragonte climbers will need to track down or make for Las Herrerías.

From Villafranca, the **Official Route** –known as the **Camino de Pradela** , even though it avoids the village centre – hives up a cobbled street, c/ Pradela, immediately after crossing the río Burbia. Continue a steep climb for the first kilometre, before the path becomes

gentler; enjoy superb view. After a further climb past communication masts, and through woods, continue on, ignoring sign for Pradela. [However it is 1km to the Albergue in Pradela

1 **Lamas** Pr 10 €10 N M|B|W|@ *677 569 764* c/ Principal | miguellamaspra@gmail.com https://alberguelamas.business.site

itself, so turn right here to use it]

The descent takes us to Trabadelo (9.4km R|B|S|P), having climbed up over 300m and

2 **Municipal** M 36 €6 N K|W|D|@ *687 827 987/ 987 566 447* | Camino de Santiago s/n albergue@trabadelo.org | www.trabadelo.org

3 **Parroquial** Pa 20 €7 Y* K|W|D|@ *624 674 904* c/ de la Iglesia s/n | fcraya@hotmail.com | * Except 1–15 Nov.

4 **Casa Susi** Pr 10 €12 N M|B|@ *683 278 778* c/ Camino de Santiago 25 | alberguecasasusi@gmail.com

5 **Crispeta** Pr 32 €6–8 Y M|B|K|W|D|@ *620 329 386* c/ Camino de Santiago 1 | osarroxos@gmail.com

6 **Camino y Leyenda** Pr 8 €17 (+ 5 Priv. €26/35) N M|B|W|D|@ *602 321 154* | c/ Camino de Santiago alberguecaminoyleyenda@gmail.com

7 **Pensión El Puente Peregrino** €39+ Dbl. *987 566 500* | Camino de Santiago 153 elpuenteperegrino@yahoo.com

8 **Hostal Nova Ruta** ** €40/50+ *696 978 652* Lugar Trabadelo 1 | www.hostalnovaruta.com

9 **Casa Rural Os Arroxos** €35+/40+ *987 566 529* Camino de Santiago s/n www.osarroxos.es | As Crispeta Albergue/Bar

back down by nearly the same. Back in the village, the 17th century **church of San Nicolás** contains an earlier seated image of the Virgin and Child, and a Baroque altarpiece. There is also the **chapel of Nuestra Señora de la Asunción.**

The Road Route is for all when there is bad weather, but the hazard is still the traffic on the N-VI, despite the recent A-6 motorway (high above), and there is some recent barrier protection for pilgrims. Take care when crossing over, as you will do several times. From Villafranca, after crossing the Burbia, do not hive off as for the Pradela route, but then turn right to stay on the right bank of the second river, the Valcarce. After a further 4.5km arrive in **Pereje** (B).

10 **Municipal** M 30 €5 Y K|W|@ 987 540 138
c/ Camino de Santiago | www.pereje.org

11 **Casa Rural Las Coronas** €36/46 699 512 004
Camino de Santiago s/n

The Cluniac monks at Villafranca assumed the village to be theirs until the Aurillac monks at Cebreiro built a pilgrims' hospital and church here. Everyone from Alfonso VI to Pope Urban II and Queen Urraca got involved in the turf war, and in 1118 the dispute was resolved in favour of Cebreiro. The main purpose of the hospital was to house pilgrims who could not make it over the pass when it had snowed. Today, the **church of Santa María Magdalena,** covered in dingy render, has a Santiago Peregrino statue and a Baroque altarpiece. A further 4.5km brings us to **Trabadelo** where the two options meet.

Continuing, now on the converged *Camino de Pradela* , from Trabadelo, follow the N-VI, parts of the old road, and the Valcarce, to **La Portela de Valcarce** (13.5km R|B|S|).

12 **El Peregrino** Pr 26 €10 (+ Hostal €28/40) N M|B|W|D|@ 987 543 197 | Ctra. Antigua N-VI, s/n www.laportela.com

13 **Vagabond Vieiras** Pr 9 Don (€15 suggested) (+ 2 Priv. €75+ Dbl.) N M|B|W|D|@ 669 329 821 Ctra. Antigua N-VI https://vagabondvieiras.com

14 **Hotel Valcarce** *** €30/50 987 543 180 | Ctra N-VI km 68 | www.hotelvalcarcecaminodesantiago.com

La Portela   *mochilaosabatico/shutterstock.com*

Its name in Galician means narrow pass. The small **church of San Juan Bautista,** is Baroque from the 17th and 18th centuries, and being made of local materials, is typical of the area. There is also a 19th century **forge,** preserved as a museum. A short distance later, enter another attractive riverside village, **Ambasmestas** (R|B|S) where the río Balboa flows into the

15 **Camynos** Pr 10 €10 (+ Hostal €35/45) NM|B|W|D|@ 629 743 124 | Ctra. N-VI 43 www.camynos.es

16 **Casa del Pescador** Pr 24 €10–12 N M|B|K|W|D|@ 603 515 868 | casitadelpescador@gmail.com

17 **Hotel El Rincón del Apóstol** * €17 individual / €30+/40+ 987 543 099 | Ctra. Antigua N-VI 1 www.elrincondelapostol.com

18 **Hotel Rural Ambasmestas** *** €30/45 987 543 247 Ctra. Antigua N-VI 19 | www.ctrambasmestas.com

Valcarce – and then **Ambascasas** (R|B|S|), and on to **Vega de Valcarce** (16.3km ∞).

19 **Municipal** M 64 €8 N K|W|@ 601 501 687 c/ Pandelo s/n | alberguemunicipal@vegadevalcarce.net

20 **El Paso** Pr 26 €13 N K|W|D|@ *628 104 309*
Ctra. Antigua N-VI 6 | www.albergueelpaso.es

21 **La Magdalena** Pr 9 €10 (+ 3 Priv. €30+Dbl.) N
M|B|W *643 979 017* | Ctra. Antigua N-VI 48A
alberguemagdalenavega@gmail.com

22 **El Roble de Veis** Pr 18 €10 Y M|B|W|@
618 401 515 | Ctra. Antigua N-VI s/n
https://albergue-el-roble-de-veis.negocio.site

23 **Pensión Fernández** €25+/32+ *987 543 027*
Pl. del Ayuntamiento 3

24 **Casa Rural El Recanto** €47+/52+ *987 543 202*
Ctra. N-VI 83 | www.elrecanto.com

25 **Casa Rural Mesón Las Rocas** €35+/45+
987 543 208 | Camino de Santiago s/n
mesonlasrocas@gmail.com

There have been accommodation options in the earlier villages, to rest up before the climb to O'Cebreiro; here is a larger village with additional facilities such as bank and pharmacy. From here, you can climb up (45 minute round trip) to the ruined 15th century **Sarracin Castle** –nothing remains of the earlier fortification – and also visit the **church of la Magdalena**. One of the traditional houses with rounded thatched roof, a *palloza*, is preserved; we will see more of these as we travel into Galicia. **Remains** of the pilgrims' hospital and cemetery can also be seen.

On the approach to Ruitelán (B), the

26 **Pequeño Potala** Pr 14 €20 M+B&B
Y W|D|@ *987 561 322* | Ctra. Antigua N-VI
pequepotala@hotmail.com

27 **El Rincón de PIN** Pr 10 €10 (+5 Priv. €38 Dbl.)
Y M|B|W|D|@ *616 066 442* | Ctra. N-VI 41 A
alberguepin@gmail.com (Closed during 2022)

church of San Juan Bautista is charming. The **shrine of San Froilán** is where he, around 850, lived a hermit's life in a cave while trying to organise a crusade, at a time when the Moors in the south were slaying priests and monks. He founded three monasteries in the then border lands, at Viseu and near Zamora, and became bishop, then patron, of León. According to legend, while Froilán was praying, his mule was attacked by a wolf; he spoke to the wolf,

who cowered, and it then became a companion, or alternatively, the mule perished, so the wolf carried the hermit's saddle bags. Once through the main part of Ruitelán, turn off to cross the river via a **Roman bridge** (rebuilt 15th century) after which the highest Dragonte route joins, as we all enter Las Herrerías (19.8km R|B|S).

28 **Las Herrerías** Pr 17 €7 N M|B|W|D *654 353 940*
c/ Iglesia 1 | alberguelove@gmail.com

29 **Casa Lixa** Pr 30 €12–15 (+ 4 Priv. €40+/48+) N
M|B|W|D|@ *987 134 915* | c/ Camino de Santiago 35
www.casalixa.com

30 **Pensión Casa Polín** €33+/40+ *987 543 039*
c/ Camino de Santiago 6 | info@casarestaurantepolin.es

31 **Casa Rural El Paraíso de Bierzo** €47+/56+
627 457 959 | Ctra. General 1
www.paraisodelbierzo.com

The village's name derives from more of the iron forges that were a feature of the area.

On the *Dragonte Route*, after crossing the Burbia, and having said goodbye to pilgrims turning right for the Pradela route, and again to those heading off for Pereje, cross the second river, the Valcarce, and continue, passing by the motorway tunnel, and following signpost for Dragonte. After a nearly 6km steep climb, on National Footpath GR11, reach Dragonte. If it already feels like a mistake, you can right-turn on any of the roads/tracks to go down into the Valcarce valley to join the road route. There is a less steep climb now, as the track widens, and after the highest point at 1073m we turn off right by the GR11 signpost on a path that joins a road, which runs into Moral de Valcarce. Continue the descent as you go through this village, and at a stream turn right. Now ascend through the woods, and emerge at the **church and site of the monastery of San Fructuoso**. This route was used by medieval pilgrims, including those carrying infectious diseases, where the monastery, with its spring renowned for its healing powers attended to them. You are in the small village of **Villar de Corrales**, and after the fountain, continue climbing along a small road, veering right onto a track as the road goes off left. Reaching the second high point (1055m) there is now the corresponding descent, past the old quarry, and into the newer workings themselves – the next village San Fiz do Seo, is visible as a marker. After crossing the river, pick up the public road, turn right and take the next left, climbing, into **San Fiz do Seo**. The tiny **church** is dedicated to Our Lady of Sorrows, to whom they hold a fiesta on September 15th – turn left here. There is a campsite here, with restaurant. After walking through the village, follow level around the hillside, then start a gradual descent, crossing a stream. Now we begin the third climb, through woods, and do not take the path signed for GR1, but continue up, into **Villasinde** (S).

Villasinde   *Guillermo Camuñas CC BY-SA 3.0*

This is another point at which you can go down to accommodation, at Vega de Valcarce. If conditions allow, continue up past the **church of San Pedro Apóstol** (restored in 2003, and worth a look if open) and up the hill, picking up the GR11 sign. Pass the first in a series of communication masts at another 1000m+ point, then after the fountain and with more masts in sight, begin the descent down to the valley floor. This section of path can be covered with encroaching growth, as non pilgrims have plenty of other options in this area, and it is steep, but improves once you reach woods. Then reach the river, and the **convergence** with the main route, and into **Las Herrerías**.

A reminder, it is a further 8km to O'Cebreiro. The **church of San Julián** (18th century) boasts a fine coffered ceiling, and there is a 16th century figure of Christ and a Baroque image of the saint. The buildings at the far end of the village all belonged to, or are on the site of, the Hospital Inglés. It is mentioned in a papal bull of Alexander III in 1178, but nobody is sure whether the hospital was built by the English, or was primarily for English pilgrims, or relates solely to royal patronage, as king Henry II is said to have stayed here on his pilgrimage to Santiago. According to legend, the fountain is linked to Suero de Quiñones, the knight of the bridge at Órbigo. There is a separate cyclists' way – continuing on the road – and if the weather is bad, walking pilgrims are advised to take this, and so missing out the next village. If not, then hive off the road and after 2km and a further steep climb, we reach **La Faba** (23.2km R|B).

32 **La Faba** A 52 €8 N K|W|D|† *637 025 929*
c/ de la Iglesia s/n | http://lafaba.weebly.com/

33 **Tito's La Faba Rooms** Pr 8 €12 (+ 2 Piv. €45+)
N M|B|W|D|@ *622 475 871* | c/ Santiago 8
titoshouserestaurant@gmail.com

The **church of San Andrés** is a mix of 16th and 18th centuries, reflecting its rebuild in the latter, and has recently undergone restoration as part of a Spanish-German project. **Evening Mass**. The Albergue is also run by a German association. Sadly another Albergue here – El Refugio – burned down on New Year's Eve 2021 (it was closed at the time). Continue up and out of the village, and soon we are in the last village on the long trek through Castilla y León, **La Laguna**.

34 **La Escuela** Pr 29 €14 (+ 2 Priv €40 Dbl.) N
M|B|W|D|@ *987 684 786* | c/ Camino de Santiago 10
baralbergueescuela@hotmail.cs

The first of the stone waymarkers that provide good information for pilgrims throughout their Galicia Camino appears here, even though we haven't quite yet crossed the boundary. The retreat of Sir John Moore's British army had become more desperate than at Cacabelos, by the time they reached Pedrafita in the valley below. Gold, horses, treasure, and the women folk who had come along with them – most from a spree in Villafranca where their supposed allies were based – were sacrificed in the biting cold. Moore later restored order as they reached A Coruña; before he was killed by the pursuing Marshal Soult's feared French army.

O'Cebreiro Palloza   Stanislava Karagyozova/shutterstock.com

O'CEBREIRO (R|B|S)

The municipal Albergues in Galicia have been organised and opened by the Regional Government – Xunta. Many are purpose-built while others are converted from school and other buildings. They provide basic facilities, including kitchens that are NOT equipped with cooking utensils. Most do not provide meals. Most still do not have internet. Almost all now have washers and driers.

35 **Xunta** X 106 €8 Y K|W|D|@|Cred *660 396 809*
O Cebreiro s/n

36 **Casa Campelo** Pr 10 €15 (+ 4 Priv. €50) N W|D|@
679 678 458 | casacampelo@outlook.com

37 **Pensión Casa Carolo** * €40/48 *982 367 168*
O Cebreiro 20

38 **Hostal Mesón Antón** €73+ Dbl. *982 151 336*
O Cebreiro 15

39 **Hotel O Cebreiro** * €40+/49+ *982 367 182*
O Cebreiro 10 | www.hotelcebreiro.com

40 **Casa Rural Venta Celta** €46 *667 553 006*
O Cebreiro 19

41 **Casa Rural Valiña** €40/50 *982 367 125*
Rúa Cebreiro | hotelcebreiro@gmail.com

42 **Casa Rural Navarro** €40/45 *982 367 007*
Rúa Cebreiro 9 | www.casaturismoruralnavarro.com

Finally, we arrive in this Galician village, in the province of Lugo, and a national monument of Spain. After the solitude of much of the options leading up here, the large car park alerts you to this being one of those 'visited' places – a destination in its own right. There are a handful of souvenir shops as well. So, try to put that to one side as we appreciate the significance of this place to pilgrims and to Spanish and Galician culture. Firstly, ringed by stone walls, there are well preserved *palloza* houses, one of them an ethnographic **museum**. O'Cebreiro is a point of arrival for the pilgrim; at the end of an arduous climb, it is approximately 635km from Roncesvalles, with 155km to go to Santiago. The lush green scenery (and often the weather that produces it), slate and granite, small farms, and quaint architecture will be with us for most of the final part of the journey. Yet, as a point of departure, it is also a reminder that we have not yet arrived, neither physically nor in spirit, as the Prayer of La Faba – displayed on a board – reminds us.

Although I have traveled all the roads,
Crossed mountains and valleys from East to West,
If I have not discovered the freedom to be myself,
I have arrived nowhere.

Although I may have shared all of my possessions
With people of other languages and culture;
Made friends with Pilgrims of a thousand paths,
Or shared an albergue with saints and princes,
If I am not capable of forgiving my neighbor tomorrow,
I have arrived nowhere.

Although I may have carried my pack from beginning to end
And waited for every Pilgrim in need of encouragement,

Or given my bed to one who arrived later than I,
Given my bottle of water in exchange for nothing;
If upon returning to my home and work,
I am not able to create brotherhood
Or to make happiness, peace and unity,
I have arrived nowhere.

Although I may have had food and water each day,
And enjoyed a roof and shower every night;
Or may have had my injuries well attended
If I have not discovered in all that the love of God,
I have arrived nowhere.

Although I may have seen all the monuments
And contemplated the best sunsets;
Although I may have learned a greeting in every
language
Or tasted the clean water from every fountain;
If I have not discovered who is the author
Of so much free beauty and so much peace,
I have arrived nowhere.

If from today I do not continue walking on your path,
Searching and living according to what I have learned;
If from today I do not see in every person, friend or foe
A companion on the Camino;
If from today I cannot recognise God,
The God of Jesus of Nazareth
As the one God of my life,
I have arrived nowhere.

© *Fray Dino OFM. La Faba - O Cebreiro*

Its **church of Santa María la Real** is partly 9th century, and as such is believed to be the oldest surviving church that has attended to pilgrims' needs along the route. Built on the site of a Celtic temple, in the style of Asturian churches of the time, and originally part of a Benedictine monastery, it was handed to the French order of St Gerald de Aurillac by Alfonso VI (the Brave) in 1072. It was handed back, with papal approval, to the Benedictines by Ferdinand and Isabella in 1487, as part of the monastery of San Benito el Real at Valladolid, and then fell into disuse from 1853, sometime

after the start of the secularisation of the 19th century. It was restored in 1962. The church's side chapel is the setting for a 14th century **Eucharistic miracle**. A peasant farmer, Juan Santín, from the neighbouring village of Barxamaior, trudged through a blizzard to attend Mass. As the only member of the congregation, the celebrant monk scorned the man's dedication and, in a further lapse of faith, questioned the purpose of preparing the sacrament, at which point the bread became flesh and the wine blood. It is said that a 12th century statue of the Virgin inclined her head as a gesture of approval. From that point, the village became a place of pilgrimage on its own, besides taking on a greater significance to those on the Way. In 1486 the Catholic Monarchs donated a reliquary to contain the remains, which is displayed along with the Paten and the Chalice. The latter, donated by an earlier pilgrim, became known as the 'Holy Grail of Galicia'. Galicia is derived from the word chalice, and the present coat of arms features one with a host, although an original design of the kings of Galicia bore three. The monk and the peasant are both buried here. So too is **Don Elias Valiña Sampedro** (1929–1989) the parish priest of O'Cebreiro, who is credited more than most with the revival of the pilgrimage to Santiago, and there are signs here of the gratitude of pilgrims to him.

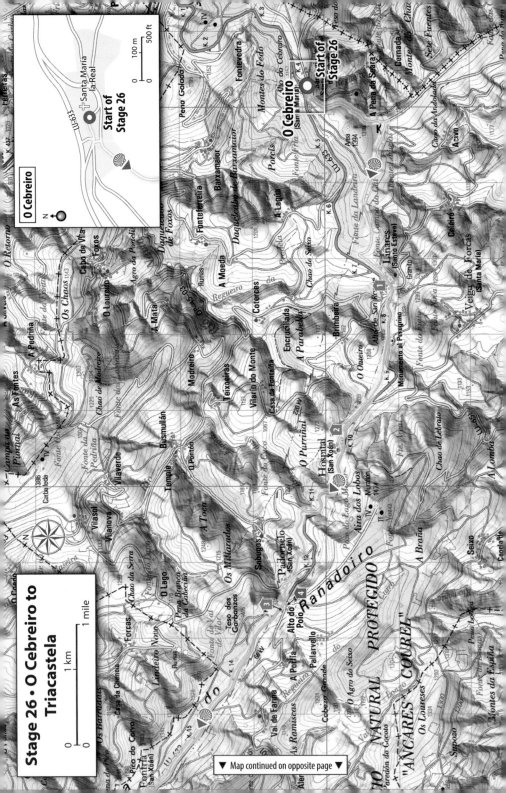

Stage 26 • O Cebreiro to Triacastela

O Cebreiro

▼ Map continued on opposite page ▼

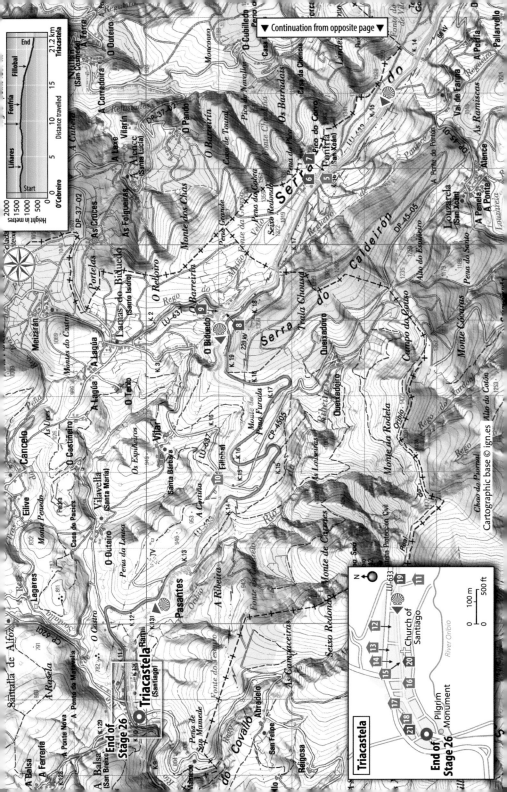

▼ Continuation from opposite page ▼

Triacastela

End of
Stage 26

Church of Santiago

Pilgrim
Monument

River Oribio

N

0   100 m
0   500 ft

LU-633

Cartographic base © ign.es

THE FINAL STAGES

As a reminder, to obtain the Compostela, pilgrims must walk at least the last 100km – traditionally this is from Sarria although the Camino has been re-waymarked with the 100km marker now just beyond it – (or cycle, ride the last 200km roughly from Ponferrada). Those only doing the last 100km must obtain stamps with dates at each day's start and end point (including where the end and the next day's start are the same stamp – twice) and along the way. Arriving in O'Cebreiro, we are approaching 100 miles from Santiago, and for those who have already covered a lot of ground, the Camino should have become noticeably busier by now. This only increases markedly from Sarria itself, and then two more Caminos, the Primitivo and Norte join respectively from Melide and at Arzúa.

TO TRIACASTELA (21.2km)

In complete contrast to 'yesterday's stage', today's is 22km long and, until the descent of the last 7km – a drop of over 500m around the side of *Monte Calderon* – is fairly level. After 3km through the forest, arrive at the former flax producing village of **Liñares** (B|S).

1   **Linar do Rei** Pr 20 €12 N K|W|D|@|Cred
616 464 831 | Liñares s/n | linardorei@gmail.com

The **church of San Esteban** is 12th century, with very early 8th century origins, but like its neighbour back in O'Cebreiro, was rebuilt in the early 1960s. The Baroque altarpiece is unlikely to be viewed, as the building mostly remains closed.

Following the road more or less, the path climbs up for a kilometre to the *Alto de San Roque*, where a large modern **statue** of a medieval pilgrim strides out towards Santiago. There is also a small **chapel** here. A further climb – weather permitting, the views are stunning – takes us to **Hospital de la Condesa** (5.7km R|B), and its **church of**

2   **Xunta** X 18 €8 Y K|W|D *660 396 810*
Hospital da Condesa

San Juan with a rare cross of Santiago atop the tower. It too has early origins, while what you see here is 11th–12th century with very recent external restoration. Nothing remains of the hospital. As the track leaves the road temporarily, we come to **Padornelo** and the **Ermita San Juan**, the dedications reflecting that this area was assigned to the order of Malta. Its interior contains a Baroque altarpiece and several sculptures. We are still at over 1200m up, but a further short, steep climb brings us to **Alto do Poio** (8.5km R|B), at 1337m

Alto do Poio   *Jesus Solana CC BY 2.0*

3   **El Puerto** Pr 16 €8 (+ 4 Priv. €25 Dbl.) Y M|B
982 367 172 | at the foot of the LU-633

4   **Hostal Santa María** €31+/40 *982 367 167*
Alto do Poio | www.pensionsantamariadopoio.com

the highest point in Galicia on the Camino Francés. The path returns to parallel the road, before tracking right again, and into **Fonfría** (R|B|S).

5   **A Reboleira** Pr 50 €12 (+ 8 Priv. €40/45) Y
M|B|W|D|@ *982 181 271* | Fonfría 15
https://reboleirafonfria.com

6   **Pensión Casa Lucas** €40/45 *690 346 740*
Fonfría 25 | www.casadelucas.es

7   **Casa Rural Nuñez** €40/45+ *982 161 335* | Fonfría 15

The small village is named after a cold **fountain** which survives, but the hospital that famously gave light, salt, water and two blankets to the able-bodied, and additionally an egg, bread and lard to the sick, is no longer there to administer to modern pilgrims; however, as with all the previous villages on this stage, there is modern accommodation. The **church of San Juan** is 16th century. We start the descent gently.

We have travelled just over 12km from O'Cebreiro, and now, following the Albergue, we continue to track the road for most of the 2.5km into █O'Biduedo█ (14.3km **R|B**).

8 **Casa Rural Quiroga** €45 Dbl. *982 187 299*
O Biduedo s/n

9 **Casa Rural Xato** €25/30 *982 189 808* | O Biduedo 4

At the start of the village, the charming **Ermita de San Pedro** is claimed by some to be the smallest on the Way. From now on, the descent proper begins. After 3.5km cross a minor road and then pass under the main road, and through the hamlets of █Fillobal█ (**B**),

10 **Fillobal** Pr 18 €12 (+Priv. €30/40) Y K|W|D|@
666 826 414 Fillobal 2 | alberguefillobal@yahoo.es

█As Pasantes█ and █Ramil█.

TRIACASTELA (∞)

Triacastela   *Ikonya/shutterstock.com*

11 **Xunta** X 56 €8 Y K|W|D *982 548 087*
Rúa do Peregrino, s/n

12 **Lemos** Pr 12 €12 (+ Pensión €50 Dbl.) Y B|K|W|D|@
677 117 238 | Av. de Castilla 24
www.pensionalberguelemos.com

13 **Refugio del Oribio** Pr 27 €10 Y K|W|D|@
982 548 085 | Av. de Castilla 20
albergueoribio@gmail.com

14 **A Horta de Abel** Pr 14 €11 (+ 3 Priv. €35/40) N
K|W|D|@ *608 080 556* | Rúa do Peregrino 5
ahortadeabel@hotmail.com
http://alberguehortadeabel.es

15 **Atrio** Pr 20 €10 (+ 2 Priv. €40 Dbl.) N
M|B|K|W|D|@ *699 504 958* | Rúa do Peregrino 1–3
https://xoan65.wixsite.com/albergueatrio/inicio

16 **Complexo Xacobeo** Pr 36 €12 (+ Pensión €50 Dbl.)
Y* M|B|K|W|D|@ *982 548 037* | Rúa Santiago 8
www.complexoxacobeo.com | *Closed 21 Dec.– 31 Jan.

17 **Aitzenea** Pr 38 €10 N K|W|D|@ *982 548 076*
Pl. Vista Alegre 1 | www.aitzenea.com

18 **Berce do Camiño** Pr 27 €9 N K|W|D|@
982 548 127 | Av. Camilo José Cela 11

19 **Pensión García** €38+ Dbl. *621 200 607*
Rúa do Peregrino 1 | https://tinyurl.com/2rbehvcp

20 **Pensión Casa Simón** ** €49+ Dbl. *982 548 438*
Praza Iglesia 3 | www.pensioncasasimon.es

21 **Hostal Vilasante** €35/45 *982 548 116*
Av. Camilo José Sela 7 | pensionvilasante@gmail.com

The end of the 11th stage in Aymeric Picaud's Guide, and home to several hospitals and a monastery, Triacastela was the first town of note for pilgrims, having tackled the mountains after Villafranca. In truth, it never amounted to most of the other prior principal stops. The name suggests it once had three castles, and images of them are carved on the tower of the **church of Santiago**, just below a Santiago Peregrino in a niche. The tower is Baroque, otherwise the narrow single nave church is Romanesque with some 18th century remodelling, while internally the decoration is Baroque and Neoclassical. A tradition is remembered, whereby pilgrims would help with the construction of the cathedral at Santiago in lifting up a piece of limestone from the quarry outside the town, and carrying it to the kilns at Castañeda 90km away, to be made into mortar.

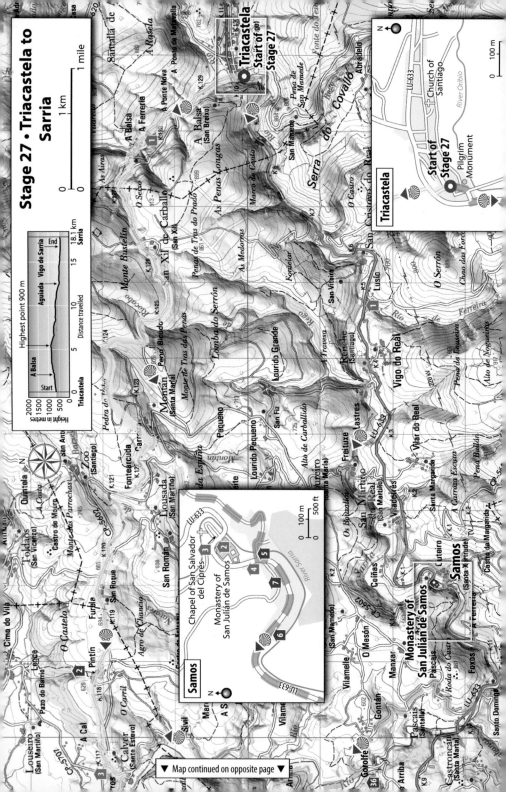

Stage 27 · Triacastela to Sarria

TO SARRIA (18.1km)

For pilgrims, there are two distinct choices, the *official route* via San Gil (San Xil) or the *option* that allows exploration of the monastery at Samos, a major site in its own right. The official route is just 17.2km long, but involves a climb. It is attractive and peaceful, the only roads it follows being minor ones.

The separation of the options – a junction – is a few steps from the departure from Triacastela. Here, there is a **pilgrim monument** – another statue of Santiago Peregrino, atop an obelisk of local stone.

For the *official route* turn right (just before the monument) and cross the main road (LU-633), following a minor road. Turn off right to **A Balsa**

1 **El Beso** Pr 16 €10 N M|B|W 633 550 558
A Balsa s/n | albergue@elbeso.org | www.elbeso.org

and, once across the river, a steep climb, past the small **chapel of San Antonio**. After more dense woodland, rejoin the road at a rest area that has a pond and enormous scallop shell marking a fountain, and into **San Gil** (3.7km). From this hamlet, the steep climb continues to the high point, *Alto de Riocabo* at approx. 900m. The path continues, looking down on the village of **Montán** (and its **Romanesque church**) which the old path used to pass through, until it descends into the hamlet of **Fontearcuda** (R|B)(again, to see the church, you have to divert: the road that you cross straight over also leads to the right to **Zoó** and its **church of Santiago**) and rejoins the road down to **Furela** (10km B). Pass another small **chapel**, dedicated to San Roque.

Then turn onto and over the road, to **Pintín** (11km R|B); this and the next village

2 **Pensión Casa Cines** ** €49 Dbl. 982 090 837
Pintín 5 | www.casacines.com

have accommodation.

Rejoin the road and enter **Calvor**.

3 **Xunta** X 22 €8 Y K|W|D 660 396 812 | Calvor

Pintín   lkonya/shutterstock.com

After **Aguiada** (B) at the hamlet of **Hospital**, the *Samos option* joins.

At **San Mamede del Camino** (14km B), it is 4km to Sarria itself. Continue to follow the minor road through a series of hamlets, until the connected village of **Vigo de Sarria** (R|B|S) on the outskirts of the town. Perhaps

4 **A Pedra** Pr 23 €12 (+ 4 Priv. €35/45-50 Dbl.) N
M|B|K|W|D|@ 652 517 199 | Vigo de Sarria 19
info@albergueapedra.com

5 **Oasis** Pr 27 €12 Y K|W|D 605 948 644
Vigo de Sarria 12 | reservas@albergueoasis.com

6 **Camping Vila de Sarria** €70 (Bungalow)
671 681 333 | Ctra. de Pintín 1km
www.campingviladesarria.com

7 **Pensión de Ana** * €44/61 982 531 458
Cimo de Agra 11 | www.pensionana.com

8 **Pensión Siete en el Camino** €35+/45+
615 334 367 | Ctra. de Pintín 10
www.sieteenelcamino.com

9 **Hostal dpCristal** ** €32+/44+ 669 799 512
Rua Calvo Sotelo 198 | www.dpcristal.com

stop at the information office of the Association of Friends of the Camino de Santiago. Cross the busy road, Rúa Calvo Sotelo to join Rúa do Peregrino, and then across the **bridge** over the Sarria river. Continue left up the stepped street to Rúa Maior and the main sights.

MONASTERY OF SAMOS AND ALTERNATIVE ROUTE TO SARRIA (25km to Sarria)

For pilgrims, the route out of Triacastela that takes in the monastery is longer, and while it follows the río Oribio, it also involves crossing the busy LU-633 besides a stretch right alongside it. It is also popular, one of the better used options. Leave Triacastela, turning off left at the junction to pass the pilgrim monument, which acknowledges the tradition of taking a stone to Castañeda. Cross the river, and the path runs alongside the main road for 3.5km. You have to cross the main road to take the road into San Cristobo do Real,

1   **Casa Forte de Lusío** X 60 €8 Y K
659 721 324/682 157 378 | Lusío 5 – 400m off Camino – restored 18th century monastery bldg.

from where the route becomes more peaceful. This village offers a pastoral scene, with the mill and weir on the river. Its **Palacio de Lusío** with its foundry (said to have made the gates to Lugo cathedral) dates from 1551, and the **church** features a 17th century altarpiece. A papal bull of 1175 mentions this and the next village belonging to the monastery of Samos.

Cross the river and follow the path for 1 km before crossing back over by a **chapel** and meeting the main road again in Renche (B), whose **church of Santiago** – another with visible Romanesque origins – contains a Santiago Peregrino in the main altarpiece. Continue away from the road and back down to and over the river, to climb a hill to the **chapel** in the hamlet of Freituxe (7km). Descend the hill and over the river again, and up to San Martiño do Real with its whitewashed **church** with decorated corbels. As with all the churches and chapels on the route to and from the monastery, it is a case of 'if' they are open; this church

has an interesting frescoed interior. It may have formed part of an early monastery of the 8th century. There is now a good view of Samos (9.5km ∞),nestled in the narrow

2   **Monasterio** Pa 66 Don N Basic †
982 546 046 | Av. de Compostela 1
www.abadiadesamos.com | Hospedería Hotel
€35+/40+ No meals. *643 639 226*
hospederiaexterna@abadiadesamos.com

3   **Tras do Convento** Pr 10 €12 (+ 2 Priv. €26+ Dbl.)
N M|B|W|D|@ *982 546 051* | Rua do Salvador 1
trasdoconvento@gmail.com

4   **Val de Samos** Pr 50 €15 N K|W|D|@
982 546 163 | Av. de Compostela 16
info@valdesamos.com | https://valdesamos.com

5   **Pensión Santa Rosa** €25+ *633 430 219*
Rúa Colledeiro 5 | Self-service kitchen.
www.samospensionsantarosa.com

6   **A Veiga** * €38+/48+ *982 546 052*
Av. de Compostela 61 | www.hotelaveiga.com

7   **Casa Rural Licerio** €45/55 *692 022 323*
Av. de Compostela 44
https://casalicerio.wixsite.com/casalicerio

Samos Monastery   lunamarina/shutterstock.com

valley; make a descent.

The **monastery of San Julián de Samos** is, quite simply, one of the oldest-established and largest in western Europe. Its origins are from about 655, when it is said to have been founded by San Martín Dumiense, and initially was home to a community of hermits. In the early 8th century, Alfonso I of Asturias underwent an education here, but Moorish incursions meant the monastery was abandoned and his successor, Fruela I, continued his father's lifelong *reconquista*

Upper gallery of the main cloister Jl FolpoC CC BY-SA 4.0

Altarpiece Jl FolpoC CC BY-SA 4.0

struggle by recapturing the area; when he was assassinated, the monastery gave refuge to his family. Nothing remains from that time; however, the tiny **chapel of San Salvador del Ciprés** is 9th century and has the eponymous tree right up against its structure. Most of today's monastery structure dates from the 16th and 17th centuries, following a serious fire in 1558. It has an 18th century **façade** (without its planned towers) and **steps**, with another fire in 1951 necessitating major reconstruction. It has mostly been home to a Benedictine community, who remain today in greatly reduced number, but there were power struggles, which included installing the Cluniac order in the 10th century, and abandonment in 1835. The institution produced seven bishops, and perhaps its most famous son was Benito Jerónimo Feijóo, a leading figure in the Spanish Enlightenment. His statue is in the **large cloister** – Baroque or classicist in style – and the largest in Spain. He commissioned the **monastery church**, built from 1734 to 1748. Its main altarpiece contains a statue of the patron by José Ferreiro. Another, A Inmaculada by Francisco de Moure, features a statue of the Virgin. The **Small cloister** – neo Gothic in style – contains the **fountain of the Nereids**, said to

be designed by Velázquez; it is 'supported' by serpentine bodies with the heads of women. The **library** holds 25 000 volumes; it was once considered one of the most important in the country, but was badly depleted of originals in the later fire. The monastery is open every day, with later opening at 12.00 on Sundays and public holidays. Guided tours €5; **Mass with Pilgrim blessing** at 7.30pm. There is an Albergue and Hospedería retreat plus hotel as part of the monastery, and a range of other accommodation in the town.

Leaving Samos, follow the main road out of the town, where, after a short while, the river joins. At Teiguín, the small **chapel** is dedicated to Santo Domingo. Cross the road and turn off on a path [recommended – though some people prefer to walk all along the road into Sarria instead and save 2.5+km] to Pascais, climbing, left onto a path and left again by the **church of Santa Eulalia**, which preserves its Romanesque apse and north door. Another 2km, now of undulating descent, and heading northwest, brings us to Gorolfe (15.3km) and its **chapel**. Continue, to rejoin the river, and after another 5km – via Sivil (B) and through a tunnel under the

8 **Pensión A Fonte das Bodas** €49+ Dbl. *637 138 636* | Sivil 1 | https://afontedasbodas.com

road at Aguiada – join the official route, and continue into Sarria.

Sarria

SARRIA (∞)

⑩ **Xunta** X 40 €8 Y K|W|D|Cred *660 396 813*
Rúa Mayor 79

⑪ **Monasterio de la Magdalena** Pa 110 €12
N K|W|D|@|Cred *982 533 568* | Av. de la Merced 60
www.alberguesdelcamino.com

⑫ **San Lázaro** Pr 27 €10–12 (+ 4 Priv. €28/35) N
W|D|@|Cred (order ahead) *659 185 482* | Rúa San
Lázaro 7 | www.alberguesanlazaro.com

⑬ **Barullo** Pr 20 €11–14 (+ Priv. €32+ Dbl.) N
B|K|W|D|@ *698 108 755* | Pl. de Galicia 40
barullosarria@gmail.com | https://alberguebarullo.com

⑭ **Alma do Camiño** Pr 100 €13 (+ Priv. available) N
B|K|W|D|@|Cred *629 822 036* | Rúa Calvo Sotelo
199 | www.almadelcamino.com

⑮ **Credencial** Pr 28 €12 Y M|B|W|D|@|Cred
982 876 455 | Rúa do Peregrino 50
www.alberguecredencial.es

⑯ **Puente Ribeira** Pr 28 €12 (+ 8 Priv. €27+/47+) N
B|W|D|@|Cred *982 876 789* | Rúa do Peregrino 23
www.alberguepuenteribeira.com

⑰ **Casa Peltre** Pr 22 €12 N K|W|D|@|Cred *606 226 067*
Rúa Escalinata Maior 10 | hola@alberguecasapeltre.es

⑱ **Mayor** Pr 16 €12 N K|W|D|@ *680 110 093*
Rúa Mayor 64 (Entrance at R/ Pedreiras 1)
alberguemayor@gmail.com | www.alberguemayor.com

⑲ **O Durmiñento** Pr 38 €10 N M|B|W|D|@|Cred
600 862 508 | Rúa Mayor 44
durmiento_sarria@hotmail.com

⑳ **Internacional** Pr 38 €10+ (+ Priv. €45+) N M|B|W|D|@
982 535 109 | Rúa Mayor 57
www.albergueinternacionalsarria.es

㉑ **Obradoiro** Pr 38 €11 N K|W|D|@ *982 532 442*
Rúa Mayor 49 | reservas@albergueobradoirosarria.es

㉒ **Los Blasones** Pr 42 €11 N M|B|K|W|D|@|Cred
600 512 565 | Rúa Mayor 31
https://albergueselosblasones.com | Also Pensión

㉓ **Don Álvaro** Pr 40 €15 (+ 7 Priv. €40+/50+) Y
K|W|D|@ *982 531 592* | Rúa Mayor 10
info@albergueduonalvaro.com | Also Pensión

㉔ **Matías Locanda** Pr 32 €10 (+ 42 Priv. €35+ Dbl.) N
M|B|W|D|@ *982 886 112* | Rúa Mayor 4
info@matiaslocanda.es

㉕ **El Bordón de la Casa Batallón** Pr 6 Don (+ 4 Priv.
€12/24) Y K|M|B|W *982 530 652* | Rúa Mayor 29
www.casabatallon.com

㉖ **Hostel Andaina** Pr 26 €13 N K|W|D|@|Cred
628 232 103 | Rúa Calvo Sotelo 11
https://hostelandaina.com

㉗ **Sleeping Sarria Hostel** €48 Dbl. *689 319 941*
Ctra. Esqueiredos 1 | sleepingsarriahostel@gmail.com

㉘ **Pensión Casa Matías** €27+/45 *659 160 498*
Rúa Calvo Sotelo 39 | https://casamatias39.com

㉙ **Pensión Escalinata** €40/50
982 886 540/627 321 765 | Rúa Mayor 76

㉚ **La Casona de Sarria** ** €49+ Dbl. *982 535 556*
Rúa San Lázaro 24 (Reception at Rúa Porvir 50 –
Posada Hostal hotel) | www.lacasonadesarria.es

㉛ **Baixo a Lua – Rooming** €60 Dbl. *698 177 153*
Rúa do Peregrino 37 | https://baixoalua.com

㉜ **Pensión Estación** ** €28+ Dbl. *658 094 994*
Rúa Matías Lopéz 106 (2nd fl.)

㉝ **Hotel Mar de Plata** * €42+/50+ *982 530 724*
Rúa Formigueiros 5 | www.hotelmardeplata.com

㉞ **Hotel Novoa** * €58/68 *982 605 021* | Pl. de la
Constución 4 | https://hotel-novoa.negocio.site/

㉟ **Hotel Alfonso IX** **** €50+/60+ *982 530 005*
Rúa do Peregrino 29 | www.alfonsoix.com

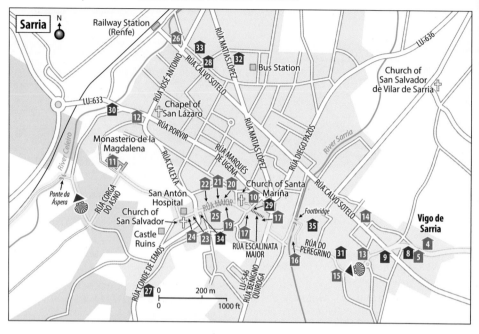

by King Alfonso IX of León and Galicia, who died here in 1230 while making his pilgrimage to Santiago, to give thanks to the Saint for his victory over the Moors at Mérida. After that tragic event, the town's importance only grew; a couple of the seven pilgrims' hospitals survive today. Its influence continued through the 16th century, the patronage of Ferdinand and Isabella dispensed by the Marquises of Sarria, one of whom built a new hospital, **San Antón**, which now houses the law court. Among the town's famous sons and daughters is Gregorio Fernández (1576–1636) the master sculptor whose works we have seen in so many churches. Nowadays a modern town of over 13 000 inhabitants (Municipality), there are also some notable 19th century buildings. Industries include furniture production; it is a centre of agriculture and, of course, tourism. Sarria is also a centre for antique shops and fairs.

Archaeological finds attest to thousands of years of habitation in this area, including Celts and Swabians, and Romans, but the town was founded at the end of the 12th century

The **rail and bus stations** are on the northwest side of town, this being a major point of arrival for those who are walking *in*

Church of Santa Mariña

effect the last 100km to Santiago to collect the Compostela; there are direct and connected routes from all over Spain. To cater for all arrivals, there are many albergues and other accommodation, but they do fill up.

Beginning at the bottom of Rúa Maior, climb the steps, and on the right is the **church of Santa Mariña**, dedicated to a Galician saint. It is actually a 19th century church, built over a 13th century one.

Credencials can be stamped at the church – don't forget to start your pilgrim's passport with your first *selo* (stamp) before you leave Sarria on the day of departure if you are starting your Camino here. And you have to get a stamp at your stopping place, and then another at the same place when you start the next day, with written dates – and so on. It is still possible to start it after you leave Sarria – *see Ferreiros on P222* – but not advisable, so why not make a symbolic start here?

The small **church of San Salvador** has a late Romanesque ground plan, and early

Gothic façade, with later belfry. There is some fine carving on both portals and the corbels, together with ornamental iron work in the north gate. After this and the former hospital of San Antón, you can see what remains of the castle – a tower and a section of wall – destroyed during the 15th century Spanish peasants' revolt, but rebuilt, then later abandoned. Turning right, up Rúa da Mercede, the **former prison** is a neoclassical green and white coloured building. At the end of the avenue, is the **Monasterio de la Magdalena**. It was founded in 1200 by Italian friars, who sought the permission of the bishop of Lugo to look after pilgrims, initially in a hermitage. The church was built in the 13th century, and retains Romanesque features and Isabelline Gothic decoration. There are several tombs and a cloister. Since 1896 the monastery has been home to a community of fathers of the order of Mercy. Then, the **chapel of San Lázaro** (Separately: towards the rail station along Rúa Porvir, turn right onto Rúa José Antonio) is all that remains of the pilgrims' hospital dedicated to the care of lepers, founded in the 16th century; the chapel itself is 18th century. **Mass schedules** in the town include San Lázaro (7pm Mon–Sat), Magdalena (8pm in summer, 1pm Sundays), and Santa Mariña (7.30pm in summer, 12pm Sundays).

Chapel of San Lázaro   Norrin strange CC BY-SA 4.0

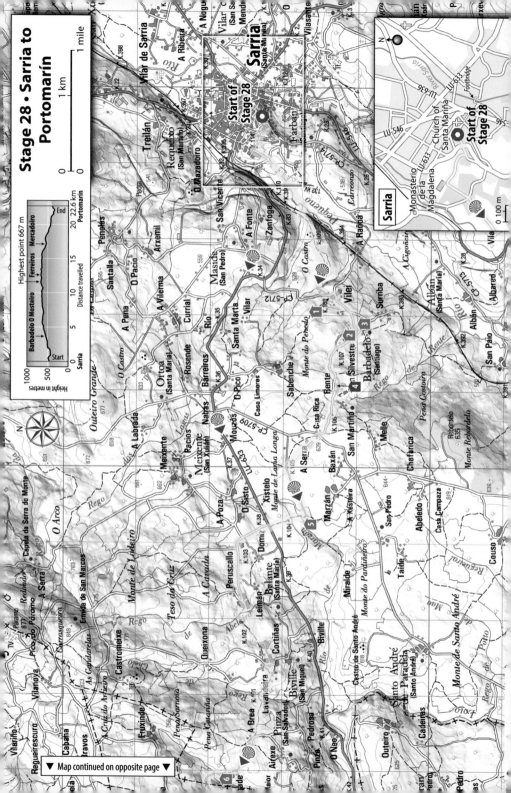

Stage 28 · Sarria to Portomarín

Highest point 667 m

Height in metres

Start — Sarria

Barbadelo 0 Mostairo

Ferreiros · Mercadoiro

End

Distance travelled

Sarria ... Portomarín

Sarria

▼ Map continued on opposite page ▼

TO PORTOMARÍN (22.6km)

After the Monasterio de la Magdalena, descend the hill to cross the río Celeiro at the **Ponte da Áspera** and down towards the rail line, eventually passing underneath it and the CG-2.2 motorway. Cross a stream and continue up through beautiful, mainly oak woodland. Join a road, and continue into **Barbadelo Vilei** (R|B)

1 **Casa Barbadelo** Pr 48 €12 (+ 11 Priv. €60 Dbl.) N
M|B|W|D|@|Pool 982 531 934 | Vilei 108km
www.barbadelo.com

(*Vilei is arrived at first*) and then into **Barbadelo O Mosteiro** (3.6km **B**).

2 **Xunta** X 18 €8 Y K|W|D 982 530 412 | O Mosteiro

3 **O Pombal** Pr 12 €12 N K|W|D|@ 686 718 732
Surriba-Barbadelo
www.albergueopombal.blogspot.com

4 **Casa Rural Casa Nova de Rente** €25+/30+
982 187 854 | Rente, 1km on from O Mosteiro
casaruralnovaderente@hotmail.com

Barbadelo   *José Antonio Gil Martínez CC BY 2.0*

Its Romanesque **church of Santiago** was once part of a monastery, and while its robust appearance with carved tympanum and archivolts may attract you, it is the interior that has earned the church the designation as a national monument, with carved capitals and Santiago Peregrino polychrome altarpiece.

Continue along the road, and cross over a lane north of **Baxán** (B|S). Pass the restored mill by the río Marzán.

5 **Molino de Marzán** Pr 15 €12 N M B W D @
679 438 077 | Lugar de Molino de Marzán
inf.marzan@gmail.com

Cross over the main LU-633 to **Leimán** for a further 4km [past **B**] through several more hamlets, including **A Brea** (B), before reaching **Morgade** (B).

6 **Casa Morgade** Pr 6 €14 (+12 Priv. €52+/52+)
N M|B|W|D|@ 676 535 369 | Morgade s/n
www.casamorgade.com

Pass a **chapel**, and another kilometre brings us to **Ferreiros** (12.5km R|B).

7 **Xunta** X 20 €8 Y K|W|D 982 157 496/660 396 815
Ferreiros s/n

8 **Casa Cruceiro** Pr 24 €12 (+2 Priv. €50 Dbl.) N
M|B|W|D|@|Cred 639 020 064 | Ferreiros 2
www.casacruceirodeferreiros.com

The waymarking has been changed, and so here you are just over 100km to Santiago, and it's your last chance to start your Credencial at the Albergue's café/restaurant.

The small Romanesque **church of Santa María** – at **Mirallos** (R) – was moved stone by stone from its original location. The café/restaurant here no longer offers Albergue or other lodgings. The ascent becomes steeper as we pass through **Pena** (B) and **Rozas** (B), with a high point at *Pena dos Corvos* (660m). We can see the reservoir – *Embalse de Belesar* – of the río Miño ahead. We are not far from the río Loyo and the scant **ruins** of the monastery that was the spiritual home of the order of Santiago. Hamlets to pass through include **Moimentos**, **Mercadoiro** (R|B),

9 **Mercadoiro** Pr 22 €12 (+ 4 Priv. €50+ Dbl.) N
M|B|W|D|@ 982 545 359 | Aldea de Mercadoiro 2
https://www.mercadoiro.com

Moutras (S), and **A Parrocha** (B). At **Vilachá**, (R|B) pick up the road, descending on some

10 **Vilachá** Pr 10 €13 N M|B|W|D|@ 696 004 491
Vilachá 10 | alberguevilacha@gmail.com

11 **Casa Banderas** 9 €27 MB&B N W|D|@|Picnic
682 179 589 | Vilachá 5 | https://casabanderas.com

Portomarín Bridges   ©Javier stock.adobe.com

Portomarín   *El fosilmaníaco CC BY-SA 3.0*

new path, and cross the modern road bridge high above one of northern Spain's principal rivers, towards the town. Climb up the old steps to enter Portomarín, or go left to bypass and continue your day's journey.

PORTOMARÍN (∞)

12 **Xunta** X 86 €8 Y K|W|D *660 396 816*
Rúa Fraga Iribarne (at Travesía de Lugo)

13 **Casona da Ponte** Pr 47 €13 (+ Pensión €60 Dbl.) Y
B|K|W|D|@ *982 169 862* | Camiño da Capela 10
casonadaponte@gmail.com

14 **Pons Minea** Pr 24 €12 (+Priv. €40/50) Y M|B|W|D|@
686 456 931 | Av. de Sarria 11
info@ponsminea.es

15 **Ferramentiero** Pr 130 €13 N B|K|W|D|@
982 545 362 | Av. Chantada 3
info@albergueferramenteiro.com

16 **Folgueira** Pr 32 €12 Y M|B|K|W|D|@ *982 545 166*
Av. Chantada 18 | www.alberguefolgueira.com

17 **Aqua Portomarín** Pr 10 €12 (+ 3 Priv. €40+/45+)
N B|K|W|D|@ *608 921 372* | Rúa Barreiros 2
albergueaquaportomarin@hotmail.com

18 **Ultreia** Pr 14 €12 (+5 Priv. €30+/35+) Y K|W|D|@
982 545 067 | Rúa Diputación 9
info@ultreiaportomarin.com

19 **Porto Santiago** Pr 7 €15+ (+ 4 Priv. €45+/55+) Y
K|W|D|@ *618 826 515* | Rúa Diputación 8
www.albergueportosantiago.com

20 **El Caminante** Pr 15 €12 (Pensión at Rúa Sánchez
Carro 2 €33+/47+) N M|B|W|D|@ *696 071 565* | Rúa
Benigno Quiroga 8 | http://alberguelcaminante.com

21 **Villamartín** Pr 22 €12 N M|B|K|W|D|@
982 545 054 | Rúa dos Peregrinos 11
https://alberguevillamartin.webnode.es/

22 **Huellas** Pr 6 €14+ (+ 3 Priv. €34/37) Y
K|W|D|@ *681 398 278* | Rúa dos Peregrinos 15
https://alberguehuellas.com

23 **Novo Porto** Pr 22 €12 N K|W|D|@ *610 436 736*
Rúa Benigno Quiroga 12 | www.albergenovoporto.com

24 **Casa Cruz** Pr 16 €12 N M|B|K|W|D|@ *982 545 140*
Rúa Benigno Quiroga 16 | info@casacruzportomarin.com

25 **Pasiño a Pasiño** Pr 30 €12 Y K|W|D|@
665 667 243 | Rúa de Compostela 25
alberguepasoapaso@gmail.com | www.pasinapasin.es

26 **Casa do Marabillas** Pr 16 €12–14 (+ 2 Priv. €30/35)
N B|K|W|D|@ *744 450 425* | Camiño do Monte 3
casadomarabillas@gmail.com
www.casadomarabillas.com

27 **Manuel** Pr 16 €12 (+ 4 Priv. €28/30) Y K|W|D|@
982 545 385 | Rúa do Miño 1
https://alberguemanuel.com

28 **Baires** Pr 5 €15-18 (+ 3 Priv. €39+) Y W|@
645 118 958 | Barreiros 1

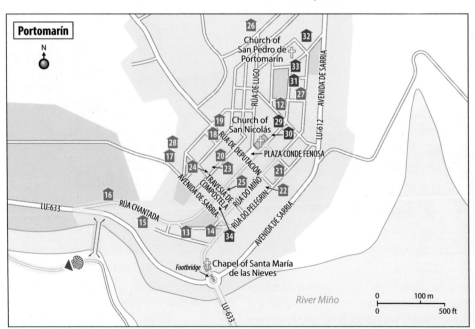

29 Pensión Mar * €35+/50+ *622 611 211*
Rúa Fraga Iribarne 5 | www.pensionmar.com

30 Casa do Maestro *** €55+/65+ *626 510 806*
Rúa Fraga Iribarne 1 | www.casadomaestro.com

31 Hostal El Padrino *** €60/70 *665 586 070*
Rúa Fraga Iribarne 18 | http://hostalelpadrino.com/

32 Hotel Pousada de Portomarín *** €56
M+B&B+Picnic | Pilgrim's package *982 545 200*
Av. de Sarria s/n | www.pousadadeportomarin.es

33 Hotel Pazo de Berbetoros ** €60+/ 75+ *982 545 292*
Rúa San Pedro s/n | www.pazodeberbetoros.com

34 Hotel Vistalegre ** €80+ Dbl. *982 545 076*
Rúa de Compostela 29 | www.vistalegrehotel.com

Portomarín: San Nicolás   *Cruccone CC BY-SA 3.0 ES*

The town you see today only dates from 1962. The original is under the reservoir, after the Miño was dammed here and further upstream. However, the two oldest surviving churches – both Romanesque – were dismantled and rebuilt on the higher ground of the new town; the numbers on the stones were put there to aid reconstruction. Habitation in the area predates the Romans, who had a settlement here, but the medieval town's precise origins are subject to differing accounts. There was a series of military clashes, including between Queen Urraca and her husband Alfonso I of Aragón, in which the main bridge was destroyed, before later being rebuilt. At one point, three orders, the Knights Templar, the order of Santiago, and the order of St John, all had bases here, with the knights of Santiago having their own bridge that connected with a road to the monastery of San Xoán de Loio. The town was divided into two districts, San Pedro and San Nicolás, with the order of St John occupying the latter. The town is well known for its brandy, its eel pies, and its tarta de Santiago. There are some attractive green spaces for those who want to enjoy their picnic of local produce.

At the entrance to the town, a small part of the **old bridge** – originally Roman – has been preserved, unusually doubling as steps out of the (now submerged) old town, to the **chapel of Santa María de las Nieves**, which is located in the arch. It was probably the chapel to the hospital run by the order of St John. The main street, Rúa Xeral Franco, is part colonnaded, to replicate what was in the old town. It leads to the Plaza Conde Fenosa, where we find the **church of San Nicolás**. Alternatively named the church of San Juan, in honour of the order who built it, this sturdy tower church has a distinct military look to it. Its main feature is the pleasing west façade, with its geometric rose window over a tympanum carved with a Pantocrator, and archivolts featuring a representation of the 24 elders of the Revelation. The east end is also decorated with a smaller rose, and carvings. The north portal shows scenes from the Annunciation. The south portal is also finely carved. So much so, that the exterior has been attributed to Master Mateo, he of Santiago cathedral. Inside, there is much less decoration, but the highlight may well be a 14th century polychrome Crucifix. The **Pazo del Conde da Maza** is a palace that was similarly salvaged. At the upper end of the town, we find the second Romanesque church, the smaller **church of San Pedro**, with an attractive portal.

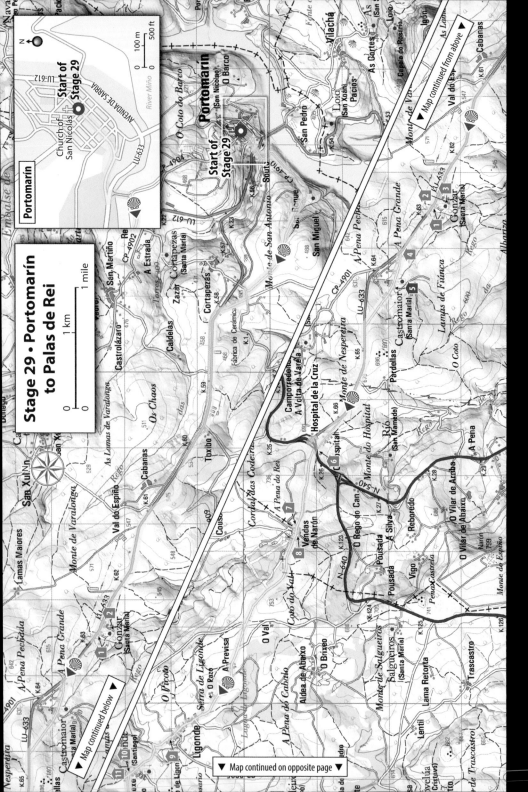

Stage 29 • Portomarín to Palas de Rei

Portomarín

Church of San Nicolás

Start of Stage 29

AVENIDA DE SARRIA

River Miño

Embalse de

Start of Stage 29

Portomarín (Ben Nicolao)

O Barco

O Coto do Barco

San Pedro

Vilachá

As Cortes

Loio (San Xoán)

Pacios

Igón

Cabanas

Val do Est

K.61

K.62

Monte de Va

A Pena Grande

Gonzar (Santa María)

K.63

Monte de San Antonio

San Miguel

A Pena Pecha

A Pena Grande

LU-633

CP-4901

Castromaior (Santa María)

Pardellas

Lamas de Fránca

O Coto

Rego

A Pena

A Previsa

O Val

O Brixeo

O Pato

Aldea de Abaixo

Serra de Ligonde

Ligonde

O Picoto

A Pena do Cabalo

Monte de Salgueiros

Salgueiros (Santa María)

Lama Retorta

Lentil

Trascastro

Pena Castrela

Vigo

Reboredo

A Silva

Pousada

Pousada

O Rego do Can

O Vilar de Arriba

O Vilar de Abaixo

Monte do Hospital

Río (San Mamede)

Monte de Nespereira

Hospital de la Cruz

A Volta de Varela

Camporredon

Cousso

A Pena do Rei

Cabanas

Val do Espiño

As Lamas de Varalonga

Monte de Varalonga

Lamas Maiores

San Xul/N

Ox Chaos

Caldelas

Castrolázaro

A Estrada

San Martiño

Cortapezas (Santa María)

Zazar

Fábrica de Cerámica

Toxibo

Cordal das Codorñas

Veñdas de Narón

Narón

Castromaior (Santa María)

A Pena Grande

Gonzar (Santa María)

A Pena Pechada

▲ Map continued from above ▲

▲ Map continued below ▲

▼ Map continued on opposite page ▼

N

0   100 m
0   500 ft

0   1 km
0   1 mile

Cartographic base © ign.es

The Church of San Salvador

Palas de Rei

End of Stage 29

Church of San Tirso

See map on page 231 for details of accommodation in Palas de Rei.

End of Stage 29

Palas de Rei

Highest point 725 m

Height in metres

Portomarín — Castromaior — Eirexe — Palas de Rei

Distance travelled

Start — End

25.1 km

End of Stage 29

Ponterroxán

TO PALAS DE REI (25.1km)

To leave Portomarín on the Camino, go back down to the rivers and reservoir and go right uphill from yesterday's crossing, or along Avda./ Rúa Chantada and turn left. Traditionally, one crossed the high rusty iron-railing footbridge, over the río Da Barrela: however, thankfully for many, this has been closed in recent years (perhaps to aid digestion of breakfast!) and now you cross via the road bridge. Keep right. Begin a gentle climb through woodland, coming out to criss-cross the road by some factories at Toxibó (4.7km). A track away from the road leads to Gonzar (R|B) and its small

1 Xunta X 28 €8 Y K|W|D Gonzar s/n

2 Casa García Pr 26 €10 (+ 4 Priv. €35 Dbl.) N
M|B|W|D 982 157 842 | Gonzar 8

3 Albergue-Hostería de Gonzar Pr 20 €10–12 (+ 13 Priv. in Hostería €45/55) N M|B|W|D|@|Pool 982 154 878 | Gonzar 7 | https://hosteriadegonzar.com

Romanesque **church of Santa María** (statue of the Virgin from same era and 16th century altarpiece) – 7km from the river crossing in Portomarín. A kilometre later, at Castromaior (9.2km **B**), the remains of the *Castro* are on the

4 Ortiz Pr 12 €12 (+ 4 Priv. €25/45-50) N M (on request)|B|W|D|@ 982 099 416 | Castromaior 2 | info@albergueortiz.com

5 Casa Perdigueira €40 Dbl. 690 852 026 Castromaior 9

hill; we pass its own small Romanesque **church**. At Hospital de la Cruz (2.5km **B**), nothing

6 Xunta X 32 €8 Y K|W|D At exit of the village

remains of the pilgrims' hospital that gives the village its name; cross over the N-540 main Lugo to Ourense road. Ventas de Narón (13km R|B)

7 Casa Molar Pr 18 €10 (+ 2 Priv. €30 Dbl.) N M|B|W|D|@ 696 794 507 | Ventas 4casamolarventas@gmail.com

8 O Cruceiro Pr 26 €12 (+ 6 Priv. €30/35) N M|B|W|D|@ 658 064 917 | Ventas 6 www.albergueocruceiro.blogspot.com

also had a pilgrims' hospital, with the **Ermita de Santa María Magdalena** being most of what remains. Earlier, in 840, it is said to have been the scene of a battle between Christian and Moorish forces, but this is not the same Narón (near Ferrol) where in 825 Alfonso II of Asturias scored one of his victories. We continue to climb the sierra de Ligonde, to the high point at 750m (path is approx. 30m lower).

Descend to **Lameiros** and **Ligonde** (R|B),

🚰 **Fuente del Peregrino** A 9 Don N M|B *687 550 527*
Ligonde 4 | www.lafuentedelperegrino.com

passing the **ruins** of the pilgrims' hospital. The cemetery was originally for pilgrims; the **Casa de Carneiro** hosted Charles V on his way to be crowned Holy Roman Emperor in 1520, and also Philip II on his way to La Coruña and England, to marry Mary Tudor in 1554.

At the hamlet of **Eirexe** (17km R|B), the

🔟 **Xunta** X 20 €8 Y K|W|D *679 816 061* Airexe 7

⓫ **Pensión Eirexe** €25/40* *982 153 475* | Airexe 18
pensioneirexe@yahoo.com | * Also 4 bunk places in a room @ €10. Open Easter to November.

cruceiro de Ligonde is one of the most famous wayside crosses on the Camino; standing in front of an old oak tree, on one side is an image of Christ on the Cross and on the other, an image of the Virgin and Child, with images of the Passion such as the crown of thorns, hammer and nails; it is dated 1670. The **church of Santiago** is Neoclassical but with the Romanesque façade recovered from the previous church. At **Portos** (19.2km B), 2km

⓬ **A Paso de Formiga** Pr 11 €13 (+ 2 Priv. €50/70) N M|B|W|D|@ *618 984 605* | Portos 4
www.apasodeformiga.com

on, there is the opportunity to detour (5–6km round trip) right, to **Vilar de Donas** to see the church of the knights of Santiago, their tombs and the frescoes. Alternatively, it can be done later by taxi from Palas de Rei. **Pilgrims' Mass** at 7pm (6pm winter).

THE CHURCH OF SAN SALVADOR AT VILAR DE DONAS

Closed Mondays. The custodian will take great care in explaining the church's features, but not in English. The order of Santiago in 1184 took over a monastery that had been a convent, which had given the village the name, *Donas*. They built the single nave Romanesque church, which has three apses;

Vilar de Donas fresco

ruins of the monastery cloister can also be seen. The Romanesque **doorway** is protected by a glass canopy and framed on one side by a carved **anteportico** that was another part of the monastery; its five carved archivolts and richly decorated capitals have much of the fine detail preserved. There is further detail around the windows.

Inside, the upright **tombstones** of some of the knights of Santiago greet you in the **porch** *(see page 14)*. More tombs of the knights, who died, sometimes defending the

Altar stone   *Lameiro CC BY-SA 4.0*

Camino in Galicia, are to be found in the church. The **altar stone** depicts the miracle at O'Cebreiro.

There is a Gothic stone **baldachin** dating from the 15th century. The church is famed for its **frescoes**, considered the most important in Galicia. Painted in the 14th century, some depict the founding ladies, while others include the Annunciation and the Resurrection.

The path continues through Lestedo ,

13 **Casa Rectoral** €65+/73+ *982 196 563* | Lestedo s/n
www.rectoraldelestedo.com

14 **Hostería Calixtino** €57+/72+ *670 500 900* | Os Valos
www.hosteriacalixtino.com

where the former pilgrims' hospital, which later became a rectory, has been restored and converted into a boutique hotel.

At A Brea (21.5km **R**), the path joins briefly parallel to the N-547, before moving on to Rosario . The hamlet looks up to *Alto do Rosario*, or 'Holy Mountain'. Here, most pilgrims would recite the Rosary, for they believed that this is the mountain where Queen Lupa sent James' followers to re-bury his remains, and where they tamed a dragon and oxen *(see page 12)*.

Resume tracking the main road and then a park to enter the busy pilgrim town of Palas de Rei .

PALAS DE REI (∞)

15 **Os Chacotes** X 112 €8 Y K|W|D|@ *607 481 536*
Rúa As Lagartas s/n [Os Chacotes 1km before Palas de Rei]

16 **Palas de Rei** X 60 €8 Y K|W|D *660 396 820*
Ctra. de Compostela 19

17 **Mesón de Benito** Pr 78 €12 N M|B|W|D|@
636 834 065 | Rúa da Paz
www.alberguemesondebenito.com

18 **San Marcos** Pr 70 €12–15 (Also Pensión €60 Dbl.)
N B|K|W|D|@ *982 380 711* | Travesía de la Iglesia
www.alberguesanmarcos.es

19 **Outeiro** Pr 64 €12 N K|W|D|@ *630 134 357*
Pl. de Galicia 25 | www.albergueouteiro.com

20 **Zendoira** Pr 50 €12–15 (+6 Priv. €30+/40+)
N B|K|W|D|@ *608 490 075*
Rúa Amado Losada 10 | www.zendoira.com

21 **Castro** Pr 60 €12 Y M|B|W|D|@ *982 380 321*
Av. de Ourense 24 | info@alberguecastro.com

22 **Buen Camino** Pr 42 €12 N M|B|W|D|@
982 380 233 | Rúa do Peregrino 3
www.alberguebuencamino.com

23 **A Casiña di Marcello** Pr 17 €15–20 Y M|W|D|@
640 723 903 | Rúa Camiño da Aldea de Abaixo (exit from the town) | albergueacasina@gmail.com

24 **Hostel O Castelo** €40–50 Dbl. *618 401 130*
Rúa do Cruceiro 14 | www.hostelocastelo.com

25 **Pensión O Cruceiro** *** €55/60 *982 380 205*
Rúa do Cruceiro 13 | www.pensionocruceiro.com

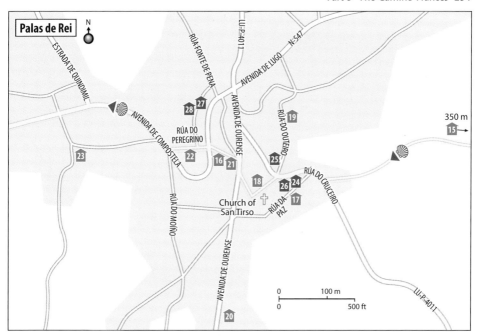

Palas de Rei

N

RÚA FONTE DE PENA
ESTRADA DE QUINDIMIL
LU-P-4011
AVENIDA DE LUGO
N-547
AVENIDA DE COMPOSTELA
AVENIDA DE OURENSE
RÚA DO PEREGRINO
RÚA DO OUTEIRO
RÚA DO MOÍÑO
RÚA DO CRUCEIRO
RÚA DA PAZ
AVENIDA DE OURENSE
LU-P-4011

350 m
15

Church of San Tirso

28 27
23
22
16 21
18
19
25
26 24
17
20
15

0   100 m
0   500 ft

🏨 **Hotel Mica** * €50/70 *982 179 311*
26   Rúa do Cruceiro 12 | www.hotelmica.com

🏨 **Pensión Arenas Palas** ** €36/50 *982 380 326*
27   Av. Compostela 16 | www.arenaspalas.com

🏨 **Pensión Casa As Hortas** *** €59/79 *626 518 388*
28   Rúa das Hortas 7 | https://pensionashortas.com

Church of San Tirso   *Ikonya/shutterstock.com*

The **church of San Tirso** has retained its Romanesque portal, but is otherwise rebuilt, a

quite common feature in these parts. The end of the 12ᵗʰ stage in the Codex Calixtinus, Palas de Rei is nowadays a modern town, with its historic monuments lying outside in the wider municipality. The town takes its name from *Pallatium Regis*; Visigothic King Witiza (reigned c.694–c.710) is said to have built a palace here. Further west, there are turnings off south to the **Castle of Pambre**. Built on a rock above the river Pambre in the late 14ᵗʰ century by the powerful Ulloa family, in response to peasant uprisings, it is one of the finest surviving examples of military architecture in Galicia. It is possible to go inside in summer, and although there is not very much to see, efforts are being made to resolve this. Approx. 1 hour (4.5km) from Casanova with accommodations at **Sambreixo** and **O Vilar de Remonde**.

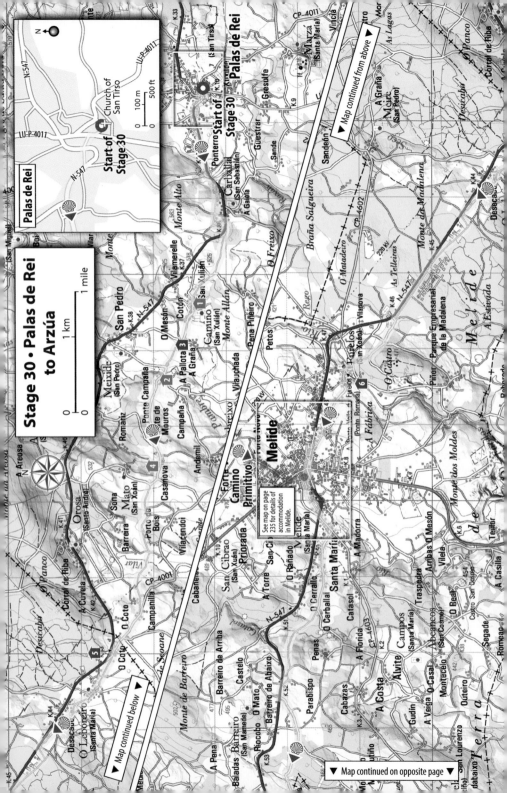

Stage 30 • Palas de Rei to Arzúa

Palas de Rei

inset map:
N
LU-P-4011
N-547
N-547
Church of San Tirso
Start of Stage 30
0 100 m
0 500 ft

Start of Stage 30
Palas de Rei

▼ Map continued from above ▼

0 1 km
0 1 mile

Ponterro
San Tirso (San Tirso)
Carballal (San Sebastián)
A Gaiola
Guéstar
Sande
Giesulfe
Marzá (Santa María)
Sandeón
A Graña
Mácre (San Pedro)
Monte da Madalena
As Lagas
Corral de Riba
Corral de Riba
Monte Alto
Viamerelle
Cotón
O Mesón
1 San Xulián
Camiño (San Xulián)
3 A Pallota
A Graña
Braña Salgueira
O Mataduoiro
As Telleiras
Pena Piñeiro
Petos
O Frezo
Vilaova
Pardos (San Xoán)
O Castro
Piñor
Parque Empresarial de la Madalena
A Estrada
M e l i d e
Meixide (San Pedro)
San Pedro
Romaníz
Ponte Campaña
2
Campaña
te de Mouros
4
Vilauchada
Vilaucha
Andimil
Viauchada
Arxeixo
Melide
6
O Cátiro
A Fábrica
See map on page 235 for details of accommodation in Melide.
Forte
Camiño Primitivo
Meide
(Santa María)
A Madorra
O Mesón
Arribas
Vilela
Vilela
Monte dos Moldes
Teijor
A Casilla
Sóña Mato (San Xoán)
Casanova
Vilacendói
Porto Bois
San Cibrao (San Xulián)
Prioraba
San-Ci
A Torre
O Rañado
O Carballo
Santa María
Santa María
Catasol
Traspedra
O Beat
Romea
Segade
Orosa (San Andel)
Barreira
Cabañeiro
Campanilla
Penas
A Florida
Campos (Santa María)
A Costa
A Veiga
Gudín
Outeiro
A Coto
O Cato
Barreiro de Arriba
Castelo
O Mato
Riocobo
Parabispo
Cabazas
O Casal
Montrucelo (San Cosme)
Castro San Cosme
A Casilla
A Cuvela
Corral de Riba
Descaba
O Panco
5
O Coto
Monte de Barreiro
Barreiro de Abaixa
A Costa
Abcanoo (San Cosme)
San Lourenzo
A Pena
Báladas
Barreiro (San Mamede)
5 O Cato
Leboreiro (Santa María)
Desecáu

▼ Map continued below ▼

▼ Map continued on opposite page ▼

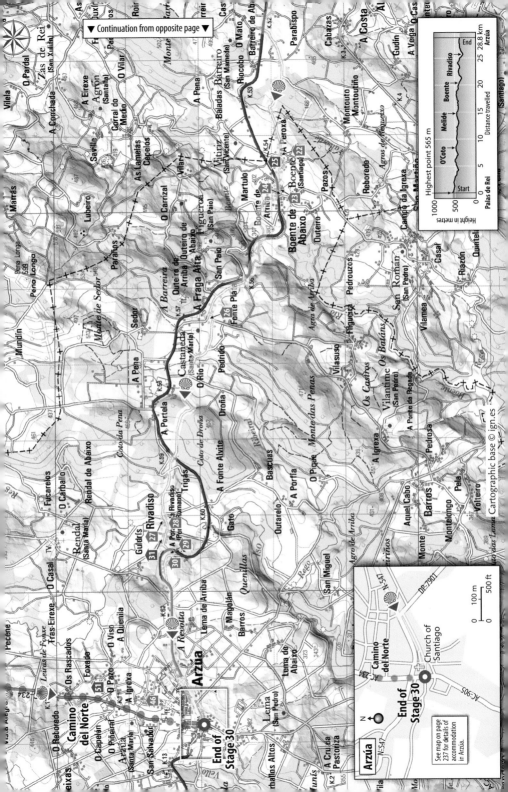

TO ARZÚA (28.8km)

Stopping at Arzúa, it leaves, potentially, an even shorter final two stages into Santiago, but note that Melide is also a significant stop. The options are more deliberately flexible because *when* you plan to arrive at this Holy City can be special to the pilgrim, so more about that a little later. The N-547 has, very recently, got a completed section of the A-54 Santiago to Lugo motorway near to it startng west of Arzúa. The Camino always involved crossing this busy, single road a few times, in order to get back on to dedicated paths through more peaceful and safer surroundings, but now, is much quieter from there, but still an important consideration prior to it. By now, the Way no longer includes scaling the peaks and sides of mountains, however, the river valleys and the paths themselves can still take their toll.

Three kilometres after leaving behind Palas de Rei, via Carballal, we come to San Xulián do Camiño (B) and its beautiful little

1 O Abrigadoiro Pr 16 €12 N M|B|W|D *676 596 975*
San Xulián do Camiño | oabrigadoiro1@gmail.com

2 Casa Domingo Pr 18 €14 N M|B|W|D|@
630 728 864 | Ponte Campaña, 1km on from San Xulián | www.alberguecasadomingo.com

3 La Pallota de San Cristobal * €70+ Dbl. *659 070 510* A Graña (after San Xulian)
https://lapallotasancristobal.com

Romanesque **church**. Built in the late 12th century, and dedicated to Julian the Hospitaller, at the east end, there is a *hórreo* – a Galician raised grain store – at the entrance to a farm. Many pilgrims pause here, and unlike so many others, it has been unlocked during the day

with a volunteer custodian. Otherwise, your best chance of seeing the interior is to stay in one of the Albergues in the village, and attend Mass. Cross the río Pambre to Casanova (5.6km B) and then after the highest point

4 Xunta X 20 €8 Y K|W|D *982 173 483 /660 396 821* Mato-Casanova

of the stage – some 515m – we pass into A Coruña province at O'Coto (B).

5 Hostal Rural Casa de los Somoza ** €60/75 *981 507 372* | O Coto s/n | www.casadelossomoza.com

We come to the **church of Santa María** at O'Leboreiro (9km) The Romanesque-Gothic church has an image of the Virgin and Child carved in the tympanum. According to a local legend, a wooden image of the Virgin was uncovered from the ground outside, and placed in the church, but it kept reappearing outside, until the image was carved above the doorway. There is a thatch roofed *Cabazo*, a variant of a *hórreo*. The **Casa de la Enfermería** opposite was the pilgrims' hospital, and displays the shield of the Ulloa family, who had it built. After crossing the río Seco via a medieval bridge, we come close to the main road and pass an industrial park. The order of Santiago has erected a series of modern **monuments** here. Ten kilometres after leaving Palas, we pass through Desecabo (R) and then after passing an industrial area, reach Furelos (R|B) via

6 Casa Adro *** €85 Dbl. *616 678 206* c/ Ponticela s/n www.casaadro.com/en

another bridge. The **church of San Juan** once had a pilgrims' hospital attached. The Albergue 'Melide' is the first of several.

MELIDE (14.5km ∞)

7 Xunta X 156 €8 Y K|W|D *659 582 931* Rúa San Antonio s/n

8 Melide Pr 49 €12 N B|K|W|D|@ *627 901 552* Av. De Lugo 92 | www.alberguemelide.com

9 Arraigos Pr 20 €11–13 Y B|W|D|@ *600 880 769* Rúa Cantón de San Roque 9 Entpl. albergue.arraigos@gmail.com https://www.alberguearraigos.com

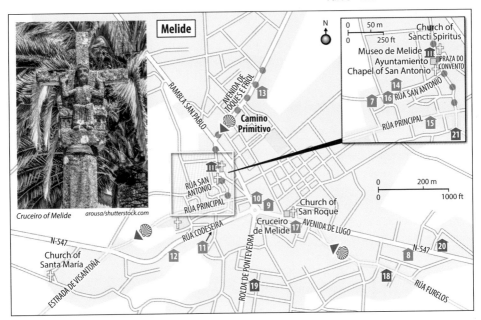

Cruceiro of Melide   arousa/shutterstock.com

O Cruceiro Pr 88 €12 N K|W|D|@ *616 764 896*
Ronda de A Coruña 2 | www.albergueocruceiro.es

To reach next two albergues, turn left off Camino

Pereiro Pr 45 €11–12 (+4 Priv. €35+) Y B|K|W|D|@
981 506 314 | Rúa Progreso 43
www.alberguepereiro.com

Montoto Pr 50 €14 N K|W|D|@ *646 941 887* | Rúa
Codeseira 31 | https://alberguemontoto.negocio.site

Alfonso II El Casto Pr 34 €12 N B|K|W|D|@ *608
604 850* | Camino Primitivo – Av. Toques y Friol 52
info@alberguealfonsoelcasto.com

San Antón Pr 36 €13–15 N B|K|W|D|@ *698 153 672*
Rúa San Antonio 6 | www.alberguesananton.com
Also Pensión ** €40/70

O Candil Pr 12 €18 (+ Priv.€50 Dbl.) B&B N K|W|D|@
639 503 550 Rúa Principal 21 | www.ocandil.gal

O Apalpador Pr 12 €13 N B|K|W|D|@ *981 506 266*
Rúa San Antonio 23 | https://alberguoapalpador.com/

Ezequiel Pr 19 €12 K|W|D|@ *686 583 378*
Rúa Sol 7 | pulperiaezequieldemelide@gmail.com

B&B A Lúa do Camiño €40 Dbl. *620 958 331*
Rúa Circunvalación Campo Feira 15 (entrance to
town, left) | https://tinyurl.com/4j49u86f

Pensión Ferradura *** €61 Dbl. *601 650 660*
Rúa Luís Seoane 8 | https://tinyurl.com/2zey2rsm

Hotel Carlos 96 * €45+/68+ *981 507 633*
Av. de Lugo 119 | https://hc96.com

Pensión Esquina ** €40/60 *981 505 802*
Rúa Ichoas 1 | www.pensionesquina.com

We now enter this busy town, which possesses
several worthy monuments. The **church of
San Roque** has a fine Romanesque portal with
carved archivolts, but is otherwise a rebuild
of the former church of San Pedro/chapel of
San Roque. The **cruceiro de Melide** (c.14th
century) is considered the oldest in Galicia, and
like the one at Ligonde, has a different figure
on each side; Christ in Majesty and Christ
Crucified; it may have been part of one of the
original churches. Passing a large plaza, and
over a busy crossroads, the Camino heads for
the old town. In the Plaza del Convento, the
church of Sancti Spiritus was formerly part
of a Franciscan convent, was rebuilt in the 15th
century, and has 18th century additions. Inside
are Ulloa family tombs and altarpieces of the
Baroque and Neoclassical styles. Opposite, on
the site of the former pilgrims' hospital, is the
town's **museum**. Adjoining the Ayuntamiento

Church of San Roque   *bepsy/shutterstock.com*

is the **chapel of San Antonio**. Here is where the Camino Primitivo – from Villaviciosa on the coast, via Oviedo and Lugo – joins the Camino Francés. Melide is renowned for its restaurants and bars serving the Galician speciality, Octopus – *Pulpería* – and its Sunday market.

Leave the plaza via rúa San Antonio, go past the cemetery. The **church of Santa María** (12th century) is on Camino on the way out of town, a pleasing single nave Romanesque church of pure form, and some interesting external decoration. Inside are a series of early 14th century paintings on and around the apse.

Continuing out of Melide, cross the small river at O'Caraballal, and briefly rejoin the N-547. The path continues through attractive woodland, of eucalyptus trees, which with pine, begin to dominate over the deciduous oak and chestnut we have been used to. Raído and Parabispo (B) are two of the hamlets you pass. Enter Boente (5km from Melide B)

22 **El Alemán** Pr 40 €16 N M|B|W|D|@|Pool
981 501 984 | Boente de Arribas/n
www.albergueelaleman.com

23 **Boente** Pr 42 €14–15 (+ Pensión €40/55) N
M|B|W|D|@|Pool 981 501 974 | Boente
www.albergueboente.com

24 **Fuente Saleta** Pr 22 €13 Y M|B|W|D|@
648 836 213 | Boente | fuentesaleta@hotmail.com

25 **Rectoral de Boente** ** €68+/88+ 684 238 323 | Lugar
Boente de Arriba 16 | https://rectoraldeboente.com

with its **church of Santiago** and Matamoros figure above the door; inside there are images of Santiago Peregrino and San Roque. Little appears of its 12th century origins. You are right beside and over the road through here. After crossing the río Boente and passing under the main road, join a minor road into Castañeda (R|B).

26 **Santiago** Pr 4 €13 N M|B|W|D|@ 699 761 698
A Fraga Alta | hostsantiago2022@gmail.com

It is here that the kilns (which have not survived) accepted the limestone rocks pilgrims brought from Triacastela, to be turned into mortar for Santiago Cathedral. Continue to climb to Portela, cross above the main road. Continue alongside a minor road through woodland, starting the descent to Ribadiso (25.4 km R|B|S), and enter, crossing the river

27 **Xunta** X 60 €8 Y K|W|D 660 396 823 | Ribadiso s/n

28 **Los Caminantes** Pr 68 €12–13 (+ 9 Priv. €32/46) N
K|W|D|@ 647 020 600 | Also 2nd Albergue in Arzúa
info@albergueloscaminantes.com

29 **Milpés** Pr 24 €12 N M|B|W|D|@ 981 500 425
Ribadiso 7 | www.alberguemilpes.com

30 **Mirador de Ribadiso** Pr 10 €12 Y W|D 722 297 498
Ribadiso 8

31 **Pensión Ribadiso** *** €65+ Dbl. 981 500 703
Ribadiso 22

via another single arch medieval bridge (12th century). The 15th century former pilgrims' hospital of San Antón once again caters to the (modern) pilgrim, as the riverside Xunta Albergue. From here to Arzúa is a further 3km, tracking the main road and ignoring signs for another walking route.

ARZÚA (∞)

32 **Xunta** X 56 €8 Y K|W|D 660 396 824
Rúa Cima de Lugar 6

33 **De Selmo** Pr 46 €12–14 N B|K|W|D|@ 981 939 018
Rúa de Lugo 133 | info@oalberguedeselmo.com

34 **Santiago Apóstol** Pr 92 €12 Y M|B|K|W|D|@
981 508 132/660 427 771 | Rúa de Lugo 107
www.alberguesantiagoapostol.com

35 **Don Quijote** Pr 48 €12 N M|B|W|D|@ 981 500 139
Rúa de Lugo 130 | www.alberguedonquijote.com
+ Also https://pensionrua.com

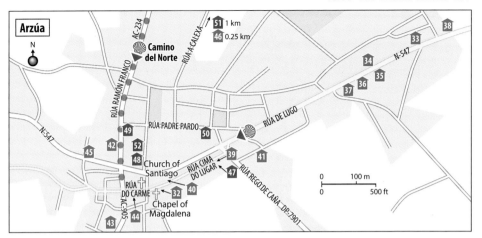

36 **Ultreia Pr** 39 €12 **Y* M|B|K|W|D|@** 981 500 471
Rúa de Lugo 126 | info@albergueultreia.com
*In winter, Groups only res.

37 **De Camino Pr** 46 €14 N **B|W|D|@** 981 500 415
Rúa de Lugo 118 | www.decaminoalbergue.com

38 **Los Tres Abetos Pr** 42 €15–17 **K|W|D|@** 649 771 142
Rúa de Lugo 147 | www.tres-abetos.com

39 **Cima de Lugar Pr** 14 €12 (+ 8 Priv €45/55) **Y* W|D|@**
661 633 669 | Rúa Cima do Lugar 22
https://acimadolugar.com | (*Closed Jan & Feb)

40 **Casa del Peregrino Pr** 14 €12 N **K|W|D|@**
690 813 566 | Rúa Cima do Lugar 7

41 **Arzúa Pr** 14 €12 (+ 4 Priv. €35–45) **K|W|D|@**
981 508 233/608 380 011 | Rúa Rosalía de Castro 2
pensionarzua@gmail.com

42 **Del Peregrino Pr** 20 €15–18 N **W|D|@** 981 500 145
Rúa Ramón Franco 7 | informacion@hsuiza.com

43 **Vía Lactea Pr** 150 €15 **Y K|W|D|@** 616 759 447
Rúa José Neira Vilas 26 | info@albergvevialactea.com

44 **San Francisco Pr** 28 €15 (+ 2 Priv. €35/45) **Y B|W|D @**
881 979 304 | Rúa Carmen 7 (Rúa do Carme)
www.alberguesanfrancisco.com

45 **Los Caminantes Pr** 26 €12 N **K|W|D|@** 647 020 600
Rúa Santiago 14 | www.albergueloscaminantes.com

46 **A Conda – Pensión Vilariño Moscoso Pr** 18 €20
(Pensión €52-62 Dbl.) N **K|W|D|@** 670 385 351
Rúa A Calexa 92 (800m from centre)
www.pensionvilarino.com

47 **Hostel Cruce de Caminos** €14–20 per person
B|K|W|D 604 051 353 | Rúa Cima do Lugar 28
www.crucedecaminosarzua.com

48 **Pensión Luís** €55/65 687 586 274
Rúa Alcalde Juan Vidal 5 | info@pensionluis.es

49 **Pensión Begoña **** €50+/50+ 981 500 517
Rúa Ramón Franco 22 | www.pensionbegona.com

50 **La Casona de Nené** €49+/75+ 981 508 107
Rúa Padre Pardo 24

51 **Pazo Santa María** €132/144+ 981 500 702
north of Camino (turn off at Rúa do Piñeiral)
www.pazosantamaria.co

52 **Casa do Cabo** €45+/63+ 698 100 213 | Rúa Alcalde
Juan Vidal 13–15

A town of over 6000 and many facilities. Here we meet the *Camino del Norte* , and pilgrims who have walked from as far away as Irún near the border with France. The town is famous for its cheese, which has its own festival on the first Sunday in March. Although it owes its origins to the Caminos, there is not much history on view today. However, behind the main Plaza, lies the rebuilt **church of Santiago** and the 14th century Gothic **chapel of Magdalena**. The latter was part of an Augustinian monastery and hospital which followed the same rule as that at Sarria; it is restored and open as a cultural centre. The church has Santiago Matamoros and Peregrino images, and altarpieces from the 18th and 19th centuries.

Stage 31 • Arzúa to
O Pedrouzo

0 ———— 1 km
0 ———— 1 mile

Arzúa

Start of Stage 31

Camino del Norte

100 m
0

Camino del Norte

Church of Santiago

Start of Stage 31

Arzúa

A Cruña
Pastoriza

Pastoriza a Vella
A Riva

Lema de Abaixo

Lema
(San Pedro)

Carballos Altos

Munís

A R

Os Rascados
Foxedo
O Pazo
A Igrexa

A Cañota
Vista Alegre
A Riba

Os Brazados

K9

K1

234

O Reboredo
O Pazo
O Capelán
O Piñeiral
Arzúa
(Santa María)
San Salvador

K13

Seixas

Chinelo
K12

Bosende
K11

Bosende

Busade
K10

A Grada Bosende

CP-0604

Rouris

As Quintas

Outeiro

A Valada

Sesar

Soutullo

Sebio

Os Pazos

A Ponte do Ladrón

Peroxa

Cortobe

A Ampaxcada

Fondevila

Raído
K65

Pregontoño

Pregontoño

K66

N-547

A Curiscada
K67

O Castro

A Riba

A Riva

Pastoriza a Vella

Trastonfao

Fondevila

O Puman
(Santa Estevo)

Pantiñobre
(Santa Estevo)

Pousada

As Corredoiras

O Sixto

Pedride

Corrado
481

Ermida do

Baiobre

A Ponte Nova

A Igrexa
A Igrexa

Os Planás

K68

1

Burres
(San Vicente)

Ciacuncís

Longüello

Soutullo

Salmonte

K19

Casilla de Salmonte

Coto de Branzas

Ermida de
Santa Isabel

K20

Cas de Buares

K21

Baiobre

K22

Baiobre

Pena Grande

Coto de Salmonte

AC-240

A Cruz

A Úceira
Finca da Úceira

Fontelas

A Cruz

2
Casa do Alto

O Cruceiro
K69

Os Planás

As Quintas

A Calzada
K70

Monte da Pedreira

Monte do Boto

Monte do Roio

N-547
K71

Rouris

Monte de Castro

O Castro

O Vilar

AC-240

220 KV

Casanova

O Casal

O Reboredo

Fonte Outeiro

Carballido

A Igrexa
Xirirín
(Santa María)

Dodro

Curras

Ramil

Pedro da Chantada

Manedo

Rio Dodro

Casas do Rial
Muíño do Calvo

O Pazo

Ois
Vila do Seso
Monte de Secabo

Suso

O Casal

Regas

A Xesta
K74

A Torre

A Ponte

Ramil

Monte de Ramil

Frechazo
Primeiro

Marganide

Cimadevila

Monte do Burato

A Igrexa
O Outeiro

3

A Calle
K72

Taboada

Ferreiros
(San Breixo)

Fontequeijo

O Casal

Suso

Ferreiros
(San Mamede)

San Mamede

4

Aquelavila
Montes de Aquelavila

Tenzas de
Cachofás

Frechazo
Último

220 KV

A Aldea do Monte

O Castro

Aldea de
Abaixo

Granxa de Doroño

Boavista
K74

Quintas

▼ Map continued on opposite page ▼

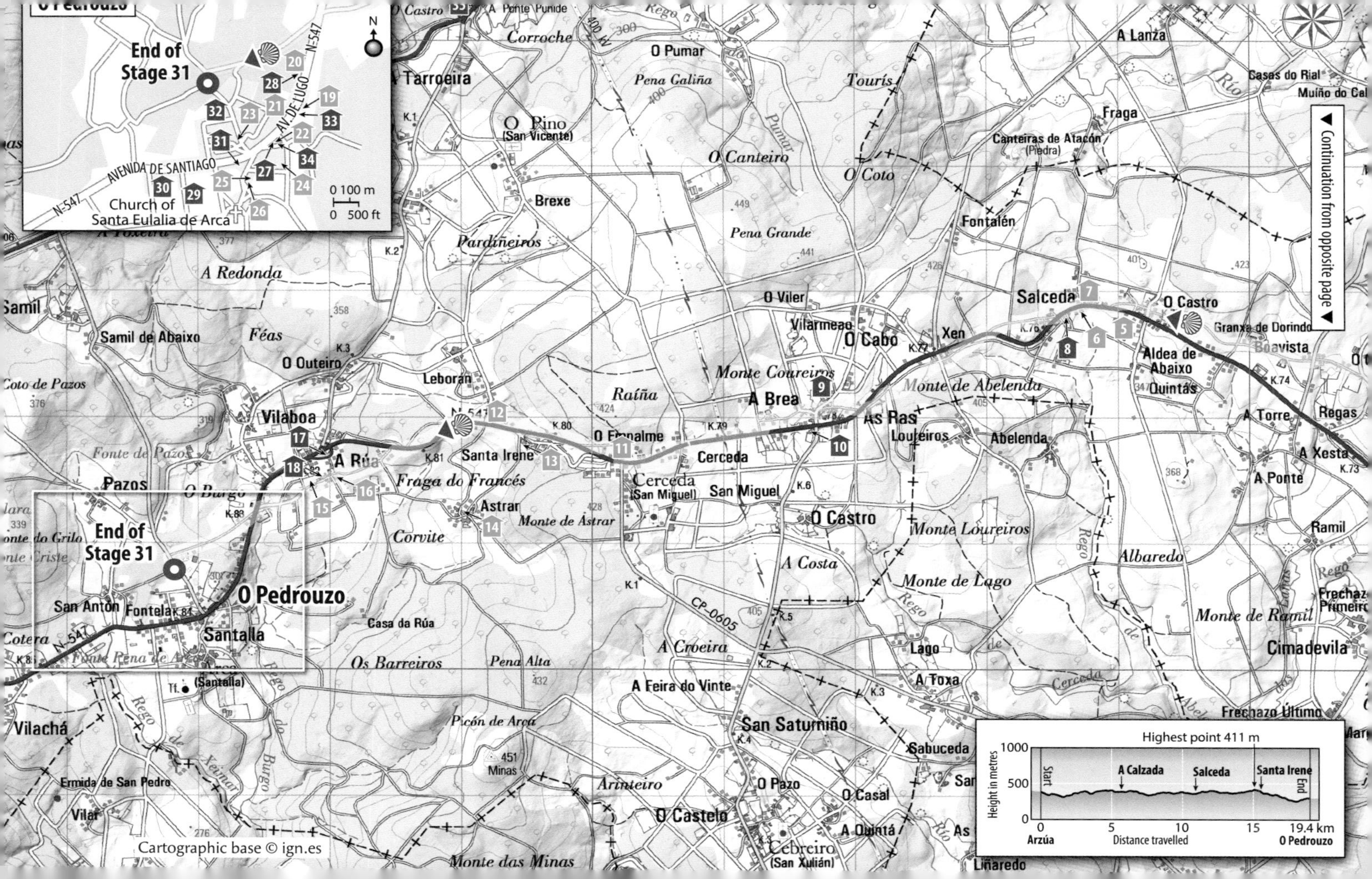
▼ Continuation from opposite page ▼
End of Stage 31
O Pedrouzo
AVENIDA DE SANTIAGO
AV. DE LUGO
N-547
Church of Santa Eulalia de Arca
0 100 m
0 500 ft
A Tarroeira
O Pino (San Vicente)
Brexe
Pardiñeiros
A Redonda
Samil de Abaixo
Féas
O Outeiro
Coto de Pazos
Leborán
Vilaboa
A Rúa
Pazos
O Burgo
San Antón
Fontelas
Santalla
Casa da Rúa
Os Barreiros
Pena Alta
Picón de Arca
Minas
Arinteiro
Vilachá
Ermida de San Pedro
Vilar
Monte das Minas
Santa Irene
Fraga do Francés
Astrar
Monte de Astrar
Corvite
O Empalme
Cerceda
Cerceda (San Miguel)
San Miguel
O Castro
A Costa
A Croeira
A Feira do Vinte
San Saturniño
O Castelo
O Pazo
O Casal
A Quintá
Cebreiro (San Xulián)
CP-0605
Raíña
A Brea
Monte Coureiros
O Viler
Vilarmeao
O Cabo
As Ras
Loureiros
Abelenda
Monte de Abelenda
Monte Loureiros
Monte de Lago
Lago
A Toxa
Sabuceda
Xen
Salceda
Aldea de Abaixo
Quintás
Granxa de Dorindo
Boavista
A Torre
Regas
A Xesta
A Ponte
Ramil
Albaredo
Monte de Ramil
Cimadevila
Frechazo Último
Frechaz Primeiro
O Pumar
Pena Galiña
Tourís
O Canteiro
O Coto
Pena Grande
Fontalén
Canteiras de Atacón (Piedra)
Fraga
A Lanza
Casas do Rial
Muiño do Cal
Corroche
Highest point 411 m
Height in metres
1000
500
0
Start
A Calzada
Salceda
Santa Irene
End
0
5
10
15
19.4 km
Arzúa
Distance travelled
O Pedrouzo
Cartographic base © ign.es

TO O PEDROUZO (19.4km)

The planning of your arrival in Santiago means that the last stage might be very short, in order to enter the city in the morning, collect your Compostela from the Pilgrim's office, and then attend the Midday Pilgrims' Mass. Others will decide to get a good night's sleep in the city, perhaps in a hotel, before attending Mass. All the 'stages' are advisory only, so it follows that these final stages are very flexible indeed. Today's (ending in the hamlet of O Pedrouzo, part of the larger parish of Arca and village district of O Pino) is 19km; tomorrow's is less than 20km, well below the recommended daily 25km, and there are only – perhaps – the journey-lengthening mixed senses, as we approach the point of arrival.

Leave Arzúa via rúa do Carmen, passing the site of the pilgrims' hospital of **San Lázaro** and its surviving **chapel** (deconsecrated). Onto a

Pazo de Santa María is an overnight option in Arzúa

wooded track, that passes under the N-547, through hamlets, and crosses over a series of streams and a small river. After the river bridge beyond A Peroxa (B|P) you can detour (past the roundabout commencement of the new A-54) a total of 800m to an Albergue-Pensión that is by the N-547:

1 **Camiño das Ocas** Pr 30 €12 (+4 Priv. €30+/40+) N K|W|D|@ 648 404 780 | Bebedeiro s/n www.caminodasocas.com

Otherwise, pass through As Quintas (R)

2 **Taberna Vella** Pr 8 €17+ M|K|W|D 687 543 810 Lugar de Taberna Vella | heidi.tasin@gmail.com Heidi's place. Not always open, phone ahead or call in.

After A Calzada (Burres), cross the río Lengüello and commencing a climb, we come to A Calle de Ferreiros (7.5km R|B|S).

3 **A Ponte de Ferreiros** Pr 30 €15 Y M|B|W|D|@ 665 641 877 | A Ponte de Ferreiros 1 http://albergueaponte.hol.es

4 **Hotel Rural A Casa do Horreo** €60+ Dbl. 626 616 758 | A Calle 6 http://hotelruralcasadohorreo.com

After passing through Boavista (R|B) we come back to the main road at Salceda (11km R|B|P).

5 **Salceda** Pr 8 €15 (Also Pensión €60+ Dbl.) Y M|B|W|D|@ 981 502 767 | N-547 (300m off Camino, left) | www.albergueturisticosalceda.com

6 **Alborada** Pr 10 €15 (Also 4 Priv. €55 Dbl.) N W|D|@ 620 151 209 | N-547 Lugar de Salceda s/n pensionalberguealborada@gmail.com

7 **Corona** Pr 20 €15 N K|W|D|@ 675 149 086 | Lugar de Salceda 22 | alberguelacorona22@gmail.com

8 **Pensión Casa Tía Teresa** €50 Dbl. 628 558 716 | Salceda 14

From here, there is a series of crossings, back and forth, of this route that was much busier prior to the new A-54. A Brea (O Pino) (R|B)

9 **Mar de Frisia** ** €62–102 Dbl. 622 471 762 A Brea 36 (150m from Camino) https://www.mardefrisia.es

10 **Pensión O Mesón** * €30/42+ 981 511 040 A Brea 16 | www.pensionomeson.com

offers more accommodation and cheesemakers. At Santa Irene (16km R|B), the Baroque

11 **Andaina** Pr 15 €12 Y M|B|W|D|@ 609 739 404 O Empalme de Santa Irene 11 albergue.andaina@gmail.com

Santa Irene   Bene Riobó CC BY-SA 4.0

12 **Xunta** X 32 €8 Y K|W|D Santa Irene s/n

13 **Santa Irene Pr** 15 €14 N M|B|W|D|@
981 511 000 | Santa Irene s/n (cross the main road)

14 **Rural Astrar Pr** 24 €12–14 N B|K|W|D|@ 981 511
463 | Astrar 18 (700m from Camino, left)
albergueruralastrar@gmail.com
www.albergueruralastrar.com

chapel is across the road (left) via the tunnel; it is dedicated to Irene of Tomar, the Portuguese martyr, and its fountain was believed to have healing properties. We are at the highest point, at some 400m. Descend to A Rúa (R).

15 **Camping Peregrino Pr** 112* €10–12 N B|W|D|Pool
662 456 093 | A Rúa 28 | www.campingperegrino.es
* Places shared in tents, 4 beds in each.

16 **Espíritu Xacobeo Pr** 32 €13 (+ 3 Priv. €55 Dbl.)
N K|W|D|@ 620 635 284 | A Rúa 49-50
www.espirituxacobeo.com

17 **Hotel O Pino** * €32+/45+ 981 511 035 | A Rúa 9
www.hotelopino.com

18 **Hotel Rural O Acivro** €80 Dbl. 981 511 316
A Rúa 28 | www.oacivro.com

Pilgrim sign, Arca   *P.Lameiro CC BY-SA 3.0*

Meeting the main road again, from here, pilgrims who do not want to visit O Pedrouzo can cross the road and continue to San Antón. Otherwise, turn left; follow the road into functional O Pedrouzo (Arca, O Pino) (∞) and your accommodation.

19 **Xunta** X 150 €8 Y K|W|D|@ Av. de Lugo 30

20 **O Burgo Pr** 14 €14 (+5 Priv. €40+/45+) N W|D|@
630 404 138 | Av. de Lugo 47
www.albergueoburgo.es

21 **Mirador de Pedrouzo Pr** 50 €13-15 N B|W|D|@ Pool
(€) 686 871 215 | Av. de Lugo 2
www.alberguemiradordepedrouzo.com

22 **O Trisquel Pr** 78 €13+ N K|W|D|@ 616 644 740
Rúa Picón 1 | informatrisquel@gmail.com

23 **Otero Pr** 34 €12 N W|D|@ 671 663 374
Rúa Forcarey 2 | www.albergueotero.com

24 **Edreira Pr** 44 €12–13 N W|D|@ 660 234 995
Rúa da Fonte 19 (Left off Camino at Rúa Minas)
info@albergue-edreira.com

25 **REMhostel Pr** 50 €13 N B|W|D|@
981 510 407 | Av. de la Iglesia 7
reservaalberguerem@gmail.com

26 **Cruceiro de Pedrouzo Pr** 94 €10–12 N K|W|D|@
Sauna 981 511 371 | Av. de la Iglesia 7
www.alberguecruceirodepedrouzo.com

27 **Pensión Una Estrella Dorada** * €57/75 630 018 363
Av. De Lugo 10-1°

28 **Pensión Compás** €27/40 981 511 309
Av. De Lugo 47 | www.pensioncompas.com

29 **Pensión Codesal** * €35/45 600 506 351 | c/ Codesal 17

30 **Peregrina Pensiones** €50+ Dbl. 672 196 046
Av. Santiago 37 (4 properties close to one another;
ideal for small groups) https://peregrinapensiones.com

31 **Pensión 9 de Abril** €40+ Dbl. 606 764 762
Av. Santiago 7-1°C | www.pension9deabril.com

32 **Pensión Lo** * €55+/65+ 608 989 100
Rúa Mollados 43 | www.pensionlo.com

33 **Pensión Platas** ** €50/70 981 511 378
Av. De Lugo 26 | www.pensionplatas.es

34 **Pensión A Solaina** €41+ Dbl. 633 530 918
Rúa do Picón 3, 1–1C | https://pensionasolaina.co

35 **O Muiño de Pena** ** €82+ 673 820 033 | A Ponte
Puñide 24 (O Pino) https://omuinodepena.com

The next municipality from O Pino is Santiago de Compostela.

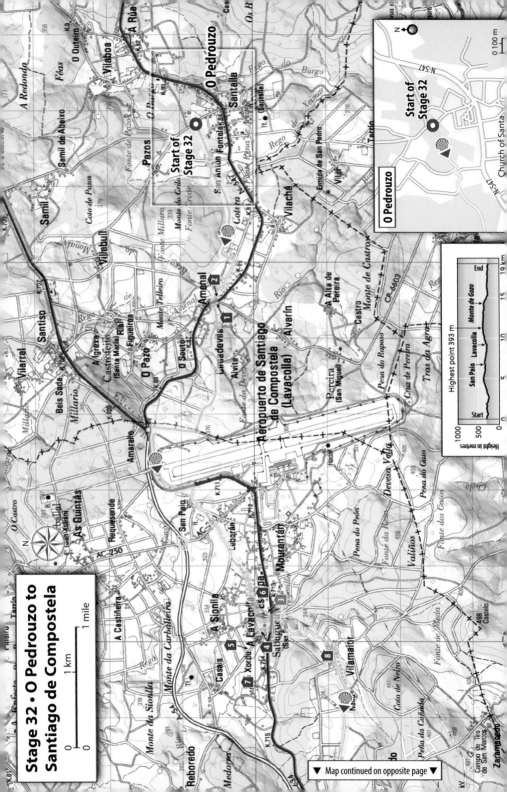

Stage 32 • O Pedrouzo to Santiago de Compostela

0 1 km
0 1 mile

Start of Stage 32

O Pedrouzo

Highest point 393 m

End 19 km

Monte de Gozo

San Paio · Lavacolla

Start

Height in metres
1000
500
0

O Pedrouzo

Start of Stage 32

Church of Santa

N-547

N-547

▼ Map continued on opposite page ▼

O PEDROUZO TO SANTIAGO DE COMPOSTELA (19km)

The final stretch: this stage means an early start if you have stayed in the O Pedrouzo area and plan to attend today's Pilgrims' Mass. There is only a short, final piece of Galician countryside to enjoy, streams to ford, before the soulless, largely unshaded trek to Monte de Gozo, then braving the highway junction, bridge, and modern suburbs of the city. But if you are visibly suffering, in some distress, the locals are quite likely to stop what they are doing and encourage you on your last steps; such is their pride in the Camino, and understanding of its significance. Alternatively, you may be approaching the final steps with renewed vigour. When you arrive in the Praza do Obradoiro, there should always be a sense of achievement, and the opportunity to share the same with fellow pilgrims.

If you have been to O Pedrouzo, leave by turning right off the main road onto Rúa Concello, and then left by the football pitch onto a track. Continue through woods to San Antón, and at Amenal (3.2km R|B|S) cross

1 Hotel Amenal ** €55+ Dbl. 981 510 431
Rúa Amenal 12 | reservas@hotelamenal.com

2 Kilometro 15 €43/53 981 814 300 | Rúa Codesal 11
https://barkilometro15.negocio.site

the river and go through the tunnel under the main road. Climb a hill up to Cimadevila from where a track (right, onto it and then left) takes us past the end of the runway of Santiago de Compostela **airport**, where a number of pilgrims have placed crosses made of twigs in the wire of the perimeter fence. Close to a major road junction, a stone scallop shell sign bids welcome to the municipality of Santiago de Compostela.

We are at San Paio (B) with its little **church of Santa Lucía**. After passing through a tunnel, the next village is Lavacolla (9.5km R|B|S),

3 Lavacolla Pr 32 €13 Y K|W|D|@ 722 117 891 Lugar
Lavacolla 35 | reservas@alberguelavacolla.com

4 Hostal A Concha €43+ Dbl. 981 888 390 | Lavacolla 1

5 Hotel Garcas * €50+ Dbl. 981 888 225 | Rúa Noval 2
https://hotelgarcas.com

6 Hotel Ruta Jacobea *** 69+ Dbl. 981 888 211
Lavacolla 41

7 Pazo San Xordo €79 Dbl. 981 888 259
c/ San Xordo 6 | https://pazoxanxordo.com/

or 'wash what hangs below!' which is being polite – cola actually means tail! Here, medieval pilgrims were directed to wash themselves and their clothes in the river, to prepare for entry to Santiago. It is most likely that this was for the purely practical reason, to reduce the spread of disease with so many people at the same location, at journey's end, rather than making themselves presentable before visiting St James' remains. It is possible, though, that for some, this act took on the significance of purification. These days, this suburb caters for business people and airport passengers, besides just a few pilgrims. The **chapel of San Roque** lies a short distance off Camino, off right by the church, past the bandstand. The Camino continues left, around the 19th century **church of Cruz de Beneval**. Cross the airport road and follow a service road.

We begin the climb to Monte de Gozo,

8 Casa Rural de Amancio €72+ Dbl. 981 897 086
Lugar Vilamaior 9 | www.casadeamancio.com

passing first through Vilamaior and then past the stations for TV Galicia and then after the next turn, TV España [At the top of the road, at a junction by a campsite, make the said turn left, and then go right]. We reach San Marcos

9 Hotel Akelarre * €50+ Dbl. 981 552 689
Av. San Marcos 37B | www.akelarrehotel.com

(R|B) some 7.5km from the end of the airport runway.

Monte do Gozo (15km ∞), meaning 'mount

Monte do Gozo – pilgrim statues Pmk58 CC BY-SA 4.0

of joy', was where pilgrims would gain their first sight of Santiago Cathedral. The first in the group to spy it would earn the title, King or *Rey*, and such was the pride in gaining this honour, that the family name often changed accordingly. The **Chapel** is very simple, but welcoming. At the top of the hill the huge sculpture, erected to commemorate the visit of Pope John Paul II in 1989 has now been removed, save for four commemorative plates. A Polish-run Albergue is a part of the Centre that was established near the site. Looking over to Monte Gaiás, the enormous **City of Culture** complex – part-opened in 2011 – is so ambitious and costly it will not now be completed. On your way down towards the city, is the vast, modern **pilgrims' complex**, an Albergue with 500 beds and facilities, built for the Holy Year of 1993.

10 **Xunta** X 500 €8 (+ en-suite rooms €74+ B&B) Y M|B|K|W|D|@ 660 396 827/ 981 558 942
Rúa do Gozo 18 | https://montedogozo.com

11 **Juan Pablo II** Pa 68 €10 N M|B|K|W|@|† 981 597 222
Rúa das Estrelas 80 | ceperegrinacion@alfaexpress.net
Rooms available (closed during 2022)

12 **Hotel Santiago Apóstol** *** €49+/62+ 981 557 155
Cuesta de San Marcos 1
www.santiagoapostolhotel.com

At the end of the complex, there are steps down to the road junctions, road and railway bridges.

For the final hour's walk, negotiate the slip roads and high bridges, much improved but still one with wooden planks; care is required. Back on *Terra firma*, we walk along the paved main street (N-634), passing the **Palace of Congress** and **monument to the order of Santiago**. On the opposite side, behind the Education Museum, the first of the main city's Albergues catering for pilgrims entering along the Francés is located. The **church of San Lázaro** is in modern surroundings, but in the eponymous district of the city where lepers were confined. Turn off the main drag (N-634), but still on rúa do Valiño, as it becomes Rúa das Fontiñas. At the major junction, this road in turn becomes Rúa dos Concheiros (scallop shell wearers), which after making a right-fork at a square where there is a Cross, in turn becomes Rúa San Pedro. The neoclassical **church of San Pedro** was built on the site of a monastery. We continue to the traditional entry point to the old walled city, the **Porta do Camiño**, and along the Rúa das Casas Reais and Rúa das Ánimas, and into Praza de Cervantes. The monuments we are passing are described in the guide to the city that follows. We are really close now; down the Rúa da Azabachería and enter the Praza da Immaculada, with the north façade of the Cathedral on your left. Finally, we walk down the slope and under the arch of the Pazo do Xelmírez, and out into the wide open **Praza do Obradoiro**. Turn around and face the magnificent, recently cleaned **west façade**, with its staircase, and, at the central element, statues of St James dressed as a Pilgrim welcoming you.

You do not need to go to the Pilgrim's Office immediately to collect your final stamp and certificate, but many make this their next call. Its location has changed (again!). With the west façade in front of you, turn around left 180 degrees, walk alongside the Parador but down the pedestrian ramp (Costa do Cristo) to the ramp (right) or steps to turn immediate right onto Rúa das Carretas (not Rúa das Hortas ahead); the office is at No. 33 on the left after the Post Office.

SANTIAGO DE COMPOSTELA (∞)

1 **San Lázaro** X 80 €8 Y K|W|D Rúa da Vesada 2 off r/ San Lázaro (Behind Museo Pedagógico – blue sign)

2 **Dream in Santiago** Pr 60 €18–23 N K|W|D|@
981 943 208 | Rúa San Lázaro 28
https://dreaminsantiago.com

3 **Fin del Camino** Pa 112 €14 N K|W|D|@
981 587 324 | Rúa de Moscova 110
https://alberguefindelcamino.com

4 **Monterrey** Pr 36 €14–18 N W|D|@
655 484 299 | Rúa das Fontiñas 65-A. Bajo
www.alberguemonterrey.es

5 **La Credencial** Pr 36 €12+ N K|W|D|@
981 068 083 | Rúa Fonte dos Concheiros 13
reservaslacredencial@gmail.com | https://lacredencial.es

6 **SCQ** Pr 24 €18+ B&B N K|W|D|@ 622 037 300
Rúa dos Concheiros 2c | www.alberguescq.com

7 **SIXTOS no Caminho** Pr 40 €15–20 N B|W|D|@
682 721 194 | Rúa dos Concheiros 2
https://sixtosnocaminho.com

8 **Santos** Pr 24 €15+ N W|D|@ 881 169 386 | Rúa dos Concheiros 48 | as.alberguesantos@gmail.com
https://albergue-santos.negocio.site

9 **La Estrella de Santiago** Pr 24 €10–22 N W|D|@
881 973 926 | Rúa dos Concheiros 36–38
www.laestrelladesantiago.es

10 **Porta Real** Pr 20 €16–20 N W|D|@ 633 610 114
Rúa dos Concheiros 10 | reservas@albergueportareal.es

11 **Seminario Menor** Pa 169 €16–19 (+81 Priv. €18+–36+)
N K|W|D|@ 881 031 768 Av. Quiroga Palacios 2
www.alberguesdelcamino.com

12 **La Estación** Pr 24 €16 N K|W|D|@ 639 228 617
Rúa de Xuana Nogueira 14
https://www.alberguelaestacion.com

13 **Meiga Backpackers** Pr 30 €14–18 N K|W|D|@
981 570 846 | Rúa dos Baquiños 67
info_meiga@yahoo.es
https://www.meiga-backpackers.es

14 **O Fogar de Teodormiro** Pr 20 €13–18 Y K|W|D|@
881 092 981 | Pl. de Algalia de Arriba 3
www.fogarteodomiro.com

15 **The Last Stamp** Pr 62 €19–25 Y K|W|D|@
981 563 525 Rúa do Preguntoiro 10
reservas@thelaststamp.es | www.thelaststamp.es

16 **Azabache** Pr 20 €16–25 Y K|W|D|@ 692 105 603
Rúa Azabachería 15 | https://albergueazabache.com

17 **Km.0** Pr 50 €15–16+ Y K|W|D|@|Cred (Fisterra) 881
974 992 | Rúa das Carretas 11 | www.santiagokm0.es

18 **Blanco** Pr 20 €18+ (+ Priv. 40+ Dbl.) Y W|D|@ 881
976 850 Rúa das Galeras 30 | www.prblanco.com

19 **Mundoalbergue** Pr 34 €20+ Y B|K|W|D|@
696 448 737 | Rúa San Clemente 26
www.mundoalbergue.es | info@mundoalbergue.es

20 **A Fonte de Compostela** Pr 30 €14–18 Y K|W|D|@
604 019 115 | Rúa Estocolmo 172
https://alberguesafonte.com

21 **Linares** Pr 14 €16+ Y W|D|@ 620 153 190
Rúa Algalia de Abaixo 34 | linares@grupogescaho.com
(See also Linares Rooms)

Most Albergues in Santiago allow an extra night's stay. Price ranges for beds higher in summer.

OTHER ACCOMMODATION:

22 **Linares Rooms** €36+/43+ 981 943 203 | Rúa Algalia de Abaixo 34 | www.linaresroomssantiago.com

23 **Pensión Pazo de Agra** * €25+/35+ 981 583 517
Rúa Calderería 37

24 **Pensión Mar Azul** €35–78 Dbl. 688 193 036
Pr. De Galicia 3 – 4th fl. | https://marazulpension.com

25 **PR Fornos** *** €33+/43+ 981 585 130
Rúa do Hórreo 7 (2°–3°) | www.fornossantiago.com

26 **Hostal México PR** *** €30-40/41-60 981 598 000
Rúa República Arxentina 33 | https://hostalmexico.com

27 **Hospedería San Martín Pinario** €41+/53+*
981 560 282 | Pl. de la Immaculada 3
www.hsanmartinpinario.com (*email/call for Pilgrim rooms)

28 **Hotel Nest Style Santiago** *** €41+/45+
981 563 444 | Rúa Doutor Teixeiro 15
www.neststylehotels.com

29 **Hotel Atalaia B&B** €47+/52+ 981 566 373
Algalia de Arriba 44 | www.atalaiahoteles.com

30 **Hotel Altaïr** *** €106+ Dbl. 981 554 712
Rúa dos Loureiros 12 | www.altairhotel.net

31 **Hotel Monumento San Francisco** **** €99+/105+
981 581 634 | Campillo San Francisco 3
www.sanfranciscohm.com

32 **Parador Hostal Dos Reis Católicos** *****
€ 130–149/166–226 (B&B Pilgrim's rate)
981 582 200 | Pl. do Obradoiro 1 | www.parador.es

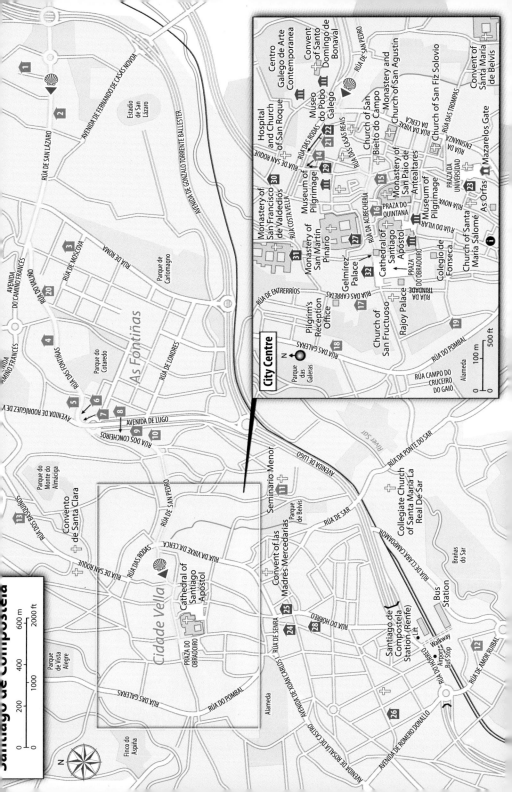

Rúa do Vilar

We have seen already that the city of Santiago de Compostela owes its establishment and growth to the veneration of what are understood to be St James' remains, albeit that there were Celtic/Suebian and Roman settlements there before – each with their own 'burial grounds'. The focal point of the city has always been the Cathedral, with a surrounding infrastructure of monuments that served the Pilgrimage, and the Bishopric. The old town was given the UNESCO World Heritage designation in 1985, the same year as the Camino Francés. With its four principal squares, or *Prazas*, it is notable for its use of locally sourced granite, of a type that seems to change colour as often as the weather in these parts. Today, the population is 95 000; this is substantially less than the other Holy Cities, Jerusalem and Rome, and there are, inevitably, a lot less religious shrines

and monuments to see than in either of those locations. However, the University of Santiago de Compostela has also shaped the city, having been formally established by the bull of Pope Clement VII in 1526. It was under the instigation of the Archbishop of Santiago, Alonso Fonseca III, and so has even earlier origins, making it one of the world's oldest universities in continuous operation, and one of Spain's leading academic institutions. Fonseca was also responsible for a new wave of building in the city, which had undergone a decline following the rise of Toledo as Spain's religious centre. Besides, the city served as the capital of the Kingdom of Galicia, and latterly the seat of the autonomous community of Galicia. Regional newspapers, radio and television are here. At the same time, new industries, such as automotive, electronics, and banking have established themselves.

Alonso Fonseca III

The Obradoiro façade

©Formatoriginal stock.adobe.com

THE CATHEDRAL OF SANTIAGO APÓSTOL

The building we see today is essentially Romanesque, but with Renaissance and Baroque additions, the west façade being the most notable among the latter, of course. Remains of the two earlier churches, along with those of a section of the defensive walls and a tower, are beneath the Cathedral. Furthermore, archaeological finds include a refashioned altar originally dedicated to Jupiter, and the tomb of Bishop Theodemir. When Bishop Diego Gelmírez took over the building works in 1111, they were at an early stage, allowing this most ambitious and influential of clerics to grow his own power and wealth at the same time as the Cathedral and the city surrounding it, which he did over nearly four decades. He is responsible for the apse and its chapels, the crossing, and the canons' choir. One of the greatest controversies he caused was replacing the original tomb of St James, which was attributed to the saint's followers. The Portico of Glory was added half a century later by Master Mateo, who was commissioned by King Ferdinand II of León in 1168 to continue the works, and it is also his galleried, vaulted interior that we see today. Gelmírez's cloister was later replaced with Fonseca's, along with the addition of the double staircase and hospital in the Praza Obradoiro. It was the continuing rivalry of other religious cities in Spain – Ávila joined the fray with a bid for St Teresa to share patronage with St James – that propelled wealthy Santiago on a fourth building splurge from the mid 17th century. Besides the remodelling of the old city that you see today, the Holy Door, Portico Real de la Quintana, clock tower and main altarpiece of the Cathedral's Capilla Mayor, were all further Baroque additions in this time.

The principal architect of the **Obradoiro façade** was Fernando Casas y Novoa, whose second tower, and central object, with arches and balustrades, statues and pinnacles of

Statue of Master Mateo

stone filigree have formed one of the most recognisable images of the Christian world. Under the staircase is a door leading to the **crypt of Master Mateo**. This was a device to resolve the difference in level between the chancel and the Praza, and was also used to support the Portico of Glory above it. With a large central pillar, there are decorated capitals and keystones of the vaults.

The next step (so to speak) would be to climb the stairs and go inside the west door, but this is no longer possible. First we shall deal here with the other Cathedral façades. Walking off right, around the cloister, brings us to the **Puerta de las Platerías**. Named after the silversmiths (whose workshops were outside) rather than being anything to do with the architectural style of this south façade, this is the only one open to the outside that retains the original Romanesque. The double portal features the Temptations of Christ (left) and

Praza da Quintana

scenes from the Adoration of the Magi and the Passion (right). The frieze and the door posts include a number of statues of saints, from different periods. Above are two windows with lobed arches, which suggest Moorish influence. Set into the cloister wall, are some shops selling jewellery made from jet – a traditional pilgrim souvenir – and others from silver. The **Casa do Cabido** (chapter house) – designed by Clemente Fernández Sarela in 1758 and one of the most beautiful Baroque houses you will see – is across the square, with the **fountain of the horses** in the centre. The house now forms part of a complex, including one of the city's **Pilgrimage museums** (in the Casa Gotica). The **Casa do Deán** – once the Dean's house and still owned by the Diocese– off the square is also by Sarela.

Then, on the east side, just beyond the apse chapels are two more doors, the **la Quintana and Puerta Santa façade**. The Praza da Quintana is on two levels, joined by a staircase. The lower level was a cemetery, known as the *Quintana de Muertos*, whereas the upper level is known as the *Quintana de Vivos* or square of the living. The Quintana portal is also known as the **Puerta Real** (Royal Door) and was completed in 1700; its ornamentation is typically Baroque. To the

right is the **Puerta Santa**, or Holy Door, which is of similar style and vintage. Also known as the Door of Pardon, it is only opened in a Holy Year, initially on December 31st of the preceding year, in a solemn ceremony. 24 statues are inset into the door surround, separated by pillars, but the statues themselves were removed from the original stone choir of Master Mateo. Santiago Peregrino appears above, flanked by two of his disciples, Athanaseus and Theodorus. There is one further door, the **Abbots' Door**, located on the stairway, which connects to the Corticela Chapel in the Cathedral. Here is the best place to view the superb **clock tower**, designed in the early 1700s by Domingo de Andrade; the clock faces only having one hand to mark the hour. Finally, go around to the north side, to the **Azabachería façade**, in the Praza da Immaculada. Begun in 1759, the lower part of the façade is more florid than the upper part, upon orders from the Royal Fine Arts Academy in Madrid to dispense with the Baroque in favour of the more geometric Neoclassical. This was once the location of the Romanesque 'French Door', through which pilgrims from the Camino Francés originally would pass after bathing in the square's fountain (later relocated to the cloister).

As indicated, even prior to the recent restoration it is not possible to follow the pilgrim's progression, through the Obradoiro doorway, and then the earlier **Portico of Glory**. It can only be viewed from the inside as part of the Museum entrance policy and fee (*see panel on page 255*). It was never the only entrance and as we have seen, many pilgrims would enter from the north door, however given the significance of the arrival on the west side, this cannot be seen as a minor hindrance. The undoubted magnificence of the restoration and the apparent overriding need to protect it, calls into question the triumph of art over pilgrimage in this place of pilgrimage, instead of serving it as was intended. Until the building

Portico of Glory – before restoration   © *Santiago de Compostela Turismo*

of the Obradoiro, this *was* the west façade of the Cathedral. If you manage to get a ticket, look up to see where once there was a stained glass rose window. The Biblical story being told to medieval pilgrims in the three arches, columns and tympana, is the Triumph of the Apocalypse, as relayed by St John in the Book of Revelation – the triumph of good over evil, and the consequent beginning of a new age – a fitting message, no doubt, for the passing through the doorway on completion of the journey, and the suffering, of pilgrimage. The 24 elders are there around the central arch archivolt, in animated conversation, with medieval musical instruments, some with cups, having just played some tunes. St James looks calmly down at you from the central column. They include those in the central tympanum, the multitude of the blessed. Also here is a large figure of Christ in Majesty, showing His wounds and surrounded by the Evangelists, while below them are angels holding instruments of the Passion. The column itself is a Tree of Jesse, the genealogy of Christ – indeed some say that James was a brother of Jesus, although the positioning may only refer to his being sent as Christ's Apostle. Over the centuries, millions of pilgrims have put the fingers of their right hand in the Tree while asking for a blessing and you could see the indentations. In the left arch there are figures representing the Ten Tribes of Israel. The right arch represents the Last Judgement. On the side pillars, more animated conversation between Apostles and Prophets, including a smiling Daniel. The liveliness and the detail of the figures are more common of the later Gothic sculpture, and so Master Mateo and his workshop of sculptors have been seen as leading the art in this direction. Just beyond the portico, on the back of the central column, there is a kneeling curly-haired figure. It is believed to be Master Mateo, admiring his work, or offering it to God. It is traditionally known as the 'Saint of the Bumps' as another tradition was for visitors to touch their head on his, in the hope that some of his gifts would be bestowed on them.

Our next visit as pilgrims is down the nave to the Capilla Mayor and its **High Altar** and **Burial Crypt**. There is a Gothic dome above a Baroque-looking drum, and it is beneath here that the giant incense burner, the famous **Botafumeiro** ('smoke spreader') with its ropes and pulleys, is located. It weighs 53kg (more than 60kg when full) and can reach speeds of 70mph. It is swung high up towards the galleries and controlled by a team of eight *tiraboleiros* and is quite a spectacle when in operation. It is mentioned in the Codex Calixtinus, which refers to it as the *Turibulum Magnum*. Here is where the daily Pilgrims' Mass takes place, with a congregation regularly in excess of 1000. The altar itself is made from Mexican silver. The choir dates from 1606. To the right, one can climb some steps and embrace the **image of St James** (closed at 1.30pm, reopening at 4pm), the **shrine** housing the polychrome statue of the Saint seated. Below, this time to the left, a passageway leads to the **crypt** and, finally, the silver urn, housing the remains of the Saint. The urn was made by local silversmiths upon the rediscovery in 1878. Above the altar and shrine is a huge gold-covered baldachin; the crowning element is a Santiago Matamoros figure.

So, having offered thanks to St James, in moments of solemnity and joy, it is time to explore the rest of the Cathedral, beginning with the chapels leading off the ambulatory. Starting clockwise, the **chapel of San Bartolomé**, behind a wrought iron grille, has a Plateresque altarpiece and the fine marble tomb of Diego de Castilla, a canon of the Cathedral (d.1521). The **chapel of San Juan** contains a large statue of the Apostle, and above it is a smaller statue of Santa Susanna, who along with St James is co-patron of the city. The **chapel of Nuestra Señora la Blanca** has statues of the Immaculate Virgin by Gregorio

Fernández, c.1747 and also a statue of the Virgin of Walsingham, of special interest to English visitors. Central to the ambulatory is the **chapel of el Salvador**, the first part of the construction of the Cathedral. Bishop Diego Paláez and Alfonso VI are remembered in sculptures on the entrance capitals.

Pause at the **Holy Door**, which has bronze panels with images of the life of St James, and a sculpture either side from Master Mateo's workshop. The **Lily chapel** (sometimes referred to as San Pedro, also the Prebends' chapel) has the recumbent statue of its founder Mencía de Andrade, with a dog at her feet, on her tomb. Next to this is the **Mondragón chapel**, an interesting central relief of the flamboyant Gothic altarpiece being a depiction of the Descent from the Cross in terracotta. The **Chapel del Pilar** is the last of the chapels behind the main altar. A tabernacle set into the altarpiece depicts the Virgin atop a marble pillar, the statue having been carved in Zaragoza.

To the left of the main altar and ambulatory, are a series of chapels. In the far corner, accessed by a passageway, the **chapel of la Corticela** was actually a separate church. Built in the reign of Alfonso II, it pre-dates the Cathedral and was only incorporated in the structure in the 18th century. Even in those days, confession was available in different languages, and is known officially as the Pilgrims' and foreigners' parish church – which means pilgrims can get married here – but check for regular Mass and confession in English as it may well be moved elsewhere. Back out again, to the crossing (next to San Bartolomé chapel) is the **chapel of la Concepción**. By Juan de Álava, there is a statue of the Virgin and Child by his contemporary Cornelis de Holanda, housed in an altarpiece by Simón Rodriquez. On the other side of the crossing, still on the north side, is the **Communion chapel**. Rebuilt in 1784 in the neoclassical style, it houses the tombs of two archbishops, Bartolomé Rajoy and the 15th century Lope de Mendoza. Then, the **chapel of Cristo de Burgos** is dedicated to the much venerated image housed in that other great cathedral of Spain, Burgos.

We are nearly back at the Portico of Glory, and it is now time to cross over and visit the exhibits around the cloister. Enter through a passageway. The **reliquary chapel** is by Juan de Álava. Among the most notable of 140 relics are the head of St James the Less (*Santiago Alfeo*) in a silver bust inlaid with precious stones and with ceramic face, a similarly designed bust of Santa Paulina, and an undecorated one of St Teresa containing a tooth. The chapel also serves as a Royal Pantheon, including Ferdinand II of León and his son Alfonso IX, who as we have seen, died short of completing his pilgrimage. On the other side of the passageway, the exhibition continues as the **Treasury**, also known as the chapel of San Fernando. Among many exhibits, we see the large silver-gilt and enamel monstrance (16th century) by Antonio de Arfe. The silver hammer is used to strike at the Puerta Santa in Holy Years. We go out into the courtyard of the Plateresque **cloister**. The floor is some three metres lower than the Cathedral, one of the reasons why the original Romanesque one fell into disrepair and a challenge for the architect. Juan de Álava is once again responsible, completing the initial phase up to his death in 1537. Don't miss the view of the Praza Obradoiro from the gallery of the west façade, which also houses the **Tapestry Museum**. Back down below, the **Archive** is only generally open to researchers, housing Chapter records, the records of the construction of the Cathedral and, of course, the Codex Calixtinus. However, it is possible to book a guided tour if you have a group of 6 to 20 people. Next, the **Library**, with ceiling paintings depicting the life and miracles of St James. The **Chapter House** has a stuccoed ceiling in white and gold, Flemish tapestries, and a statue of St James. A second more recent Botafumeiro made of

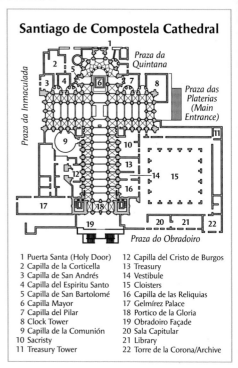

Santiago de Compostela Cathedral

Praza da Inmaculada
Praza da Quintana
Praza das Platerias (Main Entrance)
Praza do Obradoiro

1 Puerta Santa (Holy Door)
2 Capilla de la Corticella
3 Capilla de San Andrés
4 Capilla del Espiritu Santo
5 Capilla de San Bartolomé
6 Capilla Mayor
7 Capilla del Pilar
8 Clock Tower
9 Capilla de la Comunión
10 Sacristy
11 Treasury Tower
12 Capilla del Cristo de Burgos
13 Treasury
14 Vestibule
15 Cloisters
16 Capilla de las Reliquias
17 Gelmírez Palace
18 Portico de la Gloria
19 Obradoiro Façade
20 Sala Capitular
21 Library
22 Torre de la Corona/Archive

silver is usually kept here. The **Archaeological Museum** includes some fascinating insights to the earlier churches that stood on this site, as well as a reconstruction – from original materials – of Master Mateo's stone choir. On the mezzanine, the **Museum of Painting and Sculpture** includes some exquisite pieces, with the Gothic and Renaissance periods particularly well represented.

Admission to the Cathedral is free, but the Museums and therefore, parts of the cloisters are not. A number of paid guided tours are available; they include parts that are otherwise inaccessible, such as the Cathedral excavations, and the rooftop – these have to be booked at least a day in advance – check online.

PILGRIMAGE INFORMATION

No backpacks allowed in the Cathedral.

Confession: 9am – 2pm and 5pm – 8pm; Available in a number of languages; confessionals in the ambulatory.

Masses: Pilgrims' Mass, Main altar, 12.00pm daily; other Mass times 7.30am, 9.30am, 11am (Corticela chapel), 7.30pm.

Mass in English: has been in the chapel at the Pilgrim's Office since 2020, but check with the Cathedral or search online.

Botafumeiro: Used on 11–12 Feast Days, and by arrangement with groups (donation/s required) such as at the Pilgrims' Mass, i.e. it is not guaranteed to be used at every Pilgrims' Mass. There is often a group attending the Pilgrims' Mass who donate in advance! A figure of c. €400 has been mentioned before, as a trigger to get it swinging. botafumeiro@catedraldesantiago.es

However, from 2013 it is also deployed every Friday (except Good Friday) at 7.30pm. Call the Pilgrim's Office or write at peregrinos@archicompostela.org

Feast Day: Martyrdom of St James July 25th – Fiesta lasts for two weeks; includes a fireworks display on July 24th. Also 'national' holiday in Galicia.

Contact: Fundación Catedral de Santiago, Casa do Deán, Rúa do Vilar 1, E-15705 Santiago de Compostela. Tel: 981 569 327; Sacristy Tel. 981 583 548
www.catedraldesantiago.es
www.facebook.com/CatedraldeSantiago

Museum: Basic entrance €4 for pilgrims, €10 incl. Portico of Glory. Timed tickets. Pazo de Gelmírez Entrance.

Pilgrim's Office: Oficina de Acogida al Peregrino, Rúa das Carretas 33, E-15705 Santiago de Compostela. Tel: 981 568 846. Open 8am to 8pm Easter to October and 10am to 7pm November to Easter.
https://oficinadelperegrino.com/en

AROUND THE CATHEDRAL

The other attraction that is included in the price of the Cathedral Museums ticket, is Archbishop **Gelmírez' Palace** – as with the Portico of Glory viewing to the left of the Obradoiro façade of the Cathedral. Still the seat of the Archbishop, the palace has played host to the most illustrious pilgrims, rather than the humble ones. Lope de Mendoza and Fonseca III both made additions in the 15th and 16th centuries. Interior highlights are Romanesque structural stonework on the ground floor, and carved corbels of figures enjoying a banquet in the upstairs refectory.

On the north side of the 'Place of Workshops' (where the Cathedral stone masons among others had their base), you cannot fail to be impressed by the **Hospital de los Reyes Católicos**, whether or not you

have splashed out on a stay at the most famous hotel in the *Parador* chain. It draws obvious comparisons with the Hospital of San Marcos at León, only the long façade here is more Renaissance and sparing in its decoration, than lavish Plateresque. Built by order of Ferdinand and Isabella in 1499, there was a succession of architects, beginning with Enrique Egas, while Gil de Hontañón worked on the interior and two of the courtyards. Later, two more courtyards were added by the Baroque architect Manuel de los Mártires. The portal does display elements of Plateresque; medallions of the founders are in the corners, while above are Adam and Eve, and the 12 Apostles. Other highlights include the chapel and the staircase. The first 10 pilgrims to arrive before each mealtime receive a free breakfast, or lunch, or dinner. On the west side, is the huge neoclassical **Rajoy Palace**, built by Archbishop Bartolomé Rajoy as a Seminary for Cathedral choirboys. We could be in Paris, judging from the style of the architecture, if not the colour of the stone. The central pediment features a relief of the Battle of Clavijo, above which is a Santiago Matamoros. It is nowadays the seat of the city, and offices of the autonomous community of Galicia. Completing the square is the **College of San Jerónimo**. It was built by Fonseca III for poor students attending his university. Only the portal is decorated, and this was transported from a former pilgrims' hospital in the Praza Azabachería. It is now the seat of the University Rector and administration.

A couple of sights lie just behind the buildings of the Obradoiro. The **church of San Fructuoso** is down the steps at the side of the Rajoy Palace. Built in 1757, the church is the first one comes to if taking the Camino Finisterre. Behind the College of San Jerónimo is the **Colegio de Fonseca**. Originating from the 16th century, and housing the University Library, it is noted for its fine Renaissance cloister with statue of the founder. The other

Rajoy Palace

side of the building is the Praza de Fonseca, where there are many cafés and bars.

One monument you will have noticed opposite the Quintana façade – so bare of decoration it almost looks like a wall to the square – is the **monastery of San Paio de Antealtares**. It is dedicated to Paio or Pelayo, a Galician child martyr – so, not to be confused with the hermit who discovered the tomb, but it is Alfonso II's monastery erected to guard it. A Baroque structure largely replaces the 9th century one. The Benedictine monks were replaced by the cloistered nuns who reside today, and who offer tasty almond tarts. Inside, a **museum** of sacred art can be visited (entrance at the rear), which includes the original Cathedral altar that accompanied the Apostle's tomb. Another monument you will have noticed, this one on the opposite side of the Praza da Immaculada, is the **monastery of San Martín Pinario** – another Benedictine

institution that cared for the Apostle's tomb. It was founded in the 10th century, originally part of a 9th century oratory that included the Corticela chapel. Having accumulated considerable wealth, the monastery was rebuilt from the 16th century, and incorporates Renaissance, Baroque and Neoclassical styles. It is nowadays part Seminary, part Diocesan archive, part University faculty, and an 81-room hotel open to visitors in summer. The church has several altarpieces, including the main one designed by Casas y Novoa. This, together with the exceptional choir, a **museum**, reliquary chapel, sacristy, and the old pharmacy, can all be visited; there are also two cloisters. Further east, behind the monastery and other University buildings, the second **Museum of Pilgrimage** to be mentioned here (Rúa de San Miguel, 4) includes statues of St James, and pieces in silver and jet. There are accounts from pilgrims from centuries past, and the displays link Santiago

Monastery of San Martín Pinario

to pilgrimage sites across the globe. Admission free.

THE NORTH OF THE OLD TOWN

Further north of the San Martín Pinario monastery, we find the **monastery of San Francisco de Valdediós** dedictaed to perhaps the city's most famous pilgrim. It was founded by Francis of Assisi during his visit in 1214, the money raised from the miraculous discovery of a treasure, and the land leased from the monks of San Mariño for the annual rent of a basket of trout. There is a modern monument to St Francis outside, while the altarpiece also contains an image of him. In the cloister gallery

is a 'Holy Land' museum. The other parts of the monastery now form a hotel.

Going east along Costa San Francisco, via Costa Vella and Rúa do Hospitaliño, turn left onto Rúa de San Roque (junction with Rúa das Rodas if coming from the east). The **hospital and church of San Roque** was constructed from 1578 to help cope with the plague outbreaks that were still common. It was remodelled in the 18th century, but with a Renaissance façade. Besides a beautiful cloister, the Baroque church has one of the most important of Simón Rodríguez's altarpieces. Further up the street, the **Convento de Santa Clara** is another of Rodríquez's. The highly decorated façade to one side of the building is intriguing for its 'curtain' effect, that continues up for three 'levels'. Originally founded in 1260 in part from the dowry of Doña Violante of Castile, wife of King Alfonso X (the Wise) as a cloistered convent of Poor Clares, the main altarpiece in the church is dedicated to the Immaculate Conception, to whom the Franciscan orders have much devotion. A surviving tradition among Santiago's citizens is that if it rains on your wedding day, you should offer a basket of eggs to the convent.

To get to the next two sights, one can come back down San Roque and turn left before the hospital/church, and along Rúa de Ramón del Valle Inclán. The **Centro Galego de Arte Contemporanea** was designed by Portuguese architect Álvaro Siza, and given the fine views of the old city afforded from its terraces and rooms, aims to complement its surroundings. There are works by internationally acclaimed artists, as well as opportunities provided to those from the region. Closed Mondays; admission free. Next is the **Museo do Pobo Galego** (Museum of the Galician People) in the former **Convent of Santo Domingo de Bonaval** in front of the **gardens**. Separate rooms are dedicated to the sea, the land, trades, costume, music, the living environment, and architecture. There is a pantheon of major Galician figures. Closed Mondays; admission free on Sundays. The convent itself was founded in 1220 by St Dominic – Santo Domingo de Guzmán – on his pilgrimage. It was remodelled into Baroque, with Domingo de Andrade responsible for the triple spiral staircase.

Back towards the Cathedral, the **monastery and church of San Agustín** is at the east end of the Praza de Cervantes. It was built by the Count of Altamira for the calced Augustinian order, and while the church and cloister by Fernández Lechuga are Baroque, there is a neoclassical façade. Nowadays, the monastery is a University hall of residence, and the church

Museo do Pobo Galego   santiago lopez-pastor CC BY-SA 2.0
(inset: Baroque staircase © Turismo Santiago de Compostela)

is maintained by the Jesuits. In the Praza, we also find the small **Jet Museum** and the **church of San Bieito do Campo** and its exhibition of religious art.

THE SOUTHEAST OF THE OLD TOWN

Leading off the Praza de Cervantes, by San Agustín, Rúa de Ameas has several dining options. It leads to the city's **market** – Mercado de Abastos de Santiago – and on to the **church of San Fíz de Solovio**. According to the legend of the discovery of the Apostle's tomb, this was the simple dwelling place of the hermit, Pelayo (or Paio). The early church was destroyed in a raid by Alamanzor, and rebuilt by Gelmírez in the 12th century, then again in the 18th century by Simón Rodríguez. The Romanesque façade remains, however, complete with polychrome

Convent of Santa María de Belvís

tympanum representing the Adoration of the Magi. There are several University buildings south of here – including the former Jesuit church, now the **university church** – and then the **Convent of las Madres Mercedarias**, facing the **Mazarelos Gate**, the only one remaining of the old city wall. It was founded in 1671 by Archbishop Antonio Girón, whose tomb is here. The most outstanding feature of the neoclassical façade is a relief of the Annunciation by Mateo de Prado.

Heading southwest onto the colonnaded Rúa Nova, we find the **church of Santa María Salomé**. Dedicated to the Apostle's mother, it is another church commissioned by Gelmírez, which retains aspects of its Romanesque façade; there is a 13th century seated Virgin besides 15th century statues of the Virgin and the Angel of the Annunciation. Nearby, in Rúa das Orfas, the church of what is now a school can be visited at the **convent of As Orfas**. The façade has much detail.

You can reach the **convent of Santa María de Belvís**, which sits together with the Seminary and a major Albergue of the city, if you go east from San Fíz (behind the church) and through the park. The alternative is to book in at the Albergue before completing your Camino. It was founded in the 14th century, originally with the daughters of nobles taking Dominican orders; about 30 nuns are in residence today. Rebuilt in the 18th century, its church is by Casas y Novoa (visible only during Sunday Mass at 12.30pm). His façade of the **communion window** and the **chapel of the Virgen del Portal** is what most people come to see. Here was originally the gatehouse to the convent, where an image appeared during the original construction; the 17th century nuns repeatedly moved it to the church, but each time it returned, hence the building of the simple chapel. The Virgin began performing miracles, in particular healing the sick, and so has a special place among the people of the city, who make the pilgrimage on September 8th.

There are several more convents, monasteries, churches and chapels, besides palaces and old colleges, many of which can be visited at least in part, so time permitting, keep an eye out as you walk around the city.

THE COLLEGIATE CHURCH OF SANTA MARÍA LA REAL DE SAR

Set aside from the Baroque-dominated old city, this important church is a leading example of Spanish Romanesque architecture, and so shares that distinction with the Cathedral. If exploring or staying in the southeast of the city, you can walk down the southern part of the Parque de Belvís, and then work along to Rúa de Sar, which passes under the main Avenida de Lugo (N-550). Alternatively, it is a 20-minute walk from the Cathedral.

A monastery was founded in 1136 by Munio Alfonso, a canon of the Cathedral chapter, and consecrated by Archbishop Gelmírez. It housed the first Augustinian community in Galicia. The present church dates from shortly after that period, around 1168. It became a parish church in 1851.

The exterior, of granite ashlar, is supported by flying buttresses added in the 17th and 18th centuries, but behind them – along the **north wall** – we see much of the Romanesque. The **west façade** was remodelled in the 18th century, with the loss of one rose window and the introduction of square ones; there remains a rose window above the central apse. The three **apses** are again typically Romanesque – the central one is polygonal and the side ones semi-circular. The short **belfry** is also noteworthy.

If you can access the interior, the **arches** either side of the central barrel vaulted nave slant back towards the side naves. Nobody is sure why. Through the sacristy, one accesses the **cloister**. One side is from the 13th century, while the others are Baroque. The Romanesque part, as you would expect, features beautifully decorated capitals, attributed to the workshop of Master Mateo. The whole, with its peaceful courtyard garden, is very pleasing. The **priory** houses a museum of religious art.

Open Monday – Saturday 10am to 1pm and 4 to 7pm; Sundays and Holidays 10am to 1pm. In summer Mass is at 8pm Monday – Saturday; Sundays and feast days 10.30am and 12.30pm. Entrance €2 bookable on the Cathedral website. The **chapel of Santas Mariñas** is nearby. The 3-day fiesta is in mid August.

Part 6
CAMINO FINISTERRE – INCL. MUXÍA EXTENSION

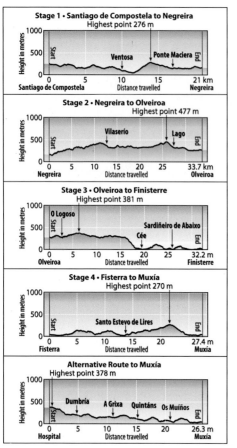

Stage 1 · Santiago de Compostela to Negreira
Highest point 276 m

Stage 2 · Negreira to Olveiroa
Highest point 477 m

Stage 3 · Olveiroa to Finisterre
Highest point 381 m

Stage 4 · Fisterra to Muxía
Highest point 270 m

Alternative Route to Muxía
Highest point 378 m

and is certainly a question frequently asked of one pilgrim from another, *Are you going on to Finisterre?* As the Galician countryside opens to sparse landscape – interspersed with beautiful white sand beaches – and this 'mini Camino' reaches an abrupt cliff edge topped by a lighthouse, the goal is to see the sun falling as though into the sea – or way beyond it (*See also p.10*). The place has special resonance among those who follow the Celtic traditions, as well as the spirituality of the 'New Age'.

And, as we have already acknowledged, according to tradition, St James continued here, perhaps to gain inspiration in his struggle to evangelize Iberia, or to fulfil his Master's call to the Apostles to spread the Christian message to the ends of the known world – literally. Another legend has it that James' disciples came up to Dugium – near modern Fisterra – to ask permission of a Roman general to bury his remains; the general imprisoned them, but they escaped when the bridge at Ponte Maceira collapsed in front of their pursuers. This is mentioned in the Codex Calixtinus, undoubtedly encouraging pilgrims to visit the area. Cabo da Roca in Portugal is actually the westernmost point in mainland Europe, and not everyone is overwhelmed, but it may be one of those places where you do not know how you will react until you have visited; or perhaps you already made up your mind that your Camino – physically to *join* the mind – must not end in Santiago.

The 83km three-stage route direct to Cape Finisterre can be done in the opposite direction, as some make the return journey to Santiago on foot, or to visit Muxía first (the Alternative Stage departing at Hospital). To add to the attraction, this Camino has a completion certificate all of its own, the *Fisterrana*; be sure to use your *credencial* all along the way or obtain a fresh one. The Pilgrim's Office in Santiago issues the standard *credencial* (don't queue again at the verification desks) or you can go to the Galicia Tourist Office inside the Pilgrim's Office (not

All roads lead to Santiago: well, not quite all. The journey to Cabo Fisterra – the 'end of the earth' *finis terrae* of Roman legend and we believe Biblical reference – is considered special by those who take it, following their journey to Santiago de Compostela. It is believed that people have made this way since the beginning of the pilgrimage – and a long time before. Today, it is becoming gradually more popular, the City one in Rúa do Vilar) and obtain a Fisterra *credencial* with additional information about the route. Either version is accepted. Muxía issues this little route's own certificate – the **Muxíana** – subject to stamps being obtained at least from Lires if you are walking from Fisterra, or along the initial stages of the Finisterre if coming via Hospital. You can get both certificates regardless of which you visit first – Fisterra or Muxía – provided you have the stamps. And/or if you walk back to Santiago from the coast (Fisterra and Muxía): cover at least 100km with the stamps to prove it and the Pilgrim's Office will issue you a Compostela. Having originally been separate with the Muxía a semi-official extension, both are now officially joined up. So, you could make this a road that leads to Santiago after all.

Indeed, for those who want more, there is the 30km stage along the craggy coast to Muxía – or you can include it after Olveiroa, via Dumbría instead of Finisterre or to make a circuit to include both. Apart from another stunning sunset and more seafood, the main reason to visit Muxía is for the **sanctuary of Nuestra Señora de la Barca**, the only shrine to the Virgin Mary associated with the legend of St James in Spain, apart from the Basilica of the Pillar at Zaragoza. The legend here is similar, that the Virgin, still alive at the time, interceded directly with James' faltering mission, this time arriving in a stone boat.

The final part of that voyage might not have been easy; in contrast to the calmer Rías Baixas to the south, where James' disciples later landed with his body, this stretch of Galicia has become known as the *Costa da Morte* on account of the large number of shipwrecks that have occurred on the offshore rocks, including some recent oil tanker spills. But it might also refer to the pagan belief that this spot where the sun goes down, marked the point of death, whereas the Christians who followed would regard it as the point at which new life begins.

Muxía sunset

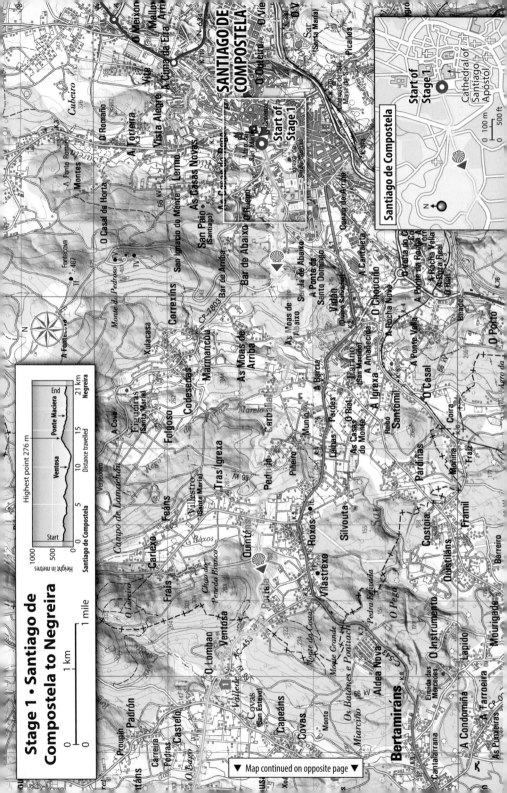

SANTIAGO TO NEGREIRA (21km)

To begin, exit the Praza Obradoiro at its northwest corner, by the Rajoy Palace, down the ramp, taking the steps down past the aforementioned **church of San Fructuoso** (on

your left).

Along Rúa das Hortas, continue straight – crossing a large junction onto Rúa Poza de Bar – for 1km, and reaching a small park, the Carballeira de San Lourenzo. The old Franciscan **monastery of San Lourenzo de Trasouto** is alongside but barely visible as you walk through the

park – it is used as an events centre. Down Costa do Cano to cross the river at Ponte Sarela. At the road leading to Sarela da Baixo, see if you can glimpse your last view of Santiago Cathedral. After **O Carballal** (R|B), cross the medieval **bridge** over the río Roxos, a popular rest spot with another, **Alto do Vento** (R|B), a short distance further on (8.4km from the start). We leave the municipality of Santiago de Compostela here.

After **Ventosa** (9.8km R|B), join the

A Casa do Boi Pr 20 €15–16 (+ 2 Priv. €45 Dbl.) Y M|B|W|D|@ *981 890 967* | Ventosa 92 https://www.acasadoboi.com

Ponte Maceira

AC-453 road, departing it for a short distance, before rejoining near the medieval **bridge** at **Augapesada** (11.5km B|P). A steep ascent of more than 200m takes us to *Alto do Mar de Ovellas*, before beginning a measured descent at **Carballo** (B). From here, it is 3km to the highlight of the stage, the medieval village of **Ponte Maceira** (*Pontemaceira*) (16.8km R|B|P).

The attractive río Tambre is dammed, with stone watermills, one of which is now a restaurant. Across the beautiful 13th century **bridge** – with its legendary Roman origins – the **chapel of Carmen or San Blas** is indecisively dedicated. Elsewhere, the Romanesque **church of Santa María** at **Portor** is worth seeking out. From the bridge, it is less than 4km to the end of the stage; the path includes alternate stretches of river and the AC-544, and the

Negreira: Pazo de Cotón

hamlets of **Barca** and **A Chancela**.
Negreira (∞) is a small market town with
a modern face, but with Roman origins. The
noble **Pazo de Cotón** is especially impressive.
There are several churches in and around,
including the Romanesque-originating **San
Pedro de Gonte** – a short Camino detour
from the next stage – and **Santa María de
Covas** (north, direction Muxía) is 17th and 18th
century, but the latter probably only worth it if
you can see the interior.

2 **Xunta** X 22 €8 Y **K*** *664 081 498* | Rúa do
Patrocinio s/n (on way out of town) * Reminder: no
kitchen utensils in Xunta Albergues.

3 **Anjana** Pr 20 €14 N M|B|W|D|@ *607 387 229*
Chancela 39 | www.albergueanjana.com

4 **Alecrin** Pr 40 €14 N M|B|K|W|D|@|Cred
981 818 286 | Av. de Santiago 53
https://www.albergueennegreira.com

5 **San José** Pr 50 €14 (+ Pensión €25/35–45) Y
K|W|D|@|Cred *881 976 934* | Rúa Castelao 20
info@alberguesanjose.es | www.alberguesanjose.es

6 **Lua** Pr 40 €14 N K|W|D|@ *698 128 883*
Av. de Santiago 22 | alberguelua@gmail.com

7 **El Carmen** Pr 30 €14 + **Hostal La Mezquita** €40/55
Y M|B|W|D|@ *636 129 691* | Rúa del Carmen 2
www.alberguehostalmezquita.com

8 **Bergando** Pr 28 €15 (+ 5 Priv. €55+) Y K|B|W|D|@
659 447 204 | Monte Bergando (800m from
Camino, r. after car dealerships – or call albergue)
albergueberagando@gmail.com

9 **Albergue Turistico de Logrosa** €17+ per person
639 606 918 Logrosa 6 (700m from Camino, turn
left at Chancela, before Negreira; transfers may be
available) http://alberguelogrosa.com

10 **Hotel Millán** ** €50/60 *981 885 201*
Av. de Santiago s/n | www.hotelmillan.es

11 **Casa Néboa** €68/73+ *680 521 335*
c/ Vilachán de Arriba 5 | https://casaneboa.com

Stage 2 • Negreira to Olveiroa

▼ Map continued from below ▼

0 — 1 km
0 — 1 mile

N

Start of Stage 2

Negreira

▲ Map continued on opposite page ▲

▼ Map continued above ▼

Negreira

Start of Stage 2

N

0 — 100 m

🏛 Pazo de Cotón

AC-447

AC-441

AC-546

Río Barcala

Cartographic base © ign.es

Highest point 477 m

Height in metres

1000
500

Start — Negreira — Vilaserio — Lago — End — Olveiroa

Distance travelled — 33.7 km

Olveiroa

N

End of Stage 2

Church of Santiago de Olveiroa

DP-3404

0   100 m
0   500 ft

DP-3404

End of Stage 2

Olveiroa

TO OLVEIROA (33.7km)

The end of this longer stage is the only settlement that calls itself a town; however there are accommodation options on the way. The highest climb reaches 477m near *Vilar do Castro*, some 26km from the start. The Camino passes through Negreira via the río Barcala, and passes the Pazo de Cotón. Follow the main road, and then turn right at the **church of San Julián**. The path climbs through woodland, to rejoin the road and into Zas (**S**) to turn off right through Camiño Real (**S**) and Rapote, to A Peña (*Piaxe*) (9km **B**).

1 **Alto da Pena Pr** 20 €17 (+ 2 Priv. €50 Dbl.) Y M|B|W|D *609 853 486* Piaxe 5 albergue.altodapena@yahoo.com

2 **Rectoral San Mamede da Pena Pr** 24 €17 (+5 Priv. €40/60) N W|D|@ *649 948 014* | Piaxe 8 rectoraldapena@yahoo.com https://www.hoteleswebs.com/albergue-mamede-pena

The **church of San Mamede** has an unusual belfry consisting of an open metal frame. Rejoin the road on exiting the village, and then follow a path for 2km, before returning to the road for a similar distance before reaching Vilaserío (**R**).

3 **Municipal M** 14 Don Y Basic *981 893 506* Vilaserío s/n (end of village)

4 **O Rueiro Pr** 30 €12 (+Pensión €57 Dbl.) Y M|B|W|D @ *981 893 561* Vilaserío 28 | jesuspubal@gmail.com www.restaurantealbergueorueiro.com

5 **Casa Vella Pr** 14 €14 (+ 3 Priv €35/50) N M|B|K|W|D *981 893 516* Vilaserío 23 | cvvilaserio@gmail.com

Rejoin the road, before turning right into O Cornado and the end of the typically small enclosed fields of Galicia, the farming becoming more intense following land consolidation. This is easier terrain, as we pass over a bridge and through Maroñas, and Santa Mariña (**R|B**)

6 **Santa Mariña Pr** 34 €12 N M|B|K|W|D|@ *655 806 800/981 852 897* | Santa Mariña 14 casaantelo@gmail.com

7 **Casa Pepa Pr** 38 €14 (+ 6 Priv. €45/50) N M|B|W D|@ *981 852 881* Santa Mariña 4 alberguecasapepa@yahoo.es www.alberguecasapepa.es

where there are more facilities, besides a traditional parish **church**. We begin to climb, via Bom Xesús before reaching Vilar Do Castro which, as the name implies, has a nearby fort on the higher *Monte Aro*, with views down to the reservoir, Embalse de Fervenza. Next stop on the Camino is Lago (27.5km **B**) after which there

8 **Monte Aro Pr** 30 €14 N M|B|W|@ *682 586 157* Lago 12 | www.alberguemontearo.com

is a possibility to visit A Picota (∞) by road

9 **Picota Pr** 6 €17+ (+2 Priv €45 Dbl) Y K|W|D|@ *649 311 523* | Av. 13 de Abril 94 correo@alberguepicota.com

10 **Hotel Casa Jurjo** €49/64+ *981 852 015* Av. 13 de Abril 91 | www.casajurjo.com

11 **Hostel Camino de Finisterre** €48+/55+ *678 621 047* Rúa do Cine 1 (a.k.a. El Horreo del Camino)

(left at bus stop) if you require more facilities, with continuation to A Ponte Oliveira. But look out for a recently marked path earlier as the Camino turns sharply right at Vilar do Castro (after Santa Mariña). Adds approx. 1.3Km to the route if taking this left turn (a claimed

4.3km to A Picota; 3.6km to P. Olveira).

After the detour options and some granite outcrops, the **church of San Cristovo** at **Corzón** (R) has Romanesque origins and its position alongside the graveyard and cruceiro makes for another typical scene. Soon after, cross the bridge over the río Xallas at **Ponte Olveira** (R|B).

12 **Ponte Olveira** Pr 14 €15+ (+ 7 Priv €40–50)
N M|B|K|W|D|@ 666 950 223 | Ponte Olveira 3
info@albergueponteolveira.com

Here, in 1809, Galician peasants fought unsuccessfully to halt the advance of French troops. Finally, 1.8km on from the bridge, we reach **Olveiroa** (R|B|S).

13 **Xunta** X 40 €8 Y K 981 744 001
Olveiroa s/n | https://dumbriaturismo.com

14 **Casa Manola** Pr 18 €15 (+ 7 Priv €35/45+) Y
M|B|W|D|@ 981 741 745 | Olveiroa 24
www.casamanola.com

15 **Hórreo/Casa Loncho** ** Pr 48 €14 (+ Pensión €50 Dbl.) N* M|B|K|W|D|@ 981 741 673/617 026 005
Olveiroa s/n | casaloncho@gmail.com
www.casaloncho.com | * Albergue

16 **Santa Lucía** Pr 10 €12 (+ 4 Priv. €25/35) Y K|W|D|@ 683 190 767 | Olveiroa s/n
www.alberguedeolveiroa.com

17 **Pensión As Pías** *** €40/50+ 981 741 520
Olveiroa s/n | www.aspias.net

Even here there are limited facilities, with dining options in the lodgings plus a bar. The town has a **church** dedicated to St James, and several **hórreos**. Nearby, is the first of three fountains believed to provide miraculous healing properties: The fountain at the **Ermita de Santa Lucía** is said to be able to cure diseases of the eyes; there is a local pilgrimage here on Whit Monday (end of May or start of June).

Stage 3 • Olveiroa to Finisterre

N

1 mile

1 km

Start of Stage 3

Olveiroa

Alternative route to Muxía
(see pp. 288/289 for full description)

Hospital

Dumbría
(Santa Eulalia)

Church of San Xián

Highest point 381 m

Sardiñeiro de Abaixo

End

Cée

O Logoso

Start

Height in metres

Olveiroa

N

Start of Stage 3

Church of Santiago de

DP-3404

DP-3404

100 m

▼ Map continued on opposite page ▼

TO FINISTERRE (32.2km)

At Hospital, after some 6km of this final stage on the original Camino Finisterre, there is the **option** to get to Fisterra in 'reverse', taking the inland route up to Muxía and then coming down to Finisterre; otherwise continue on to Fisterra and then decide whether to do the 'extension' stage, in which case you can walk back to Hospital from Muxía using the option in 'reverse', or decide to bus from Muxía to Santiago. The option from Hospital passes through the market town of Dumbría.

Both Cée, and then around the ría neighbouring Corcubión, have several accommodation options between them, with many more at Fisterra 10km further on. The cape and lighthouse are an additional 3km from the town of Fisterra.

Soon after the built up part of Olveiroa, the Camino turns left off the street onto a path, which further descends and crosses a stream. The hills include wind turbines, frequent around here, and views of the Xallas below. After 3.5km from the start, pass through **O Logoso** (R)

1️⃣ **O Logoso** Pr 40 €14 (+ Pensión €35-40/40-45) Y M|B|K|W|D|@ *659 505 399* | Logoso 12 alberguelogoso@gmail.com | https://ologoso.com

2️⃣ **A Pedra** €35-40/40-45 +Apts. *652 864 623* Logoso 8 | monicaapedra@gmail.com https://restauranteapedra.com

where there are remains of a Castro – and climb about 55m to **Hospital** (B).

3️⃣ **O Casteliño** Pr 18 €14 Y M|B|K|W|D|@ *615 997 169* | Hospital 10 | jeeennytah06@gmail.com Check-in at Bar over 500m before Albergue.

Pilgrim information centre on the options and circuit

The name, at least, is a reminder that this route was part of the medieval pilgrimage infrastructure, though the hospital itself was destroyed by the Napoéonic army. It is nearly 14km to the next settlement, the town of Cée, and so the bar here is popular. Follow the main road and at the roundabout, the **Muxía** **option** is available by turning right, otherwise to continue direct to Finisterre turn left.

After continuing on to Finisterre, passing a large factory, leave the road (right) onto a path. After another 2.5km, pass the **cruceiro Marco do Couto** and, weather permitting, enjoy more fine views. After a further 2km we come to the **sanctuary of Nuestra Señora de las Nieves** (15th century with 18th century remodelling) and the second of the fountains. The water is believed to improve breast milk both in women and livestock. The pilgrimage to the Lady is on September 8th. Another 3.5km brings us to the third fountain, at the **Ermita de San Pedro Mártir**. Curative properties are directed towards rheumatism, warts, but most important of all, sore feet – with a recent large scallop shell plaque above the flowing water, though in truth the previous shrine is the more popular rest stop for pilgrims. Its pilgrimage is the Sunday following Ascension Day. Not far further, on a clear enough day, you will get your first sight of Cape Finisterre, as a 4km-plus steep descent to Cée begins.

Cée (∞) is a modern looking town, combining industry and a port with a beach. It

4️⃣ **O Bordón** Pr 24 €15 Y B|K|W|D|@ *981 197 562* Camiños Chans-Brens | albergueobordon@gmail.com

5️⃣ **Moreira** Pr 14 €14–15 (+ 4 Priv €35 Dbl.) N K|W|D|@ *620 891 547* | Rúa Rosalía de Castro 75 info@alberguemoreira.es

6️⃣ **A Casa da Fonte** Pr 40 €14 N K|W|D|@ *699 242 711* | Rúa de Arriba 36 guzmanroget@gmail.com

7️⃣ **Tequerón** Pr 14 €14-17 (+ 4 Priv. €40+/45+) Y K|W|D|@ *666 119 594* | Rúa de Arriba 31 hostelalberguetequeron@hotmail.com https://www.alberguetequeron.com

8 **Pensión Beiramar** €40+/50+ (+ Bunks €10) *981 745 040* | Av. Finisterre 220 (on leaving the town) www.pensionbeiramar.com

9 **Hotel La Marina** * €36+/54+ *981 747 381* Av. Fernando Blanco 26 | www.hotellamarina.com

10 **Hotel Larry** ** €50+/60+ *981 746 441* Rúa Magdalena 8

11 **Hotel Oca Insua** *** €60+ *981 747 545* Av. Finisterre 82 | www.hotelinsua.com

is difficult to navigate through in order to stay on the official route, however if in doubt, look for signs to the next settlement, Corcubión, and Avenida Fisterra, or stay close to the beach with the water on your left. Besides its 18th century **castle** above the port, the older aspects of the town include the **church of Santa María de Xunqueir**, in the late 16th century Gothic *Marinero* style, and while the exterior was remodelled in the 19th century, the interior retains much of the Gothic original. The statue of the Virgin found in nearby reeds, that inspired the building of the church, was destroyed in a fire said to have been caused by Napoléonic troops.

Corcubión's (21.5km ∞) history is more apparent, with its *Pazos* (noble houses), fishermen's cottages and *Modernista* resort houses along the promenade.

12 **San Roque** M/A 14 Don Y M|B *679 460 942* San Roque s/n (on Camino out of town) info@amigosdelcamino.com | (Association)

13 **San Pedro** Pr 4 €17+ B&B (+ 2 Priv. €45+ Dbl.) Y B|K|W|D|@ *670 395 045* | A Amarela 17 (After San Roque, before Estorde) sanpedroalbergue@gmail.com

14 **Hotel Playa de Quenxe** * €50 Dbl. *676 745 134* Lg. Praia de Quenxe, 43

15 **Hotel As Hortensias** €59+ Dbl. *981 747 584* Rúa as Hortensias | www.ashortensias.es

16 **Pensión MarViva** €65+ Dbl. *628 276 773* Pl. José Carrera 4

17 **Casa da Balea** *** €68/75+ *652 424 200* Rúa Rafael Juan 44 | www.casadabalea.com

At the beginning of the town, on Campo de San Antonio is the **chapel of San Antonio,**

originally 17th century. Facing Cée's castle across the ría is the **Castle of Cardeal**, and together they protected the ría and the two towns' inhabitants. Pirates were one of the causes of several fortifications along this coastline. Next to Quenxe beach, there is a small **maritime museum**. Above on the hill, there was a Castro of which there are scant **remains**. Beyond the Camino, on the southern tip of Cape Cée (left at the cemetery then keep going) there is a **lighthouse**. The **church of San Marcos** was built in the 14th and 15th centuries in the Romanesque and Gothic styles, and modified in the 19th century. It is notable for its seated statue of St Mark, said to have been brought by ship from Venice. It may have been commissioned in the late 16th century by the Countess of Altamira, whose family was seated here, however the legend is that the ship went aground here a century earlier and did not shift until the image was taken ashore and placed in the church. The Camino turns right here, and up the steps.

To leave the town on the Camino, at the top of the steps by the church, fork right and follow Rúa Mercedes, then onto Campo do Rollo by a children's playground. A left turn takes us up a steep road that comes onto the **Campo San Roque**, and the Xunta Albergue, officially in the village of Vilar. To visit the **church of San Pedro de Redonda** go left at the Albergue. The church is early 13th Century Romanesque; there is also a cruceiro, while inside are images of saints and three of the Virgin Mary. The Camino alternates between the main road (AC-445) and paths twice more as we make a steep descent through **Amarela** to **Estorde** (24.5km R|B).

18 Hotel Playa de Estorde *** €40+/60+ 981 745 585
Playa de Estorde | www.restauranteplayadeestorde.com

We have crossed the peninsula of the shorter Cabo de Cée and are again within sight of our destination. A white sandy beach here, and another, 1km on at **Sardiñeiro de Abaixo** (R|B), look tempting to rest awhile on a warm

19 Pensión Playa de Sardiñeiro €50+/55+ 981 743 741
Av. Coruña 68 | https://playadesardineiro.com

20 Hotel Merendero € Enquire 981 743 535
Av. Alvariña 1 | www.hotelrestaurantemerendero.com

sunny day. There are more path and road combinations, but they can be avoided by staying with the road and utilising the beaches, including the next one at **Langosteira**

21 Hotel Mar de Fisterra ** €68+ 981 740 204
Rúa Cruz de Baixar 1 | www.hotelmardefisterra.com

22 Hotel Langosteira *** €56+ Dbl. 698 138 921
Av. Coruña 61 | www.hotellangosteira.com

(R|B|S|P). At the end of the gentle arc of sand intersected by a river, by the Punta San Roque, join the Rúa Cruz de Baixar, and then the main road into **Fisterra**.

FISTERRA (∞)

23 Xunta X 26 €8 Y K|W|D Rúa Real 1
alberguefisterra@hotmail.com

24 Cabo da Vila Pr 32 €15 (+ (+ Pensión €30+/40+)
Y B|K|W|D|@ 607 735 474 | Av. de A Coruña 13
www.alberguecabodavila.com

25 De Sonia-Buen Camino Pr 50 €17 N K|W|D|@
619 529 343 | Rúa Atalaya 11
www.buencaminofinisterre.com | sofari4@hotmail.com

26 Do Sol e da Lúa Pr 15 €15 (+3 Priv.)Y M|B|K|W|D|@
617 568 648 | Rúa Atalaya 7
alberguedosol@hotmail.com
http://alberguedosol.blogspot.com

27 Mar de Rostro Pr 23 €14 N K|W|D|@
981 740 362/637 107 765 | Rúa Alcalde Fernández 45
alberguemarderostro@hotmail.com

28 Por Fin Pr 11 €17 N B|K|W|D|@ 636 764 726
Rúa Federico Ávila 19 | albergueporfin@gmail.com

29 Mar de Fora Pr 34 €16 (+2 Priv. €35-50) N
B|K|W|D|@ 648 263 639/981 740 298
Rúa Potiña 14 | www.alberguemardefora.com

30 O Encontro Pr 14 €12–15 B&B (+4 Priv. €40+) Y
K|W|D|@ 696 503 363 | Rúa Fonte Vella 22
hildamarino13@gmail.com

31 La Espiral Pr 12 €14 (+ 2 Priv. €30–40 Dbl.) Y
B|K|W|D|@ 607 684 248 | Rúa Fonte Vella 19
alberguelaespiral@hotmail.com

32 Arasolis Pr 16 €13 (+3 Priv.) N K|W|D|@ 638 326
869 | Rúa Arasolis 3 | alberguearasolis@yahoo.com

33 De Paz Pr 14 €15 (+ 3 Priv. €36 Dbl.) Y W|D|@ 687
624 092/981 740 332 | Rúa Victor Cardalda 12

34 Finistellae Pr 20 €12 (+6 Priv. €30/35) N W|D|@
637 821 296 | Rúa Manuel Lago País 7
www.finistellae.com

35 Fin da Terra e do Camiño Pr 12 €15 (+ Pensión
€25/40) N K|W|D|@ 675 361 890 | Rúa Alfredo
Saralegui 15 | alberguefindaterra@gmail.com
https://alberguefindaterra.wixsite.com/inicio

36 A Pedra Santa Pr 22 €14+ N B|K|W|@ 613 017 062
Travesía de Arriba 6 | apedrasanta2021@gmail.com

37 Hostel Oceanus Finisterre ** €17 per person/€40
Dbl. | Albergue facilities | 609 821 302
Av. A Coruña 33 | www.oceanusfinisterre.es

38 Pensión Mirador Fin da Terra ** €39+ 648 918 929
Rúa Montarón s/n | https://tinyurl.com/4kymf4zb

39 Hostal Mariquito €34+/44+ 981 740 084
Rúa Santa Catarina 44–46 | www.hostalmariquito.com

40 Hotel Tematico do Banco Azul ** €90+ Dbl. 981 712
391 | Rúa Pescadores 1 | www.hoteldobancoazul.com

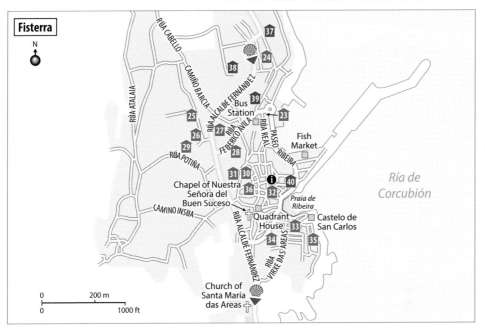

The Costa da Morte Tourist Office & Pilgrims' Centre, where you **collect your *Fisterrana***, is located at Plaza Constitución 31. Here, close to the harbour, are ATMs, shops, and numerous seafood restaurants. The **bus station** for those wishing to return to Santiago this way, is back up towards the entrance to the town where Federico Ávila meets Real at Pr. Santa Catarina. The gift shop opposite (next to the kiosk) sells tickets if you want to purchase in advance.

The main service is operated by Monbus www.monbus.es and after three hours will allow a change at the bus station for the airport (if going straight out of the city). Mon–Fri 7 departures; Sat, Sun & Hols. 4 departures. Allow 3 hours for the journey. Arriva operate between Fisterra and Muxía calling at Cée, 5 times Mon-Fri and only once a day weekends, taking 40–45 mins. As ever, schedules and operators are subject to change; always ask or check timetables.

The harbour has its medieval **tower**, and modern **fish market** *(Lonja/Lonxa)*. To the southwest at Plaza de Ara Solis, the **Quadrant House** is believed to be the 13th century pilgrims' hospital, rebuilt in 1604 with a sundial and the coat of arms of Juan Diaz de Valdivieso. In the same square is the **Chapel of Nuestra Señora del Buen Suceso** (18th century Baroque). The **San Carlos castle** was built in the 18th century during the reign of Charles III of Spain and has recently been restored.

The final 3.5km of the stage is to Cape Finisterre.

TO 'WORLD'S END' (3km from Fisterra)

The journey as a walking pilgrim to the lighthouse and cape at Finisterre, a climb of approximately 120m, will most likely be timed to allow an hour or so of daylight before the sunset, more if you want to visit two more points of interest. Leave the town via the main road.

The first site, and of particular interest to the pilgrim, is the **parish church of Santa María de las Areas** (Virgin of the Sands) with the **chapel and image of the Holy Christ**. The life-like image is similar to the one at Burgos, with hair and nails, which have been said to grow, along with perspiration claimed to have been observed. Legend has it that in the 14th century, a box was seen to have been thrown overboard a boat which had run aground during a storm, allowing it to drift away. Once ashore, the box was discovered by some sailors who opened it and were amazed to see the image, attributing

it to Nicodemus, who was reputed to have carved several images whose features were too wondrous to have been created only by mortals. Most of the events of the pilgrimage are held in Holy Week, beginning with the Palm Sunday Mass, the Novena, a depiction of the Last Supper on Holy Thursday, and the *Desenclavo* – taking down of Christ – procession on Good Friday. It is the largest celebration on the peninsula, involving most of the community and attracting tens of thousands of people.

The church itself is Romanesque and Gothic, partly rebuilt in the latter style, leaving some ruins of the former. The domed chapel housing the image is 17th century Baroque, while the bell tower is a century or so earlier, Renaissance. The patron is carved in stone in the main chapel, while there are three further chapels. There is a small 'Holy Door' and a 17th century Santiago Peregrino.

Up **Monte do Facho**, 300m before the Lighthouse, a road to the right leads to a track,

which in turn, leads to the remains of the **Ermita de San Guillermo** – we don't know for sure which one it was dedicated to, but many think it to be William of Aquitaine. It is next to the site of the **Ara Solis** stone, which was believed to directly resolve infertility among couples and presided over by a 7th century hermit; the activity of visiting couples was eventually considered lewd, so it was partly destroyed. It was originally one of a series of stones used in Celtic rituals involving sun worship. Some of the rocks remain; the rocks swayed, according to one legend, to determine whether or not a Druidess was a virgin. They too were Christianised, as the **Pedras Santas**, afforded belief that the Virgin Mary presided over them, and who moved them when pilgrims had a request granted. Prior to that, it is, according to another legend, the 'resting' place of a fearsome witch, Orca Vella, who is said to have buried herself alive with a shepherd after surrounding the grave with snakes. This is a long trek; allow two hours or more in total.

The present **lighthouse** – *Faro de Fisterra* – dates from 1868, and is the most important

along this, at times, treacherous coast. The large rock ahead right, is the **Centolo**, or Devil's rock, which has accounted for several wrecks over the years. To the left, the granite mountain on the 'mainland' is *Monte Pindo*. There is also an interesting modern **cemetery**, off the road left after the Pilgrim monument, which has not been taken up very much by local families, who prefer to be nearer the town, but could stir a pilgrim as a possible final resting place.

🏨 **Hotel O Semáforo de Fisterra** €99+– 150+ Dbl
981 110 210 | Ctra. del Faro s/n
www.hotelsemaforodefisterra.com

Faro de Fisterra ©ARCAM stock.adobe.com

Stage 4 • Fisterra
to Muxía

0 — 1 km
0 — 1 mile

▲ Map continued on opposite page ▲

▲ Map continued lower right ▲

N

Castrexe
Casa do Lo
Casa do Lo
Faro
Tourinán
(San Martiño)
O Virtú
Vilachán

Praia do Rostro
Rostro Beach

Suarriba
Buxán

Tourinán
Cabanela
O Regueiro
As Pontella
Monte de Cardosa
O Seixo
Basachos
Trás da
Guisamon

Castro
Castelo

Monte do Castelo
O Cornido
Rial
Os Sabu
Cruz da Rapadoira

Alto da Mina
Cuarzo
Cruceiro Monte
Vao do Mel
A Lamela
Monte do Serradeiro
Fonte Caban

Praia de Arnela

Castrominán
Os Canceliños

San Cristovo
Cristovol
San Cristovo
Castro
Loalo
Prado de Le

Robaleira

Denle

Monte de
Anxela
O Castro
de Duio

Vilar de Duio
San Salvador
de Duio
Duio
(San Vicenzo)
Vigo
Capela
Mallas
O Bispo
Ermedesuxo de Arriba
Ermedesuxo
de Abaixo
O Carballido
As Escaselas

Vilela de Nemiña
Monte Nemiña
Monte da Croa
Monte do Vao
A Retorta
Casa da
Pedra Furade
6

Pinelas
Montenén
de Nemiña
Nemiña

Vaosilveira
A Granxa

Veladoiro
A Nave
San Martiño
de Arriba
Monte Pión
San Martiño
de Duio
San Martiño
de Abaixo
Corticeiras
Praia da
Enseada

Praia de Lires
Punta Mellón
Piscifactoría
2
1
5
Lires
(Santo Estevo)
4

Start of
Stage 4
Punta do Cabelo
Fonte de
A Atalaia
O Porcallón
Punta do Almace
Punta Gavoteira
Punta Uña de Ferro
Praia do Mar de Fóra
Punta dos Abeláns
A Insua
A Salgueiroa
Fisterra
(Santa María)
Fonte Cardei
Fisterra
Praia da Ribeira
Petón Alto
Praia do Corveiro
Petón dos Corvos

Area Pequena
Area Grande
do Cortello
Fte. Soleiros
Monte de Baixo
3
Monte Gerval
Monte da Poza
A Cañosa
Ru
As Bouzas
Tedín
de Lagoa
Vermello
Monte da Vela
esgueira
Mixírica
Monte do Couto

Mexadoira
Padrís
Castrexe
O Sisto
O Pedrouzo
Casa de Prado C
Campo do Cego

Cartographic base © i

Fisterra

N

AC-445

Start of
Stage 4

Hotel Arenal

Langosteira
Beach

0 — 100 m
0 — 500 ft

AC-445

de Cabanas

Rostro Beach

Suarriba
Buxán
Monte de
O Cornido
Areeiros
Agra de Prado
Alto do Caribio
Monte

▲ Map continued from above left ▲

Sardineiro de Arrib

TO MUXÍA (FROM FISTERRA) (27.4km)

As with several stretches of the Camino del Norte, this northerly coastal route, though less than 30km in length, can take its toll, with some steep climbs and more dramatic descents. Facilities are in line with the number of pilgrims – more limited than the Camino Finisterre. Retrace steps back through Fisterra, to Langosteira beach, as far as the Hotel Arenal.

Look out for yellow arrow pointing left (remember, there is the option to walk back to Santiago which explains the arrows pointing straight ahead) and take it to depart the Camino Finisterre. Pilgrims walking from Fisterra to Muxía, bear in mind that others might pass you coming from Muxía to Fisterra.

Follow the road into **San Martiño de Duio** (R) with its small Baroque **church**. Offshore under the waves – with some ruins still visible at times – is reputed to be the site of ancient Dugium, where the disciples came and were imprisoned during Roman occupation. It is also believed by some to have been a seat of Queen Lupa, she of the parallel legend with the disciples, the oxen and the dragon at Alto do Rosario. Celtic and Suebic tribes probably settled here, with excavations of pottery and tools indicating that this was so.

Another kilometre brings us to **Escaselas** (3km R|B|S) and following a left turn, the next settlement, **Hermedesuxo de Baixo** (B).

The paved road continues straight for a time-and-distance-saving (c. 2km) *variant*, known as *Rostro*, that will get you onto a path and then the beach of the same name

Praia do Rostro   *amaianos CC BY 2.0*

(Seasonal Bar/Degustation further up at Praia

da Mexadoira), before rejoining the official route at **Padrís**.

Otherwise, continue on the *official route* by forking off right onto a path that reaches **San Salvador**. After San Salvador, the official route climbs up about 80m through forest, before descending to **Rial**, and then on to **Buxán** (B), 4.5km from the split. Turn right to enter more forest. Back on asphalt, you can see the dunes and playa O Rostro. At **Castrexe**, we are down in a valley, as we ascend to **Padrís**. Continuing to climb – through a stretch of forest – we are still enjoying the best scenery of the route, even though we are now beyond parallel to the superb beach. The descent begins before **Canosa** and finally enters the only village with a range of facilities, **Santo Estevo de Lires** (13.5km R|B). Make sure you get

1 **As Eiras** Pr 30 €15–20 (+ Hotel ** €60+ Dbl.) M|B|W|D|@ 662 261 818 | Lires 82 reservas.aseiras@hotmail.es | https://ruralaseiras.com

2 **Casa Lourido** €38+/45+ 981 748 203 | Lires 15 www.casalourido.es

3 **Casa Jesús** €40+/50+ 981 748 393 | Lires 86 www.turismoruralcasajesus.com

4 **Casa Raúl** €40+/50+ 678 420 859 Lires 5 https://www.casaraul.es

5 **Aparthotel Ría de Lires** €72+ Studio 625 270 080 Lires 12 | https://aparthotelriadelires.com

your *credencial* stamped at one of them. The **church** is 17th century, while the estuary is known for its diversity of birds.

Hórreos mark the exit from Lires. Turning right, cross the río do Castro via the new footbridge, and continue up to **Frixe** (*Frije*) (B).

The **church of Santa Leocadia** is a short detour and is worth it to observe the 12th century Romanesque features and decoration that are well preserved, with a small statue

6 **Casa Ceferinos** * €60+ 981 748 965 | Frixe 11 www.casaceferinos.com

of the patron placed in a niche. Continue through forest, crossing a road on the way, to

MUXÍA (∞)

Church of Santa Leocadia   amaianos CC BY 2.0

Guisamonde (18.8km), 9.4km from Muxía. After 2km, with the climb now including paved road, enter **Morquintián**. The **church of Santa María** is another not directly on the route, and is from the same period, with many original features. A kilometre further along the route, there is reportedly still confusing signage: one sign encourages you to fork left while yellow arrows on the asphalt road encourage turning to the right; pilgrims are advised to follow the arrows on this occasion rather than the official sign. Continue to climb up to the highest point, *Facho de Lourido* (270m) where in the days before lighthouses, bonfires were lit to warn ships, before a very steep descent. After 2km, pass through **Xurarantes** and a further 1.5km, follow the road parallel to the dunes rather than going on the beach. Link up with the road to enter the town.
There are a few accommodation options,

7 **Xunta X** 32 €8 Y **K** (no utensils) @
Rúa Enfesto 22

8 **Da Costa Muxía** Pr 8 €15 N K|W|D|@ *676 363 820*
Av. de Doctor Toba 33 | www.dacostamuxia.com
dacostamuxia@gmail.com

9 **Muxía Mare** Pr 16 €13–14 (+ 2 Priv €45 Dbl.)
Y K|W|D|@ *664 102 205* | Rúa Castelao 14
www.alberguemuxiamare.es

10 **@Muxía** Pr 44 €15 Y K|W|D|@ *609 615 533*
Rúa Enfesto 12 | info@alberguemuxia.com

11 **Arribada** Pr 40 €15–18 (+ Priv. €48/64) Y K|W|D|@
981 742 516 | Rúa José María del Río 30
muxia@arribadaalbergue.com
https://www.arribadaalbergue.com

12 **Bela Muxía** Pr 44 €16 (+ Pensión €60+ Dbl.)
Y K|W|D|@ *687 798 222* | Rúa Encarnación 30
albergue@belamuxia.com
https://www.belamuxia.com

13 **Pensión Casa Isolina** * €35+ Sgl.
630 581 744/981 742 367 Rúa Real 52
www.pensionalberguecasaisolina.com

14 **Habitat Cm Muxía** *** €49+/55+ *981 742 148*
Rúa Real 40

15 **Pensión Rustica Alemana** €75 Dbl. *986 064 877*
Rúa Virxe da Barca 3–7
https://www.hotelesyo.com/pension-rustica-alemana

16 **A de Loló** * €42+ Dbl. *981 742 422 /646 390 101*
Rúa Virxe da Barca 37 | https://adelolo.com (Also
Four Rooms & other lodgings)

17 **Parador Costa da Morte** **** €132+ B&B Pilgrim
rate | *881 161 111* | Lugar de Lourido s/n
www.paradores.es

from the Xunta to private Albergues, to a new *Parador* that was for a long time a controversial construction site. With a population of well over 5000 the town shares with Fisterra fishing and tourism as its main activities, with sampling the seafood a major attraction. For pilgrims going back to Santiago by **bus**, monbus.es operate 3 departures daily with one calling at Cée and Fisterra (3 hours total; the other two more direct services take just over 2 hours.) Arriva also operate several departures a day weekdays between Muxía and Fisterra (via Cée) but with

only one daily departure on Sat. & Sun. There are also services to A Coruña. Always double check the timetables, as the services are subject to change.

To obtain the *Muxiana* certificate with your stamped credencial visit either: the Tourist Office, c/ Virxe da Barca 49 (3.30-8.30PM), the Town Hall, c/ Real (Mon-Fri 8.30AM-3PM) or the Xunta Albergue (from 1PM).

The aforementioned important pilgrimage shrine here, the **sanctuary of Nuestra Señora de la Barca**, suffered a serious setback on Christmas Day 2013, when the church caught fire following an electrical fault. The roof was destroyed, and the image of the Virgin severely damaged but salvaged. The restoration of the 17th century sanctuary – itself rebuilt from the 12th century original – is complete, and if closed during the day/early evening you can see inside through a grille in the doorway. Three replacement images have been carved, and some of the fundraising has been imaginative.

A tall stone sculpture has recently been added. Approach it below **Monte Corpiño** on a path known as *Camiño de Pel* (skin) because it contained a fountain where pilgrims would wash before the sanctuary. There are more sacred stones nearby, the **Pedras de Abalar**, three of which are believed to be the remains – keel, rudder, and sail – of the boat of legend. It is customary to place oneself underneath the stones, in order to relieve gastritis and other similar problems. Someone standing on top, who causes the stone to rock, is deemed entirely free of sin. The sail – Pedra dos Cadrís – is said to cure back problems, so it is worth a try crouching underneath and rubbing against it. Again, as at Fisterra, belief in these spiritual properties is likely to have originated in pre-Christian times. It is a 3km walk from the sea front, to this exposed promontory frequently lashed by stormy seas. The major fiesta, *Romaría da Virxe da Barca*, is celebrated on the second Sunday in September (except when that

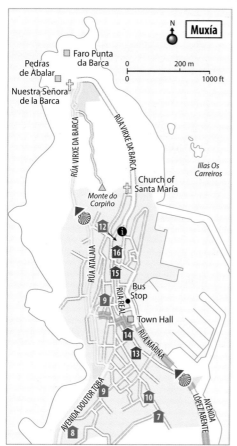

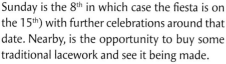

including in an interesting Rosary Chapel. The wooden **poles** nearby are for drying salted conger eel, a method now claimed to be unique to the town.

For those who do not take the route from or to Hospital (*see page 288–289*), the other significant site to look out for is the **church of San Julián de Moraime**. It may have been founded as early as the 8th century, and then became a Benedictine monastery. Future Alfonso VII took refuge here during the fighting with the forces of his mother, Queen Urraca. Later additions include the Baroque tower to twin with the more Gothic one. The west portal shows 26 (eroded) Elders of the Apocalypse, with some believing it to be an earlier 'trial' work of Master Mateo prior to the Portico of Glory. Inside, the frescoes (uncovered in 1970) have been significantly worn away by humidity; there are disputing theories as to how old they are. The capitals are carved with the typical Romanesque plant motifs, as is a beautiful north door, rediscovered in 1975. Those excavations also uncovered a Roman burial ground, all of which suggest a more extensive establishment than what we see today. Generally, however, the place is in a poor state of repair and investigation, though nonetheless fascinating and evocative.

Sunday is the 8th in which case the fiesta is on the 15th) with further celebrations around that date. Nearby, is the opportunity to buy some traditional lacework and see it being made.

On the way back to the town taking the other side of the promontory, up against Monte Corpiño with its belfry built into rock, the parish **church of Santa María** is a Romanesque-Gothic *Marinero* transition. In 1203 the original church was donated by Pope Innocent III to the monastery of Carracedo at the time of its re-dedication. Although plain looking, with its austere walls, rectangular apse and gable roof, closer examination reveals carved doorways. Inside, the quality of the carving continues,

Ría de Camariñas

End of Alternative Route
de Xaviña
as Cruces
eñora da Barca
lo da Pel
uxía
(ta María)
Pedriña

Ría de Camariñas

Muxía

End of Alternative Route

Nuestra Señora
de la Barca

Monte
Corpino

0 ___ 200 m
0 ___ 1000 ft

Illas Os Carreiros
Pedra dos Corvos

Praia da Cruz
Punta
das Chans

Furna
do Barro

Praia de Fornelos

Praia da Espiñeirido

Corpiño de
Chorente

As Figueiriñas

Piscifact.

Vilela

Merexo

Nosa Señora
(Santa María)

Allo do Enfesto
A Baiuca

Praia de
Borreiros

Mte. de Merexo

Serdón

A On

Pardiñas

teira

margidas

lina

Vilar de Figueiras
Figueiras de Abaixo

Area do
Coto

Chorente
Fras de Arriba
K2
Capela de S. Roque

Area
Maior

O Peón

San Martiño

San Martiño
de Ozón

Insua

Pena da Serra

A Gaseira

Pardiñ

Area de
Lourido

A Carrúa

Petón Grande
As Casas Novas
K3

9
Moraime
(San Xulián)

Os Pexegos
Vilar de Sobremonte
Os Muíños

6

Quintáns
pela de San Isi

Gorulleiros

Oruxo

Os Gotros
Os Muíños
8
K5

AC-440
K6

K7
Ozón
K8
7

TV
Lourido
O Facho
312

Xuraranfes

O Castro
Serantes

Labexo

Monte de Labexo

Cebráns

Tras da P

Xazón

As Agreiras
K1
Albergueria

A Casa do Monte

As Devesas
Armear

Monte Maior

Castelo

Os Castelos
O Cruce

A Raposa

Fonte Grande

Armear

Monte da Raposa

Fonte Pedreira

Risamonde
K2
As Brañas

Monte Miñoa

Fumiñeo

O Castro

Cartel

O Vilariño

Añobres

Ribas

Canles do Cao

Vilamaior

A Estivada
K3
Baltar

Prados da Braña

Rego do Lobo

Cotro de Bouzas

As Lagoas

Cruz de Santos

Bouzas

Vaseixiño

Casa de Bergantiños

A Brea
Allo das

orquintián

O Aveeiro

A Fieiteira

Morpeguite

intoulo
quintián
a María)

O Foriña

Prado de Anselmo

Prado

Santa Mariña

A Rumbada

Os Pasantes

Capela de Santa Rita

Vilastose
A Grixa

5 Cibrán
4

As Esti

Faro de Prado

A Casanova

A Casanova

Agrodosío

arvelle
on
Bardullas
(San Xoán)

Capela de Santa Mariña

A Aveeira
K5

Vilarmide

K4
Sena

A Grixa

As Falloas

Prado Vilarvello

Fonte Branca

Mobial

Fte. das Gateiras
K6

Couciero
(San Pedro)

Montecelos

CP-3403

143

Tras da Bouza

As Gándaras

Sorna

Vilar de Outeiro

Devesa de Agar

Montesiños

Agar

A Toxeira

O Pedregal

K7

Agar

Casas de Ponte
Ca

Cartographic base © ign.es

▲ Continuation from opposite page ▲

HOSPITAL TO MUXÍA OPTION – 'ALTERNATIVE ROUTE' (26.3km)

This is a waymarked (though not always 'straightforward') 26.3km option; so that makes 32.3km if you have stayed overnight at Olveiroa, to do it in one go *(see p. 274 and map on p.272 for route out of Olveiroa to Hospital incl. accommodation)*. Furthermore, the main stop on the way with facilities, Dumbría, is only 4km from the split at Hospital – where there is an Albergue *(see p. 274)*. Many of the other villages have at least a bar, but accommodation is limited until you reach Muiños and Moraime,

both close to Muxía.

Turn right at the roundabout (for DP-3404) after Hospital and its bar. Start a descent, and continue it having turned left onto a path. Cross a small river, then the road, then onto a path that flattens out bends in the road. Return to the road and path combination, including a track through woods, and into **As Carizas**, right by a hórreo onto its street.

We follow minor roads back to the main one to enter **Dumbría** (R|B|S|P).

The striking Albergue is flanked by sports

1 **Xunta** X 26 €8 Y K (with utensils)|W|D|@ 981 744 001 | next to football pitch | www.dumbria.com

2 **Casa A Pichona** *** €68+ Dbl. 609 649 252 c/ Castro 8 (400m from Camino west of As Carizas) https://casapichona.com

3 **O Argentino** €30–40 981 744 051 | c/ Dumbría s/n argentinod@gmail.com

facilities. The **church of Santa Eulalia** is Romanesque in origin, but rebuilt in the late 17th/early 18th century; the cruceiro and the very large hórreo complete a pleasing trio. At the medical centre, turn left, and cross the río Fragoso, then cross the AC-552 with care. Over

the other side, the route is flanked by walls for 2km until you reach **Trasufe**. The **Capilla de la Virgen del Espiño** (Baroque) is better known as the Capilla da Santina de Trasufre, with its fiesta on September 21ˢᵗ attributed by some to the Virgin of Arantzazu, far away in the Basque Country, as this is also a Virgin of the thorn bush. The fountain is believed to cure warts. There is a series of hórreos; after the village cross the río Castro, and after a series of right turns, reach **Senande** (B|S). After the bar and shop (turn left), continue on the road signed to Agrodosío, Vilastose and Casanova. Continue straight-right, into **A Grixa/Vilastose** (11km B), with its cruceiro, hórreo, and its **church of San Ciprián de Vilastose** that has its belfry on

4 **O Cabanel** Pr 12 €15 (Priv. €45) Y M|B|K|W|D|@
*600 644 879 | A Grixa 39 | www.albergueocabanel.com
reservas@albergueocabanel.com*

5 **Casa Rural Liñeiros** €95/100 *981 732 237/683 281 829 | Vilastose 29 by church | https://lineiros.es*

the hill opposite. Turn left onto a local road, but then the Way departs right onto a path.

Follow road and woodland path combination for about 3km into **Quintáns** (R|B|P), with its 17ᵗʰ century **Capilla de San Isidro** – a distance of 5km from Senande. The village plaza has facilities; veer left here.

6 **Et Suseia** Pr 10 €15 N K|W|D|@ *689 946 840* Lugar Pedragás 1 (600m after Quintáns) *info@etsuseia.com*

7 **Pensión Plaza** * €32+–36+/38+–43+ *981 750 452* Quintáns 194 | www.plazapension.com

Follow this road, through a junction, until a minor road is reached to turn left, then onto a dirt road, and then a paved one before turning right onto a minor road with wall, and come down into **San Martiño de Ozón** (B|P). The hórreo, at over 27 metres and supported by 22 pairs of legs, is one of the longest in Galicia. To see the Romanesque origins of the **church of San Martín** one needs to view the east side, where two apses are preserved – there were

three – accessed through an arch. They are fine of form, with carved capitals; the 1708 Baroque butchery and its presiding priest are recorded in an inscription inside, where, again, the apses are the points of interest. By that time, it had ceased to be a monastery. The surviving buildings are home to an alternative community who welcome pilgrims to rest awhile. Continue through the village, turning left uphill, looking out for a right turn as it gets steeper.

After entering woods, and beginning a descent, you should see the coast and Camariñas across the estuary. Join the road and, with the village of Merexe behind you, enter **Os Muíños** (R|B|P), 4km on from San

8 **Pensión O Relax do Río** *** €78+/86+ *613 488 718 | Os Muíños 100 | https://pensionorelaxdorio.es*

Martiño. Head to the centre, and turn onto the bridge over a river. Head in the direction of Playas de Os Muíños, but 600m further on turn left by a house to the Romanesque **church of San Julián de Moraime** at **Moraime** (21.5km R|B) (*see p. 285 for description*)

Church of San Julián de Moraime   Stanislava Karagyozova/shutterstock.com

9 **Monasterio de Moraime** Pr 38 €18 (+ Pensión €75+) Y M|B|W|D|@ *881 076 055 | Moraime 2* https://hostelmonasteriodemoraime.com

Continue up steps, and left uphill. Enter woods, and the **chapel of San Roque** is notable for its carving of the saint as a pilgrim, with a child and a dog at his feet. After this, the small village of **Chorente** signals a descent after its last house. The route leads down to the Praia de Espiñeirido; you can enter **Muxía** alongside the beach or on the official path.

Part 7
DEVOTIONS AND PERSONAL REFLECTIONS

DEVOTIONS

PRAYERS BEFORE, ON & AFTER THE CAMINO

See also the La Faba Prayer of Fray Dino (p. 206–207)

The following Devotions have been selected by Andrew Nunn, Dean of Southwark.

GOD OF OUR JOURNEY

God of our journey
who led your pilgrim people by day and by night
and saw them to their journey's end:
send your blessing on these your servants
as they travel the pilgrim road
in honour of your Son
and of his companion St James.
Make them sure footed,
joyful in heart
courageous and humble
and a blessing in themselves
to those they will meet on the way;
through Jesus Christ
who always went ahead of his disciples
and leads us now.
Amen. [1]

CELTIC BLESSING – FOR GALICIA

May the road rise up to meet you.
May the wind be always at your back.
May the sun shine warm upon your face;
the rains fall soft upon your fields
and throughout this day,
may God hold you in the palm of His hand.
Amen.

ARRIVAL IN SANTIAGO DE COMPOSTELA

May all who come to Santiago de Compostela,
following in the footsteps of Christian pilgrims
from many different times and places,
be renewed in the faith which comes to us from the apostles,

in union with the whole church
may we with them commit ourselves generously
to follow Jesus Christ,
who alone is the way, the truth and the life.
Amen. [1]

THE END OF THE PILGRIMAGE – THE CONTINUATION

St James,
for this pilgrimage we needed
your zeal and courage.
Continue to teach us, apostle and friend of Our Lord,
the WAY which leads to him.
Open to us, preacher of the Word,
the TRUTH you learned from the Master's lips.
Give to us, witness of the Gospel,
the strength always to love the LIFE
which Jesus gives,
as in his name we pray.
Amen. [2]

Thank you, Lord, for being with us on the Way;
thank you for bringing us safely home.
May I and my companions
continue the journey
that leads to you
and come to your Heavenly City
for all eternity.
Amen. [1]

Merciful God, whose holy apostle Saint James,
leaving his father and all that he had,
was obedient to the calling of your Son Jesus Christ
and followed him even to death:
help us, forsaking the false attractions of the world,
to be ready at all times to answer your call without delay;
through Jesus Christ your Son our Lord,
who is alive and reigns with you,
in the unity of the Holy Spirit,
one God, now and forever.
Amen. [3]

1 © Very Revd. Andrew Nunn

2 © Libreria Editrice Vaticana (A prayer before the Tomb of St James by Pope Saint John Paul II, August 19th 1989)

3 © The Archbishops' Council 2000 ('Collect for the Feast of St James' from Common Worship: Services and Prayers for the Church of England)

PERSONAL REFLECTIONS

Wherever you are on your personal journey, use this space to record your reflections.

Part 8
GLOSSARY

CONVERSATION

ENGLISH	SPANISH
Yes	Si
No	No
Please	Por favor
Thank you (very much)	(muchas) Gracias
You're welcome	De nada
No Thankyou	No gracias
Hello	Hola
Greetings	Saludos
Goodbye	Adiós
Good morning	Buenos dias
Good day	Buenas tardes
Good evening/ night	Buenas noches
So long	Hasta la vista
Good way/walk!	¡Buen camino!
Excuse me	Desculpa
Sorry	Perdón
Do you have some	Tienes
Do you have a	Tienes una (f)/ un (m)
I would like to have	Me gustaría tener
Give me	Dame
I don't want	No quiero
How many?	¿Cuántos?
How much?	¿Cuánto cuesta?
OK	Vale
I don't know	No sé
(very) Good	(muy) Bien
Bad	Malo
Here	aquí
Over there	Por ahí
This	esta
That one	Aquél
Up	arriba
Down	abajo
Left	Izquierda (f)/ Izquierdo (m)
Right	Derecha (f)/ derecho (m)
Straight on	todo recta (f)/ recto (m)
Wrong way!	¡sentido contrario!
Do you speak English?	¿Habla Inglés?
I don't speak Spanish	No hablo Español
I don't understand	No entiendo
Understand?	¿Comprender?
Do you have a bed?	¿tienes una cama?
Do you have a room?	¿tienes un cuarto?
Where are you from?	¿De donde eres?
I am	Soy
American	Estadounidense
British	Británica (f)/ Británico (m)
Irish	Irlándes
Canadian	Canadiense
Australian	Australiano
a New Zealander	Neozealándes
South African	Sudafricano
One, two, three, four	Uno, dos, tres, quatro

EMERGENCIES/HEALTH

I am ill	No siento bien
It is urgent!	¡Es urgente!
Call a doctor	Llame a un médico
Call the Police	Llama la Policia
Fire!	¡Fuego!
Get out!	¡Sal!
Go away! (rude)	¡Vete ya!
Leave me alone!	¡Déjame en paz!
Pharmacy	Farmacia
Hospital	Hospital
Health Centre	Centro de salud
Medicines	Medicamentos
Plasters/ Dressings	protectoras/ apósitos
Orthopedic support	Suporte ortopédico/ Corsé ortopédico
Cream	Crema
Spray	Rociar/aerosol
Sunblock	Bloqueador solar
Blister	Ampolla
Cut	Corte
Fracture	Fractura
Ache/Pain	Dolor
Foot	pie
Toes	Dedos de los pies
Leg	Pierna
My back	Mi espalda
My shoulder	Mi hombro

FOOD, DRINK, MEALS

Breakfast	Desayuno
Lunch	Almuerzo/Comida
Dinner	Cena
Desserts	postres
Coffee	café
Tea	té
With milk	con leche
Large coffee with milk	Café con leche doble
Small coffee topped with milk	Cortado
Cold/hot	frío/caliente
Beer	cerveza
Wine – red/white/ rosé	vino – blanco/tinto/ rosado
Orange juice	zumo de naranja
Water with/ without gas	Agua con/ sin gas
Toast (large)	Tostadas
Butter	mantequilla
Bread	pan
Jam [strawberry]	confitura [fresa]
Honey	miel
Ham	jamón
Cheese	queso
Egg/s	huevo/s
Fish	pescados
Shellfish	mariscos
Chicken	pollo
Pork	cerdo
Beef steak/ sirloin	bistec/ solomillo
Lamb	cordero
Spicy sausage	chorizo
Country sausage	salchícha
Blood sausage (black pudding)	morcilla
Potatoes	patatas
Rice	arroz
Tomatoes	tomates
Cucumber	pepino
Salad	ensalada
Grapes	uvas
Plums	ciruelas
Apple	manzana
Banana	plátano
Almonds	almendras
Fried	fritos
Boiled	hervido
Scrambled	revueltos
Grilled	a la parilla
Griddled	a la plancha
Stewed	estofado
Sauce	salsa
(without) Salt	(sin) sal
(with) Pepper	(con) pimienta
Sugar	azúcar
Sandwich (in Spanish bread)	bocadillo
Savoury pie	empanada
Omelete with potatoes	tortilla
Knife	cuchillo
Fork	tenedor
Spoon	cuchara
Cup	taza
Glass of wine	una copa de vino
Plate	plato
Can I see the menu?	¿Puedo ver el menú?
The bill please	La cuenta por favor

Part 9
INDEX

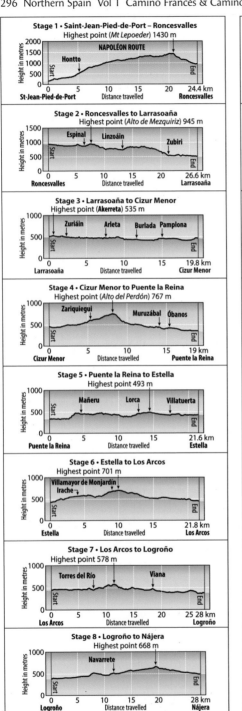

Stage 1 • Saint-Jean-Pied-de-Port – Roncesvalles
Highest point (Mt Lepoeder) 1430 m

Stage 2 • Roncesvalles to Larrasoaña
Highest point (Alto de Mezquiriz) 945 m

Stage 3 • Larrasoaña to Cizur Menor
Highest point (Akerreta) 535 m

Stage 4 • Cizur Menor to Puente la Reina
Highest point (Alto del Perdón) 767 m

Stage 5 • Puente la Reina to Estella
Highest point 493 m

Stage 6 • Estella to Los Arcos
Highest point 701 m

Stage 7 • Los Arcos to Logroño
Highest point 578 m

Stage 8 • Logroño to Nájera
Highest point 668 m

Stage 9 • Nájera to Santo Domingo de la Calzada
Highest point (Cirueña) 744 m

Stage 10 • Santo Domingo de la Calzada to Belorado
Highest point 826 m

Stage 11 • Belorado to San Juan de Ortega
Highest point 1159 m

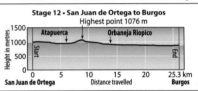

Stage 12 • San Juan de Ortega to Burgos
Highest point 1076 m

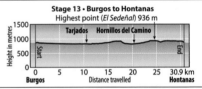

Stage 13 • Burgos to Hontanas
Highest point (El Sedeñal) 936 m

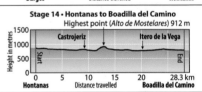

Stage 14 • Hontanas to Boadilla del Camino
Highest point (Alto de Mostelares) 912 m

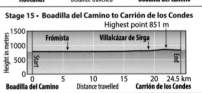

Stage 15 • Boadilla del Camino to Carrión de los Condes
Highest point 851 m

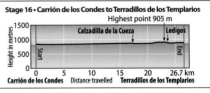

Stage 16 • Carrión de los Condes to Terradillos de los Templarios
Highest point 905 m